THE INTUITIVE PRACTITIONER

THE INTUITIVE PRACTITIONER
On the value of not always
knowing what one is doing

Edited by
Terry Atkinson and Guy Claxton

Open University Press
Buckingham · Philadelphia

Open University Press
Celtic Court
22 Ballmoor
Buckingham
MK18 1XW

e-mail: enquiries@openup.co.uk
world wide web: http://www.openup.co.uk

and
325 Chestnut Street
Philadelphia, PA 19106, USA

First Published 2000

A catalogue record of this book is available from the British Library

ISBN   0 335 20363 9 (hb)   0 335 20362 0 (pb)

Library of Congress Cataloging-in-Publication Data
The intuitive practitioner: on the value of not always knowing what one is doing/
[edited by] Terry Atkinson and Guy Claxton.
     p.   cm.
  Includes bibliographical references and index.
  ISBN 0-335-20363-9. – ISBN 0-335-20362-0 (pbk.)
   1. Teaching – Psychological aspects.   2. Intuition.   I. Atkinson. Terry, 1948–   .
II. Claxton, Guy.
LB1025.3.I59   2000
371.102–dc21   99–16162
                                                                                        CIP

Typeset by Type Study, Scarborough, North Yorkshire
Printed in Great Britain by St Edmundsbury Press, Bury St Edmunds, Suffolk

Contents

Notes on contributors   vii

Introduction
Terry Atkinson and Guy Claxton   1

**Part 1: Perspectives on intuition in professional learning and
practice**   13

1   Intuition and the crisis in teacher professionalism
    John Furlong   15
2   The anatomy of intuition
    Guy Claxton   32
3   Trusting your own judgement (or allowing yourself to eat the
    pudding)
    Lucy Atkinson   53

Part 2: Intuition and initial teacher education   67

4   Learning to teach: intuitive skills and reasoned objectivity
    Terry Atkinson   69
5   Awareness and intuition: how student teachers read their own
    lessons
    Peter John   84
6   The role of intuition in mentoring and supporting beginning
    teachers
    Elisabeth Lazarus   107
7   Elaborated intuition and task-based English language teacher
    education
    Arlene Gilpin and Gerald Clibbon   122

Part 3: Intuition and continuing professional development   135

8   The development of professional intuition
     Agnes McMahon   137
9   The formal and the intuitive in science and medicine
     Richard Brawn   149
10   Complex decision making in the classroom: the teacher as
     an intuitive practitioner
     Laurinda Brown and Alf Coles   165
11   Developing intuition through management education
     Gill Gregory   182

Part 4: Intuition and assessment   197

12   Assessment and intuition
     Patricia Broadfoot   199
13   Measurement, judgement, criteria and expertise: intuition
     in assessment from three different subject perspectives
     Roger Curtis, Paul Weeden and Jan Winter   220
14   Intuition, culture and the development of academic literacy
     David Johnson   239

Part 5: *The Intuitive Practitioner*: a critical overview   253

15   *The Intuitive Practitioner*: a critical overview
     Michael Eraut   255

Index   269

Notes on contributors

Terry Atkinson is a senior lecturer in education at the University of Bristol. He has worked as a secondary school teacher and as a teacher trainer. He has written on and carried out research into professional learning and the impact on learning of information and communications technologies.

Lucy Atkinson has worked in all phases of teaching from nursery to higher education and has extensive experience of special education. Her last appointment was as deputy head of an inner city primary school and she is now a freelance consultant and trainer working in the areas of literacy and learning support.

Richard Brawn teaches and researches in the Graduate School of Education at the University of Bristol. His primary interests and work are in the realm of professional learning and development, and in this context he has worked closely with medical tutors and general practitioner trainers. He is active in initial teacher training, is a core tutor on the University's Teaching and Learning Programme for new academics and coordinates the Graduate School's Professional Learning and Development Centre.

Patricia Broadfoot is Professor of Education and Dean of the Faculty of Social Sciences, University of Bristol. She has published widely in the area of assessment, including *Education, Assessment and Society* (Open University Press 1996), and is editor of the international journal, *Assessment in Education*.

Laurinda Brown worked in curriculum development as mathematics editor at the Resources for Learning Development Unit, after teaching mathematics at Backwell School, Avon for fourteen years, latterly as head of department. She is now a lecturer in education and mathematics at the University of Bristol, Graduate School of Education and her research interests include the effective teaching and learning of mathematics and ways of knowing.

Guy Claxton is Visiting Professor of Psychology and Education at the University of Bristol, Graduate School of Education. His previous book *Hare Brain, Tortoise Mind: Why Intelligence Increases When You Think Less* was Anthony Storr's book of the week in the *Times Educational Supplement*. A new book *Wise Up: The Challenge of Lifelong Learning*, was published in October 1999.

Gerald Clibbon is a part-time lecturer at the University of Bristol, Graduate School of Education, where he works on the MEd programme in the Teaching English as a Foreign Language specialism. He has been a teacher, teacher educator and materials writer in Saudi Arabia, Greece and the UK. His interests are in the professional development of English language teachers.

Alf Coles taught in Zimbabwe, Eritrea and London before teaching at Kingsfield School, Bristol, where he is currently second in the mathematics faculty. He is enrolled on a Masters in Education course at the University of Bristol, Graduate School of Education and in 1998 was awarded a teacher research grant by the Teacher Training Agency.

Roger Curtis has worked in secondary schools for over twenty-five years in a variety of roles including head of department and head of faculty and as a member of a senior management team with responsibility for assessment, reporting and recording. He has worked as an advisory teacher and has been involved in both GCSE and A level examinations as a trainer, examiner and syllabus developer. He has also been involved in the development of exemplification materials for the art national curriculum. He is currently the PGCE tutor for art at the University of Bristol.

Michael Eraut is Professor of Education at the University of Sussex. Since 1991 his work has focused on professional knowledge and learning across a range of professions. Since the publication of his book *Developing Professional Knowledge and Competence* (1994) he has studied non-formal learning in the workplace and the interaction between tasks, context and mode of cognition.

John Furlong is a professor of education at the University of Bristol. He has written and researched extensively on policy and practice in initial teacher education. His most recent books include *Teacher Education in Transition* (Open University Press, forthcoming), *Initial Teacher Education and the Role of Higher Education* (1996) and *Mentoring Student Teachers: The Growth of Professional Knowledge* (1995).

Arlene Gilpin has worked in the field of Teaching English as Foreign Language since the early 1960s, first as a language teacher and, for the past 20 years, as a teacher educator in a wide range of countries. Her research interests are adult and professional learning, task-based approaches to learning languages and teaching, and learning in higher education.

Gill Gregory is an independent training and development consultant. She is currently undertaking her PhD on a part-time basis. She is researching the notion that managers can become more innovative problem solvers by developing their intuition.

Peter D. John is currently a lecturer in education at the University of Bristol, Graduate School of Education. His research interests focus on the policy and practice of teacher education, teacher professionalism and cross-professional learning. He is the co-author of *Professional Knowledge and Practice* (Cassell, 1996) and editor of a forthcoming volume entitled *Mentoring Across the Professions*.

David Johnson is a psychologist and senior lecturer at the University of Bristol, Graduate School of Education. His research interests include literacy, learning and cognition and he is engaged in a number of research projects in a wide range of countries. Of these the most significant are studies on literacy in 5000 schools in the Punjab province of Pakistan and the impact of design and technology on literacy and learning in primary schools in South Africa. He has published extensively on the topics of literacy and learning in international and comparative contexts.

Elisabeth Lazarus is a lecturer at the University of Bristol, Graduate School of Education where she coordinates the PGCE modern languages programme. Her previous professional experience as a secondary school teacher and as head of a languages faculty has shaped her teaching and research interests. These focus on the teaching and learning of foreign languages and on the professional development of teachers. Her current research and recent publications investigate the role of mentors in schools in a number of national settings.

Agnes McMahon is a senior lecturer at the University of Bristol, Graduate School of Education. Her research and publications are in the field of education management and policy with a particular focus on continuing professional development for teachers, teacher appraisal, school leadership and headteacher development.

Paul Weeden is a lecturer in education at the University of Birmingham, formerly having held a similar post at the University of Bristol. He is the author of articles in the fields of assessment and geographical education. Recently completed contracts have included authoring and trialling Key Stage 3 geography optional tasks and tests for both SCAA and ACAC, and children's understanding of national assessment requirements for QCA (LEARN). His current research interests are in Key Stage 3 and Key Stage 4 assessment and how self-assessment can be used to improve students' learning.

Jan Winter taught in schools in Bristol before becoming a mathematics advisory teacher for Avon LEA. She now works at the University of Bristol, Graduate School of Education as an education lecturer. Her research interests include assessment and teachers' professional development. She contributed a chapter on teachers' professional learning to *Liberating the Learner* (1996) and completed a short research project in 1997 for SCAA (now QCA) on the transition from GCSE to A level mathematics. She is currently working on research projects on pupils' experiences of assessment (for QCA) and on evaluation of new mathematics units (for Nuffield).

Introduction

Terry Atkinson and Guy Claxton

This book is about what professionals do, and how they learn to do it. Focusing mainly on the professional world of teachers, but with illustrative discussions of medical and business practice, the book takes issue with the dominant tradition which sees rational, explicit, articulate understanding as the central ingredient in both practice and development, and which, in consequence, stigmatizes or ignores other ways of knowing. It is self-evident that much of what teachers and others do, in the heat of the moment, is not premeditated; it is intuitive. A situation arises; the teacher responds, and only later, if at all, will she or he pause to 'figure out' what was going on, and why they did what they did. What then is the relationship between the rational and the intuitive; the explicit and the tacit; articulated comprehension and 'gut feeling'? Without at all being anti-rational or anti-intellectual in tone or intent, the contributors, in their different ways, are seeking for a more subtle, differentiated and dynamic understanding of the ways in which these different types of learning and knowing interact.

Put more formally, the overall purpose of the book is to investigate, both conceptually and empirically, the role of intuition in professional practice, and its significance for professional development, especially (though not exclusively) within the world of education. Its aims are:

- to explore the relationship between articulate/rational/explicit and inarticulate/intuitive/implicit ways of knowing and learning in the context of adult professional practice and development;
- to question the current tendency to interpret 'reflection' solely in terms of articulation, and to reassert the value of other forms of reflection;
- to illustrate the working relationship between reason and intuition in a variety of case studies in distinctive educational and professional settings, and to make links and comparisons between them;
- to extract and highlight practical lessons which this reassessment of

intuition has for the initial and continuing professional development of educators and others.

Over the last 30 years, a variety of models have vied with each other as accounts of professional learning, and each in turn has become suspect or discredited. Crudely, in the old-style 'apprenticeship model', student teachers, for example, were supposed to soak up knowledge through a mixture of observation and trial and error: 'sitting by Nellie'. In the 'scholastic model' which replaced the apprenticeship model in the 1960s, students imbibed academic knowledge, and learned how to put it into practice. In the 'craft–knowledge model' that superseded it, seasoned practitioners attempted to render their intuitive expertise into explicit maxims and theories, often with the help of a researcher, and then to feed this back to students. While in the 'reflective practitioner model', it was students themselves who were required to unearth and formalize their own reflex responses and tacit beliefs.

It is not the intention of *The Intuitive Practitioner* to argue for any one of these simplified models. Rather we seek to deepen the debate about professional learning by focusing on one vital underlying way in which these models differ. Each presupposes a different relationship between conscious comprehension and spontaneous performance – if you like, between reason and intuition. At one extreme, the apprenticeship model relies on unreflective induction: experience is deemed both necessary and sufficient for professional learning to occur. Competence need not be explained or theorized at all, and the professional becomes merely a skilled technician. At the other, the scholastic model gave a central place to highly intellectualized understanding, which was then supposed to dissolve, in a straightforward way, into competence through practice. Both research and experience reveal that it doesn't. In between, the craft–knowledge model has been shown to produce accounts of professional practice, but to leave unexplained how these constitute a pathway that leads beginners towards competence. And the reflective practitioner model, at least in its more extreme forms, seems to lead tutors to a denial that there is any valuable knowledge which they can transmit, and to underestimate both the emotional tolerance and the learning prerequisites which reflection requires.

The Intuitive Practitioner explores some of the many reasons – political, philosophical and psychological – why none of these models has proved satisfactory.

In particular, we believe that the importance of the deliberate, conscious articulation of knowledge, whether others' or one's own, may in the current intellectual climate be overestimated, while intuitive forms of knowledge and ways of knowing have tended to be ignored and under-theorized. The assumption that professional competence is best acquired when you 'know' – are able to explain and justify – what it is you know, needs questioning. There may be valid socio-political arguments for establishing a self-conscious professional rhetoric – to afford collective protection against government interference and attempts at 'deprofessionalization', for example – but such considerations should not be confused with an implicit psychology of adult professional learning: 'what works best'. It may be, for instance, that explicating and theorizing one's competence through discussion and reflection is a process that needs to come later in the course of professional development, once considerable tacit expertise has already been established, and that tutors and mentors who try to start the process too soon may impede the development of that very expertise. Certainly, the attempt to get student teachers, nurses and others to be 'reflective' often proves frustrating and unrewarding for tutors and students alike. What exactly is being asked of students, and why?

The Intuitive Practitioner teases out some of the complex, subtle issues that need to be addressed if we are to develop a more satisfying and comprehensive model of adult professional learning. The book draws together, in a variety of ways, both personal experience and a range of scholarly literatures from psychology and sociology, in order to explore the functions of intuition in professional learning and practice, and to uncover the ways in which explicit knowledge and implicit 'know-how', reason and intuition, are braided together in professional contexts. Are there times and/or stages in learning when one can think too much, or when explicit instruction can get in the way of learning? What are the pros and cons of becoming 'self-conscious'? Can intuition be cultivated, and its quality be improved? Can intuition in the sense of personal reflection make teachers and managers more creative? Does intuition have a valid, and valuable, place in the context of assessment? Is intuition a 'way of knowing' that has particular value in dealing with complexity?

And does it necessarily support professional learning to make the implicit theories of students, mentors or tutors, explicit? *The Intuitive Practitioner* is, in a sense, a sequel to *Liberating the Learner* (Claxton *et al.* 1996), in which some of the same authors explored the tacit beliefs held by teachers and students, and the ways in which these might serve to inhibit learning. Throughout that book ran, more or less consistently, the currently conventional assumption that one could be released from the restraining power of these unconscious assumptions by making them conscious – by 'reflection'. But a gathering unease has brought many of these authors to question that belief, and this book represents the collective fruits of the collaborative and multidisciplinary enquiry that resulted: an enquiry that has implications not only for how we structure professional training and development, but which illuminates some of the increasingly controversial assumptions at the heart of contemporary educational models of knowing and learning, and indeed in western culture at large.

In Chapter 2 Guy Claxton describes the principal characteristics of intuition and the different ways in which intuitive thinking is used in everyday life. As he notes, the term intuition is capable of widely varying interpretations. In the succeeding chapters, many of these are applied to professional contexts of teaching and teacher development. The reader may feel as if the term intuition is used as a catch-all for those aspects of professional thinking that are not readily understood or rendered into words or, worse still, as John Furlong warns against in Chapter 1, as a hedge against the very proper demand for accountability. However, the editors and other contributors are inviting the reader to develop a sense of intuitive practice through a serendipitous exploration of this somewhat eclectic set of studies rather than through a rational formulation of the concept. The various chapters differ in many respects but in sum they amount to a consideration of intuition as it manifests in professional practice and development.

Teaching is a highly specific process but one which nevertheless has similarities with others involving the performance of complex and diverse skills in real time and in contexts that are unpredictable and constantly evolving. A comparison to speaking a foreign language points to some of these similarities. The putative linguist may have formal knowledge about language acquired through study in school or university but then has to apply this knowledge in order to perform the largely practical task of communication. One approach to this problem is to orient the learning process towards the development of communication strategies and the performance of communicative tasks. Language users who have learned in this way may then be able to manage effectively those situations for which they have been prepared but may struggle with unfamiliar tasks and may be unable to articulate their knowledge of language in any systematic way. Similarly, knowledge about teaching and learning can be described, prescribed and acquired in professional training contexts but remains difficult to apply in the classroom. This is due in part to the nature of formalized knowledge which is usually explicit, conscious, language-based and constructed as a theoretical model. By contrast, the development of teaching skills through experience can result in competent performance in a specific context, the acquisition of know-how, but not necessarily the ability to give an account of the learned expertise or to perform it in a different context.

Any attempt to describe professional practice in order that the resulting knowledge be applied by practitioners fails to take account of either the cultural or the individual nature of cognition which depends less upon factual recall and more on the adaptation of knowledge to the individual's purposes, emotions, preferences, cognitive framework, world view, and to the shared memories and meanings of the culture. Cognition and memory are, in truth, our servants and not our masters. We remember selectively for reasons of efficiency and personal or cultural choice. It is this essentially subjective aspect of memory and cognition which is manifest in intuitive practice and intuitive thinking. The way in which a professional must operate is dictated by the choices that have been made throughout the period of professional training and experience. Generalizable knowledge about teaching and learning will never fully reflect or be reflected in the individual cognitive framework of practitioners.

The concept of the intuitive practitioner offers new ways for understanding and interpreting professional practice. Essentially, it represents a reconceptualization and rehabilitation of Schön's (1983, 1987, 1991) original concept of the reflective practitioner, a concept which has been simplistically interpreted to refer to conscious and deliberative reflection on practice. Schön was seeking a more effective way of understanding the intuitive and implicit thinking of professionals than that afforded by rational analysis: 'If the model of Technical Rationality is incomplete, in that it fails to account for practical competence in "divergent" situations, so much the worse for the model. Let us search, instead, for an epistemology of practice implicit in the artistic, intuitive processes which some practitioners do bring to situations of uncertainty, instability, uniqueness, and value conflict' (Schön 1983: 49).

Here, then, Schön is arguing that the attempt to account for the thinking, action and knowledge embodied in professional practice through a series of rational propositions drawn from relevant disciplines such as pedagogy, didactics, psychology or sociology is, at best, incomplete. What is lacking in the rational approach is that which cannot be readily accounted for because it is implicit in the context and depends upon the individual's intuitive capacity to perceive, apprehend and act. Schön delineates a view of professional practice in which the knowledge and thought of a practitioner is evident most fully in the actions of the practitioner. The terms used are 'knowledge in action' and 'reflection in action'. Eraut (1994) and Munby and Russell argue that these terms do not imply conscious knowledge or reflection but rather, that 'The reflection that Schön is calling attention to is *in the action*, not in the associated thinking about action' (1992, original emphasis). The teacher is not reflecting consciously but is functioning intuitively. Thus, Eraut (1994) sees Schön's theory as one of metacognition rather than of reflection. It is a theory of different forms of perception, thought and knowledge. This is not to argue that practitioners neither use, or need to have, theoretical or procedural knowledge relevant to their craft. Rather, it is to say that they do not necessarily make reference to such knowledge while engaged in professional activity because, as Brown and McIntyre (1993: 53) point out:

teachers have no time to wring their hands, reflect on complex theories of learning or of motivation, and make sophisticated choices between alternative courses of action. They have to act quickly, spontaneously and more or less automatically, immediacy is the essential characteristic of the situation, and any implicit theory the teacher may use must be such that it can swiftly produce the appropriate course of action.

Intuition can provide a holistic way of knowing – it appears to be unconscious insight but it is not, therefore, without basis. Rather, its basis is the whole of what has been known but which cannot, by nature of its size and complexity, be held in consciousness. Reason, by contrast, is concerned with conscious analysis of knowledge which confines it to the level of detail. Eraut (1994: 142) contends that:

there are severe limitations to what can be achieved by a purely positivist approach in the complexities of the real world, as it is only capable of tackling simple or simplified problems . . . the technical rationality model fails to take account of how professionals work in practice in order to achieve their desired goals. Technical rationality is inadequate both as a prescription for, and as a description of, professional practice.

Guy Claxton proposes that babies and animals operate only by intuition, lacking language and self-awareness. Thus, Descartes may have reasoned 'I think [i.e. bring intuition to awareness via language] therefore [I know] I am', but thinking at such a conscious level may lead to a self-awareness that is counterproductive since the effectiveness of experienced teachers is 'dependent on a fluency of action which would be possible only if the action was spontaneous, largely automatic, and based on only very limited conscious examination of available options' (Brown and McIntyre 1993: 106). There is a balance to be struck between the role of conscious and subconscious mental activity. Nørretranders (1998) ascribes to consciousness the ingenious function of deciding on what is important but considers that the sorting and interpretation required for it to know what is important is not conscious. He concludes that subliminal perception and sorting is the real secret behind consciousness.

As a practical skill, teaching makes similar demands to certain performance arts. One can experience the nervousness of stage fright or muff one's lines or hit a mental block. Experienced professionals perform fluently and with real artistry despite unexpected or hostile events. This is made possible by the development of routine procedures that are second nature to the practitioner, having been run through so many times. Rehearsing for a stage performance is an accepted technique which can also be used in teaching. The rationalist project has emphasized content and objectives whereas intuition allows us to focus on how a lesson will develop under real-life conditions.

Professional practice is characterized by complexity, is dynamic and interactive and happens in a very specific and constantly changing context. Images, whether visual or metaphorical, can be used more readily than verbal reasoning by practitioners. Pattern recognition allows them to read the context at a glance and to adapt the preconceived plan in the light of the changing context. The fluent performance of an experienced professional may depend, in part, on the ability to carry out a complex series of actions without the need for conscious thought until the subconscious brings to awareness that which is important.

The intuitive practitioner also makes use of more deliberate thinking in order to analyse objectively certain problems such as a newly-encountered scenario or an unexpected or unusual difficulty; to plan in advance the learning aims, teaching methods, resources etc; and to reflect on and evaluate the outcomes and the events of a lesson with a particular emphasis on self-monitoring. Thus, three main thinking processes underpin teaching: the intuitive thinking that underlies action and rapid decision making, the analytical and objective thinking that allows teachers to plan for learning and the reflective thinking that is crucial to monitoring and learning from experience.

The interconnectedness of the three thinking processes is represented cyclically in Figure 1. Intuitive thinking is characteristic of experience and its

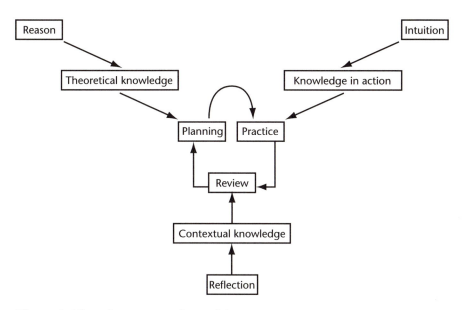

Figure 1 Thought processes in teaching

product is tacit knowledge in action which is evident in and supportive of practice. However, practice alone is inadequate and calls for both preparation and review. At the preparation stage, rational thinking makes use of theoretical knowledge in order to draw up a plan of what is to be done. At the review stage, reflective thinking allows lessons to be learned from practical experience that build into local, contextual craft–knowledge which can support further planning.

In this book we are concerned with and will pay particular attention to intuitive thinking. It is inevitable, therefore, that it will be given more prominence than other forms of thinking and that a distorted picture will be painted. There is no intention here to devalue other thought processes. Our purpose is to make the case for intuition in professional development and professional practice so that it may take its rightful place alongside reason and reflection.

The editors and all but one of the other contributors are active researchers within the University of Bristol, Graduate School of Education. They are all currently engaged in teaching and research relating to the initial and/or in-service education and training of schoolteachers, trainers and lecturers. The book draws upon their diverse and extensive expertise as facilitators of professional learning, and as researchers, in exploring a novel and important theme which has largely been neglected hitherto in the literature. This collection is distinguished from most edited works in that there has been unusually tight collaboration between the contributors throughout the process of researching and writing the chapters. Each piece of research has been developed in the light of the other contributions.

The book is divided into five parts, the first of which offers a number of perspectives on intuition. In the opening chapter, John Furlong sets out what he sees as the key political and epistemological challenges to professional autonomy faced by teachers today. Politically, governments are increasingly adopting interventionist forms of public management; epistemologically, teachers' autonomy is undermined by the collapse of certainty in the 'grand narratives' of earlier periods. The four main responses to these challenges, he argues, are the 'reflective practitioner' movement; the reassertion of the importance of theory and the 'rationalist' project; the critical education movement deriving from Habermas and others; and a humanistic approach that emphasizes emotional, personal, and intuitive sides of professionalism. Advocates of the fourth approach (which this book largely represents) must face two issues. First they need to recognize the degree of legitimacy of political demands for greater control. A concern with intuition must not be used as defence against intervention. Second, they need to engage with, rather than ignore, the rationalist attempt to articulate explicit criteria of 'good teaching' and 'good professionalism'.

This is followed by a chapter by Guy Claxton that offers a conceptual and psychological overview of intuition, designed to complement the socio-political and professional perspective of Chapter 1. The word intuition has been used in a host of different ways, and if it is to be discussed profitably, these need disentangling and tidying up. One of the reasons why education has been wary of intuition is the mysterious, if not supernatural air that hangs over it. Guy Claxton shows that, while there are some usages of intuition which are indeed somewhat mystical, there are others that are psychologically quite straightforward, such as learning and performance without explicit comprehension and awareness; the use of implicitly generated analogies; the detection of 'inklings' that manifest through imagery or bodily responses; and holistic judgement. He reviews recent empirical work that bears on these forms of intuition, and lays out some of the distinctions which the subsequent contributions will make use of and develop.

In Chapter 3, Lucy Atkinson examines the divergence that people exhibit in their use of intuition. She considers the possible link between trusting in one's own judgement and acting on intuition, and hypothesizes that lack of trust in judgement can lead to an unwillingness or inability to perform such actions. In order to pinpoint possible causes of this divergence, some aspects of the initial nurturing environment of infancy are considered. The interaction and balance of these aspects are hypothesized as being crucial to the development of trust in judgement. The chapter then looks at how this divergence in acting on intuition may affect the learner in subsequent environments such as school, higher education and professional training, concluding with a review of the implications of this perspective for the providers of these environments.

In the second part of the book, we focus on intuition in early professional learning, particularly in the context of initial teacher education. In Chapter 4, Terry Atkinson considers the ways in which intuition and reflection interweave at different stages of teachers' development. In the first stage, student teachers, as is widely documented, arrive with a variety of largely implicit beliefs about teaching which condition their 'intuitions', judgements and reactions. But do these need addressing head-on, as many advocates of 'reflective practice' claim? In the second stage, students are exhorted to be as methodical, thoughtful and explicit in their planning and evaluation as possible. But is this the best way of learning? In the final stage, Terry considers the place of intuition in the art of teaching itself. Do practising teachers leave the phase of self-consciousness behind, and if not, how does reflection best serve their changing needs?

Following this, an empirical chapter by Peter John takes a detailed look at the intuitive ways in which new teachers understand the contexts in which they find themselves, and their own performance and reactions. Drawing upon case study data gathered using stimulated recall interviews, participant observation and process trace methodologies, Peter explores, first, the sorts of meanings student teachers attribute to their classroom practice, and, second, the sorts of ways in which their intuitive understandings of their subjects, their pupils and their classrooms influence their emerging teaching styles. The chapter focuses particularly on the developing 'know-how' – as Peter puts it, the routines, recipes and rituals – that enables the teacher to 'sense the mood' of a class, and make good intuitive decisions 'on the hoof'.

Still in the realm of teacher education, Elisabeth Lazarus in Chapter 6 draws on her experience of initial teacher and mentor training in a range of national cultures, including Malaysia and the UK, to explore the relationship between intuition and reflection in the interaction between new teachers and their mentors, and asks how best mentors can be prepared to share both their 'know-how' and their knowledge. How does the effort to explicate their own expertise impinge on mentors' own professional development? And what kind of knowledge, delivered in what kinds of ways, at what kinds of rates and stages, offers maximal facilitation for the beginning teacher? Elisabeth particularly asks: how can mentors best be trained to use their intuition?

The balance and relationship between explicit knowledge and implicit, intuitive competence is hotly contested in many professional areas, not least that of the teaching and learning of foreign languages. In Chapter 7, Teaching English as a Foreign Language (TEFL) teacher education specialists Gerald Clibbon and Arlene Gilpin outline some of the different positions that have been taken in their field on the need for, and the status of, explicit knowledge in the context of language learning, and in learning to teach languages. There is a current fashion in teacher education, for example, for the use of 'awareness raising' activities that are supposed to form a bridge between teachers, learners and language. The authors review a range of such activities, present a framework for evaluating them, and explore its applicability in other areas of professional training. The widely encouraged activity of 'reflection' turns out to be more complex and problematic than is often assumed.

In the third part of the book we focus on the role of intuition on more mature areas of professional practice. In Chapter 8, Agnes McMahon examines the framework of national standards and qualifications for the continuing professional development of teachers that is being developed by the Teacher Training Agency (TTA), and questions whether it will facilitate the development of intuitive and reflective modes of learning. The TTA is rightly concerned that a professional development curriculum for teachers should focus on the knowledge and skills that teachers will need to exercise their responsibilities within schools, but it would be unfortunate if this was interpreted to mean a narrow, competency-based approach to professional development. The chapter discusses approaches to continuing professional development for teachers which recognize the importance of intuition and reflection, as well as the acquisition of more practical skills.

Nowhere is intuition treated with more distrust than in science, and this attitude may spill over into the professional attitudes of science teachers and teacher educators, inhibiting their use of imagination, intuition and 'hunch' in the design and delivery of classroom activities. In Chapter 9 Richard Brawn contrasts this 'culture of rationality' with the tolerance, indeed prizing, of intuition in another discipline that is also seen as essentially scientific: medicine. Both the classroom teacher and the medical practitioner are required to exercise their 'clinical judgement', which often goes beyond, and is sometimes at odds with, the dictates of reason. Yet both receive a training that places a premium on the explicit, analytical weighing of evidence, and the rational justification of decisions. Using data from interviews with both teachers and doctors, Richard asks whether the medical world contains a more productively ambivalent attitude towards intuition, and if so, whether the world of science education might not have valuable lessons to learn from the comparison.

The literature contains suggestions that intuition, in one of its forms, is a way of knowing that is pre-eminently suited to complex situations. In Chapter 10 Laurinda Brown and Alf Coles, drawing on the work of Bruner, Damasio, Fischbein and Gattegno, develop a model of the teacher as an intuitive actor in a complex world. In this model, intuition is viewed as a way of knowing which gives a holistic sense of purpose and feeling that then functions as the 'ground' that allows reason and analysis to make fast, effective decisions. This model requires a reappraisal of the traditional dichotomies between 'reason' and 'emotion', and 'analysis' and 'intuition', and is illustrated through a variety of practical examples and vignettes from teacher training and classroom practice. This model is of particular interest in that it provides a way of integrating the learning of both students and teachers.

Finally in this section, Gill Gregory investigates the relationship between creativity and intuition in management education. She explores the attitudes to creativity, and the cultures that either support or inhibit it, in the world of business. Drawing on the literature that links creativity and intuition via the concept of 'incubation', Gill argues that professionals, if they are to develop their creativity, need to nurture the development of certain psychological qualities and dispositions, and also the development of a conducive climate. Both of these, she suggests, require a reappraisal, one private, the other public and corporate, of the value of intuition, and its relationship to reason.

Part 4 looks at the relationship between intuition and assessment. In a largely theoretical chapter, Patricia Broadfoot sets the scene for the following two chapters, which focus on the place of intuition in professional assessment and evaluation, again in different settings. She argues that educational assessment, and its preoccupation with measuring and comparing, reflects the rise of technical rationality since the Enlightenment of the eighteenth century. In contrast to the current *Zeitgeist* of league tables and measurable performance indicators, she argues that it is possible to conceive of assessment much more intuitively, as the product of an essentially human interaction between assessor and assessed. The price that has been paid for the domination of a measurement approach, as against the recognition of assessment as a humanistic project, is discussed. Chapter 12 concludes by exploring the potential for a more intuitive approach to educational assessment.

In Chapter 13, Roger Curtis, Paul Weeden and Jan Winter focus on the place of intuition in teachers' assessment of children. Looking at teachers' assessment practice across a range of subjects, the authors explore the kinds of judgements commonly made and the evidence on which they are based. The emphasis in recent years has shifted towards 'objective' forms of evidence, with an implied distrust of teachers' unsupported evaluations. Yet there is little doubt that much of what teachers know about students' performance and potential, as a result of hundreds of hours of personal contact, cannot be captured by such 'measurements'. If, as the evidence suggests, the quality of intuitive judgements can be both increased and undermined, the distrust of teachers' intuition runs the risk of becoming a self-fulfilling prophecy. The way forward may be to seek to develop the validity and reliability of intuition, not to abandon it. Interviews with teachers of art, mathematics and geography explore their views and confusions about the relationship between intuitive/subjective and rational/objective judgement, and highlight the generic issues that are raised.

One of the jobs of a university tutor is to encourage the development of discipline-specific literacies: students' ability to write in appropriate academic genres. But how do they do this? In Chapter 14, David Johnson presents the results of an empirical investigation in which lecturers were asked to judge either intuitively or 'objectively' the quality of student scripts, in terms not of content knowledge but of how well they conformed to a particular genre. On the basis of this data, David explores the relationship between the two types of judgement, and asks when it is useful for the intuitive to be made explicit. Drawing on the work of Owen, he suggests that while professionals have an extensive 'tacit knowledge of structural properties of text', they are rarely able to intervene, as teachers of literacy, at levels above those of word choice or sentence construction.

The final part of the book comprises a single chapter: a critical overview of the preceding chapters by the only author from outside the Bristol Graduate

School of Education. Michael Eraut considers the extent to which the contributors have met the challenge laid down in John Furlong's opening chapter. Have they collectively advanced our understanding of professional practice, professional learning and 'professionalism'? Has the case been made for the role of intuition in professional learning and development? It was felt that this task would best be accomplished by someone outside of the group of contributors who had worked together for some time on these ideas. Michael synthesizes the arguments put forward in many of the earlier chapters while adding his own perspective. He also notes the contradictions inherent in a book which brings together diverse views on a complex and, until now, little understood dimension to professional learning and practice. He concludes with a rousing analysis of what is to be done in schools and colleges to shake off the shackles of managerial orthodoxy, thus bringing the book full circle with an affirmation of the impact on learning to be made through liberating the intuitive practitioners of the teaching force.

References

Brown, S. and McIntyre, D. (1993) *Making Sense of Teaching*. Buckingham: Open University Press.

Claxton, G.L., Atkinson, T., Osborn, M.J. and Wallace, M. (eds) (1996) *Liberating the Learner: Lessons for Professional Development in Education*. London: Routledge.

Eraut, M. (1994) *Developing Professional Knowledge and Competence*. London: Falmer Press.

Munby, H. and Russell, T. (eds) (1992) *Teachers and Teaching: From Classroom to Reflection*. London: Falmer Press.

Nørretranders, T. (1998) *The User Illusion*. New York: Viking.

Schön, D.A. (1983) *The Reflective Practitioner*. New York: Basic Books.

Schön, D.A. (1987) *Educating the Reflective Practitioner*. San Francisco, CA: Jossey-Bass.

Schön, D.A. (1991) *The Reflective Turn*. New York: Teachers College Press.

 **Part 1**

Perspectives on intuition in
professional learning and practice

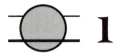 1

Intuition and the crisis in teacher professionalism

John Furlong

What is good, Phaedrus, and what is not good – need we ask anyone to tell us these things?

It is what he was saying months before in the classroom in Montana, a message Plato and every dialectician since him had missed, since they all sought to define the Good in its intellectual relation to things.

(Pirsig 1976: 389)

Introduction

I recently had cause to pick up Pirsig's *Zen and the Art of Motor Cycle Maintenance* (1976) nearly 25 years after first reading it (my son was reading it at the time) and was immediately recaptivated by its romance: the excitement of taking on the big boys in philosophy; the belief that there was another way of looking at the world that was lost on those (the dialecticians) dominated by over-rationalistic perspectives. On reflection, I was also struck by the similarity between the hero Phaedrus' project – struggling with understanding complex and intangible concepts such as Good and Quality – and the project the contributors to this volume had set themselves. They too have been concerned with defining Good and Quality, though in their case it is quality in professional learning and practice that they are interested in. Moreover, like Phaedrus they recognize that there is an essential element in professionalism that has largely been overlooked in conventional rationalist accounts. For them, that missing element is defined as 'intuition' and this book is devoted to its exploration.

One of the challenges of writing a book on a topic such as intuition is that as a concept it is so hard to pin down. Different dimensions, different nuances of meaning move in and out of focus in the hands of different writers. Moreover, as Claxton demonstrates in Chapter 2, the potential of meanings around the notion of intuition vary considerably from the mystical (a perspective that

I suspect Pirsig would probably be happy with) to the rational to the mundane. Equally variable are the forms or 'manifestations' of intuition which include physical sensations, hunches and aesthetic responses.

But it is not my aim in this chapter to enter the debate over the nature of intuition. That is for the other contributors. Rather it is to 'situate' the current debate, asking how it is that an issue such as intuition in professionalism has emerged as an important topic for consideration at this particular juncture. For as Apple argues, 'Authors are not mechanically determined by ideology, or class or history. However, authors are very much *in* the history of their societies "shaping and shaped by that history and their social experience" (Said 1993)' (Apple 1996: vii).

I will be arguing that it is no accident that a group of educationalists have become concerned with an intangible such as intuition at this particular time, for the background to this concern lies in the current crisis of confidence in the nature of professionalism. Traditionally, as Hoyle and John (1995) suggest, debates around the notion of what it means to be a professional have focused on three central issues: knowledge, autonomy and responsibility. As I will outline in the next section, each one of these dimensions of professionalism has been fundamentally challenged in recent years. As a result, the teaching profession has found it progressively more difficult to respond to an ever-increasing barrage of 'technical rationalist' forms of management and control.

The overriding question facing the teaching as well as many other professions at the turn of the century is therefore how to respond to this crisis; I will argue that the current concern with intuition is part of that response. However, a concern with intuition is only the latest in a long line of such responses. In the second half of my chapter I will therefore discuss three other schools of thought within the contemporary literature on professionalism. The first is the idea of the reflective practitioner, an approach which draws on the interpretive tradition of knowledge; the second, which I call the 'new rationalism', draws on forms of positivism. The final approach, critical theory, rejects both interpretive and positivist views of knowledge and instead focuses on a process – 'the pursuit of truth'. In the conclusion of the chapter I will reflect on the success of these other responses to the current crisis in order to identify two fundamental challenges or difficulties that I believe those interested in the idea of intuition need to address if the concept is to contribute effectively to the rebuilding of our confidence in teachers' professionalism.

The crisis of professionalism

As I suggested above, the background to the current interest in intuition is the crisis in professionalism. That there is such a crisis is widely acknowledged (Schön 1983, 1987; Hargreaves 1994; Whitty 1996; Barnett 1997; Clark and Newman 1997; Bottery 1998). It encompasses all three of the traditional dimensions of professionalism identified by Hoyle and John (1995): knowledge, responsibility and autonomy. The questioning of one has led progressively to the questioning of the others.

Knowledge

The idea that professionals have access to specialized bodies of knowledge is central to traditional definitions of professionalism. Doctors, lawyers, and to a lesser extent teachers, have been seen as possessing technical or specialist knowledge which is beyond the reach of lay people. However, the sort of knowledge that has been seen as important is very different to that which might be involved in intuition. As Hoyle and John (1995) argue, traditionally professionals' knowledge is seen as having two component parts: first it is objective knowledge tested by scientific method through which it acquires validity; second it is supported by a variety of theoretical models and case descriptions which allow it to be applied in specific cases. It is because professionals need to learn this body of external, objective knowledge that they need long periods of training, significant parts of which need to go on within higher education: 'professionals, through specialist and usually long periods of training, are taught to understand this research validated knowledge and to apply it constructively and intelligently according to the technical rules governing the conduct of the profession' (Hoyle and John 1995: 46).

However, in recent years, the certainty that there is indeed an objective body of knowledge available to practitioners to 'guide their practice', and into which new recruits need to be inducted, has been profoundly challenged. As a result there is now a serious 'epistemological crisis' within the professions. That crisis has two interrelated dimensions. At the most fundamental level there has been increasing uncertainty that objective knowledge exists at all. As Barnett (1990: 11) has said:

> from various theoretical quarters – philosophy of science, sociology of knowledge, epistemology, critical theory and post-structuralism – the ideas of objective knowledge and truth have come under a massive assault. What if anything is to replace objective knowledge is unclear. Pragmatism, relativism, 'metacriticism' and even 'anything goes' are all proposed. The very diversity of the alternative opinions is testimony to the collapse of some of our basic epistemological tenets.

At the same time, the notion that theoretically-based knowledge (even if it did exist) could actually 'guide' practice has also been questioned. As Hirst (1996) reminds us, controversy over the role of 'theory' in professional practice has a long history; the debate has been highly complex, largely partisan and has shown little sign of resolution. Where there has been agreement however is in dissatisfaction with the notion that technical rationalist forms of knowledge (and most particularly the four 'ologies' of education: sociology, psychology, philosophy, history) can guide professional action. This questioning of technical rationalism in professional knowledge has been most clearly articulated by Schön (1987: 3–4): 'Technical rationality holds that practitioners are instrumental problem solvers who select technical means best suited to particular purposes. Rigorous professional practitioners solve well-formed instrumental problems by applying theory and technique derived from systematic, preferably scientific knowledge.'

In reality, Schön suggests, professionals work in a very different way. Rather than inhabiting the 'high ground' of professional certainty, they have to work in the 'swampy lowlands' of everyday life, facing situations that are complex and messy, defying easy technical solutions: 'the problems of real-world practice do not present themselves to practitioners as well-formed structures. Indeed they tend not to present themselves as problems at all but as messy indeterminate situations' (1987: 4).

Of course to those with an interest in intuition, such a description is hardly novel. None of the contributors to this volume would expect professional practice to be reducible to a technical following of rules derived from abstract knowledge. However, the public's growing recognition that the professionals' knowledge is not so objective after all and does not and cannot 'guide practice' has given rise to a progressively deepening crisis of confidence both in professional education and in professionals themselves.

Responsibility

The other traditional dimensions of professionalism identified by Hoyle and John (1995) – autonomy and responsibility – are closely interrelated. Professionals, they suggest, are traditionally seen as working in complex and unpredictable situations which necessitate autonomy: 'as professionals work in uncertain situations in which judgement is more important than routine, it is essential to effective practice that they should be sufficiently free from bureaucratic and political constraint to act on judgements made in the best interests (as they see them) of the clients' (Hoyle and John 1995: 77). Of critical importance here is the suggestion that professionals make judgements on behalf of clients *as they see them*. Given the complexity of the situations they face, they necessarily have to interpret those interests. To draw a distinction utilized by Hoyle and John, they do not act as an 'agent' of someone else (for example the government); they act as a 'principal', making their own judgements.

However, exercising judgement in relation to clients' interests is a complex matter. It does not simply demand the application of specialist knowledge. Such judgements also entail the utilization of values, for if professionals are to balance their own and their clients' interests, then they have a responsibility to develop a 'voluntaristic commitment to a set of principles' (Hoyle and John 1995: 104) that will govern their day-to-day professional activity.

The interconnectedness of the three dimensions of traditional conceptions of professionalism should now be clear. It is because professionals face complex and unpredictable situations that they need a specialized body of *knowledge*; if they are to apply that knowledge, it is argued that they need the *autonomy* to make their own judgements; and given that they have that autonomy, it is essential that they act with *responsibility* – collectively they need to develop appropriate professional values.

However, in recent years, the belief that professionals such as teachers do indeed act with responsibility in relation to their clients (teachers, parents, industry, the country) has been questioned and as a consequence of that questioning there has been a growing challenge to their autonomy. Instead of acting with responsibility, the teaching profession has been accused of failing to serve its clients' interests. Too frequently, it has been argued, teachers have interpreted their clients' interests in ways that are of convenience to the profession rather than the clients themselves. Teaching, like so many other professions has, it is suggested, become subject to what has been termed 'producer capture'.

Producer capture is seen to occur when a service appears to be organized more to suit the needs of producers than consumers: 'The professionals create a technical language which serves only to bamboozle ordinary people and they organise the system for their convenience rather than to respond to the demands of its consumers. The result is inertia and resistance to change' (Ransom 1990: 8). This interpretation of the work of professionals is well illustrated by O'Hear (1988) in his critique of one professional group, initial teacher educators. According to O'Hear, 'a large vested interest has arisen in the form of a teacher-training establishment, which runs, directs and assesses the courses in teacher training. In assessing the value of this training, we shall thereby, indirectly consider whose interests it *really* serves' (1988: 6, emphasis added). For those who support these interpretations of teachers' work, no progress will be made in reforming the educational system until the autonomy of the 'educational establishment' is broken.

Autonomy

The development of teachers' professional autonomy in England and Wales has a long history but it reached its height in the post-war period. Between the 1940s and the early 1970s, teachers, both as individuals and as a profession, achieved significant control over many aspects of their professional lives including the school curriculum (Grace 1987). Yet as all of us are acutely aware, that autonomy has been fundamentally challenged in recent years with developing external control of almost all dimensions of educational activity: the curriculum, pupil assessment, teachers' terms and conditions of work, the organization and management of schools, colleges, universities, and teacher education. The questioning of professional autonomy first began with Callaghan's Ruskin speech of 1976, but in reality, Callaghan did no more than throw down the gauntlet. It was left to successive Conservative governments in the 1980s and 1990s to develop a twofold strategy to make that challenge to teacher autonomy a reality. First, in England and Wales, as in many other parts of the English speaking world (Whitty *et al.* 1998), there were moves to develop a more devolved system of education with a greater degree of institutional autonomy and parental choice. These sorts of policy initiatives were intended to introduce a 'market', or rather 'quasi-market' (Le Grand and Bartlett 1993), element into the provision of educational services. Increasingly therefore, teachers' autonomy (including their right to utilize their intuition in making professional judgements) has had to be moderated by the need to respond to that competitive market in which the 'currency' of competition has become 'objective' performance indicators.

Second, the introduction of market forces was accompanied by increased direct central control. As Whitty *et al.* (1998: v) say: 'in many contexts, devolution of responsibilities to individual schools was accompanied by increased powers of surveillance on the part of central and state governments'. This central intervention has taken many forms: the national curriculum, assessment schemes, league tables, competency frameworks and progressively more invasive inspection regimes. And as Patricia Broadfoot in Chapter 12 points out, in nearly every case, these new mechanisms of control are based on, and promote, external objectivist forms of knowledge; they are the antithesis of more subtle and complex 'ways of knowing' that are central to a notion of intuition.

As I have argued elsewhere (Furlong 1992: 169), this new language of control:

> creates the impression of disinterestedness and objectivity in education.
> It implies that there is a common framework for people with fixed goals.
> In the words of Popkewitcz (1987) it 'flattens reality and obscures the
> struggles which fashion and shape our world'. Yet underneath, such
> approaches often remain deeply ideological. The 'neutral professional' is
> in reality asked to deliver an education that is increasingly defined by a
> political process over which the individual teacher has little control.

Overall, therefore, we can now gauge the depth and breadth of the current crisis of professionalism in the field of education. Teachers' relative autonomy from external intervention (which might allow them to utilize their own judgement and intuition) has been profoundly challenged and they now find themselves having to be responsive both to the demands of the market and to central government in professional decision making. However, arguing against such increased control is highly problematic given the progressive undermining of the profession's confidence in its own professional knowledge. In the past, it was expert objective knowledge that was the cornerstone of professionalism; it was because professionals were seen as possessing such knowledge that society granted them autonomy to make key decisions about the most fundamental aspects of our lives – about our health, about our finances, about our legal affairs and about the education of our children. But once the certainty of that knowledge has been called into question, the basis of professionalism itself starts to crumble. After all, if all knowledge is relative, who can argue that common sense, ideology or the market should not determine educational policy and practice; the voices of 'expert teachers' have no more right to be heard than anyone else's.

Responding to the crisis

How then can professions like teaching respond to this crisis? Or perhaps we should first address the prior question of *whether* they should respond. Is the lack of current confidence in professionalism a problem for anyone else but the professionals themselves? I would suggest that it is and that given the central role that professionals continue to hold in our society, constructing an effective response is vital to the strength of our democracy. The epistemological and ethical questions that have been raised in relation to the nature of professional knowledge and values are profound. Professional practice does involve the utilization of highly complex forms of knowledge; it also constantly involves teachers in the execution of moral judgements demanding an explicit recognition of the centrality of values in professional life. These complexities cannot simply be swept under the carpet by inventing more and more performance indicators and other explicit forms of external control. To ignore them is to devalue the professionalism of teachers and in turn to devalue education itself. The current low morale of many within the teaching profession and the increasing utilitarianism of many young people in their attitude towards education are perhaps testaments to the consequences of this approach.

Finding ways of responding to the difficulties that have been raised is therefore important and I would suggest that an exploration of intuition is one such response. The recognition that there are many different 'ways of knowing' that have been ignored and silenced in the traditional obsession with objective knowledge is vitally important. Indeed it is the crisis with conventional conceptions of professional knowledge that opens up the possibility of exploring alternatives.

However, as I have already indicated, examining intuition is not the only response that is possible and in this second half of the chapter I want to set out three other alternative responses. They are: the notion of the reflective practitioner; 'new rationalism' which is now leading to the call for 'evidence based practice'; and the critical theory perspective loosely based on the work of Habermas. Each of these responses focuses on professional knowledge, perhaps recognizing that it is here that we can find the heart of our current difficulties. As we will see, they each address the issue of knowledge in rather more conventional ways than those responses concerned with intuition. Despite this, I believe that a consideration of these three schools of thought is valuable in that if they are scrutinized carefully, they can teach us some important lessons about how the concept of intuition needs to be developed if it is to help us build a new and richer understanding of professionalism.

Reflective practice

The most frequently articulated response to the crisis in professionalism has been through the development of the notion of reflection. As the Modes of Teacher Education research project (Barrett *et al.* 1992; Furlong *et al.*

forthcoming) clearly demonstrated, throughout the 1990s the overwhelming majority of those leading teacher education programmes in England and Wales claimed that their courses were explicitly informed by a notion of reflection.

The idea of reflection and its role in professional knowledge is notoriously difficult to pin down. As many commentators have observed, there are probably as many different definitions of reflection as there are individuals using the term to describe their practice. Much has been written on the subject during the last decade (for some useful, conceptually-based summaries, see Calderhead and Gates 1993; Zeichner 1994; Furlong and Maynard 1995) and I therefore do not intend to spend too much space here exploring these differences. However, for the purposes at hand, it is important to describe the way in which reflection, however it is defined, responds to the crisis in our understanding of professional knowledge.

One of the most influential writers on the subject of reflection in recent years has been Schön (1983; 1987); a consideration of his work will therefore provide a useful starting point. As we saw before, Schön explicitly presents his ideas as a response to the crisis in professional knowledge. It is precisely because traditional forms of specialist knowledge do not relate to contemporary practice that it is necessary, he argues, to develop a new 'epistemology of practice'. For Schön that is characterized as reflection.

At first sight, Schön's presentation of reflection appears to have much in common with intuition. Rather than seeing professional practice as based on rational decision making, he characterizes it as a form of artistry. However, he goes on to argue that the difficulty with terms such as artistry, wisdom, and indeed intuition, is that (according to him at least) they can close off enquiry – they can too easily become junk categories 'attaching names to phenomena that elude conventional strategies of explanation' (Schön 1983: 32). Instead, he argues, we need to develop a new body of research-based knowledge that is the product of a careful examination of what professionals actually *do*.

As a result of such careful observation, Schön presents his classic threefold definition of professional practice involving different 'levels' of consciousness or explicitness in thinking. The three different levels are 'knowing-in-action' in which thinking is entirely implicit, embedded in the act of doing itself; 'reflection-in-action' when, because of some problem or difficulty, we draw our interpretive processes to the level of consciousness but without stopping what we are doing; and 'reflection-on-action' which takes place after the event, when we try to articulate, to ourselves or others, some of the processes that were going on in our actions.[1]

As I have indicated, there are many different conceptions of reflection and Schön's work, however influential, differs in key respects from a number of other formulations. But what it has in common with the majority of conceptions of reflection is two things. First it focuses on a cognitive or thinking process. Professional practice is still seen as being based on a notion of *knowledge* and this knowledge and the thinking processes associated with it can be captured, at least in part, in language. From this perspective therefore, professionals can claim to have a distinctive body of expert knowledge but it is

much more complex and grounded in real, live contexts than has traditionally been imagined. Second, the vision of professional knowledge being advo-
cated is based firmly in the interpretive tradition. Because each context that a
professional faces is so different, it is for the individual themselves to develop
their own principles as to what constitutes sound professional practice. In
marked contrast to technical rationalism, professional knowledge for the
reflective practitioner is essentially personal and relative. Professional education from this point of view is therefore a process of encouraging trainees to
engage with different forms of professional knowledge – some of it derived
from formal propositional knowledge, some of it derived from experience
itself. It is through using each to critique the other that individuals are able to
reach their own conclusions as to what constitutes sound professional practice.

Despite its popularity, the notion of reflection has proved a weak defence in
the battle to support professionalism. Professionals themselves may believe
that writers such as Schön capture more of the complexities of their day-
to-day lives than the traditional theoretically-based accounts of a previous
generation. But when it comes to arguing against ever more invasive forms of
central control, the argument that professional knowledge is essentially personal and situationally specific has not proved particularly robust.

A rather different approach, which potentially could be more politically
effective, involves a reconceptualization rather than an abandoning of
rationalism. Here, the contemporary work of Hirst (1996) provides a useful
starting point and it is to a consideration of his arguments that we now turn.

'New rationalism'

'To fail to equip young entrants to the profession with as clear and critical a
grasp of at least the most defensible goals and practices of education leaves
them and their pupils at the mercy of prejudice and ill-considered ideology. It
is also to render almost impossible the systematic development of education
in any truly coherent and rational way' (Hirst 1996: 167).

Like Schön, Hirst begins from a recognition that there is a current crisis in
the epistemological bases of professional life that has resulted from the overly
rationalist approach to professional knowledge that was propounded in the
post-war years. This approach, as we have already seen, was based on the idea
that 'theory' derived from the foundation disciplines could directly guide
practice. In the 1960s, Hirst himself was significantly associated with this perspective (e.g. Hirst 1966). However, as he now says, it soon became apparent
that the disciplines of education could not begin to provide clear answers to
the immensely difficult theoretical questions that they addressed; and even
when there seemed to be answers, these could not begin to add up to the
answering of the extremely complex practical questions that they were
expected to tackle. For Hirst, this is because 'practice' is far more complex and
multi-faceted than was recognized at the time. It involves far more than cognitive knowledge:

> Engaging in [educational practice] may involve elements of knowledge, belief, judgment, criteria of success, principles, skills, dispositions, feelings, elements encompassing any or all of our capacities and their achievements. These elements are inextricably locked together in any given practice, each taking its distinctive character in part from its relationship to other elements, the whole constituting the very nature of the practice.
>
> (Hirst 1996: 170)

For Hirst, such 'practices' could never be captured in the propositional knowledge that can be derived from the foundation disciplines of education. That was nothing more than 'an over-intellectual myth'. However, Hirst argues that the response to this realization must not be to turn our back on rationalism; that is merely an evasion of responsibility. Professional practices may be much more complex that we originally thought, but they can still be rationally developed and defended. Professionalism must still aspire to use 'reason' to articulate the most defensible practical ends of education and the best means of achieving these.

However, developing our sense of 'the best', Hirst suggests, involves doing something different from that which was done in the past; it involves developing forms of *practical* rather than *theoretical* reason. Within theoretical reason, 'concepts and propositions are developed solely in understanding and explaining our world in the pursuit of truth irrespective of any practical purposes' (Hirst 1996: 171). By contrast, the object of practical reason is the development of 'practical principles': 'practical principles are the outcomes of successful practice, generalisations are valid only insofar as they capture what successful practice entails . . . In the critical examination of practices in the terms of practical discourse itself, new and more rational, that is successful, practices can be conceived and experimentally assessed' (1996: 171).

Practical reason for Hirst must have a number of distinctive features if it is to help advance professionalism. First, it must be a public not a private process, based on open professional collaboration and critical enquiry undertaken by significant social groups. Second, it must be systematically structured. What we need, Hirst suggests, is well considered experimentation in which more refined discourse is generated to embody widely applicable practices open to public examination, criticism and transmission. Finally, such an approach must continue to engage with theoretically-based knowledge. Theoretical reason may not itself be able to provide the basis for generating rational practices, but Hirst suggests that it does provide crucially important knowledge and understanding of ourselves and our physical and social context. Such knowledge sets out the boundaries, the framework within which rational practices can be developed:

> We have yet to learn effectively two linked truths; that rational practices for the achievement of our good must in all areas be practically not theoretically developed but also that if our efforts are not to be constantly thwarted they must be illuminated by all the insights fundamental

theoretical critique can provide [without that] the experimental development of rational practices in any area is proceeding on inadequately
examined presuppositions.

(Hirst 1996: 172)

In the last two years, support for such a reassertion of the rationalist bases
of professional knowledge in education has emerged in the context of the
debate about the quality and value of educational research in Britain. In arguments that have an interesting resonance with those of Hirst, Hargreaves
(1996) has argued for the development of teaching as a 'research-based profession'. At present, he suggests, teaching compares badly with medicine
where some of the most important research is conducted by practitioners
themselves, evaluating the effects of one treatment or one technique, rather
than another: 'The significant difference between the two professions is that
whereas doctors are demanding and getting more evidence-based research,
teachers are not even seeing their severe lack of evidence-based research as a
problem in urgent need of remedy' (Hargreaves 1994: 4).

However, this is hardly surprising, Hargreaves argues, because most educational research is currently irrelevant to the needs of teachers. It rarely
addresses their practical questions and even on the occasions when it does, it
seldom gives them answers in forms that they can use – in Hirst's terms, it is
largely based on 'theoretical' rather than 'practical' reason. As a result, Hargreaves suggests, there are few areas which have yielded a corpus of research
evidence regarded as scientifically sound and a worthwhile resource to guide
professional action: 'One must ask the essential question: just how much
research is there which (i) demonstrates conclusively that, if teachers change
their practice from x to y, there will be a significant and enduring improvement in teaching and learning and (ii) has developed an effective method of
convincing teachers of the benefits of, and means to, changing from x to y'
(Hargreaves 1994: 5).

The Teacher Training Agency (TTA) has taken up Hargreaves' critique of
educational research as well as his plea for a new approach with enthusiasm.
It has started to commission its own research and 'Ultimately the TTA hopes
to develop a culture of using evidence in the classroom for continuing
improvement of classroom practice' (Millett 1997). As in medicine, the aspiration is to build a new form of 'evidence-based' professionalism 'in which
clinical, managerial and policy decisions are based on sound information
about research findings and scientific developments' (Department of Health
1997, para. 1.1).

As I have argued elsewhere (Furlong 1998), there are a number of criti-
cisms that can be made of these arguments, particularly concerning the idea
that objective knowledge in a profession such as teaching is possible. The
belief that through rational analysis we can come to know, even for a
moment, what the best, the most rationally justifiable practices actually are
and that these can then guide professional practice, is, I would suggest, problematic. Such an approach to professional knowledge apparently ignores the

epistemological debates of the last 20 or 30 years. It also ignores what we know about the impact of research on teachers. Studies of teachers' thinking have repeatedly demonstrated that prior beliefs and values (things they have learned in childhood; ideas that are closely associated with their identities) profoundly influence their practice and how they receive research know-ledge. As Kennedy (1997: 7) says, 'the potential for research to contribute to practice depends on its ability to influence teachers' *thinking*' (original empha-sis). And the final response to the current crisis that I want to examine – criti-cal theory – does indeed assert that a particular sort of thinking is the best defence of professionalism.

Critical theory

As I have already indicated, the first two approaches to rebuilding profession-alism that I have discussed (reflection and rationalism) are based on an attempt to reconceptualize professional knowledge. Their implicit argument is that if confidence in professional knowledge can be rebuilt, then pro-fessional autonomy can be re-established. However, as we have also seen, these two movements are based on diametrically opposed conceptions of knowledge. The notion of the reflective practitioner clearly stands within the interpretive tradition, arguing for a recognition of the subjectivity and situa-tional specificity of professional knowledge. In sharp contrast, notions of 'evi-dence-based practice' remain within the positivist tradition.

Critical theory begins from a critique of both the positivist and interpretive conceptions of knowledge. As Carr and Kemmis (1986: 145) explain, posi-tivist social science 'has made a shibboleth of "truth" – as if it stood above social life, could be objectively ascertained and could prescribe wise practice without understanding the human, social, economic, political, historical and practical constraints within which real practice occurs'. Moreover, critical theorists suggest that such an approach will not necessarily lead to greater professional autonomy. On the contrary, as the current interest of the TTA in 'evidence-based practice' demonstrates, it is a short move from 'objective knowledge' to hierarchical or bureaucratic control.

On the other hand, interpretive social science is equally flawed in that it:

> makes a shibboleth of practical judgment, which is informed by know-ledge grounded in the actor's own understanding and circumstances. It thus uses the single criterion of authentic knowledge in arriving at con-clusions about actions: it aims to transform consciousness but may not transform practice because it does not provide a systematic critique of the conditions under which the practice occurs.
>
> (Carr and Kemmis 1986: 145–6)

In contrast to these approaches, critical theory would suggest that profession-alism cannot be reconstituted through any appeal to objective 'truth' in know-ledge, whether subjectively or objectively defined. Truth certainly matters and a commitment to it is seen as being at the heart of professionalism. However, following Habermas (1970; 1974), critical theorists would suggest that truth is not an end point: 'Rather truth is the description we give to a particular kind of human transaction' (Barnett 1990: 59). This transaction is a conversation, but not just any kind of conversation. In normal conversation (what Habermas calls 'communicative action'), individuals tacitly and uncritically accept the norms, social practices and belief systems of everyday life. In 'discourse' on the other hand, participants explicitly criticize the background consensus concerning belief systems, norms, values and ideologies taken for granted in everyday life: 'During everyday communicative interaction, situations arise in which validity claims concerning beliefs and values become problematic; through discourse one questions their validity and engages in argumentation in which validity claims which have become problematic are made the topic and are examined for their justification' (Roderick 1986: 82). It is the commitment to engage in such discourse in relation to one's knowledge and one's values that, for critical theorists, constitutes the heart of true professionalism.

Of course, this sort of intellectual debate is not cosy or easy. It imposes certain demands on participants. They have to listen attentively to others and have to be sincere, coherent and committed. But most fundamental of all, according to Barnett (1990, 1997), is the willingness to expose one's viewpoint to the critical gaze of others. Such 'discourses' can only happen between participants who come together as equals. Habermas conceptualizes this form of life in terms of the 'ideal speech situation' which requires equality and freedom from inner and outer constraints for all participants. He argues that this ideal, 'although counterfactual', is in reality 'anticipated' in all communication (Roderick 1986).

In reality, most professional situations are not constituted in this fashion; as a result they are characterized by 'communicative action' rather than 'discourse'. However, Barnett (1990) suggests that situations approaching this ideal are to be found within the university seminar, and for this reason many would argue that higher education must remain central to professional education (Furlong 1996). In addition, Carr and Kemmis (1986) argue that such idealized situations can be created when teams of professionals work together on forms of action research. But whether or not such conditions of freedom ever in reality exist in their pure form, the importance of the 'pursuit of truth' in relation to professional knowledge and values is seen as central to the notion of professionalism itself.

Critical theorists therefore do not reject either the objective knowledge of positivism or the subjective knowledge of relativism. Both are important forms of knowledge; they are however seen as significantly flawed. True professionalism depends on a continued commitment to hold up knowledge, from wherever it comes, to public, collaborative scrutiny. It also depends on the commitment to create and maintain those spaces within professional life (and perhaps most especially professional education) where critical discourse can flourish. For it is only through this form of discourse that professional knowledge can be freed from its tendency to deteriorate either into subjectivity or into technicism.

Conclusion

These then are the principal arguments that have been advanced in recent years in response to the crisis in professionalism. To date none of them has been particularly successful in stemming the tide of ever more detailed control over professional practice. Indeed it now seems that the current government is interested in utilizing the promise of evidence-based practice to institute even greater control. By sponsoring studies of pedagogy – what Millett (1997) calls 'the last corner of the secret garden' – the aspiration would seem to be to use research to tell teachers *how* to teach as well as *what* to teach. However, it would be wrong to judge the validity of these arguments simply in terms of their political effectiveness. For the most part, they have rightly been part of an internal conversation within the profession itself, driven as much by our need to re-establish confidence in ourselves and our own professional judgements as by any concern with politics. The same is true I suspect in relation to the current exploration of intuition.

In considering the potential contribution of the notion of intuition to an understanding of professionalism, it is valuable to recognize that each of the three approaches I have described above concentrates on a fairly conventional definition of professional knowledge. Those concerned with reflective practice call for a recognition of the importance of subjective knowledge, while those interested in evidence-based practice reassert the need for objective knowledge. Critical theorists, in contrast, consider both forms of knowledge profoundly flawed; as a consequence, they insist that the only route to secure professional knowledge is through a commitment to the pursuit of 'truth' through critical discourse.

However, as the rest of this volume will demonstrate, the idea of intuition is different in that it does not prioritize knowledge as it is conventionally defined. Instead, intuition focuses on 'ways of knowing' – obviously including knowledge but much more besides: feelings, hunches, ways of recognizing complex patterns. In reality, such an approach has a long history; it can for example be recognized in Aristotle's concept of *phronesis* – what Smith (1996) terms 'practical wisdom'. Yet our exclusive contemporary focus on more conventional ideas of knowledge has led us to overlook this tradition. As a result, until now there has been little contemporary exploration of what such practical wisdom might be and how it can be acquired and nurtured. A further elaboration of professionalism from this perspective is therefore to be welcomed.

Despite this, if the notion of intuition is to make a serious contribution to the debate about teachers' professionalism, I would suggest that there are two important lessons to be learned from the other responses to the current crisis of confidence that I have described. The first is to recognize that the demand for accountability in professional practice will not, and in my view, should not, go away. Professionals do need to be able to account for what they do. As James Callaghan said in his Ruskin speech 25 years ago, there is nothing wrong with non-educationalists, even prime ministers, talking about education. Indeed one might say that in a modern democracy there is a great deal that is right about it. The mechanisms so far established to ensure greater accountability such as league tables and inspection reports are recognized as crude and partial by the majority of the population. But the voracity with which the information they provide is consumed, despite its faults, is an indicator of the fact that people do now expect professional accountability. This particular genie is unlikely to be persuaded back into the bottle.

In these circumstances, a call for a recognition of the value of intuition will not find much support if it is utilized simply as a strategy to re-establish privacy within the profession – the creation of some new level of professionalism that demands for accountability cannot reach. The lack of public credibility for the reflective practitioner movement has been precisely because of its unclear definition – its insistence that all professional knowledge is so personal and so situationally specific that it cannot be defined or held up to account. Intuition must not fall into the same trap. Careful empirical and analytical work of the sort presented in this volume is essential.

The second lesson is also connected to this need for accountability. As we have seen, one of the strengths of the new rationalism is its concern with the development of public and explicit definitions of quality. Hirst, for example, wants prospective teachers to be equipped with a 'clear and critical grasp of at least the most defensible goals and practices of education' (1996: 142). Hargreaves (1999) wants us to be able to use research findings to help find out 'what actually works'. I would fully accept the point made by critical theorists that the 'objective' knowledge that such rationalists argue for is partial, and itself must be held up to constant scrutiny if professionalism is to maintain its integrity. I therefore believe that the teaching profession needs vigorously to defend the few remaining opportunities it has to engage in a critical discourse about its own work. I would also accept that publicly defined goals and practices of education are necessarily partial and will change over time. However, the aspiration to define (with all the necessary caveats) publicly defensible principles in relation to the goals and practices of education remains a vitally important project. Without that sort of exploration, all that is left is subjectivity and relativism. Intuition therefore needs to take its place *alongside* rationalism and the constant need for critical discourse; it cannot be seen as a substitute for either of them.

As the chapters in this volume clearly demonstrate, the notion of intuition has much to contribute to our understanding of teachers' professionalism. We have come a long way since the 1960s when it was thought that a further elaboration of the foundation disciplines (sociology, psychology, philosophy and history) was all that was needed in order fully to understand professional practice. But in reviewing the contribution of other approaches as I have done, we can recognize an important gap in our understanding of professionalism which a properly developed understanding of intuition might fill. In doing so, our aim should be to help the profession regain its confidence in its own judgements and then its optimism about its future. As Phaedrus said in the closing moments of his long motor cycle journey when he had finally come to understand the nature of Quality: 'It's going to get better now. You can sort of tell these things' (Pirsig 1976: 406).

Note

1 'Knowing-in-action' clearly has close links to some conceptions of intuition, despite Schön's dislike of the term (see for example Chapter 10 of this volume). However, there are important differences too, particularly concerning his emphasis on knowledge and thinking as opposed to 'ways of knowing'.

References

Apple, M.W. (1996) *Cultural Politics and Education.* New York: Teachers College Press.

Barnett, R. (1990) *The Idea of Higher Education.* Buckingham: Open University Press.

Barnett, R. (1997) *Higher Education: A Critical Business.* Buckingham: SRHE/Open University Press.

Barrett, E., Whitty, G., Furlong, J., Galvin, C. and Barton, L. (1992) *Initial Teacher Education in England and Wales: A Topography* (Modes of Teacher Education research project). London: Goldsmiths' College.

Bottery, M. (1998) *Professionals and Policy: Management Strategy in a Competitive World.* London: Cassell.

Calderhead, J. and Gates, P. (eds) (1993) *Conceptualising Reflection in Teacher Development.* Lewes: Falmer Press.

Carr, W. and Kemmis, S. (1986) *Becoming Critical: Education, Knowledge and Action Research.* Lewes: Falmer/Deakin University Press.

Clark, J. and Newman, J. (1997) *The Managerial State.* London: Sage.

Department of Health (1997) *Research and Development: Towards an Evidence-based Health Service.* London: Department of Health.

Furlong, J. (1992) Reconstructing professionalism: ideological struggle in initial teacher education, in M. Arnot and L. Barton (eds) *Voicing Concerns: Sociological Perspectives on Contemporary Educational Reforms.* Wallingford: Triangle.

Furlong, J. (1996) Do student teachers need higher education? in J. Furlong and R. Smith (eds) *The Role of Higher Education in Initial Teacher Training.* London: Kogan Page.

Furlong, J. (1998) Educational research: meeting the challenge. Inaugural lecture, University of Bristol, 30 April.

Furlong, J. and Maynard, T. (1995) *Mentoring Student Teachers: The Growth of Professional Knowledge.* London: Routledge.

Furlong, J., Barton, L., Miles, S., Whiting, C. and Whitty, G. (forthcoming) *Teacher Education in Transition: Re-forming Teacher Professionalism?* Buckingham: Open University Press.

Grace, G. (1987) Teachers and the state in Britain: a changing relation, in M. Lawn and G. Grace (eds) *Teachers: The Culture and Politics of Work.* Lewes: Falmer Press.

Habermas, J. (1970) Towards a theory of communicative competence. *Inquiry,* 13: 89–113.

Habermas, J. (1974) *Theory and Practice.* London: Heinemann.

Hargreaves, A. (1994) *Changing Teachers, Changing Times: Teachers' Work and Culture in the Post-modern Age.* London: Cassell.

Hargreaves, D. (1996) *Teaching as a research-based profession: possibilities and prospects* (The Teacher Training Agency annual lecture 1996). London: TTA.

Hargreaves, D.H. (1999) The knowledge-creating school. *British Journal of Educational Studies*, 47: 122–44.

Hirst, P. (1996) The demands of professional practice and preparation for teaching, in J. Furlong and R. Smith (eds) *The Role of Higher Education in Initial Teacher Training.* London: Kogan Page.

Hoyle, E. and John P. (1995) *Professional Knowledge and Professional Practice.* London: Cassell.

Kennedy, M. (1997) The connection between research and practice. *Educational Researcher*, October: 4–12.

Le Grand, J. and Bartlett, W. (1993) *Quasi-markets and Social Policy.* London: Macmillan.

Millett, A. (1997) *Speech to TTA Research Conference*, 5 December. London: TTA.

O'Hear, A. (1988) *Who Teaches the Teachers?* London: Social Affairs Unit.

Pirsig, R.M. (1976) *Zen and the Art of Motor Cycle Maintenance.* New York: Corgi.

Popkewitcz, T.S. (1987) *Critical Studies in Teacher Education: Its Folklore, Theory and Practice.* Lewes: Falmer.

Ransom, S. (1990) From 1944 to 1988: education citizenship and democracy, in M. Flude and M. Hammer (eds) *The Education Reform Act 1988: Its Origins and Implications.* Lewes: Falmer Press.

Roderick, R. (1986) *Habermas: The Foundations of Critical Theory.* London: Macmillan.

Said, E.W. (1993) *Culture and Imperialism.* London: Chatto & Windus.

Schön, D. (1983) *The Reflective Practitioner.* New York: Basic Books.

Schön, D. (1987) *Educating the Reflective Practitioner.* San Francisco, CA: Jossey-Bass.

Smith, R. (1996) Something for the grown-ups, in J. Furlong and R. Smith (eds) *The Role of Higher Education in Initial Teacher Training.* London: Kogan Page.

Whitty, G.D. (1996) Marketisation, the state and the re-formation of the teaching profession, in A.H. Halsey, H. Lauder, P. Brown and A.S. Wells (eds) *Education: Culture, Economy and Society.* Oxford: Oxford University Press.

Whitty, G.D., Halpin, D. and Power, S. (1998) *Devolution and Choice in Education: The School, the State and the Market.* Buckingham: Open University Press.

Zeichner, K. (1994) Research on teacher thinking and different views of reflective practice in teaching and teacher education, in I. Carlgren, G. Handal and S. Vaage (eds) (1994) *Teachers' Minds and Actions; Research on Teachers' Thinking and Practice.* London: Falmer Press.

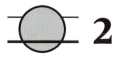 **2**

The anatomy of intuition

Guy Claxton

Introduction

On 4 October 1957 Russia inaugurated the space age by firing through the stratosphere a 22-inch electronic sphere called Sputnik-I. Though the chairman of the US National Committee for the International Geophysical Year described the achievement as 'fantastic', it was a severe blow to American scientific pride, and it inaugurated a good deal of heart-searching, one of the outcomes of which was the rapid convening of a prestigious conference at Woods Hole, Massachusetts, to analyse the shortcomings of a school system that seemed capable of producing only silver-medal scientists. Out of this gathering of expert minds, four central themes for the regeneration of education emerged (Bruner 1960). Three of them – 'structure of the discipline', 'readiness to learn' and the 'desire to learn' – had significant effects on practice, inaugurating the ideas, for example, of the spiral curriculum, discovery learning and the teaching of 'big ideas'. The fourth sank without trace. It was called the 'nature of intuition' (Fensham and Marton 1992).

The distrust of intuition, and the inability to see how (and even, perhaps, why) it could be incorporated into education, reflect 300 years of European cultural history. The Cartesian slogan *Cogito ergo sum* encapsulated the successful attempt to reduce the human mind only to its most conscious and rational regions, and to persuade people that their fundamental identity resided in the exercise of this explicit, articulate, analytical form of intelligence. The Enlightenment of the eighteenth century picked out just this single way of knowing and, in raising it to a high art, implicitly ignored or disabled any others: those that were not so clinical and cognitive, and were instead more bodily, sensory, affective, mythic or aesthetic – in a word, intuitive.

In so far as intuition was acknowledged at all in late seventeenth-century Europe, it had to be rendered mysterious and transcendental. Deprived of any conception of *unconscious* cognition, ideas that appeared in consciousness with an aura of truth, or even of profundity, could only have come from one source: God. Descartes himself, having done more than anyone to ablate the notion of unconscious intelligence from human identity, described this mystical interpretation of intuition with complete conviction: 'Intuitive knowledge is an illumination of the soul, whereby it beholds in the light of God those things which it pleases Him to reveal to us by a direct impression of divine clearness in our understanding, which in this is not considered as an agent, but only as receiving the rays of divinity' (Noddings and Shore 1984: 13).

In the nineteenth century, John Stuart Mill claimed that 'the truths known by intuition are the original premises from which all others are inferred'. And this sense of intuition as something both 'higher' and mysterious – knowledge that claims to be true, but which cannot substantiate its claim except by appeal to divine authority – lingers to this day. *Chambers' Twentieth-Century Dictionary* gives intuition as 'the power of the mind by which it immediately perceives the truth of things without reasoning or analysis: a truth so perceived; immediate knowledge in contrast with mediate'; and 'intuitionism' as 'the doctrine that the perception of truth is by intuition; a philosophical system which stresses intuition and mysticism as opposed to the idea of a logical universe'. While in the *Shorter Oxford English Dictionary* we find intuition still rendered as 'the immediate knowledge ascribed to angelic and spiritual beings, with whom vision and knowledge are identical'.

From Spinoza in the seventeenth century, through John Stuart Mill in the nineteenth to Bergson and Jung in the twentieth, there are those who have insisted on intuition as a way of knowing that is privileged and arcane. Two variants of this magical sense of intuition are alive and well in the late twentieth century. The first is the supernatural one. To be 'intuitive', to many people, I have discovered, means to be sensitive to precognition, clairvoyance and divination. A workshop I ran recently on the subject of intuition attracted many people who were deeply disappointed by the scientific tack which I was taking, and who were eager, instead, to share experiences which seemed to them to be self-evidently beyond the bounds of scientific explanation. 'Out of the blue I suddenly had the most intense feeling that something had happened to Dad . . . and sure enough, five minutes later, Auntie Jean was on the phone with news of his accident': that kind of thing. Though the interpretation of such experiences is hotly disputed (e.g. see Blackmore 1993), and I shall remain agnostic here, the prevalence of such paranormal or even 'new age' interpretations of intuition reinforces the scepticism of a rationalist establishment.

The second contemporary variant of magical intuition is the one that John Furlong warns against in his opening chapter: a fuzzy, emotional kind of 'gut feeling' that is credited uncritically with validity *sui generis*. 'I don't care what you say; I just know it, OK?', can be the cry of a kind of humanistic anti-intellectualism, a black and white epistemology in which science and rationality are contemptuously rejected as 'abstract', 'academic' or 'patriarchal', and gut feeling is falsely celebrated as infallible. Mary Field Belenky and colleagues (1986) have shown that this infatuation with 'gut feeling' may constitute a temporary stage that people pass through on their way to a more subtle understanding of the relationship between clear articulation and formative intuition, in which neither formal knowledge nor fuzzy feeling has automatic precedence, but each is allowed to inform a developing understanding which is simultaneously subjective and objective.

The secular twentieth-century professions, however, buttressed by a rationalistic and often simplistic common-sense psychology, are left simply wary of intuition, disdainful of its epistemological validity, and ignorant or suspicious of both its value and its educability. The reaction is just as black and white as the humanistic one, but in the opposite direction. 'Knowledge' or 'opinion' that is presented without a rational pedigree, lacking a tail of justification and argument, has no claim on our time or our respect. Action that is not planned or premeditated, answers that come without reasons, understandings that cannot be clearly and quickly put into words, are stigmatized as essentially second-rate. Forms of learning that do not involve articulation, and ways of judging that have no explicit criteria, are treated as lazy and inadequate. Instead, our professional and educational cultures are preoccupied with planning, deliberation, calculation, measurement, justification and accountability. Everything from development plans to attainment targets must be spelled out and nailed down.

However, even if we recognize that there are some senses of intuition that fall outside the pale of what professional cultures are willing to accept, and some claims for the universal validity of intuition which do not seem to bear scrutiny, that does not drive us inevitably into the arms of Pure Reason. If there are some senses of intuition which appear to be both obscure and grandiose, there are others, closer to everyday experience, that need not be tarred with the same mystical brush. Only if we buy uncritically a polarized view of the mind which *a priori* opposes reason and intuition, or reason and emotion, are we forced to take sides. As we shall see, hard-nosed cognitive science is reminding us that such a simplistic polarization is neither psychologically accurate nor professionally productive. Instead, we may more fruitfully ask: what are the kinds of performances for which, and situations in which, non-intellectual ways of knowing seem to be beneficial; and what is the functional *relationship* between the explicit and the implicit, in such settings? Are there cases in which certain types of intuition and certain kinds of analytical, articulate reason work productively in tandem? It is to these questions that we now turn.

Varieties of intuition

Chambers' Twentieth-Century Dictionary, in less mystical mode, describes intuition as 'immediate apprehension, without the intervention of any reasoning process', and '*the appearance of informed action or judgement without attendant thought'* which does seem, if there is one, to be the nub. But this general rubric seems to cover a number of more specific areas of professional practice and development.

Expertise

The first is simply the smooth, unreflective mastery of complex but familiar domains – such as a classroom or a clinic – which we refer to as expertise (e.g. see Dreyfus and Dreyfus 1986). Such performance is described as 'intuitive', for example, when it is unpremeditated and unselfconscious. The expert teacher may go through a whole lesson, adjusting or even abandoning their actions and intentions as they go, without being conscious of much reasoning, and without being able to say why or how they made the 'decisions' they did, or to what clues they were responding. Indeed it is well known that becoming too aware of and reflective about one's action, in the heat of the moment, may result in a loss of fluency and even, in extremes of self-consciousness, in paralysis. Thinking about what you are doing, or consciously monitoring what you are doing, as you are doing it, can be deleterious. Intuitive virtuosity unrolls, for the most part, without the help (or the hindrance) of deliberation. Occasionally the expert in mid-performance may 'stop to think', but the moments at which the flow of a lesson is interrupted may be rare.

Even in reflective mood 'after the event', the virtuoso teacher, violinist or chess grand master is often unable to articulate the basis of their skill. 'Know-how' is not automatically translatable into explicit descriptions and explanations. Many experienced professionals learning the new role of mentor, in education as elsewhere, have been struck by the gap between being able to 'do it', and being able to articulate what you are doing. The creation of 'expert systems' – the attempt to simulate the performance of experts with electronic machines – has proved elusive precisely because of the difficulty of rendering intuitive know-how into explicit detailed programing instructions.

Learning

The partial incommensurability of expert know-how and explicit knowledge means that learning, as well as fluent performance itself, may need to proceed, to an extent at least, intuitively. As Michael Polanyi (1958: 31) perceptively commented nearly 40 years ago:

> Maxims are rules, the correct application of which is part of the art which they govern . . . Maxims cannot be understood, still less applied, by anyone not already possessing a good practical knowledge of the art. They derive their interest from our appreciation of the art and cannot themselves either replace or establish that appreciation . . . [and therefore] an art which [necessarily] cannot be specified in detail cannot be transmitted by prescription, since no prescription for it exists.

It is not just that the expert has not yet got round to articulating their expertise, but could perfectly well do so, given the time and the inclination.
Polanyi's point is that virtuosity cannot *in principle* be fully explicated, for it
embodies observations, distinctions, feelings, perceptual patterns and nuances
that are too fine-grain to be caught accurately in a web of words. Thus, given
that explicit knowledge cannot be easily converted into practical know-how,
that such practical knowledge is always, essentially, incomplete, and that conscious deliberate reflection runs the risk of undermining skilled performance,
there are important questions to be asked about exactly what role such
explicit knowledge can play in any kind of learning where the primary aim is
the establishment of competence – whether it be in solving equations, trans-
lating a foreign text, or the art of teaching itself.

If the full articulation of expertise is in principle impossible, it is in practice
both unnecessary and, even, on occasion, unhelpful. Many psychological
studies of so-called 'implicit learning', in which a person tries to gain mastery
of a complex domain via an extended process of trial and error, have revealed
that such mastery emerges well in advance of conscious understanding; and
that orienting learners towards seeking such explicit comprehension can
retard the development of expertise (e.g. see Berry and Dienes 1993). Coulson (1996), in some preliminary studies, has shown that the ability to soak up
the details of a complex situation through inarticulate implicit learning is
facilitated by a state of confusion. If people have given up the attempt to try
to figure out what is going on, and simply interact with the situation in a
'mindless' but observant manner, they come to master it, at an intuitive level
– they do the right thing without knowing why – faster than those who keep
struggling for conscious comprehension. Lewicki *et al.* (1992) have also
shown that implicit learning can pick out and make use of patterns of information in a complex situation (such as a classroom) that are too subtle to be
captured in a conscious, articulate account. The implications of these studies
for the professional training of teachers and others – as discussed by several of
the contributors to this book – should be obvious.

Indeed, the presence of a phase of learning which is characterized by intuition, in which people's choices and interventions are based on 'hunch' or
'feeling' (or even seem, phenomenologically, to be pure guesswork) may even
be essential, if full mastery is to develop. Bechara *et al.* (1997) found that
neurological patients who have sustained bilateral damage to areas of the pre-
frontal cortex lack these emotional and intuitive concomitants of learning,
and are unable to achieve such practical expertise. Nevertheless, they are,
astonishingly, able to come to the same accurate, articulate understanding of
the situation as non-brain damaged people, however, this knowledge seems
to have no influence on their actual responses and choices. Such studies make
a strong case that intuition, far from being an inferior way of knowing, actually provides the 'glue' that holds together our conscious intellect and our
intelligent action (Damasio 1994).

Judgement

I have already alluded to the fact that expert judgement in many professions is often wholly or largely intuitive. The art connoisseur has a 'feeling' that the putative Giotto is 'school of', and not by the master himself. The doctor has a hunch that this combination of symptoms is not as straightforward as it looks – though they cannot say why. The experienced teacher 'just knows' that Deanne is capable of more than the tests reveal. In a whole variety of spheres, what the medical profession refers to as 'clinical judgement' is ubiquitous and indispensable, and seems to accrue gradually as a result of extensive experience, and not through erudition. Although the current emphasis on objectivity in assessment, through the use of standardized measurements of performance, is rightly intended to safeguard against the bias and injustice that is the shadow of unbridled subjectivity, the issue is again not black and white. There are costs in swinging too far in the direction of 'objectivity', not least the undermining of teachers' confidence in their own judgement, and a reluctance to use intuitive judgement when it is necessary and appropriate.

The intuitive side of judgement has again been demonstrated recently in the laboratory. Timothy Wilson and Jonathan Schooler (1991) asked students to taste and rate a number of different makes of strawberry jam. The jams had recently been the subject of a '*Which?*'-type consumer report, and those given to the students had been ranked 1st, 11th, 32nd and 44th by the 'experts'. Some of the students were told that they would be asked to explain the reasons for their preferences, and to think hard about their reactions. The results showed that those students who had been left to their own devices, and who evaluated the jams intuitively, showed a much higher agreement with the experts' choices, while those who had tried to produce explicit justifications made judgements that were more idiosyncratic. However, in a follow-up study, Schooler tested to see whether, despite this divergence from 'received wisdom', the students remained happy with their decisions over a period of time. Far from becoming more content with their choices, those students who had thought most carefully declared themselves *less* satisfied. It turns out that, in cases where much of the 'data' on which a decision is based is sensory, subtle or holistic, the attempt to force the judging process into a form that demands explicit, articulate reasoning is counterproductive. The implications here for professional practice are again significant, as a number of the contributors to the present volume point out. We might ask whether a teacher, in coming to a judgement about a child's potential, for example, like-wise draws upon a vast database of largely inarticulate impressions (as well as on the results of tests), and may be forced to neglect this rich, non-verbal, non-measurable information if forced to justify every judgement explicitly.

Sensitivity

There is a related sense of intuition as a *heightened sensitivity to clues*. To say of someone that they are 'very intuitive' can imply that they extract the maximum amount of significance from the available information: they see the meaning in the detail that others may have overlooked. Such clues may not themselves be registered consciously by the 'intuiter', yet they can still contribute to an accurate 'feeling of knowing'. This ability to be attentive to detail, whether consciously or subliminally, may underlie the kind of 'clinical judgement' which we have just discussed, and it certainly provides a non-mystical account of the famous 'sixth sense' that some people seem to display. F. Scott Fitzgerald, who was himself fascinated by the phenomenon of subliminal perception, illustrates in *Tender is the Night* how the sixth sense may actually reduce to an acute employment of the other five.

> In an inhabited room there are refracting objects only half noticed: varnished wood, more or less polished brass, silver and ivory, and beyond these a thousand conveyors of light and shadow so mild that one scarcely thinks of them as that: the tops of picture frames, the edges of pencils or ashtrays, or crystal or china ornaments; the totality of this refraction appealing to equally subtle reflexes of the vision as well as to those associational fragments in the subconscious that we seem to hang on to, as the glass-fitter keeps the irregular shaped pieces that may do, sometime. This fact might account for what Rosemary afterwards mystically describes as realising there was someone in the room, before she could determine it.
> (Fitzgerald 1934: 67)

There is now a wealth of experimental evidence that attests to the existence and the value of such subtle clues, and the abilities to make use of them (see Claxton 1997). As long ago as 1884, philosopher C.S. Peirce and his graduate student Joseph Jastrow conducted a long series of studies on unconscious perception, at the end of which they concluded that their research had

> highly important bearings, since it gives new reason for believing that we gather what is passing in one another's minds in large measure from sensations so faint that we are not aware of having them, and can give no account of how we reach our conclusions about such matters. The insight of females as well as certain 'telepathic' phenomena may be explained in this way. Such faint sensations ought to be fully studied by the psychologist and assiduously cultivated by everyman.
> (Peirce and Jastrow 1884: 83)

Creativity and problem-solving

There are more leisurely senses of intuition to do with the processes of problem-solving and creativity. In the autobiographical writings of creative scientists and artists there has been, for a long time, a recognition of the creative power of unconscious mental processes. A satisfying product may appear not as the result of conscious cognitive labour, but as a gift from 'out of the blue', and this process may be encouraged and stimulated, but it cannot be forced or controlled. Quite the reverse: the gifts appear only in a mood of relaxed rambling and rumination, when they are not being earnestly sought or worked on at all.

Now there is experimental evidence for these anecdotal conclusions, too. Janet Davidson (1995) asked people to solve simple insight problems such as: 'George wants to cook three steaks as quickly as possible, but unfortunately his grill can only cook two steaks at a time. The steaks take three minutes a side to cook. What is the shortest time in which George can cook all three steaks?' The quick, 'common-sense' response is that you cannot improve on cooking two steaks on both sides, and then cooking the third. It requires a small violation of this logic to realize that you can save time by cooking steaks A and B on one side; then the second side of A and the first side of C; and finally the second sides of both B and C.

In general an 'insight' problem is one in which people's 'first take' on the problem is likely to embody a plausible assumption which, in this case, turns out to be illicit; and/or one in which the solution depends on a holistic perception of the elements of the problem in relationship, rather than on analytical, sequential reasoning. Davidson (1995) found that people who were most successful at solving such puzzles were slower than those who became stuck and failed. Even though 'intelligence' is generally associated with faster processing, in the case of problems that require insight, rather than brute reasoning, it is 'slow and steady' that wins the race. What happens is that people who tend to rush at the problem are more likely to make some false assumptions, and get locked in to an erroneous way of thinking about the problem from which they cannot then escape.

Along the same lines, Jonathan Schooler has shown that people who are better at solving 'insight problems' are more likely to be able to let their minds go blank and admit to themselves that they are temporarily stuck. People who persist with conscious thinking are less likely to make the breakthrough. As Schooler says: 'Verbalization may cause such a ruckus in the front of one's mind that one is unable to attend to the new approaches that may be emerging in the back of the mind' (Schooler *et al.* 1993: 169). The more keenly one seeks a solution or an explanation, the more likely one is to come up with thoughts that are conventional and uncreative. Thus a student teacher, baffled by the poor reception of a well-planned lesson, may be more likely to generate a creative alternative for herself as her mind wanders drowsily in the evening than she is in a serious, anxious post-lesson debriefing with her tutor or mentor.

Rumination

The final form of intuition which I want to isolate here is linked to this last example. It concerns the seeking of insight through the act of reflecting on personal experience. The creative scientist's unconscious mind may be buzzing with data and theories of a quite impersonal kind, but the professional learner in education is much more likely to be seeking enlightenment by precipitating personal, practical forms of understanding out of their own memories. The search for meaning through reflection of this kind is fashionable in many areas of professional learning and development, and has tended to see introspection as a precursor of more articulate enquiry. First you attend to experience, and try to crystallize a description of 'what was going on'; then you get to work more deliberately, either alone or with others, to formulate explanations and theories which will form the basis of considered plans of action. As with creativity, however, there are important questions to be resolved about the relationship between these two modes – what Arnheim (1985) calls the 'intuitive' and the 'intellectual'. Does the contemporary concern with reflection in professional practice spoil the intuitive by overemphasizing the intellectual, for example? Have the more gentle, slow, ruminative or solitary forms of reflective intuition been neglected by an educational establishment that is in thrall to the explicit? Again, some of the contributors to this volume suggest that these concerns are valid.

To summarize: intuition refers to a family of 'ways of knowing' that have in common a lack of clearly articulated comprehension or rationale, but which differ in a variety of other ways. Non-mystical members of this family include:

- *expertise* – the unreflective execution of intricate skilled performance;
- *implicit learning* – the acquisition of such expertise by non-conscious or non-conceptual means;
- *judgement* – making accurate decisions and categorizations without, at the time, being able to explain or justify them;
- *sensitivity* – a heightened attentiveness, both conscious and non-conscious, to details of a situation;
- *creativity* – the use of incubation and reverie to enhance problem-solving; and
- *rumination* – the process of 'chewing the cud' of experience in order to extract its meanings and its implications.

Facets of intuition

On the basis of a comprehensive review of both the philosophical and the psychological literatures, Bastick (1982) lists some 20 properties that are ascribed to intuition, in order of their frequency of mention. He does not distinguish as clearly as I have attempted to between different members of the intuitive family, but – as in any blood family – there are certain traits that tend to characterize the family as a whole.

The most common trait is the opposition of intuition to thinking that is abstract, logical or analytical. Above all, the commentators seem to agree that intuition is a *different* way of knowing, one which does not rely on articulate fluency. Second comes a property that we met in the context of the research on the so-called 'insight problems': a sense of the relationships between the various elements of a situation or a problem. By contrast with analytical thinking, intuition is thought of as synthetic, giving a sense of the structure of the whole, which may well be greater than the sum of the parts. Third, especially in the context of creativity, there is a view that intuition involves reframing or reconceptualizing the situation. Where routine problem-solving takes the initial formulation of the problem for granted, and works from there towards a solution, intuition *qua* insight typically involves a reorganization of the perception of the problem, often as a result of breaking through an unconscious assumption which had been effectively blocking a solution.

Fourth, Bastick (1982) lists the relationship between intuition and experience. As we saw with the family members identified above, intuition is often more a matter of drawing upon and extracting meaning from a largely tacit database of first-hand experience, than it is of rational deduction. Creative individuals, the literature shows, tend to be those who have steeped themselves in the study of a particular area, and are able to draw on this well of experience in novel, flexible and integrative ways. Interestingly, this latter condition seems to exclude those who are *too* knowledgeable about the subject, for while they have the requisite database, a particular way of looking at it may have emerged that is so entrenched and habitual that it precludes taking a 'fresh look'.

Fifth, there is with intuition an essentially affective tone, an emotional involvement on the part of the knower. Intuition trades not just in conceptual understanding, but in significance – in what matters. Recently, Gelernter (1994) and others have argued that the link between creativity and emotionality emerges inevitably when the cognitive system is in low-focus, reverie-type mode.

Sixth is the familiar assumption that intuition relies upon mental processes that are not conscious: operations which may be unavailable in principle to introspection, and which may actually be impeded by the effort to make them conscious, or to bring them under conscious control. There is an emerging consensus that the Freudian image of the unconscious as a mental sump of repressed emotion characterized, at most, one small corner of the unconscious as a whole. The rest is cool and intelligent; not subversive of conscious reason but complementary to it (Claxton 1997).

Seventh, intuition comes with a kind of built-in confidence rating, a subjective feeling of 'rightness', that may vary in its strength from 'complete guess' to 'absolute certainty'. Mangan (1993) has suggested that this feeling acts as a kind of summary in consciousness of a set of unconscious processes and judgements that cannot – at least at that moment, and perhaps in principle – surface as such. He uses the metaphor of the 'menu bar' on a computer word-processing screen: a set of symbols and icons indicating the status of different variables, and the availability of various options, which act as pointers and reminders, but which do not take up very much of the limited space on the screen itself. Intuition, in general, in Mangan's view, is comprised of such shorthand references which inhabit the 'fringe' of consciousness, and he reminds us of William James' perceptive concern, in his *Principles of Psychology* (1890) with 'the reinstatement of the vague to its proper place in our mental life'.

However, this explanation of the status of the feeling of rightness in our mental life in no way entails its infallibility. The feeling may be indicative of an idea that is worth taking seriously, but it is rarely definitive. Despite famous examples of unshakeable intuitive confidence, such as Gauss' 'I have my result, but I do not yet know how to get it', the feeling of rightness – or wrongness – can be misleading. What feels like a complete guess can be shown to have significantly greater validity than its author gives it credit for. Bowers *et al.* (1990), for example, have demonstrated the undervaluing of faint hunches, inklings and even guesses. Their subjects were given clues to the solution of a puzzle one at a time, and after each one were required to come up with an attempt at the answer, even if they thought it was a complete shot in the dark. Bowers was able to show that these 'complete guesses' began to converge on an acceptable solution well before the solution itself actually appeared, even though subjects' confidence in them was non-existent. On the other hand, the feeling of rightness can be exaggerated and misleading. When people are solving analytical problems, their sense of how 'warm' they are is an accurate predictor of an imminent successful solution. However with insight problems, the feeling of warmth is actually predictive of failure. People think they are getting closer to a solution when they are actually barking up the wrong tree (Metcalfe and Wiebe 1987). The fact that intuition is corrigible deserves a closer look.

The fallibility of intuition

One of the reasons that intuition got a bad name was the apparent contradiction between the grandiose claims of incorrigibility – of direct revelation of unquestionable 'truth' – on the one hand, and the transparent fact that it can be blatantly wrong, on the other. Sometimes people's inklings and premonitions, their gut feelings and gut reactions, turn out to be perceptive and appropriate; at other times, they don't. People can end up falling in love with each other despite unfavourable first impressions. Promising hunches regularly turn out to be blind alleys. Student teachers' initial intuitions about how to manage a frisky class can be distressingly misguided.

Intuition can be mistaken and misleading; but does that mean, if we shed the inflated expectations, that it is of no value, or that it cannot be educated to become *more* reliable and perceptive? Not necessarily. Understanding the origin of mistaken intuitions can help us gain a more balanced view of the value of intuition as a whole. Take a famous example – one often used by Wittgenstein in his seminars – of a stubbornly false intuition. Imagine that the Earth is smoothed into a perfect sphere, and that a ribbon is tied snugly round the equator. Now untie the ribbon, and add just six feet to its total length. Space it out, so that the gap thus created is equal all the way round. How big is the gap? A micron? A hair's breadth? A paperback book? A foot? Most people's strong intuition is that the gap would be tiny. In fact it is easy to prove mathematically that it is nearly a foot. You could crawl under it. The intuition is false; but the interesting question is *why* is it false? It turns out that its basis is the assumption that 'if you add a little to a lot, it won't make much differ-ence'. Now there are many situations, superficially similar to Wittgenstein's puzzle, where this assumption is both valid and useful. If you were to turn the oceans into a giant cylinder, and add six gallons to it, the height would indeed rise by only a negligible amount.

The fault comes in an over-reliance on a *holistic unconscious analogy*; the unanalysed assimilation of a current problem to a class of situations to which, despite appearances, it does not actually belong. This unconscious analogizing is a vital and ubiquitous mental process – a way of getting cognition going by giving it a *prima facie* sensible guess to work on – which just happens, some-times, to be misleading (Bruner and Clinchy 1972). In many situations such intuitive analogies are either accurate, or they at least form an adequate basis on which to proceed: they 'seem like good ideas at the time', and only further experience will show whether they do, in fact, apply to the new situation. The new headteacher tacitly assumes a model of management and leadership, both consciously and unconsciously imbibed from previous experiences of being managed and led, which may be appropriate and adequate for their par-ticular personality and this particular school culture, or may not. It may be a good first guess that can be trimmed and tuned, or it may be quite the wrong place to start, that is only going to cause grief and strife. It depends. The intu-ition serves us well if we take it as a hypothesis, rather than as the God-given truth. If we take it as gospel, and try to force situations or ourselves to fit what is in fact an inaccurate template, then we may end up stymied and frustrated.

Intuitions as hypotheses

The problem with treating intuitions as guides rather than as truths is that we are often unused to taking a sceptical attitude towards what comes to us as a perception, an impulse, a gut feeling, or 'common sense'. The 'folk model of mind' which informs western education (and much of the wider culture) is one which focuses sceptical enquiry onto the positions and propositions of articulate thought, but which takes a rather 'naive realist' view of other areas of human psychology (D'Andrade 1987). Off-duty, we tend to treat our per-ceptions as if they are direct and accurate impressions of 'reality', and ignore the vital insight of the Gestalt psychologists, that 'We see things not as *they* are, but as *we* are'. We may be entertained by visual tricks and illusions that demonstrate the effects of belief, experience and culture on perception itself, but fail to take their lesson to heart: that much of our own 'knowing' comes to us already dissolved in our experience of the world. So where the uncon-scious analogies and operations that are involved in the fabrication of percep-tion, emotion and intuition are flawed, our experience will be dubious, and action based uncritically upon it misdirected (e.g. see Arnheim 1969; Gregory 1970). A balanced view of intuition is one which sees it as a valuable source of hypotheses, which are nonetheless capable of being interrogated. That delicate, often, to begin with, unfamiliar, process of self-interrogation, of seeing that one might have seen, felt, judged, differently, is one of the ways of knowing that is referred to as 'reflection'.

This simultaneous respect for the delicacy, fallibility and value of intuition is reflected time and again in the literature of creativity – artistic, scientific and pragmatic. (Creativity is a property of mundane, everyday cognition, as well as of grand products and discoveries.) An ongoing survey of Nobel science laureates by Marton and colleagues in Sweden (see Fensham and Marton 1992) – to take just one of these spheres – reveals the absolutely central place which they give to intuition. Intuition, they say, tells them which path to follow in their research, without knowing why. Michael Brown (Nobel prize for chemistry, 1985), for example, says: 'And so, as we did our work, we almost felt at times that there was a hand guiding us. Because we would go from one step to the next, and somehow we would know which was the right way to go. And I can't really tell you how we knew that' (quoted in Fensham and Marton 1992: 116). Intuition offers a vital (but still fallible) way of evaluating leading-edge results, where no explicit criteria yet exist. Stanley Cohen (Nobel prize for medicine, 1986) says: 'To me it is a feeling of "Well, I don't really believe this result", or "This is a trivial result", or "This is an important result" . . . I am not always right, but I do have feelings about what is an important observation, and what is probably trivial' (quoted in Fensham and Marton 1992: 116). And, in a classic description of intuition as sudden 'insight', Rita Levi-Montalcini (Nobel prize for medicine, 1986) says: 'You've been thinking about something without willing to for a long time . . . Then, all of a sudden, the problem is opened to you in a flash, and you suddenly see the answer' (quoted in Fensham and Marton 1992: 116).

Finally, Konrad Lorenz (Nobel prize for medicine, 1973) emphasizes both the reliance of intuition on a large database of experience, and the need for a relaxed and gentle attitude towards problem-solving:

> This apparatus which intuits has to have an enormous basis of known facts at its disposal with which to play. And it plays in a very mysterious manner, because . . . it sort of keeps all known facts afloat, waiting for them to fall into place, like a jigsaw puzzle. And if you press . . . if you try to permutate your knowledge, nothing comes of it. You must give a sort of mysterious pressure, and then rest, and suddenly BING!, the solution comes.
>
> (quoted in Fensham and Marton 1992: 116)

Balance

Rehabilitating intuition seems to be largely a matter of regaining balance: the balance between effort and playfulness, which Lorenz has just described, and the balance between intuition itself and reason. Mathematician Henri Poincaré summed it up by saying, 'It is through logic we prove; it is through intuition we discover' (quoted in Ghiselin 1952: 41). It is almost as though the well-tempered mind has available to it a number of modes that need to work in concert, each taking the lead in turn; or as if creativity demands a cycle of cognitive 'seasons', some of them involving busily planting, harvesting or threshing, and others, the fallow 'winter months' requiring patience and a tolerance for seeming inactivity, which is, despite appearances, necessary and productive. The classic model of creativity (Wallas 1926) in fact divides it into four stages: preparation, in which data is gathered, reason is applied, and eventually an impasse reached; incubation, in which the problem is not consciously worked at or attended to; illumination, in which an intuitive solution emerges into consciousness; and verification, in which purposeful analysis is applied to check the intuition out, and find ways to communicate it.

Interestingly, this balance is also acknowledged by artists. Henry Moore wrote:

> It is a mistake for a sculptor or a painter to speak or write very often about his job. It releases tension needed for his work. By trying to express his aims with rounded-off logical exactness, he can easily become a theorist whose actual work is only a caged-in exposition of concepts evolved in terms of logic and words. But though the nonlogical, instinctive, subconscious part of the mind must play its part in his work, he also has a conscious mind which is not inactive. The artist works with a concentration of his whole personality, and the conscious part of it resolves conflicts, organises memories, and prevents him from trying to walk in two directions at the same time.
>
> (Ghiselin 1952: 73)

We might wonder whether the expert teacher, perhaps about to take on the role of mentor, might agree with both of Henry Moore's points: that too much explication of their own practice might lead to a loss of fluidity; and yet that a degree of conscious, strategic 'overseeing' of their classroom practice is essential.

American poet Amy Lowell quite deliberately used 'incubation', describing how she would 'drop my subject into the subconscious, much as one drops a letter into a mailbox'. But she also acknowledged that intuition was 'a most temperamental ally': 'Often he will strike work at some critical point, and not another word is to be got out of him. Here is where the conscious training of the poet comes in, for he must fill in what the subconscious has left . . . he must have knowledge and talent enough to "putty" up his holes' (Ghiselin 1952: 110–11).

Recognition of the intricate ways in which intuition and intellect, reason and reflection, experience and explanation, balance and complement each other challenges theorists of professional development to come up with a rather more sophisticated model of adult professional learning than we have at present. The idea that what the student needs is first a conscious grasp of theory, which is then 'put into practice', has been discredited since the 1960s. The idea that expertise automatically emerges from a diet of unmediated, unreflective experience, is equally untenable. Professional development involves a shifting, dynamic interplay of different ways of knowing, and models of specific situations need to be developed which take into account their unique rhythms and 'melodies' of learning.

The voices of intuition

One of the most striking ways in which intuition differs from intellect is in the range of voices through which it speaks. Whereas the rational mind seeks articulate clarity, intuition reveals itself through channels that are hazier and more indirect. Intuitions, if they come as thoughts at all, are often faint and fleeting: ambiguous glimmerings of understanding, not bright, well worked-out solutions. Such subtle promptings may take a relaxed, attentive eye to spot. Poet Ted Hughes (1967: 56–7) described how, as a schoolboy,

> I was plagued by the idea that I really had much better thoughts than I could ever get into words . . . I became very interested in those thoughts of mind I could never catch. Sometimes they were hardly what you could call a thought – they were a dim sort of a feeling about something . . . I did not know that most people have the same trouble. What thoughts they have are fleeting thoughts – just a flash of it, then gone – or, though they know they know something, or have ideas about something, they just cannot dig those ideas up when they are wanted . . . There is [a] thinking process by which we break into that inner life . . . and if we do not somehow learn it, then our minds lie in us like fish in the pond of a man who cannot fish.

Hughes goes on, in this radio talk to children about the making of poetry, published as *Poetry in the Making* (1967), to explain how he cultivated the art of catching the gleam of an intuition, and became better at 'holding it still so as to get a really good look at it'. His argument that this art can and should be taught, though it is only slowly acquired, stands in stark contrast to those who suppose that young adults, coming to a course of professional training in, for instance, teaching or nursing, should somehow be automatically tooled-up for reflection. We might ask, of a Postgraduate Certificate in Education (PGCE) course for example, how well it 'coaches' its students in these ruminative mental arts: the ones which they will need in order to generate a stream of fresh, engaging lesson plans (rather than reaching for last year's dried crop). And, indeed, how well its graduates model the practice and the value of these arts for their students, in their turn.

As well as speaking through faint and slippery ideas, intuition also manifests itself through dreams, myths and imaginings. As we have seen, its nature is essentially holistic and analogical, so symbolism is its natural language. Intuition often alludes and hints, without unpacking itself, and if obsessively rationalistic cultures dismiss this as wilfully obscure or intellectually sloppy, they do so only by disabling the engine of insight and creativity. If creativity involves the discovery of a new pattern, a remote association, an unlikely but fruitful metaphor, these are more likely to emerge as images than as the products of earnest, purposeful thought. Studies show that creativity is enhanced in a state of reverie, in which imagery comes into its own, and people who are better able to access that state of reverie are also more creative (Lynn and Rhue 1986).

Intuition is also physical. A prompting is something that makes us want to move in a particular direction without – as Nobel laureate Michael Brown said – knowing why. A gut feeling is literally that – a bodily sensation – as is a tingling of apprehension or an inexplicable inability to take your eyes off someone who has just entered a crowded room. Paying attention to the subtle, perhaps slowly forming, sensations of the body has been shown to be enormously helpful in gaining the kind of understanding that people seek in the context of counselling or psychotherapy (Gendlin 1981). Given Gendlin's demonstration that 'focusing', as he calls it, is a teachable and learnable skill that is of general use in making sense of experience, there is no reason, other than its strangeness, why professional learning should not also make use of it.

Intuition sometimes also has an almost aesthetic quality: what another Nobel laureate, Paul Berg (Chemistry, 1980) calls 'taste': 'Taste is almost the artistic sense. Certain individuals see [a problem] in some undefinable way, can put together something which has a certain style, or a certain class to it. A certain rightness to it' (quoted in Fensham and Marton 1992: 116).

What emerges from the study of intuition is a realization that aesthetic, physical, environmental and emotional sensitivity are *forms of cognition*: they are valid ways of knowing that, properly understood and well developed, do not subvert rational thought but complement it.

Variability of intuition

If intuition is a way of knowing that can be developed (or inhibited) as a result of experience and tuition, we should expect people to differ in when, how and how well they make use of it; and they do. Jung included 'intuiters' as one of his four 'psychological types', on the basis of his clinical experience, but there is now experimental evidence for differences in intuition. Westcott (1968), for example, gave people problems to solve, and offered them a series of clues which they could take up one by one. They could opt to take only one or two clues before venturing a solution, or they could be more cautious and wait until they had more information. Westcott found that his subjects divided into four groups, according to whether they were willing to answer on the basis of a little information, or needed more; and, within each of these two groups, whether their solutions tended to be correct or not. Not all of those who waited until they had more clues solved the problems better. Some – those whom Westcott identified as the 'intuitives' – did consistently well with only a little information; others did poorly no matter how much information they had asked for.

Of particular interest were the ways in which the different groups scored differently on tests of personality. Intuitive people, Westcott (1968) found, tend to be introverted: they like to keep out of the social limelight, but feel self-sufficient and trust their own judgement. They like to make up their own minds about things, and tend to resist being controlled by others. They tend to be unconventional, and comfortable in their unconventionality. 'They explore uncertainties and entertain doubts far more than the other groups do, and they live with these doubts and uncertainties without fear. They enjoy taking risks, and are willing to expose themselves to criticism and challenge. They can accept or reject criticism as necessary, and they are willing to change in ways they deem to be appropriate' (Westcott 1968: 63).

The educability of intuition

If intuitions represent the emergence into consciousness (via routes that are not clearly articulated, and are often faint, fleeting, symbolic or sensory) of hypotheses that are based on the unconscious integration of patterns and analogies extracted from the database of previous experience, then there are obviously a number of quite straightforward ways in which the 'faculty' of intuition can be educated. We can indeed learn to improve the frequency, reliability and quality of our intuitions. And if this really is the case, then, as Westcott (1968: 191) says, 'education has a great task and responsibility which it has barely touched'. After all, intuition, in at least some of the senses in which I have defined it, is clearly the bedrock on which all other ways of knowing are constructed. Animals and babies operate only by intuition. They lack the tools of language, logic and self-awareness which conscious, deliberate rationality requires. So while reason is emerging as an outgrowth of intuition, there is no reason to suppose that it can or will supplant it. Intuition itself, as we have seen, is equally capable of elaboration and sophistication, and remains a valuable way of knowing throughout life.

To identify some of the ways in which intuition can be developed, it is useful to summarize the conditions, both situational and psychological, which support it.[1] The outer, contextual conditions include a conducive physical environment. Though stillness and solitariness are often quoted, these conditions are personal and idiosyncratic – some people have to smoke, or pace about, or look out (as Sartre did) onto an urban roofscape – and therefore learning to be intuitive involves learning what those conditions are for oneself, and developing the disposition to seek and create them. If we consider a social or professional context, the most conducive culture is one which, to quote Westcott's summary, 'encourages looseness of reaction, speculation, nonanalytic functioning and random association' (1968: 189).

Such an environment, of course, is one that is convivial, playful, cooperative and non-judgemental, as well as being purposeful and professional. Prince (1975: 258), in a review of the conditions of intuition, concludes: 'Any reaction that results in the offerer of an idea feeling defensive will tend to reduce not only his speculation but that of others in the group . . . The victim of the win–lose or competitive posture is always speculation, and therefore idea production and problem solving. When one speculates he becomes vulnerable. It is too easy to make him look like a loser'. Indeed, pressure and stress of any kind, whether competitive or not, are anathema to intuition, as they tend to focus perception and cognition on a predetermined range of strategies and information – those that are 'obvious' or 'normal' – and thus to remove the breadth and open-mindedness of vision which may be required to uncover a false assumption or a creative analogy (Easterbrook 1959). (People in the business world are fond of quoting the old proverb: 'When you are up to your arse in alligators, it's hard to think about draining the swamp.')

Intuition also requires a conducive inner, psychological environment, one that is characterized by certain dispositions and tolerances. The foremost of these is what the poet John Keats referred to as 'negative capability', which he described as 'when a man is capable of being in uncertainties, mysteries and doubts without any irritable reaching after fact and reason'. If intuition may emerge as knowledge without comprehension, one must be able to tolerate that lack of mental clarity. If intuition takes time to gestate, one must be prepared to wait – to resist the desire to end the discomfort of confusion by inducing the birth of understanding. In a classic study of creativity in artists, Getzels and Csikszentmihalyi (1976) found that the best still-life pictures were produced by those painters who played more slowly and creatively with the different elements of the composition, and who delayed foreclosing on their idea of what the painting was going to be, even until they were already part of the way through painting it.

The importance of 'daring to wait' can hardly be overstated (Claxton 1997). As we have already seen, adults who are willing to enter a state of confusion learn a complex skill faster than those who insist on seeking theories and explanations (Coulson 1996); and insight problems are solved better by those who can think slowly (Davidson 1995).

Finally, we might note the value of cultivating the skill of 'catching the inner gleam' which was mentioned earlier; and of developing the disposition to look for the unspoken assumptions – especially one's own – that may be dissolved in the very way in which a problematic situation seems to present itself.

Conclusion

Intuition refers to a loose-knit family of 'ways of knowing' which are less articulate and explicit than normal reasoning and discourse. This family has tended to be ignored, marginalized, romanticized or denigrated in mainstream educational cultures, partly because of its historical association with claims for its validity that seem grandiose or mystical; and partly because we have, until recently, lacked a cognitive psychology which makes scientific sense of its nature and its value. The members of this family include the ability to function fluently and flexibly in complex domains without being able to describe or theorize one's expertise; to extract intricate patterns of information that are embedded in a range of seemingly disparate experiences ('implicit learning'); to make subtle and accurate judgements based on experience without accompanying justification; to detect and extract the significance of small, incidental details of a situation that others may overlook; to take time to mull over problems in order to arrive at more insightful or creative solutions; and to apply this perceptive, ruminative, inquisitive attitude to one's own perceptions and reactions – 'reflection'.

Intuitions manifest in a variety of different ways: as emotions; as physical sensations; as impulses or attractions towards certain goals or courses of action; as images and fantasies; as faint hunches and inklings; and as aesthetic responses to situations. Intuitions are holistic interpretations of situations based on analogies drawn from a largely unconscious experiential database. They integrate (in an image or an impulse) a great deal of information, but may also incorporate assumptions or beliefs that may be invalid or inappropriate. Thus intuitions are instructive but fallible hypotheses which are valuable when taken as such. The intuitive mental modes are not subversive of or antagonistic to more explicit, verbal, conscious ways of knowing; they complement and interact productively with them. People vary in their facility with intuition, their willingness to trust it, and in their ability to create both the inner and outer conditions which are conducive to it. These skills, dispositions and tolerances are acquired through both informal life experience and in the course of formal education. Professional education and training thus have the opportunity, both through explicit instruction and modelling, and through the epistemological culture which they embody, either to enable people to harness and develop their intuition, or to neglect it, and so allow it to waste away.

Acknowledgements

I am grateful to Terry Atkinson and Patricia Broadfoot for their perceptive comments on an earlier draft of this chapter.

Note

1 I am concentrating here on the senses of intuition as creativity and rumination. Clearly intuition in the sense of fluid, unreflective expertise has quite a different relation to time, being often at its best when it is responding to events that are outpacing any attempt to rationalize.

References

Arnheim, R. (1969) *Visual Thinking.* Berkeley, CA: University of California Press.

Arnheim, R. (1985) The double-edged mind: intuition and the intellect, in E. Eisner (ed.) *Learning and Teaching the Ways of Knowing.* Chicago, IL: University of Chicago Press.

Bastick, T. (1982) *Intuition: How We Think and Act.* Chichester: Wiley.

Bechara, A., Damasio, H., Tranel, D. and Damasio, A.R. (1997) Deciding advantageously before knowing the advantageous strategy. *Science,* 275: 1293–5.

Belenky, M.F., Clinchy, B.M., Goldberger, N.R. and Tarule, J.M. (1986) *Women's Ways of Knowing: The Development of Self, Voice and Mind.* New York: Basic Books.

Berry, D.C. and Dienes, Z. (1993) *Implicit Learning: Theoretical and Empirical Issues.* Hove: Lawrence Erlbaum.

Blackmore, S. (1993), *Dying to Live: Science and the Near-Death Experience.* London: Harper Collins.

Bowers, K.S., Regehr, G., Balthazard, C. and Parker, K. (1990) Intuition in the context of discovery. *Cognitive Psychology,* 22: 72–110.

Bruner, J.S. (1960) *The Process of Education.* Cambridge, MA: Harvard University Press.

Bruner, J.S. and Clinchy, B. (1972) Toward a disciplined intuition, in J.S. Bruner (ed.) *The Relevance of Education.* London: George Allen & Unwin.

Claxton, G.L. (1997) *Hare Brain, Tortoise Mind: Why Intelligence Increases When You Think Less.* London: Fourth Estate.

Coulson, M. (1996) The cognitive function of confusion. Paper presented to the British Psychological Society Conference, London, December.

D'Andrade, R. (1987) The folk model of the mind, in D. Holland and N. Quinn (eds) *Cultural Models in Language and Thought.* Cambridge: Cambridge University Press.

Damasio, A.R. (1994) *Descartes' Error: Emotion, Reason and the Human Brain.* New York: Putnam.

Davidson, J.E. (1995) The suddenness of insight, in R.J. Sternberg and J.E. Davidson (eds) *The Nature of Insight.* Cambridge, MA: Bradford/MIT Press.

Dreyfus, H.L. and Dreyfus, S.E. (1986) *Mind over Machine: The Power of Human Intuition and Expertise in the Era of the Computer.* Oxford: Blackwell.

Easterbrook, J.A. (1959) The effect of emotion on cue utilization and the organization of behavior. *Psychological Review,* 66: 183–201.

Fensham, P.J. and Marton, F. (1992) What has happened to intuition in science education? *Research in Science Education,* 22: 114–22.

Fitzgerald, F. Scott (1934) *Tender is the Night.* New York: Scribner.

Gelernter, D. (1994) *The Muse in the Machine: Computers and Creative Thought.* London: Fourth Estate.

Gendlin, E. (1981) *Focusing.* New York: Bantam.

Getzels, J.W. and Csikszentmihalyi, M. (1976) *The Creative Vision: A Longitudinal Study of Problem-Finding.* New York: Wiley.

Ghiselin, B. (1952) *The Creative Process.* Berkeley, CA: University of California Press.

Gregory, R.L. (1970) *The Intelligent Eye.* London: Weidenfeld & Nicholson.

Hughes, T. (1967) *Poetry in the Making.* London: Faber & Faber.

James, W. (1890) *The Principles of Psychology.* New York: Henry Holt.

Lewicki, P., Hill, T. and Czyzewska, M. (1992) Nonconscious acquisition of information. *American Psychologist,* 47: 796–801.

Lynn, S.J. and Rhue, J.W. (1986) The fantasy-prone person: hypnosis, imagination and creativity. *Journal of Personality and Social Psychology,* 51: 404–8.

Mangan, B. (1993) Taking phenomenology seriously: the 'fringe' and its implications for cognitive research. *Consciousness and Cognition*, 2: 89–108.

Metcalfe, J. and Wiebe, D. (1987) Intuition in insight and noninsight problem solving. *Memory and Cognition*, 15: 238–46.

Moore, H. (1952) Notes on sculpture, in B. Ghiselin (ed.) *The Creative Process*. New York: New American Library.

Noddings, N. and Shore, P. (1984) *Awakening the Inner Eye: Intuition in Education*. New York: Teachers' College Press.

Peirce, C.S. and Jastrow, J. (1884) On small differences in sensation. *Memoirs of the National Academy of Science*, 3: 75–83.

Polanyi, M. (1958) *Personal Knowledge*. London: Routledge & Kegan Paul.

Prince, G.M. (1975) Creativity, self and power, in I.A. Taylor and J.W. Getzels (eds) *Perspectives in Creativity*. Chicago: Aldine.

Schooler, J., Ohlsson, S. and Brooks, K. (1993) Thought beyond words: when language overshadows insight. *Journal of Experimental Psychology: General*, 122: 166–83.

Wallas, G. (1926) *The Art of Thought*. New York: Harcourt Brace.

Westcott, M.R. (1968) *Toward a Contemporary Psychology of Intuition*. New York: Holt, Rinehart & Winston.

Wilson, T.D. and Schooler, J. (1991) Thinking too much: introspection can reduce the quality of preferences and decisions. *Journal of Personality and Social Psychology*, 60: 181–92.

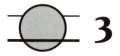 **3**

Trusting your own judgement (or allowing yourself to eat the pudding)

Lucy Atkinson

> he had, somehow, always missed the promotion he felt to be his due –
> an excellent officer, but just somehow lacking in something or the
> other, he could not understand his comparative failure, and suspected
> Kirk of having a down on him . . . Foster never did anything that was
> not absolutely correct; this, perhaps, was his real weakness, for it meant
> that he lacked imagination, both in his work and in handling the men
> under him.
>
> (Sayers 1937: 205)

> [Carlotta Adams:] No, I'm afraid I always plan a thing out very carefully
> before I do it. It saves – worry.
>
> (Christie 1933: 21)

> Miss Hemans was so mortally afraid of doing the wrong thing that she
> contrived her life so that it was practically free from any action at all. If
> one did nothing it was impossible to do the wrong thing.
>
> (Barne 1933: 27)

The role of judgement in intuition

Sergeant Foster sticks rigidly to the rulebook; Carlotta Adams makes careful plans and follows them to the letter; Miss Hemans is reduced to almost complete inactivity by her lack of self-confidence. Fictional characters, certainly; stereotypes, possibly, but surely not without plenty of counterparts in real life. What do they have in common? A deep distrust of their own ability to come up with an appropriate response to the shifting, unpredictable experiences of life. Their plan is to meet each moment with a premeditated response. They are afraid to trust their judgement.

We know that people in real life differ enormously in their willingness to trust their judgement, especially in situations that are not well-defined or where the information is incomplete. It is under such conditions that the rulebook does not suffice. Only a hunch or an intuition may be there to guide you. But is it to be trusted? What weight will it bear? Westcott (1968), for example, has shown that there are measurable differences in people's ability to demonstrate intuitive skills, and categorizes them as good or poor 'intuiters'; could it be that the 'poor intuiters' are having similar responses to events as the 'good intuiters', but are unwilling to trust their judgements?

Let us consider two vignettes of professional people:

(a) A teacher observes her newly-arrived class. Although they are reasonably quiet and well-behaved, she senses an underlying current of disturbance, of aggression and hostility. She does not know why this should be, but guesses that some incident may have taken place in the lunch break.

(b) A nurse has a 'feeling' that the condition of one of his patients has taken a turn for the worse. He is unable to pinpoint any describable symptom or change, but nevertheless feels sure that some intervention is necessary.

What action do these professionals take? Does the teacher abandon her carefully planned lesson, involving pair-work and role-play, for activities that she considers to be more 'settling'? Or does she carry on with the planned lesson in the face of her feeling that it could well prove disastrous? Does the nurse alert other members of staff, despite the fact that he may be censured for time-wasting if his fears are proved to be unfounded, or does he decide to continue to simply monitor the situation, despite his feeling that this could be detrimental to the patient?

In both these cases, the intuitive idea has arrived in the person's consciousness without justification or explanation, yet with an accompanying feeling of validity, as Guy Claxton puts it in the previous chapter. They have, again in Claxton's words, been served with an 'intuitive pudding' (Claxton unpublished). The question is, therefore, do they allow themselves to trust their own judgement, to eat the pudding and so to test the validity of the intuition by acting upon it? The intuition needs to be acted upon, or at least action must be considered. It is interesting to speculate whether the intuitive response, if continually suppressed and ignored, may finally cease to operate at all.

Judgement could therefore be seen to be a vital part of the intuitive process. If we think that acting intuitively can be a valid response to events then we need to look at the role of judgement in facilitating this testing of the validity of intuition by action. As Einhorn and Hogarth (1978: 395–416) concluded 'It is important to emphasize that judgement is primarily exercised to facilitate action.' Figure 3.1 attempts to clarify the role of judgement in the intuitive process.

How, then, do these individual differences in the ability to trust judgements arise? How is this ability to trust your own judgements developed or inhibited? Is it like that other indefinable but desirable quality, 'gumption'? It is evident, at least, that not all people have the ability developed to the same degree, otherwise if, as Bruner (1974: 104) says, 'intuition is an invitation to go further', why do some people consistently refuse the invitation?

If intuition is a 'way of knowing and learning', then like the other cognitive

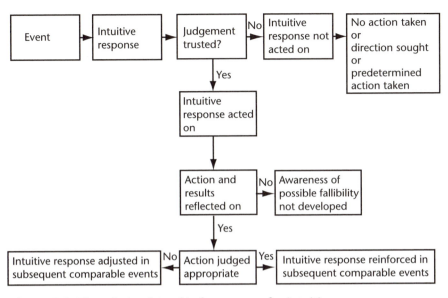

Figure 3.1 The relationship of judgement to the intuitive response

modes, it may have its roots in the person's early development, the initial nurturing environment of infancy. The ability to trust in this way of knowing, but to simultaneously acknowledge its possible fallibility, may also have its roots in this early development. By exploring some aspects of the initial nurturing environment, we may gain an awareness of the causes of the divergence in people's ability to act appropriately upon their intuitions. We may also hypothesize how aspects of nurturing environments could continue to affect the development of this ability in subsequent environments such as school, higher education and professional training.

In considering the early nurturing environment of infancy, it is necessary to try and pinpoint some aspects which may be particularly important in the formation and development of the ability to trust judgements. Three such aspects of all nurturing environments are support, structure and direction. These three components closely resemble those identified by Grolnik and Ryan (1989) as being of importance in the development of 'control beliefs', which are 'part of the self-concept, where they determine to a large extent feelings of self-esteem' (Flammer 1995: 86) Flammer further identifies control beliefs as being a combination of contingency beliefs which are based on the expectations that certain actions will result in certain outcomes, and competence beliefs which are based on one's belief in one's ability to produce the actions oneself. Grolnik and Ryan (1989) describe their three general components as follows:

- *involvement* – parent's active interest in the child;
- *autonomy support* – encouraging children to figure answers for themselves;

- *structure* – the extent to which parents provide clear and consistent guidelines, expectations and rules for behaviours.

In my model, the three components differ only slightly from these, as follows:

- *support* is the active interest described by Grolnik and Ryan (1989), extended to include persons other than parents, e.g. teachers, trainers etc., and narrowed to a notion of positive interest;
- *direction* is the extent to which 'autonomy support' is present (and the converse situation where it is actively discouraged);
- *structure* is the secure and consistent framework as described by Grolnik and Ryan, that allows for meaningful reflections on one's actions.

What, then, is the importance of these three factors in developing the ability to trust your own judgement? We could summarize the possible effects as follows:

- *Inappropriate support*: if the result of trusting one's own judgement is always negative criticism or punishment.
- *Inappropriate direction*: if one is never encouraged, or indeed allowed to act on one's own judgement, but always expected or compelled to follow the wishes and dictates of others.
- *Inappropriate structure*: if the environment in which one performs one's actions is constantly shifting and throwing back unexpected responses.

Given the presence of any of the above scenarios in a person's infant environment, we might conclude that it could be difficult for that person to successfully develop trust in judgement; given the presence of two or three of the above, then we might conclude that it could be impossible!

An environment, however, is rarely set out in these simplistic black and white terms; these factors of support, direction and structure, therefore, cannot be viewed as set points, but form continua within the nurturing environment, as illustrated in Figure 3.2. It is the balance and interrelationship of these three continua which is hypothesized to enhance or hinder the development of the ability to trust your own judgement, and although these continua are common to all nurturing environments the effect they have had in the initial nurturing environment of infancy may be carried forward into all subsequent nurturing environments. If this is so, then it will have implications for the providers of these subsequent environments.

The importance of the three continua of structure, direction and support is such that it is necessary to examine each in detail to gain an understanding of their role in the formation of the ability to trust your own judgement.

Structure

The perception of order within the world, of consistent expectations, rules, patterns and outcomes, is the underlying structure which allows for the

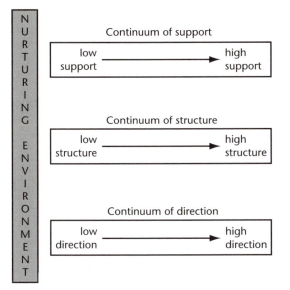

Figure 3.2 The inter-relating continua in the nurturing environment that affect the development of judgement

formation of the intuitive response and for perceiving the results of actions based on these intuitive responses. It allows for this perception to be embedded in the 'taken for granted' that Schutz (1967) expounds in *The Phenomenology of the Social World*: the infant perceives that certain actions consistently produce certain results. This 'outcome feedback' (Hammond *et al.* 1975: 293) is simply knowledge of the outcome of a judgement: 'outcome feedback can become corrective in that it permits adjustments to the general direction of judgement' (Hogarth 1986: 685). Eraut (1994: 105) writes, 'the synthesis of past experience and a knowledge of what to expect in the future . . . is the framework through which new experience is interpreted'. Eraut also contends that the 'ordinary person' perceives the world as being ordered, and this is probably true of those who have experienced medium to high structure in their initial nurturing environment. However, for those who experience a low degree of structure in infancy, the world may not be perceived as ordered, and the knowledge of what to expect in the future may be limited. For some children the world is chaotic. This chaos may arise from many different factors: parenting may be very inconsistent, with the child being submitted to a regime of alternate indulgence and severity with no apparent reasoning behind it; the close family relationships may be constantly in flux. There are many other situations which form chaotic nurturing environments, but all have in common the fact that it makes it hard for the child to develop a sense of order and pattern. Without this structural basis, it is very difficult to trust your own judgement, as the outcome feedback is constantly changing and adjusting the general direction of judgement with a frequency that is hard to cope with.

Given inconsistent consequences of actions, the perception of cause and effect is likely to be impaired. Such impairment has been shown to have an effect on emotional expression and assertiveness, the latter being of special significance for judgement: 'Children who learned cognitive problem-solving skills (finding alternative solutions, anticipating the consequences of actions, understanding cause and effect) were likely to show appropriate levels of emotional expression and assertiveness, rather than being either very impulsive or extremely limited' (Mussen *et al.* 1984: 251). The continuum of structure continues to have great importance in subsequent nurturing environments such as school, higher education and professional training. The simple infant perception of the results of an intuitively-based action can become the more complex process of reflection if the structure of the environment provides a consistent framework within which the learner is encouraged to reflect on the results of the actions that followed their intuitive responses as well as those more capable of articulation. The theories regarding the reflective practitioner concern themselves to a large extent with the rational 'reflection-on-action' (Schön 1983, 1987). That is, attempting to articulate processes underlying actions; the 'reflection-on-outcomes' which follows intuitive acts may often be unconscious and scarcely amenable to articulation, but may nevertheless be valid and formative.

For this reflection to have validity in the eyes of the learner there must be opportunities for intuitive responses to be valued. In the school situation this may take the form of problem-solving games, inference-making and predictive tasks, and detective approaches to subjects such as history. In higher education and professional training, it may be sufficient to acknowledge that the intuitive response has an important place in the academic and professional world; that students need not become 'closet intuiters'! The process of reflection when allied to intuition becomes, to some extent, a process of validation, where the results of a judgement are looked at and seen to be appropriate or otherwise; this reflection, or validation, feeds back into the intuitive process to form part of the experience that will be drawn upon in response to subsequent events. Young (1987), regarding the training of nurses, writes, 'determining the correctness of the action [intuitively] taken . . . evaluates directly the usefulness of the cues in deciding a particular action'. In this way the results of intuitive acts may be enshrined in the 'practical principles' which 'are the outcomes of successful practice' (Hirst 1996: 172). It must be acknowledged, however, that some research (Koriat *et al.* 1980: 107–18) shows that certain people disregard evidence that contradicts their current judgement.

A highly-structured nurturing environment will provide opportunities for the learner to acquire a knowledge base, which researchers into the intuitive process see as an important condition for intuition to develop: Simon (1983: 83) quotes Poincaré as saying 'inspiration comes only to the prepared mind', and Dreyfus and Dreyfus (1986) write that validating intuitive thinking is crucial, and requires this sound [knowledge] base. The providers of second-ary nurturing environments, if they wish to further the development of 'good intuition', may be wise to facilitate the acquisition of a knowledge base in a way that gives value to intuitive responses and does not inspire 'a loathing for seemingly arbitrary analysis' which Bruner (1974: 107) sees as leading to an undesirable 'uninformed intuition'.

Direction

In simplistic terms, direction is telling people what to do! It may not, however, be quite this simple; high expectations on the part of the nurturer, where these lead to the child acting in a manner which is not the choice of the child, can also be highly directive, implying 'This is what you *must* do'. This is equally true whether the direction is benevolent or malign; in fact, it can be increasingly hard to separate oneself from the wishes and expectations of a much-loved nurturer. As far as the development of the ability to trust your own judgements is concerned, receiving high direction can become a habit, and a very pleasant habit if accompanied by rewarding and reinforcing praise. But stripped of the 'security blanket' of high direction, the child who has formed the habit may find it very difficult to trust their own judgement with-out outside confirmation and permission and, at worst, be unwilling to make judgements at all, preferring to stick to courses of action prescribed by others. It is also generally much quicker and easier to do as one is told rather than to discover it for oneself, hence the highly directed child may well resent being expected to trust their own judgements in subsequent environments. An example of this problem arising in the environment of higher education is given by Beard and Hartley (1984: 99): 'Her difficulty arose from an unques-tioning dependence on authority, in this instance vested in "absolute truths" to which everything could be conveniently referred, and her assumption that, in their absence, no meaningful judgements could be made.'

Although the child from a low direction infant environment may initially have difficulty coming to terms with a more highly directive subsequent environment in school, this may be affected to some extent by prior expec-tations established in the mind of the child by the nurturer; preschool children will be told 'You'll have to do what the teacher tells you when you get to school!' An expectation of being told what to do and how to do it is also characteristic of some of those who enter professional training. Because of these expectations of being led to the Holy Grail of professional knowledge, the problems associated with high direction coupled with high support can easily lead to an over-reliance on the trainer by the trainee, as shown in Figure 3.3.

When high support is allied to low direction, however, a very different pic-ture emerges, as will be seen from Figure 3.4.

When direction is high, 'autonomy support' (Grolnik and Ryan 1989) is low. Autonomy has been identified (Hoyle and John 1995) as one of the three

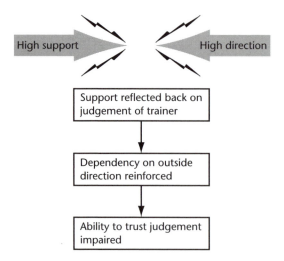

Figure 3.3 The effect on the ability to trust judgement of a combination of high support and high direction

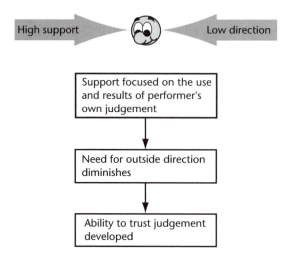

Figure 3.4 The effect on the ability to trust judgement of a combination of high support and low direction

main contributing factors in the traditional understanding of what it means to be a professional, the other two being knowledge and responsibility. If the development of autonomy has not been encouraged in the initial nurturing environment, then it may be very difficult to develop it in subsequent environments. If autonomy is one of the dimensions of professionalism, as it must be if intuitive thinking is to play any part in that professionalism, then autonomy support is essential. As John Furlong writes in Chapter 1, professionals 'need the autonomy to make their own judgements'. In a highly directive environment the development of autonomy will (a) not be enhanced and (b) the whole notion of autonomy may become undesirable and difficult to cope with for the highly directed individual.

Support

The notion of trust in your own judgement can be equated to a confidence in one's self-efficacy: 'Perceptions of one's abilities, of the probability of success, and the value of these competencies are important mediators of activity' (Eccles 1993: 147). Bruner (1974) suggests that even the initial intuitive response is 'based upon a confidence in one's ability to operate with insufficient data'. This self-confidence is part of the more general concept of self-esteem. Self-esteem can be seen as being developed through an affective route and a cognitive route. The affective route stems from positive support in the infant environment: 'self esteem is fundamentally based in affective processes; it arises early in life from the general perception that one is loved and valued' (Brown 1993: 30). The cognitive route to self-esteem is based in the person's perception of their efficacy in specific situations, for example, 'I am good at maths, I am musical, I make friends easily' etc. This perception of efficacy is also greatly affected by positive support and reinforcement, particularly as the child matures. The very young child tends to overestimate their capabilities: 'some children's self-esteem appears to be inflated, at least as compared to other people's evaluations' (Kagan *et al.* 1982: 357), and it is with maturation, particularly on entering the school environment, that this overestimation starts to be corrected: 'it is likely that schooling dampens the developmental optimism' (Flammer 1995: 69). Positive support at this stage is therefore essential to prevent over-correction of this optimism, with a resulting loss of self-esteem. In order to trust your own judgement, therefore, positive support may well be a necessity.

There are some initial nurturing environments where this support is largely denied, where the parents are disengaged from the interests of the children. This disengagement is not confined to certain social groups: 'many families appear to be quite disengaged from their children's lives, and these highly disengaged families were equally likely to live in low-risk and high-risk neighbourhoods' (Eccles *et al.* 1992: 149; see also Furstenberg 1992). The children from these highly disengaged families are likely to have a low self-esteem from an early age, having gained little perception of being loved and valued; subsequent environments may be able to enhance this low self-esteem by positive support for the specific situations that form the cognitive route to self-esteem, but the confidence to trust judgements will not have been developed at the important stage of the initial nurturing environment. It is possible that this lack of confidence may be open to remediation in a subsequent environment, but the lack will obviously affect the learner's entry status to that environment. Of the three continua of structure, direction and support, it is support that is most affected by its interaction and balance with the other two continua. In the earlier discussion of direction, it was shown that when high support is allied to high direction, the ability to trust your own judgement is impaired rather than developed. High support can also be affected in this way by its interaction with the continuum of structure (see Figure 3.5).

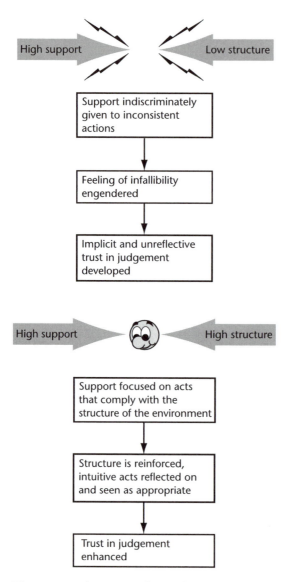

Figure 3.5 The inter-relationship of the continua of support and structure

The effect of a high support/low structure environment may be to make intuitive responses degenerate into wild guesses, since appropriate feedback is missing. When there is a desire to cling on to the intuitive response, to win the argument at all costs in the face of conflicting evidence; that is when problems arise, as pointed out by Claxton (1997).

Conclusion

The implications for subsequent nurturing environments of these three continua are twofold. First, the continua and their balance and interaction will continue to affect the development of the ability to trust your own judgement, as in the initial nurturing environment. Second, the entry status of learners into subsequent environments is, in part, a result of the balance and interaction of the continua that they have experienced in their previous nurturing environment(s). Awareness that this and other entry statuses exist, and that they can affect learning styles is, perhaps, of recent origin; according to Bourner and Flowers (1997: 77), 'The time when teaching staff in HE [higher education] could simply follow the teaching methods that they experienced as students is drawing to a close.' Many students will enter higher education or professional training with the expectation that they will be taught by the methods that they were used to in former environments.

The disparity between a former and a subsequent nurturing environment can cause considerable difficulty for students: 'Students sometimes contrast the lack of guidance at university or college with the greater direction they received at school' (Beard and Hartley 1984: 91). Similarly, in the initial teacher training environment, 'it is not uncommon for students to go through a period of resenting the pupils for forcing them to be more authoritarian than they really want to be' (Furlong and Maynard 1995: 96). The disparity may be powerful enough to interfere with meaningful learning: if a child from a highly directive home environment enters school for the first time and finds a school ethos which aims to be low directive, it can be very difficult for the child to perceive that there are any boundaries at all – they think that they can do exactly what they want in all circumstances. The process by which they find out that this is not the case can be painful for all concerned. A mature student entering a course of professional training, used to making independent judgements and confident in their ability to do so, may be highly resentful of a directive approach. The student who is used to high support for their intuitive judgements may find it hard to satisfy a trainer or mentor who requires everything to be planned out in black and white prior to the event, and who negatively criticizes intuitive acts. Conversely, the student for whom high direction/high support has become a habit can be very demanding of attention and guidance in a low direction environment.

Any subsequent nurturing environment can do nothing to alter the entry status of its learners. The question is whether the learners' capabilities and skills can be enhanced and developed from the starting point of their entry status. The ability to trust your own judgement is not one that has received much attention when the effectiveness of learning environments is considered. For instance, Hargreaves (1994: 59) notes that 'Effective schools embrace rather narrow and conventional definitions of what constitutes effectiveness . . . we do not know, for instance, what effective schools which created success in problem-solving, creativity, risk, flexibility or learning-how-to-learn would look like.' Problem-solving, risk and flexibility are at the heart of learning to trust your own judgements. If this ability is valued, which it surely must be if intuition as a cognitive mode is to be valued, then nurturing environments subsequent to the initial nurturing environment of infancy must see its development as part of their general effectiveness.

It can be concluded that there is a divergence in people's ability to access intuition as a learning style, as there is with all other learning styles. If they are unwilling to test the validity of their intuitions by action, then they will not be able to learn through these intuitions. It can be conjectured that this divergence has its roots in the initial nurturing environment, influenced by the balance and interaction of the three continua (structure, direction and support). It has been surmised that this disparity in people's ability to trust their judgement could have implications for subsequent learning environments; perhaps it also has implications for possible research. There has been extensive research into the notions of 'self-efficacy' and 'locus of control' which were mentioned in connection with the continuum of structure; however, it may be that further research to link these concepts with willingness to trust judgements could be useful. It would also be helpful to research the degree of remediation possible for those whose early nurturing experiences have not developed a trust in judgement. This could make it clearer whether subsequent learning environments can develop and enhance trust in judgement, or whether their role in this area would be simply to have an awareness of the possible disparities.

References

Barne, K. (1933) *She Shall Have Music,* London: J.M. Dent.

Beard, R.M. and Hartley, J. (1984) *Teaching and Learning in Higher Education*. London: Harper & Row.

Bourner, T. and Flowers, S. (1997) Teaching and learning methods in higher education: a glimpse of the future. *Reflection on Higher Education,* 9: 77–101.

Brown, J.D. (1993) Self-esteem and self-evaluation: Feeling is believing. Self-presentation, in J. Suls (ed.) *Psychological Perspectives on the Self: The Self in Social Perspective,* Vol. 4. Hillsdale, NJ: Lawrence Erlbaum.

Bruner, J.S. (1974) *Relevance of Education*. Harmondsworth: Penguin.

Christie, A. (1933) *Lord Edgware Dies.* London: Collins.

Claxton, G. (1997) *Hare Brain, Tortoise Mind: Why Intelligence Increases When You Think Less*. London: Fourth Estate.

Claxton, G. (1999) Professional virtuosity: knowing without knowing how or why, unpublished paper.

Dreyfus, H. and Dreyfus, S. (1986) *Mind Over Machine: The Power of Human Intuition and Expertise in the Era of the Computer*. Oxford: Basil Blackwell.

Easen, P. and Wilcockson, J. (1996) Intuition and rational decision-making in professional thinking: a false dichotomy? *Journal of Advanced Nursing*, 24: 667–73.

Eccles, J.S., Furstenburg, F., McCarthy, K.A. and Lord, S.E. (1992) How parents respond to risk and opportunity. Paper presented at the biennial meeting of the Society for Research on Adolescence, Washington DC.

Eccles J.S. (1993) School and family effects on the ontogeny of children's interests, self-perception and activity choices, in J. Jacobs (ed.) *Developmental Perspectives on Motivation*, Vol. 40. Lincoln, NE: University of Nebraska Press.

Einhorn, H.J. and Hogarth, R.M. (1978) Confidence in judgement: persistence of the illusion of validity. *Psychological Review*, 85: 395–416.

Eraut, M. (1994) *Developing Professional Knowledge and Competence*. London: Falmer Press.

Flammer, A. (1995) Developmental analysis of control beliefs, in A. Bandura (ed.) *Self-efficacy in Changing Societies*. Cambridge: Cambridge University Press.

Furlong J. and Maynard, T. (1995) *Mentoring Student Teachers*. London: Routledge.

Furstenburg, F., (1992) Adapting to difficult environments: Neighborhood characteristics and family strategies. Paper presented at the biennial meeting of the Society for Research on Adolescence, Washington, DC.

Grolnik, W.S. & Ryan, R.M. (1989) Parent styles associated with children's self-regulation and competence in school, *Journal of Educational Psychology*, 81: 143–54.

Hammond, K.R., Stewart, T.R., Brehmer, B. and Steinmann, D.O. (1975) Social judgement theory, in M.F. Kaplan and S. Schwarz (eds) *Human Judgment and Decision Processes*. New York: Academic Press.

Hargreaves, A. (1994) *Changing Teachers, Changing Times: Teacher Development*. London: Cassell.

Hirst, P. (1996) The demands of professional practice and preparation for teaching, in J. Furlong and R. Smith (eds) *The Role of Higher Education in Initial Teacher Training*. London: Kogan Page.

Hogarth, R.M. (1986) Beyond discrete biases: functional and dysfunctional aspects of judgemental heuristics, in H.R. Arkes and K.R. Hammond (eds) *Judgement and Decision Making*. Cambridge: Cambridge University Press.

Hoyle, E. & John, P. (1995) *Professional Knowledge and Professional Practice*. London: Cassell.

Kagan, J., Hans, S., Markowitz, A. and Lopez, D. (1982) Validity of children's self-reports of psychological qualities, in P.H. Mussen, J. Conger, J. Kagan and A.C. Huston (eds) *Child Development and Personality*. London: Harper & Row.

Koriat, A., Lichtenstein, S. and Fischhoff, B. (1980) Reasons for confidence. *Journal of Experimental Psychology: Human Learning and Memory*, 6: 107–18.

Mussen, P.H., Conger, J., Kagan, J. and Huston, A.C. (eds) (1984) *Child Development and Personality*. London: Harper & Row.

Sayers, D.L. (1937) *Busman's Honeymoon*. London: Victor Gollancz.

Schön, D. (1983) *The Reflective Practitioner*. New York: Basic Books.

Schön, D. (1987) *Educating the Reflective Practitioner*. San Francisco, CA: Jossey-Bass.

Schutz, A. (1967) *The Phenomenology of the Social World*. Evanston, IL: Northwestern University Press.

Simon, H.A. (1983) *Reason in Human Affairs*. Oxford: Blackwell.

Westcott, M.R. (1968) *Toward a Contemporary Psychology of Intuition: A Historical, Theoretical and Empirical Inquiry*. New York: Holt, Rinehart and Winston.

Young, C.E. (1987) Intuition and the nursing process. *Holistic Nurse Practitioner*, 1(3): 52–62.

 **Part 2**

Intuition and initial teacher education

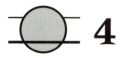

4

Learning to teach: intuitive skills and reasoned objectivity

Terry Atkinson

Introduction

Intuition as a dimension in teacher thinking has important implications for teacher education, especially pre-service teacher education. As Lucy Atkinson argues in Chapter 3, the quality of the nurturing environment provided in an educational setting can affect both the development of intuition and the confidence and judgement of learners as to when to trust their intuitions. For teacher educators, the challenge is to provide an appropriately nurturing environment in which teachers can develop their intuitive thinking skills as well as analytical and reflective thinking. To aid this enterprise, teacher educators need a clear formulation of these different kinds of thinking processes, their interaction and their development. This leads to questions such as: what is the role of knowledge about teaching in the development of intuitive practice and how can school experience best be used? Is it possible to speed up the acquisition of intuitive teaching skills and are there factors which hinder their development? How can teacher trainers ensure that student teachers trust their intuitions appropriately, having neither too little nor too much confidence in their value? What is the role of intuition in relation to other parallel processes in teacher thinking, especially reflection and the use of deliberative reasoning? How do these various ways of understanding teaching and teacher development conflict with or complement each other?

Knowledge and experience

Learning to touch-type provides an example of a learning task demanding some formal learning and a good deal of practice. The knowledge required for this task can be acquired quite rapidly in perhaps under an hour – just learn which finger goes on or reaches to which key. The practical skill has to be learned through extensive practice. Thus, we might characterize touch-typing as a low knowledge, high practice skill. What is happening during the practice phase? When an action is repeated many times with constant adjustment in the light of feedback – i.e. hitting or mishitting the keys – there is an accompanying mental development. Greenfield (1997) argues that there is a development of the neural networking that allows for very rapid processing and action. The length of practice required would be a function of the number of connections needed, and, possibly, the quality of these. This would appear to have considerable relevance for any skilled performance based upon practised ease as much as, if not more than, on explicit knowledge.

What then of teaching? The knowledge required to teach includes content knowledge, pedagogical knowledge and local knowledge – knowledge of the context and of the learners. Teaching requires extensive practice – more, for example, than touch-typing, perhaps several years even. Thus, the accumulation of the knowledge and the experience required to teach will take many years. One reason why so much practice is needed is illustrated from touch-typing. In reaching for certain keys it is very easy to hit the neighbouring key. Why? Is the brain sending the wrong message or is the body implementing it poorly? There may be interference between the different keystrokes. The expert typist has a sense of feel that tells him or her when a mistake has been made. This feel may be reflected in neurological configurations, but how are these generated? Two dimensions seem vital here: experience and feedback. Without experience it will not be possible to develop any sense of feel but feedback provides the essential fine-tuning. In typing, the feedback may be in the form of the accuracy of the finished product, in the speed rating or the comments of the typing tutor, or in the physical sensation of the finger not sitting squarely on the key. In teaching, feedback will come from a range of sources such as the reactions of pupils, their work, the teacher's own reflection and self-evaluation and the feedback from tutors and mentors. Thus, extended practice and feedback are necessary to achieve competence and, eventually, expertise in teaching.

Models of teacher education

Different models of pre-service teacher training assign differing values to knowledge about teaching and to practice. For example, 'learning by doing' was a model which relied on practice alone. It did have some successes but the novice teacher had to sink or swim and many drowned. Practice alone cannot be the whole answer because, if it were, schools would be full of ever-improving teachers, without need of initial training or continuing professional development (Smith and Alred 1993). Without feedback and reflection, ten years of teaching experience can simply amount to one year of experience repeated ten times over (Kahneman and Tversky 1990).

By contrast, knowledge-based models of teacher education involve learning about pedagogy, didactics, psychology and sociology. The problem for such models is the limited transfer of such knowledge into practice. Whether the knowledge learned is theoretical or practical in nature – for example, lesson planning, teaching and learning activities or classroom management strategies – the same problem of applicability is encountered because teaching a good lesson is not just a question of remembering the good ideas that were conveyed in the seminar room.

In the reflective model of teacher education, an attempt is made to construct practice as a learning experience. The student is expected to learn through reflection on practice. This model results in fewer drownings, but it is arguable whether reflection itself is the source of the life-saving. The mere act of reflection in isolation does not ensure any learning since it carries with it neither support nor challenge, the two key elements for growth signalled by Elliott and Calderhead (1993). It is in the shared reflection of the novice with a peer group or a mentor that these elements will be present and so lead to learning. However, it is very hard to bring teaching skills to consciousness and to give an accurate account of them in language. Sharing reflection is made easier by placing learning in a context – for example, the school placement situation. However, there is always a risk that shared reflection may be shallow and full of misunderstandings and false assumptions. How should a student teacher be able to create knowledge about teaching from early practical experience when all the king's horses and all the king's men of the educational world have been unable to construct a valid account of teaching or, at least, one from which teaching can be learned? The use of reflection upon experience can be valuable in allowing the novice teacher to learn rapidly from experience but also carries with it various dangers. The reflection may be fine but is it true to the novice teacher's practice? Does the reflection-on-action match up to the reflection-in-action? Is the student teacher ready to reflect (Atkinson 1996) or is it more important for the student to gain further experience in using certain techniques? Does reflection-on-action, with its emphasis on the explicit, militate against the intuitive and the tacit? Does conscious reflection lead to a preoccupation with detail and a failure to capture the whole?

Reflection is thus the tool of the constructivist approach forged from disillusionment with scientific knowledge for training teachers. Reflective practitioners are expected to construct their own knowledge about teaching. The outcome is simply a different knowledge set, but the application of knowledge to complex tasks remains problematic. Reflection on practice may lead to better understanding but not necessarily to better practice. The understanding built out of reflection can be applied at the planning stage when deliberative thinking is needed, but in the crucial delivery stage in the classroom intuitive thinking is required. Knowledge creation 'post hoc' cannot replace the need for thinking in action.

Models of teacher education are essentially a set of compromises revolving around the validity of knowledge and the development of skilled performance through practice. The way in which the relationship between the two is understood is crucial.

Reason and intuition in professional practice

Both reason and intuition can be viewed as tools having certain characteristics which make each more or less suitable for any given task. Teachers need to be able to use each tool and to know when to use which one or when and how to use both at the same time since, in positing different ways of knowing, we may also ascribe to them differing notions of fitness for purpose. Is intuition without thought or is it thought itself at an unconscious level? Reason can be seen as the triumph of language over thought but, for some teachers at least, their sense of their own practice is not readily given rational, linguistic expression. Brown and McIntyre (1993: 106) report that 'With a high degree of consistency we found the teachers unable to report to us the mental processes involved in their classroom decision making'. In attempting to categorize teacher action, Clandinin (1986: 45) says: 'I have lost a sense of the view of the whole teacher and her dynamic use of practical knowledge.' How then do teachers visualize their own practice? If language is either not available or not used, are there other tools? Images offer a powerful alternative. Elbaz's (1983) study of the practical knowledge of one teacher found that an important element was the images of how good teaching should look and feel, used 'intuitively'. The concept of vision conveys a sense of the ability to operate at a holistic level. Both vision and intuition represent alternative ways of knowing to that of reasoned analysis. They depend upon the ability to infer truth from knowledge without consciously articulating that knowledge. This skill is of immense value in the moment of teaching when action has to be more or less spontaneous.

The brain infers the nature of what is perceived from the minimum of information needed to reach a decision. This enables vision to work effectively and immediately. Without it, life would be slowed considerably. Of course, the brain can make mistakes as can be demonstrated by *trompe-l'oeil*. The ability to draw on the minimum of data picked up by the various senses in order to make a judgement about what is being observed is intuitive since it depends largely on assimilating and processing data unconsciously. The brain achieves this by comparing incoming data with stored data from prior observations. An apple is recognized at once as conforming more or less to previously encountered examples. Thus, prior experience is an essential component of the ability to intuit. Furthermore, this is not a uni-directional experience since each new apple encountered adds to and reshapes the concept of apple that is held.

Clandinin (1986: 17) posits image as a way of understanding the basis of intuitive decision making: 'images are seen as the mediator between the unconscious and conscious levels of being. What is known and thought at the unconscious level finds expression in a person's thought and action through a person's images. Images are thus seen as the source of inspiration, ideas, insight and meaning'. This is especially so when dealing with complexities which conscious thought and language are inadequate to capture – an image is worth how many words? The nature of images is quite diverse as Clandinin notes: 'Images may be connected to a concrete incident; have a metaphoric quality; have an affective dimension; have a moral coloring; be thought to exhibit complexity and be related to other images: and may exhibit specificity in their detailed construction and in the meaning they convey' (1986: 33).

Images that are seen repeatedly in the same or similar contexts begin to be perceived as patterns. Pattern recognition is a vital skill which can only be learned through experience. A good example concerns the ability of a teacher to scan the class and see at once certain patterns from the facial expressions and body language of the pupils. With sensitivity to these cues an experienced teacher can instantly perceive the prevailing conditions or class mood and adjust the work plan accordingly. Lacking such experience, the student teacher has to carry on with the preconceived plan regardless, often with unfortunate results.

Implications for teacher education

If we accept that there is necessarily an intuitive dimension to professional learning and to professional practice, teacher educators have to consider how this fits in with the training that they provide. Do teacher educators attach too much importance to the scientific and conscious acts of planning, reflection, evaluation and theory? Do they undervalue the intuitive skills of practice (which makes perfect), routinization, flexibility, reflection in action? How can student teachers develop intuitive skills as well as scientific ones through courses of teacher preparation? A particular concern here is the tendency of academia to predispose teacher educators towards the scientific and objectively verifiable. This in turn may alienate students who are confronted with a theory–practice dilemma.

Propositional craft knowledge

Brown and McIntyre (1993) stress that students can learn about the nature of craft knowledge in order to help them to structure their own learning, to have a sense of what is to be learned and to be able to reflect upon their learning. If procedural knowledge is to be used as an advance organizer, it has to be introduced close to the start of teaching experience for, as Eraut (1994: 120) argues, 'if the time-gap between the introduction of theoretical knowledge and its first use in professional practice is too large, that knowledge is being introduced at the wrong time in the sequence'. The experienced teacher would not normally use knowledge about teaching in the way learner teachers are expected to use it. Thus, while the novice needs to make use of craft knowledge, it is important that this is seen as an intermediate stage and not an end in itself.

Knowledge distilled from the experience of practitioners can be useful to the new teacher in helping to provide a framework for the development of intuitive insight, but this process occurs only as the novice teacher gains practical teaching experience. Elbaz (1983) reports on the case of Aileen, a beginning teacher who started out with methodical rules. Only when she became dissatisfied with her teaching did images begin to guide her on a more intuitive level. Aileen's use of methodical rules reflects the needs of an inexperienced practitioner who is not in a position to rely on her own experience and so has to use rules distilled from practice of others until her own experience builds and she develops her own images and intuitions.

Experienced teachers use knowledge about teaching only in exceptional circumstances (Brown and McIntyre 1993) – for example, when a situation is encountered that cannot be readily dealt with intuitively. In such cases, the pattern is not recognized and it is not clear what options are available and which routine set of procedures should be followed so the teacher has to analyse the problem at a conscious level, bringing to mind knowledge about how to act, often in the form of maxims, the correct application of which is part of the art which they govern (Polanyi 1958). In contrast, when a familiar situation is encountered, complex decision making can occur automatically.

Teachers and researchers tend to overlook this 'knowing-in-action', because it is not at the level of awareness. There are, then, two different sets of thinking processes that teachers may bring to bear in practice. One is largely intuitive and based upon tacit knowledge, while the other is analytical and based upon more explicit knowledge. For the novice teacher, for whom many more situations are exceptional, there is bound to be more need for conscious, analytical thinking, since the tacit knowledge needed for intuitive thinking has not yet been accumulated. The teacher educator must respond to this need in ways which nonetheless do not make the novice dependent upon explicit knowledge and which allow tacit knowledge to develop.

School experience

The student teacher's dilemma is to find the right course of action between relying on intuition without the necessary experience and following prescriptions which are distilled from the experiences of others but which may be ill-understood and which inhibit, as in the case of Aileen, the development of intuition based on experience. For example, knowing what a lesson plan is can be taught and is useful knowledge for the new teacher. However, knowing how to use a lesson plan dynamically should be a key outcome of teaching practice which is learned and applied intuitively. Brown and McIntyre (1993) describe how experienced and expert teachers perform this function in a series of steps:

1 Arrive at the class with clear goals for the pattern of activity and for the progress to be made by the pupils.
2 Make rapid initial judgements about the conditions impinging on the teaching, based on (a) cues which are evident on the occasion, and (b)

knowledge they already have about pupils, the environment, the curriculum and themselves.

3 Quickly select from their repertoire of actions those which their experience tells them are best suited to achieve their goals in the given conditions.

4 Alternatively, modify or replace their goals.

This complex set of actions and decisions must be performed rapidly and fluently. The acquisition of the necessary skills can be achieved by a mixture of formal and experiential learning. The development of skilled performance of these actions calls for extensive practice. Brown and McIntyre (1993: 84) characterize the performance thus:

> This sequence is largely automatic and repeated many times throughout the lesson as different routines (characterised by goals, conditions and actions) are brought into play in the light of the judgements the teacher makes about the circumstances facing him or her. It reflects the immediacy of teaching and implies that 'planning' for teaching has to be of a particularly flexible nature.

Thus, knowledge of lesson planning techniques must be supplemented with the flexible, fluent and intuitive application of that knowledge underpinned by automatized cognitive and perceptual skills. A lesson represents an instance of what Eraut (1994) terms a 'performance period' – a period of activity in a given professional context. Eraut's diagrammatic representation of a performance period has been adapted in Figure 4.1 in order to emphasize the key position of thinking and perceiving as parallel and largely intuitive processes which mediate between the developing classroom situation and the actions of the teacher. The model shows how teachers continually adapt and modify their goals and the actions they take to achieve them. Eraut's view is one of 'a dynamic model in which a constantly changing environment provides a changing input which leads to constant modification of plans' (1994: 150).

From this analysis, the key skills for teachers are those of reading the context, interpreting conditions and making adjustments to the lesson – skills which tutors and mentors must therefore aim to develop through teaching practice. Perhaps because such skills are implicit and difficult to access, there is a tendency to concentrate on the more explicit elements such as the lesson plan, key events or decisions in the lesson and the evaluation of the outcomes. Each of these can be discussed formally, whereas perception and intuitive thinking are less conscious processes which the student teacher cannot easily verbalize and which the teacher educator can only observe in the actions of the student. Nonetheless, these skills are essential and it is imperative that they be developed. In fact, it is inevitable that student teachers will develop the skills of rapid perception, intuitive thinking and decisions about how to adjust plans, and take actions in the light of this perception and thinking. This will have been their natural mode of operation since their earliest years, as Guy Claxton notes in Chapter 2. The task for the teacher educator is to foster

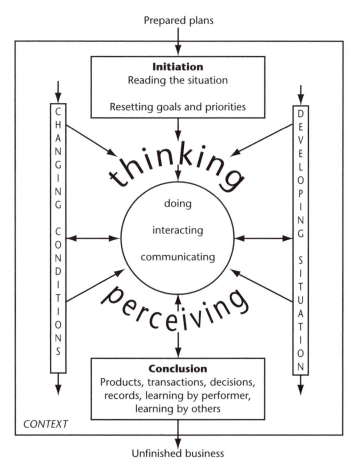

Prepared plans

Initiation
Reading the situation

Resetting goals and priorities

CHANGING CONDITIONS

DEVELOPING SITUATION

thinking

doing

interacting

communicating

perceiving

Conclusion
Products, transactions, decisions,
records, learning by performer,
learning by others

CONTEXT

Unfinished business

Figure 4.1 The performance period

this process and to ensure that appropriate principles and values underpin it. Teacher educators and student teachers readily agree that lesson planning, its analysis and evaluation, is an important part of teaching practice. However, the development of principled, flexible, perceptive and intuitive decision making in the adaptation and delivery of the lesson is equally critical but, arguably and for the reasons presented above, somewhat less clearly apprehended and, therefore, undervalued as an outcome of the practicum. It can be achieved in part by developing knowledge about the various stages and aspects of a lesson. However, the prime use of such knowledge will be to embody the principles and values which are used to reflect on and monitor the intuitive processes which lie at the heart of professional practice.

The novice teacher was born with all the neurons that he or she will ever have, but there is a massive growth of the *connections* between them which depends upon experience. In Greenfield's (1997) view, the mind is the personalization of the brain and the basic principle is that brain configuration evolves according to experience and activity. To achieve fluency requires practice which enables the mind to evolve the connections and pathways that speed up and automatize performance. One purpose and function of school experience is, therefore, to enable the development of the mental capacity to perceive the key elements of a context and to react rapidly and appropriately. Through the practicum, it is inevitable that such growth will occur but there is much to be done by student teachers and their mentors to ensure that this growth is optimal.

Eraut (1994) considers that competence is the climax of rule-guided learning and represents what can be achieved through knowledge and understanding of a given skill. He contrasts this with proficiency, which marks the onset of quite a different approach to the job: normal behaviour is not just routinized but semi-automatic; situations are apprehended more deeply and the abnormal is quickly spotted and given attention. Thus, progress beyond competence depends on a more holistic approach to situational understanding, and progress from proficiency to expertise finally happens when the decision making as well as the situational understanding becomes intuitive rather than analytic.

The role of the tutor or mentor

Mentors are also intuitive practitioners (see Chapter 6) and adopt intuitive strategies in their work with student teachers. A danger pointed out by Vonk (1997) is that the advice of the mentor carries the embedded experience of the mentor that the new teacher lacks. Vonk feels that advice has to be at the mentee's level of experience, a key principle that must underpin mentoring and one which the intuitive mentor may need to use as a maxim to monitor practice.

Intuition is developed primarily through experience. For example, Benner (1984), quoted in Eraut (1994) observes that 'in nursing, intuitive detection of change in a patient's condition often precedes more dramatic events or alerts nurses to the need for other sources of information' (p. 109). This intuitive response cannot be accounted for through rational analysis and cannot be taught as medical knowledge or understanding. Benner argues that the intuitive 'capability appears to be experientially developed' (p. 109). The implication would appear to be that it is possible to use the learning gained from experience before or even without understanding this new knowledge at a conscious level. In considering the development of intuition in nurses, Benner feels that 'there may be a significant role for tutors in accelerating the learning process' (p. 109). This acceleration may be more likely to occur if novices are enabled to work on the basis of their own experience and if a

novice's decisions are understood in the light of the experience that has produced them.

It is important here to distinguish separate and potentially conflicting mentoring functions. On the one hand, there is the need to support the development of intuitive and fluent teaching skills. On the other hand, the mentor
may wish to encourage reflection in order to challenge the thinking of student
teachers and to consolidate their learning, a process which can interfere with
performance if it is too closely linked to the event of teaching. At certain
times, the mentor or tutor will work with the student teacher on reflection-
in-action and knowledge-in-action, both of which are largely tacit but are
revealed in the actions of the student. At other times, the theatre of operations
switches to the more conscious domains of reflection-on-action and the consideration of craft knowledge in the form of propositions. The new teacher is
an intuitive learner with many implicit or subjective beliefs. Reaction against
these by teacher educators has produced a fear of intuition and a perceived
need to move from implicit theories towards more objective and verifiable
theories about teaching and learning, as discussed by many of the contributors to the current volume in Claxton *et al.* (1996). An alternative view would
be to educate the intuition of the new teacher so as to facilitate an evolution
towards legitimate intuitive practice based on principled self-monitoring.
Thus, the purpose of the mentor is both to encourage intuitive thinking and
to challenge it, thereby enabling students to be both intuitive in practice and
reflective upon practice.

If the thinking of professionals is imbued with experience (Benner 1984;
Clandinin 1986; Vonk 1997), the difficulty in the case of student teachers is
that their school experience is that of learners rather than of teachers. Hence
there is a need to reconstruct this thinking about school through the various
processes available including reflection in the light of fresh experience as a
teacher or observer. Teachers learn intuitively through the experiences provided during teacher education. Practice alone may not suffice as Smith and
Alred (1993) have noted. Thus, the spontaneous development of intuitive
thinking must be moderated by, but not be replaced by, reflection which takes
place after the event.

There is a role for the tutor and/or mentor in supporting the student
teacher's intuitive awareness. Students need to learn to trust their own intuitions and to have a sense of which intuitions to trust and which to be wary
of. Intuition is the basis for the reflection-in-action of student teachers. 'Why
did you do that?' is a deceptively simple question to ask the student in a lesson
debriefing. The fact of the matter is that the student may be only dimly aware
of the intuitive basis for decisions and may find it very hard to give rational
explanations for them. Thus, there is a need to make the student aware of
intuitive thinking so that he or she can begin to learn the vital skill of knowing when or when not to trust his or her own intuitive thinking.

Illustrative cases

The following two cases are presented to illustrate how student teachers differ in their ability to intuit and to have the confidence to trust those intuitions. A third study of the balanced ideal student is perhaps safely left to the reader's imagination. Gill Gregory reports later in this volume (Chapter 11) on techniques for measuring intuition which might also be considered by teacher educators whose task is to understand the intuitive style of each student teacher and to respond accordingly.

Case 1: the very intuitive student teacher

'I have found that lesson planning is not really as important as you tell us in our university seminars.' I was astounded to be greeted with this remark while on a school visit to observe a student teacher who was assessed by the school-based mentors as outstanding. I then proceeded to observe a lesson which amply vindicated their judgement. A very challenging class was fully engaged in meaningful and purposeful activity which lead to real and appropriate learning and very positive attitudes. The student teacher in question had rejected the paraphernalia of planning conventions: lesson templates, coursebooks, schemes of work, teaching file. In fact, she struggled to produce a lesson plan. She had used instead a process which she called 'visualization'. She had seen in her mind's eye what the students had been doing in the last lesson, what they might do in the next and what their needs might be. With this minimalist framework she was able to improvise a lesson around the various resources that she had gathered. Of course, there is some very sophisticated planning here, but it is creative and imaginative rather than analytical. By contrast, this student came close to failing the course because of the difficulty she found in articulating her intuitive understanding of teaching and learning which is assessed in the form of written assignments. Similarly, she had difficulty in convincing potential employers of her expertise because she was not able to produce well-formed rhetoric to describe her practice and provided instead an enthusiastic torrent of jumbled ideas and experiences.

Case 2: the student teacher who lacks confidence

I present here a composite of the very many student teachers who present as paralysed by fear. These students usually wait until the third or fourth week (sometimes longer) of their training course before asking the tutor when they are going to tell them what to say and do in their lessons. They have a view that teaching is an entirely conscious activity in which the teacher knows everything and simply has to tell it to their class. Their fear derives from the fact that they are conscious that they do not have this knowledge and they will not be able to teach until they are given it. For such students, the insights and intuitions which they have are either ignored or suppressed because they are not the official version of what *must be*. They are seen as subjective, personal and private and in no way relevant to the task in hand. For such students, the university seminars need to provide solutions and recipes for success – they demand lesson planning, more lesson planning and yet more lesson planning, since they themselves have no sense of their own capacity to improvise. On teaching practice, such students work conscientiously to plan the perfect lesson and yet often produce uninspired and unimaginative learning experiences as they seek to implement ill-understood ideas that derive from the experience of others. These students are intimidated by the charisma of more experienced colleagues and may seek to become their clones. Of course, in the majority of cases, they do develop as individual teachers in their own right, often to terrorize the next generation of student teachers with their own charisma, but they are only able to realize their potential when they finally allow themselves to trust in and act upon their own intuitions.

Key skills

I present here, in Table 4.1, a list of some key skills for intuitive practitioners which teacher educators might find useful to keep in mind in monitoring and supporting the development of students. Along with the key skills there are some rudimentary tasks in generic form that might assist in developing these skills. This is not a manual for teacher educators but a simple illustration. Teacher educators themselves must have the intuition to know when and how these ideas could be drawn upon.

Theory and practice

Is it possible to account for practice in a descriptive theory that can be meaningfully applied? Can we teach a theory of practice? If not, practice can certainly be learned so that we can either help or hinder that learning process. If teaching is unteachable, it is not unlearnable. Student teachers always complain that they find it hard to apply the theory that they have learned in the training institute. Perhaps this is because teacher educators and student teachers themselves are not seeing the development of practical skills as an intuitive process. It is necessary to support the development by student teachers of the key skills such as coping with uncertainty, dealing in complexity, recognizing patterns, seeing images, routinization and automation of procedures, alongside the more conscious thinking involved in self-regulation and self-monitoring, reflecting on difficulties, thinking through a new situation and evaluation. This development of intuitive, reflective and analytical thinking skills is pivotal in teacher education as in most learning contexts. The overemphasis of any one thinking process may be detrimental so it is important to signal that the aim of the present work is the rehabilitation of intuitive

Table 4.1 Key skills for intuitive practitioners

Key skill	Task for developing the skill
Seeing patterns – e.g. the mood of the class, on task versus off-task behaviour	Observation tasks – e.g. observe a lesson and note all the signs that tell you something about students: learning difficulties might be exhibited by furrowed brows, trying to copy from neighbour etc.
Fluency: build up procedures that can become routines	Plan a routine for something – e.g. calling the register. Implement, review and modify
Flexibility: student teachers in the early stages rely very heavily on detailed lesson plans but need to learn how to plan for flexibility	Timing: instead of planning how long an activity should take, plan to read the class reaction and stop the activity when it is appropriate
Decision making	Plan a lesson which incorporates alternatives between which the teacher will select *in situ* according to the needs and mood of the pupils at the time[1]
Coping with and planning for complexity	Practise visualizing the lesson (what the learners are doing and what the student teacher is doing) as a movie *before* writing the lesson plan
Being holistic, self-image and self-awareness	Student teachers make written or visual images of themselves in the practical context, an idea exploited by Swennen *et al.* (1996)

1 This idea suggested by Stephanie Charbonnier, student teacher at the University of Bristol.

thinking in order that it take its rightful place without seeking to elevate it above the other and equally important thinking processes.

Intuition and reflection

Clandinin (1986) has a view in which action is seen as being minded by key images or principles. Thus, teacher action can be spontaneous but principled. This is not to say that intuitive decision making is necessarily better or more correct. Eraut (1994) talks of the fallibility of routinized behaviour and purely intuitive decision making and suggests that there is a need for professionals to retain critical control over the more intuitive parts of their expertise by regular reflection, self-evaluation and a disposition to learn from colleagues. Over time, routines may become dysfunctional as short cuts are introduced to help cope with pressure rather than to cater for the needs of the learners. Herein lies the need for deliberative reflection and monitoring of professional practice to be ongoing and embedded.

For this process of self-monitoring to take place there is a need for the practitioner to have an awareness of intuition and of its strengths and weaknesses. Thus, while intuition is a more or less unconscious process, that is not to say that the practitioner is not or need not be aware of the intuitive process. This is awareness of the intuitive process itself rather than of the underlying reasoning. Intuition guides judgement and action but the practitioner knows that this carries with it a danger of fallibility so that more objective analysis will have to be carried out at some stage. In teaching, as in other dynamic and interactive professions, there will always be an urgent and spontaneous need to which the practitioner must react intuitively without yet having the benefit of a fully objective view of the situation. It is important that these intuitive acts are generally reliable. Practitioners must have predominantly good intuitions if they are to function effectively. They need also to be aware of their intuitions and to have a sense of safe and less safe intuitions so that self-monitoring can be a corrective process.

Conclusion

To summarize, the prime role of awareness in teaching may be to cope with atypical events and to reflect on and monitor less conscious and intuitive processes. These processes enable rapid and fluent performance and must embody appropriate principles and values. The intuitive practitioner must be reflective as well as intuitive.

References

Atkinson, T. (1996) Home thoughts from abroad, in G.L. Claxton, T. Atkinson, M.J. Osborn and M. Wallace (eds) *Liberating the Learner: Lessons for Professional Development in Education*. London: Routledge.

Benner, P. (1984) *From Novice to Expert: Excellence and Power in Clinical Nursing Practice*. Menlo Park, CA: Addison Wesley.

Brown, S. and McIntyre, D. (1993) *Making Sense of Teaching*. Buckingham: Open University Press.

Clandinin, D.J. (1986) *Classroom Practice*. Lewes: Falmer Press.

Claxton, G.L., Atkinson, T., Osborn, M.J. and Wallace, M. (eds) (1996) *Liberating the Learner: Lessons for Professional Development in Education*. London: Routledge.

Elbaz, F. (1983) *Teacher Thinking: A Study of Practical Knowledge*. New York: Nichols.

Elliott, B. and Calderhead, J. (1993) Mentoring for teacher development, in D. McIntyre, H. Hagger and M. Wilkin (eds) *Mentoring: Perspectives on School-based Teacher Education*, London: Kogan Page.

Eraut, M. (1994) *Developing Professional Knowledge and Competence*, London: Falmer Press.

Greenfield, S. (1997) *The Human Brain: A Guided Tour*. London: Weidenfeld & Nicolson.

Kahneman, D. and Tversky, A. (1990) The simulation heuristic, in D. Kahneman, P. Slovic and A. Tversky (eds) *Judgment Under Uncertainty: Heuristics and Biases*. New York: Cambridge University Press.

Polanyi, M. (1958) *Personal Knowledge*. London: Routledge & Kegan Paul.

Smith, R. and Alred, G. (1993) The impersonation of wisdom, in D. McIntyre, H. Hagger and M. Wilkin (eds) *Mentoring: Perspectives on School-based Teacher Education*. London: Kogan Page.

Swennen, A., Korthagen, F. and Jörg, T. (1996) *Working with Student Teachers' Drawings*. Glasgow: ATEE.

Vonk, H. (1997) *Improving the Effectiveness of Mentors*. Italy: University of Macerata.

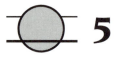 **5**

Awareness and intuition: how student teachers read their own lessons

Peter John

Introduction

The purpose of this chapter is to consider a number of issues that are central to the problem of nurturing and enhancing professional growth in student teachers. It draws upon an empirical enquiry which endeavours to describe and analyse the role that intuition plays in the thinking of novice teachers during the school experience elements of their teacher education course. In addition, an attempt will be made to appraise the findings and to consider whether a grounded conceptual framework can be constructed; one which might have an influence on both practice and research into this crucial area of professional expertise. The questions addressed by the study are: what do student teachers think about and do during their interactive teaching and to what extent, if at all, can these thoughts and actions be considered to be intuitive?

Intuition and learning to teach

The question of how teachers learn to teach is central to the enterprise of teacher education. However, only in the last two decades have researchers turned their efforts to systematic enquiry. For the most part attention has traditionally been focused on what student teachers need to know and how they might be trained, rather than on what they know and how that knowledge might be used in the classroom. Despite these foundational problems a literature has emerged which attests to the powerful influence classroom experience actually exerts during courses of professional training (Zeichner and Tabachnik 1981; Feiman-Nemser and Buchmann 1986, 1987; Calderhead 1987, 1991; Hollingsworth 1989; John 1991, 1992; Calderhead and Shorrock 1997). Nonetheless, there are still too few examples of the ways in which this experience impacts on student teachers' practice and more specifically, how their own intuition and classroom awareness affects and reacts with that experience during the practicum.

This chapter takes as its starting point the notion that intuition can be captured by researchers and practitioners. However, there are some definitional issues that need addressing before any study can proceed. The problem stems from the fact that the whole idea of intuition is so protean, often eluding exact definition, thus making the research terrain a conceptual and methodological minefield. In investigations of this kind, Dewey (1964: 46) once noted, what purports to be empirical 'too often turns out to be a process of trial and error accompanied by some degree of hope and a great deal of talk'. A caveat which should be taken as a warning rather than a deterrent.

In Chapter 2, Guy Claxton provides a detailed analysis of the concept of intuition and its various properties. Nonetheless, for the purposes of our study, a working definition was sought in order to adequately frame the investigation. This definition is therefore a practical one and resembles aspects 4 and 5 of Gill Gregory's definition (see Chapter 11), in that practitioner intuition is viewed as situation specific, triggered by problems, and related to a range of techniques which are used during particular phases of the problem-solving or creative process. A key element in this definition is the notion of professional awareness; a concept which has been central to a number of studies undertaken into the nature and character of teachers' professional knowledge (Kounin 1970; Peterson and Comeaux 1987; Berliner 1988; Tom 1994). Following Polyani and Posch (1975) this can be broken down into two distinct categories: focused and subsidiary awareness. The former represents what is being closely observed and questioned while the latter is seen as awareness which has been or will be focused on in the future. Both terms encapsulate the active role of the individual in the process of being aware and as such are essential elements in any professional performance.

The stance adopted here is that researchers and practitioners involved in teacher education at all levels should strive to reconstruct the classroom settings experienced by student teachers, thus optimizing the possibilities for students, mentors and tutors to read their practice as accurately as possible. The notion of 'reading' a situation is taken from the philosophical literature often traced to Wittgenstein's (1953) writings on ordinary language analysis and elaborated upon by others including the scientist Thomas Kuhn (1970) and Donald Schön (1983). In this literature, 'reading' a situation is part of seeing and perceiving which are in turn not only cognitively intertwined but also largely determined by the practical situation available to practitioners at key moments. In this sense 'reading' a lesson for a student teacher is both an *in situ* reflection and a *post factum* response.

For convenience, the remainder of this chapter follows a fairly conventional 'research paper' format. The next section outlines the theoretical rationale for the research and is followed by an explanation of the genesis and methodology of the project. The results are then presented and the final sections revolve around a series of reflections on the findings in the light of the current literature and the theoretical framework outlined in the opening chapter of this book.

Theoretical context

The concepts and methodology underpinning the research reported in this chapter are drawn from what has become known as the 'teacher thinking paradigm'. During the last two decades the study of teacher thinking has intensified and new insights have been gained into what Jackson (1968) termed the three phases of teaching: the pre-active, the interactive and the post-interactive. Several reviews of the literature have been published of which the most important are Shavelson and Stern (1981), Clark and Peterson (1986), Carter (1990) and Hoyle and John (1995). In general the field can be split into three overlapping categories of research: first, teachers' information processing skills, including decision-making models and expert–novice studies; second, teachers' practical knowledge, including personal and classroom knowledge; and third, pedagogical content knowledge – that is, the ways in which teachers understand and represent the subject matter to their pupils.

In general, the first category focuses typically on descriptions of the content of teachers' thoughts and their cognitive processes. Occasionally isomorphic models of the way teachers plan or think interactively have been generated. Some researchers have sought to demonstrate close parallels between teachers' thought processes and specific models of thinking, particularly the decision-making model. Other research under this heading has been of the policy capturing variety. This involves testing whether statistical or mathematical models can serve as paramorphic models of teacher thinking.

Research into pedagogical content knowledge, with its emphasis on subject matter, is aimed at uncovering what teachers know and understand about their subject, how they translate that into meaningful classroom representations and its relationship to children's learning. Research into practical knowledge, on the other hand, is more inclusive and attempts to understand the complexities of interactive teaching and thinking-in-action within the broader realms of teacher personal experience and biography. Using variants of a phenomenological epistemology researchers and scholars in this field aim to portray teacher knowledge in all its varieties and complexity – the aim being not to codify that knowledge but to illustrate its characteristics through detailed exemplification.

By sticking close to the personal and the contextual, the teacher thinking tradition endeavours to give a rich and rounded picture of the conditions under which teachers operate and the way in which they navigate classrooms and make sense of their practice. Although each category is built from a different set of theoretical assumptions all aim to uncover 'how teachers use their knowledge to make sense of the complex, ill-structured classroom world of competing goals and actions' (Carter 1990: 302).

Research design and methodology

The decision to place the study within the above tradition reflected the exploratory character of the exercise, the nature of the research questions, and the stringency of practical constraints of time and resources.

At the outset, 17 student teachers were identified (all historians) and asked to participate. Given the type of research question asked, a hybrid research model was developed blending ethnographic approaches to classroom observation with cognitively-based stimulated recall methods. In terms of the former, techniques of non-participant observation were used to gain a detailed contextual understanding of the classroom environment as well as to serve as a basis for the stimulated recall interviews. In relation to the latter, the participants were invited to comment on their classroom thinking at key moments identified in the observational data. While recognizing the difficulties and drawbacks of stimulated recall as a methodology (see Yinger 1986 for a detailed discussion), alternative approaches were considered to be either too mechanistic or time-consuming given the nature of the project. Brief outlines regarding the purposes of the project, the approaches to be used and the ethics to be observed were prepared and given to the participants before the data was collected. Two declined to become involved for personal reasons. The remaining 15 agreed to be observed and interviewed three times during a six-week period in the second section of their main school experience.

The data generated were subjected to two types of analysis: one ethnographic and one cognitive–psychological. The former involved applying Spradley's (1979) strategies of domain and taxonomic analysis to the protocols. The stimulated recall data, on the other hand, underwent a content analysis using the system developed by Marland (1977) and Marland and Osborne (1988). This involved subjecting the transcripts to a coding system based on 'thought units'. The prime categories achieved inter-coder reliability coefficients of 0.71 to 0.89, figures obtained using the Scott formula (Ober *et al.* 1971). The first step involved identifying aspects of the data that contained in-lesson thinking. The data was then segmented into 'thought units', here defined in terms of the application of cognitive process (e.g. attributing meaning to an event, recalling, evaluating, deliberating, generating, avoiding etc.) to a concrete or abstract referent (e.g. pupil behaviour, misunderstandings, a resource, information or a teaching tactic etc.). Such an analysis method allowed thinking and action to be studied in context as well as permitting the classification of thought units along a past-present-future dimension.

Presentation

The main purpose of the analysis was to try to come to a greater understanding of the nature of student teachers' thinking during lessons and how their intuition finds expression within a classroom context. However, while it is possible to detect examples of intuitive thought and action being played out in the observed classrooms we cannot say with any certainty that such things actually happened given the nature of methodology employed and the complexity of the students' thinking during particular classroom episodes. What we have then are *approximations* to their thinking. The first part of this section begins with an overview of the general findings as they relate to the sample as a whole; the second tries to give a more fine-grained feel to the data by using case material to illustrate the more poignant aspects of the analysis.

The analysis of the tabulated data regarding the 'thought units' revealed a number of insights. A breakdown of the individual datasets for each student showed a variety of responses and actions, however, when collapsed to form a general overall picture, a number of commonalities appeared. Each category is rank ordered according to the percentage of thought units presented across the sample (see Table 5.1). Each category is explained in more detail below. Again illustrative material from the transcripts is used wherever possible to aid understanding and insight.

Tactical perspectives

These tended to be considerations based on teaching methods and other courses of action taken by the student teachers. They included both retrospective thoughts about tactics used in earlier lessons and prospective thoughts related to future actions. Some were straightforward in appearance with new questions being added to Socratic sequences or basic changes being made in a task structure; others were more complex and involved shifting the whole thrust of the lesson to avoid a particular behavioural or learning problem, often not spotted during the planning stage. Comments from the stimulated recall data included the following: 'I extended the question session because they were getting a lot out of it and seemed to be enjoying it'; 'I let the role play develop – I knew the plan would have to be modified but I felt it was worth it since they were getting the idea about the relationship between the feudal system and social class'; 'the video I had used with another class on the plague just didn't work with these – so I interrupted the story and had to explain the main points'.

Table 5.1 Focus of coded thought units over 45 lessons (2250 minutes of teaching)

Rank order	Percentage (N = 1648)
Tactical perspectives	21.7
Perceptions	18.3
Deliberations	15.6
Anticipations	12.7
Pupils	10.8
Content	9.4
Aims and objectives	7.6
Feelings	6.3

Perceptions

Perceptions reported by the students focused on pupils' verbal and physical behaviour, movements, looks, comments and raising of hands. As expected, many of the thoughts were related to classroom management concerns. Those reported usually focused on low-level forms of disruptive behaviour – off-task talk, unnecessary movement, attention seeking and shouting out. Higher levels of disruption were reported but these tended to be fewer in number and were usually related to outside incidents. Examples included: 'I could see there was too much movement in the back row and particular individuals were orchestrating it'; 'I realized just from scanning the room that I would have to move certain individuals if the lesson was to progress at all'.

Deliberations

As well as contemplating what might happen, many of the students also thought about what had happened. Surprisingly these reflective moments were going on continuously throughout the lessons but tended to be more obvious during what might be termed 'key moments'. For instance, after setting a task on the plague in London, one student immediately began to evaluate the nature of his initial explanation and video footage and decided to alter the nature of the explanation, while another changed the expected finishing times and pace of a piece of extended writing on the Norman conquest. These deliberations were an attempt to see a particular situation differently from its more familiar form; they were also accompanied by changes in the descriptive language about the events used by the students.

Anticipations

This area was often associated with teaching tactics. All the observed students, to a greater or lesser extent, tried to foresee responses or reactions to topics, ideas, directions, opinions, tasks and questions. The thought units therefore tended to influence the way lessons moved and the degree of deviation from the plan during the lesson. It was during this form of thinking that the students' intuition became more obvious in both its structure and use. Trying to anticipate events and attempting to guess whether pupils would grasp new concepts or ideas forced the students, in various ways, to manoeuvre their thinking in the thick of the action. Comments included: 'I had to change tack at that point because it suddenly dawned on me that most of the group wouldn't understand what I was on about when I explained the link between the cold war and the end of the Second World War later on'; or 'I went off my intended route at that point because I could see they were going to have problems with the task unless I went about explaining the concept of evidence differently'.

Pupils

Here the students made inferences about a variety of pupil states ranging from their general attitude and approach ('they weren't in a working mood today') to their motives and intentions ('they are not interested in the detail of the Magna Carta'). Concerns regarding pupil contributions to the lesson likewise formed a common thread in the data as did the feeling pupils would either be 'intrinsically interested' or 'plain bored'. Many also commented that the time spent planning and preparing their particular lesson may have been wasted due to a lack of basic interest and many worried about coming across as 'boring' or 'dull' to the pupils. A minority mentioned their assessment of the cognitive states of their pupils, with some labelling them as clever, bright, alert, slow or poor.

Content

The issue of content was a recurring theme in the data. Being unfamiliar with the subject knowledge of the lesson to be taught was often cited as a problem as was a lack of real understanding of the issues involved in teaching that subject. This often meant a shortening of questioning sessions and an over-reliance on task-related pedagogy as a means of avoiding 'showing one's weaknesses'; of 'not being able to answer a question' or 'simply misleading or plain giving them the wrong information'. Also, in their stimulated recall interviews, a number mentioned the demand for curriculum coverage as an influence on the teaching tactic chosen. This apparent lack of subject knowledge appeared to curtail substantive interaction between the teacher and the pupils as well as forcing the teacher to rely on set lesson plans borrowed from the department and taught, as one student put it, 'on automatic pilot'.

Aims and objectives

Although every lesson plan had the obligatory list or indicative account of the general and specific expected outcomes, these played less of a role during teaching. Instead the students appeared to break the lesson down into segments while goal statements tended to be more short-term and were either related to the mood of the class or the classroom management implications of the chosen method. Thoughts therefore tended to cluster around what could be achieved within the ongoing 'hubbub' of the lesson and were therefore very general in nature. A typical example included: 'I wanted the group to identify with the characters more closely otherwise the empathy exercise on enclosure would not be successful', or alternatively, 'if I let them carry on like that they would be there all day just fiddling, never getting anywhere, so I scaled down to what might be more realistic goals'.

Feelings

Despite being a small percentage of the thoughts expressed, the feelings of the students provided some insight into the nature of their intuitive thinking. Many expressed anxiety about facing particular classes and teaching certain topics, while others declared that they experienced the whole gamut of emotions during lessons from 'extreme frustration' (the causes of which ranged from poor behaviour of individuals and groups to pupils not grasping an apparently simple concept, idea or event) to 'elation' (usually when a lesson went well or a pupil or pupils understood perfectly the topic being taught). These feelings were sometimes related to the nature of the content with some talking emotionally about how strongly they felt about the topic – for example, the Holocaust, trench warfare or the emancipation of women – and the lack of interest shown by the pupils.

   While it is possible to detect examples of intuition being used in the classroom in the above data, there is no indication that it was always at a conscious level. The ethnographic analysis of the lessons combined with the stimulated recall evidence gives us a more rounded if less scientific picture. For while the tabulated data provides interesting foundational and statistical insights it is primarily concerned with deliberations, perceptions and tactics. The lesson reconstructions that follow are created from an amalgamation of both data sets placed side by side to give a flavour of the lesson as well as allowing the reader to examine, through more detailed illustration, the categories outlined in the thought unit data above. Finally, such qualitative data gives a more fine-grained understanding of the relationship between the students' intuition and awareness while they sort through the multiplicity of stimuli which confronted them in the classroom. The two lessons were chosen because they represented the range more typically than others. However, it must be stressed that due to restrictions of space only partial reconstructions are possible.

Lesson reconstruction 1

Observed actions	*Recalled thinking*
10.10 a.m. Teacher stands by the door and greets the pupils. Settling down period and instructions given ('turn to a fresh page and take down blackboard summary'). Register taken and worksheets distributed.	I try to arrive at the classroom early if possible and stand by the door or prepare the board or whatever (*tactical perspective*). It helps control if I stand by the door and I can direct them if I need to. I can also see how they are and check what lesson they've just come from (*deliberation*).
10.14 a.m. Teacher opens with general points about aim of the lesson from	I asked them to turn to a fresh page and lay it out with title and the

blackboard and asks opening question 'Can anybody tell me what a civil war is? Some shouting out, attempt at control. Some strange answers.

words 'civil war' and the aims of the lesson, partly to settle them down (*aims and objectives*) and partly as a guide to the lesson (*tactical perspective*). It's a routine I use regularly and it can save standing there and having a confrontation. It also allows me time to do the 'housekeeping' – register and distribution of books and sheets (*tactical perspective*).

Follow-up: 'Can you give me an example of one going on today?' Again, random answers, some accurate but too much background noise and confusion, e.g.: 'This school miss!' and so on.

My opening gambit was to see whether they understood the term 'civil war' – it's been in the news recently with Rwanda and Bosnia so I thought it would spark an interesting discussion (*tactical perspective*). But even after a minute or two I could feel that there was some confusion (*perception*).

I use the question and answer method a lot – probably to start most of my lessons (*tactical perspective*). I don't plan the questions, I just have a general idea and I follow my nose. It all depends on their reaction (*perception*). Today I could tell that they were getting confused and I thought there might be problems later on (*anticipation*). I had to think quickly here (*deliberation*).

10.17 a.m. Dictionary definition of 'civil war' read out and placed on the blackboard. Pupils copy it down. Calmer atmosphere.

Luckily at this point I saw a dictionary on the shelf and so I read out the definition and then made them copy it down from the blackboard (*tactical perspective*). This gave them all a clear starting point and a reference point (*pupils*). It also gave me breathing space and a chance to settle my nerves (*feelings*).

10.20 a.m. Further question and answer session based on long- and short-term causes of the English

Some were not getting it and the answers were all over the place (*perception*). I try to stick to the

Civil War. 'Can you think back to your previous work on Elizabeth and the Stuarts? Can you pick out some long-term causes for the War? Confused answers. 'Well then can anybody tell me the dates of Eliza beth's reign?' Guesses mostly inaccurate. 'Can anybody give me some important events during and after her reign?' A few accurate answers (the Armada etc.).

Question from boy at the back: 'What is the difference between long- and short-term causes miss?'

10.25 a.m. Short delay, some chatter ing. Then a timeline is placed on the blackboard and the class asked to copy it down. A slight delay in finding the textbook. Class generally quiet during this exercise.

10.32 a.m. Teacher goes over the main points of the timeline within the context of long-term causation.

routine of 'hands up' no shouting out, but it can be difficult with some groups (*tactical perspective*).

The gap at this point in the lesson came about because of the confusion. I could tell they were confused because of the nature of the answers and the lack of them in some quarters (*perception*). The distinction between long- and short-term causes in history is difficult and I'm not sure in my own mind let alone them. John's question really threw me – he's a bit arrogant, I've picked that up already (*pupils*). I waffled an answer because I was a touch confused about the subject (*content*). I was desperately trying to think what to do (*deliberation*).

The delay before putting the time-line up on the board was because I hadn't planned it but I remembered seeing one in one of the textbooks and I was searching for it on my desk (*tactical perspective*). If it hadn't been there I would have been in a pickle because my knowledge of the period is very thin to say the least (*content*).

I decided to use the opportunity to go over the timeline and to reiterate the long- and short-term distinction on the blackboard to settle the problem and to avoid future trouble (*anticipation*): not only

10.38 a.m. Teacher introduces next segment of the lesson: 'Today we will be looking at the long- and some of the short-term causes using sources and the worksheet on your tables in front of you.' Massive audible groan from the class: 'Not another work sheet miss!' Brief instructions on completion and class asked to begin the task.

subject confusion but behavioural problems too (*perception*).

Yes, they often react like that – it still hurts me even after months of being in school. I put a lot of effort into the preparation of the materials and comments like that still grate on me. I suppose my skin isn't thick enough yet (*feelings*).

10.40 a.m. Teacher calls class together and explains in more detail what is required and goes over briefly expected answers to Source A and B questions.

Again I could tell they were confused by my instructions (*perception*). It's that glazed look they have – you can spot it instantly. So I decided there and then to go over Source A and B (*tactical perspective*) with them orally first to avoid later problems (*anticipation*). I also wanted to avoid going around the class re-explaining what I wanted twenty times over.

10.43 a.m. Class begin work using the resources. Teacher offers individual support where necessary and engages pupils with issues.

Supporting pupils is important and helps their learning (*pupils*). I try to structure it so I spend more time with particular individuals during each week, but I am always distracted by others wanting help (*tactics*). I spent more time on that side of the class today to try to engage with them a little more – too often you're just solving their basic problems without ever engaging them with the subject (*pupils*).

10.53 a.m. Two boys seek attention. From their comments they have finished and want to go further. Extra work offered.

The Richard and John problem arose because, as usual, they finished early. They were showing off a little so I asked them to read each other's answers and comment on them. In fact I could see them fidgeting out of the corner of my eye (*perception*). It's a sort of peer tutoring I suppose. I expected this to happen (*anticipation*), given what I know about them (*pupils*). I also find it useful because it keeps the group together rather than letting some fly off in other directions and at different speeds (*anticipation*). I saw this done a lot at my previous school (*tactical perspective*).

10.58 a.m. Class called together. Teacher asks for some answers to be read out. Some volunteers but teacher chooses. Interesting results – some have clearly understood the issues, others have failed to make any real headway. The two early finishers are desperate to read out but are ignored.

This is another method I use regularly – getting them to read out some excerpts from their answers. I planned it in general but I choose the pupils and comment according to the answers (*tactical perspective*).

11.00 a.m. Bell sounds. Commotion and confusion. Teacher demands attention. Threats issued regarding detention. Calm finally returns. Worksheets collected and class dismissed row by row.

Finishing is still difficult. I nearly always run over time and I could see they were irritated (*perceptions*). I could have let them go straight away but I decided against that (*deliberation*). Today I hadn't collected the papers in so I had to settle them and then collect after the bell. It's important to make sure they leave the class in an orderly way, more often than not for safety reasons, but it's also important to establish the routine with them so they know what your expectations are.

Lesson reconstruction 2

Observed actions

Recalled thinking

2.30 p.m. Orderly if noisy entry by the pupils. Teacher stands by the door and chats as they come in. Formal atmosphere but relaxed. As they enter the teacher gives them a sheaf of papers. Class are asked to sit and read the papers in silence.

I always try to give them something to do when I take the register. It helps me to settle myself and to judge their mood (*anticipation*). It was especially important today because it was last lesson and it was a role-play (*tactical perspective*).

2.35 p.m. Class called together for a brainstorm. The teacher introduces

This start is important because it allowed me to get a grip and to the lesson, explaining about the role-play. Cheers go up when announced. Warnings issued and the class are urged to take it seriously otherwise it will be changed. Brainstorm begins and the teacher writes up the answers on the board in the form of a spider diagram.

sort out any problems. Good structure is important to me and by explaining things early I can root out any potential problems – like the shouting from the back (*anticipation*).

2.40 p.m. Explanation of role-play related to the sheets. The scripts are parts to be played and the pupils have to use the information to ask a partner questions about the reasons for leaving the village and moving to the town. The whole thing is set in the 1830s.

I often use a brainstorm to go over previous things and to remind them of events and facts. It also helps in setting the scene (*tactical perspective*). It also gets around the problem of hands up – they aren't used to this so rather than impose a new routine I try to get around the problem (*pupils*). They often cheer because they think a role-play is not real work, so I have to make sure they stay on task.

2.50 p.m. Role-play begins after the teacher matches pairs. Some complaints but they settled quickly. The teacher supports individuals and asks questions and encourages.

I try to match the roles to the pupils here (*tactical perspective*). I don't plan it, I play it by ear and use what I know about them and then choose and see the reaction (*perception*). If some insist on staying with their friends (*pupils*), then I weigh up the advantages and disadvantages quickly and make an on-the-spot decision (*deliberation*). I used this role-play at my previous school and I've been waiting for an opportunity to use it here (*tactical perspective*). It fits with the topic so I though I'd use it even though it was the last lesson.

Time targets are set for the task as are likely outcomes – extended writing task and empathy exercise. 'You have just twenty minutes to complete the interviews then I'll choose pairs for the reading out.'

I always try to set targets in the lesson (*aims and objectives*). It keeps them focused and on task (*tactical perspective*). I change them if I think things are going too quickly or slowly (*perception*). I used the homework threat as a reaction and a discipline method just in case there were any problems later on (*anticipation*).

3.15 p.m. Class called together. Pairs chosen and roles played out in front of the class. Some excellent questions and clever answers: 'Miss, why did people move if things were so bad in the cities and towns?'; 'How reliable are the scripts you've given us – are they real?' Some discussion around the class after the teacher invited responses to such 'good questions'. No teacher answer given.

I was thinking about this all the way through the task (*deliberation*) and I decided to choose the ones I thought would be sensible and who had put a lot of effort in. I was a little scared here because I didn't know which way it would go (*feelings*). Playing roles out in front of the class can go either way. The question that Sara asked was very good – it showed she was thinking about the issue of evidence and selectivity. The trouble was I didn't really know the answer (*content*) – that's why I threw it open and invited responses (*tactical perspective*). I did that off the top of my head (*perception*).

3.25 p.m. Homework set around the above questions.

I thought about it and decided to set the questions they asked for homework because they were good and it gave me space to think about it for next time (*deliberation*), because to be truthful I don't really know the answer. I'm a bit shaky on the Industrial Revolution (*content*). That question was also tricky. They are made up but that doesn't invalidate them because they are based on real evidence. But that was difficult to explain and I think I made a complete hash of it (*tactical perspective*). Experienced teachers have a store of these answers. I suppose mine will develop with time.

3.30 p.m. Bell rings for the end of the day. Commotion and noise. Class settled by strong voice and threat. A short quiz gives them the incentive to settle. Class dismissed as they answer questions.

I overran slightly and I could see they were edgy and itching to go (*perception*), so I settled them under the threat of staying behind. The little quiz gave me the opportunity to get to the point of exit quickly (*tactical perspective*). I make the questions up as I go along and differentiate (*pupils*) them so everybody gets a go.

Overview

From the foregoing reconstructions, the following inferences can be made. First, both the student teachers (and others in the sample) exhibited a degree of what Schön (1983) calls re-framing or reflection-in-action. This usually came about as a reaction to particular sets of circumstances and events, some of which were anticipated while others were not. Second, much of this re-framing was underpinned or preceded by a degree of awareness and intuition. At times this was used creatively to expand opportunities and to improvise, while in others it was reactive, its purpose being to avoid problems. In this sense such re-framing mirrors the third of Bastick's (1982) properties of intu-ition outlined by Guy Claxton in Chapter 2. Third, the two lessons outlined above and most of the others were underpinned by an important sense of rou-tine. These routines were most prominent during the starts and ends of lessons but they were evident throughout the observations and provided an important anchor to the intuitive thinking used by the students. Fourth, many of the teaching tactics used – both planned and unplanned – often came ready-made in the sense that they had been seen or suggested by others (teachers, mentors, tutors etc.). These recipes were related to both content (teaching a topic in a particular way) or general pedagogy (question and answer sessions and group organization etc.). As with the routines, this recipe knowledge formed the basis upon which much of the intuitive thinking of the student teachers was based, thus emphasizing the importance of, as Claxton (Chapter 2) puts it, the 'functional relationship between the explicit and the implicit' in professional learning. Finally, the students throughout the sample showed an alertness to contextual cues but their use of these cues was limited. In general, this alertness tended to be ego-centred and was based more on personal and sometimes emotional worries rather than on wider professional concerns (Fuller 1969; Fuller and Bown 1975; John 1995).

The remainder of this chapter will try to give an overall picture of the find-ings in terms of five models of intuition-related thinking. However, it must be emphasized that theorizing intuition is itself almost a contradiction in terms and the typology should be seen as nothing more that a starting point rather than a Procrustean bed upon which a plausible theory of teacher intuition might be built.

Intuition related to problem avoidance

In this model the student teachers made a choice between two or more alternative modes of action. Their thinking can be classed as intuitive because they made their choices, as one claimed, 'by the seat of their pants'. This model is highly contextualized and is tied up with particularistic knowledge of the children, the signals that alert the teacher to the particular problem or problems and the deployment of appropriate tactics taken from a repertoire of emerging techniques and methods. The mode is characterized by evasive and anticipatory action so problems in themselves do not arise. In this sense it can be categorized as proactive intuition.

Intuition related to teacher interpretation

Here the data indicates that the student teachers' reactions to pupils and their relationships with them was often related to their own personal interpretation of pupil cues, both verbal and non-verbal. For these students, their thinking in terms of how to react appropriately involved noting the cue and the source, interpreting the meaning of the cue and then thinking about an appropriate reaction tactic. Often the tactic selected was based on personal knowledge of a particular pupil or pupils and how they might respond to the strategy. Where the pupil's reaction was out of character, the student teacher would often deliberate about how best to react and would consider a number of alternatives. Often these reactions came in ready-made form and their application depended on whether they suited individual circumstances. The actions were intuitive in the sense that the number of alternatives used gave the student the scope to 'follow their nose'. Table 5.2 gives an illustration of the model in terms of the students' interpretation during a question and answer sequence. This form of intuition tended to be more reactive in nature.

Intuition related to opportunity creation

Although less in evidence than the first two modes, this type of thinking was still noticeable in much of the data. Here the student teachers used situations to create opportunities for learning, many of which occurred during key moments in the lessons thus allowing the students to 'go with the flow'. In whole class terms this often meant permitting the lesson to move into the unknown, or in micro terms, giving individual pupils the opportunity to take their understanding further through creative use of questioning and support materials. This allowed the learners to take on new ideas, content and concepts. This form of intuition was usually proactive in nature.

Intuition related to improvisation

This mode closely resembles the previously mentioned 'opportunity' type of intuition. However, there were enough significant differences for it to be considered separately. Essentially the student would deliberately go off-plan and improvise in a reactive way because some aspect of the planned lesson had failed to work or because levels of understanding were poor and resources inappropriate or unavailable. Thus the student would change an explanation or develop a new tactic predominantly in reaction to events, often adapting

Table 5.2 Students' interpretations during question and answer

Type of pupil response to questions	Teacher interpretation
Multiple, unsolicited	If orderly and expected (e.g. brainstorming) then go with the flow If disorderly, impose order and ask for hands up
Confused, inaudible	Repeat or rephrase question or Ask for repeat answers in clearer fashion or Clarify and change tack
Private (e.g. dyadic)	Ask pupils to share answer with the class or rephrase answer for them

the lesson to perceived pupil needs. Although mostly reactive there was some evidence of proactive improvisation.

Intuition related to mood assessment

In this model of intuitive thinking, the students concerned followed a mood assessment procedure which was usually visible at the beginning of lessons (see Table 5.3). On entering classes, they looked for signs (facial expressions, attitude, movement, etc.) which they then used to decide upon class mood (lethargic, receptive, difficult, edgy, awkward, ready to engage, etc.). The teaching tactics were then adapted to suit the perceived situation (being firm, authoritative, friendly, humorous). At times this mode of thinking was also

Table 5.3 An illustration of mood assessment

Teacher thinking	Teacher classification	Teacher action
As the student teacher enters the classroom he/she assesses the mood of the class using the following cues: how they stand; facial expressions; the way they enter; reactions to the lesson outline/resources; previous lesson 'hangover' effect	The student teacher classifies the mood of the class as: lethargic; receptive; difficult; edgy; flighty	The student teacher then works the lesson around the assessment of mood: be businesslike; be friendly; use humour; set tasks early; less teacher talk; be authoritative

distinguishable during central segments of lessons sometimes preceding or accompanying a new task or approach.

Discussion

These differentiated approaches to classroom events reflected in part the enormous complexity of classroom life which in turn created a wide diversity of approaches for dealing with complex situations. The data therefore invites speculation about the links between the degree of differentiation in the student teachers' intuitive understandings of classroom life, the techniques and methods they use in their practice and the whole notion of teacher effectiveness and pupil learning. The proposition that the more effective teacher is one with a more highly tuned and highly differentiated intuition for understanding and interpreting classroom life and with a wide repertoire of appropriate models for reacting to specific situations is a plausible one. However, more research will be needed before any firm inferences can be made. It can also be argued that pupils benefit accordingly from a teacher who has the ability to predict, perceive and adapt to the subtle changes going on around him or her. Simultaneously, alleged benefits might also be contingent upon intuitive qualities inherent within the individual, as Guy Claxton points out in Chapter 2. Sensitivity to the environment is thus an important aspect of effective practice and the exercise of appropriate professional judgement.

In addition, the data appeared to validate the proactive and reactive nature of the student teachers' responses to classroom situations. The proactive approach – that is, thinking in which the intention was to initiate action and to shape classroom events rather than merely react to them – was less in evidence than the reactive. Furthermore, the practical problems confronting the student teachers at key moments in their lessons ranged from 'what to do . . .?' questions to the radically different 'what if . . .?' questions. Many of these problems were not always solved by the application of a technique, rule or procedure but required on-the-spot thinking and judgement, often backed up by the individual's own intuition. Research on the professions by Donald Schön (1983, 1987, 1991) and others has called this response a 'reflective conversation' with the immediate problem situation and suggests that to make sense of the practice of professionals (both novice and experienced) we need to understand how their intuition is used in these particular conversations.

For the students in this project, their intuition was visible during key moments which punctured their already patterned routines. These moments, although limited in number, were part of their 'unrolling virtuosity' (Claxton, this volume) and played an important role in developing their practical professional knowledge (Furlong and Maynard 1996). At these points a dialogue or conversation with themselves and with their context resulted in the construction of a new approach and a re-evaluation of their concerns as they proceeded. This was described by many as 'feeling my way through' or 'operating at gut level' or 'following my nose'. This suggests that student teachers, while lacking the fluidity, flexibility, invention and greater knowledge of their more experienced counterparts, still use their intuition as a way of coping with divergent situations. This form of in-class thinking, often articulated in a heightened sensitivity to clues, as Guy Claxton puts it, draws upon implicit and action-present cognitions rather than the more explicit and deliberative cognitions associated with *post factum* reflection (see Chapter 2).

Student's use of this intuition was, however, firmly based on the acquisition of what Hargeaves (1993) calls 'professional common-sense knowledge'. Drawing on the work of Schutz (1963) and Schutz and Luckmann (1974) this can be defined as the practical or habitual knowledge inherent in any every-day activity. In the classroom, routines are well-established formulas for organizing and structuring the classroom environment and learning. Lein-hardt *et al.* (1987) define three types of routine that characterize typical class-rooms: management routines that maintain discipline and control; support routines that define and specify behaviours; and exchange routines that spec-ify the interactive behaviours that permit a teaching and learning exchange. In the sample used in this research similar patterns of routine were evident and formed the foundation upon which much of the detected intuition was built.

In addition to these routines another defining characteristic of professional common-sense knowledge is recipes. Many of those who engage people in professional learning experiences often disparage formulas, rules or recipes for action as superficial and narrow. Practising a skill, they claim, requires judgement and reason, underpinned by a system of values and principles for action. The 'cook book' analogy is often used in a derogatory way, caricatur-ing recipes as formulaic or 'dance-step' type teaching where reason and intu-ition are forgotten. However, viewed from another perspective, recipes can take on an altogether different guise. Hargreaves (1993) reminds us not to take too lofty a view of recipe knowledge, and drawing on the work of Schutz (1963) shows that recipes allow us to bring forward 'typical means for bring-ing about typical ends in typical situations' (Hargreaves 1993: 90). In this sense they can help students construct solutions for commonplace classroom problems, thus allowing the novice teacher to construct a scheme of interpre-tation to understand events within situations as well as helping them form precepts for action. Too often it seems tutors and academics fear that students will pick up, as Hargreaves (1993) puts it, an undesirable set of recipes; ones that do not fit with their model of that continually moving mantra 'good prac-tice'.

Conclusion and implications

Casting the final section as 'Conclusion and implications' is in some senses problematic. It is traditional in most research reports to use such phraseology to help the writer gain persuasive force by terminological and practical suggestion. A form of 'moral compulsion' as Margaret Buchmann (1989) puts it. While I concede that this section is the most personal and that the conclusions which follow may not escape being *parti pris*, the purpose is to be suggestive in a practical way.

In his Chapter 2, Guy Claxton states that 'we can indeed learn to improve the frequency, reliability and quality of our intuitions'. If this is only half true then what might we as teacher educators and mentors do to help students attain Claxton's goals? First, there is some evidence that the creation of an open-ended, liberal, loose, non-analytic seminar environment is more conducive to the understanding of intuition than more ideologically dominated ones (Abercrombie 1953; John 1996). Such an environment allows students to put forward their ideas, beliefs, practices, emotions and feelings in an open and truthful way. This may prove a problem for some tutors (and mentors in school) in higher education who have their own, often deeply held, view of good practice, sometimes itself an intuitive response to their own teaching experience. Consequently, it may also be helpful, as Gendlin (1981) points out, to focus on the feelings and the practice simultaneously, thus making some seminars based on what Laurinda Brown calls 'noticing the moment' (see Chapter 10). Drawing on strategies prevalent in psychotherapy and counselling, this strategy can help students to 'unpick' the intuition in their chosen episodes of the lived experience of teaching.

Second, the dominant model of lesson planning which is increasingly supported by external effectiveness criteria and a range of proformas is perhaps in need of reshaping if intuition is to take a more formative role in student teachers' learning. Ruminating in the bath, mulling over ideas in the car, thinking about lessons in bed are perhaps as powerful as those tightly scripted plans with their narrow objectives and endless evaluations (John 1992, 1995). Furthermore, students need to learn to plan for contingency; having a flexible lesson plan, as Terry Atkinson points out in Chapter 4, can provide the student with the necessary tools to deal with the unforeseen and the unexpected. Last, if intuition cannot be forced and creativity is about the relationship of the artist to his or her context then we have to develop other models of lesson planning that fit different professional circumstances and different points in the professional learning cycle (John, in press).

School-based mentors and teachers, on the other hand, might be offered help, support and training in the application of the research methods used in the teacher thinking paradigm. This may help them improve both the supervisory and observational aspects of their role. Furthermore, 'the self-perspective' of student teachers is clearly influenced by the school context. Whether this is an element of the socializing aspect of becoming a teacher or whether it is part of a more complex juggling act is a matter of conjecture. What is clear is that novice teachers quickly learn to rely on their own resourcefulness and are adept at crafting their intuitive ideas into their practice. It is not surprising then that beginning teachers 'shop around' for curriculum ideas, activities and content that will better ensure their survival in the classroom. This can lead to an uncritical, impulsive kind of consumerism.

Therefore mentors, tutors and cooperating colleagues must help students develop a better understanding of the content they are going to teach; the potential scope, sequence and balance of lessons; the generic and specific needs of learners as well as a repertoire of routines and recipes that will enhance the quality of their teaching.

Finally, I can only partly agree with Guy Claxton (and in a sense Polanyi) in their discussion of maxims, for I believe that their use in the conversation between novice and mentor may hold the key to helping student teachers engage with that most difficult of lexicons – the language of practice (Yinger 1987; John 1996). This would allow their intuitions to interact *pari passu* with their explicit learning while at the same time allowing mentors to initiate conversations about practice in which their professional knowledge is central. For in the final analysis the way we help students to realize and use their intuitive qualities in the classroom may be the litmus test by which the quality of their learning can be gauged. Without it, students might continue to move through courses as though they were selecting from a smorgasbord – they taste a little of everything but seldom savour anything fully, or alternatively they take so much from their experiences they are stuffed full rather than nourished.

References

Abercrombie, M.L.J. (1953) Education security as a condition for change. *Health Education Journal,* 11(3): 112–17.

Bastick, T. (1982) *Intuition: How We Think and Act.* Chichester: Wiley.

Berliner, D.C. (1988) The development of expertise in pedagogy. Paper presented at the meeting of the American Association of Colleges for Teacher Education, New Orleans, February.

Buchmann, M. (1989) Teaching knowledge: the lights that teachers' live by, in J. Lowyck and C.M. Clark (eds) *Teacher Thinking and Professional Action.* Leuven: Leuven University Press.

Calderhead, J. (1987) The quality of reflection in student teachers' professional learning. *European Journal of Teacher Education,* 10(3): 269–78.

Calderhead, J. (1991) The nature and growth of knowledge in student teaching. *Teaching and Teacher Education,* 7(6): 531–5.

Calderhead, J. and Shorrock, S.B. (1997) *Understanding Teacher Education.* London: Falmer Press.

Carter, K. (1990) Teachers' knowledge and learning to teach, in R. Houston (ed.) *Handbook of Research on Teacher Education.* New York: Macmillan.

Clark, C.M. and Peterson, P.L. (1986) Teachers' thought processes, in M.C. Wittrock (ed.) *Handbook of Research on Teaching,* New York: Macmillan.

Dewey, J. (1964) The child and the curriculum, in J.A. Boyden, (ed.) *John Dewey: The Middle Works 1899–1924,* Vol 2. Carbondale, IL: South Illinois Press.

Feiman-Nemser, S. and Buchmann, M. (1986) The first year of teacher preparation: transition to pedagogical thinking? *Journal of Curricular Studies,* 18, 239–56.

Feiman-Nemser, S. and Buchmann, M. (1987) When is student teaching teacher education? *Teaching and Teacher Education,* 3: 363–408.

Fuller, F. (1969) The concerns of beginning teachers. *American Educational Research Journal*, 6: 207–26.

Fuller, F. and Bown, O. (1975) Becoming a teacher, in K. Ryan (ed.) *Teacher Education: 74th Yearbook of the National Society for the Study of Education*. Chicago, IL: University of Chicago Press.

Furlong, V.J. and Maynard, T. (1996) *Mentoring Student Teachers: The Growth of Professional Knowledge*. London: Routledge.

Gendlin, E. (1981) *Focusing*. New York: Bantam.

Hargreaves, D.H. (1993) A common-sense model of the professional development of teachers, in J. Elliot (ed.) *Reconstructing Teacher Education*. Lewes: Falmer Press.

Hollingsworth, S. (1989) Prior beliefs and cognitive change in learning to teach. *American Educational Research Journal*, 26: 160–89.

Hoyle, E. and John, P.D. (1995) *Professional Knowledge and Professional Practice*. London: Cassell.

Jackson, P.W. (1968) *Life in Classrooms*. New York: Holt, Rinehart and Winston.

John, P.D. (1991) Course, curricular and classroom influences on the development of student teachers' lesson planning perspectives. *Teaching and Teacher Education*, 7(4): 359–72.

John, P.D. (1992) A qualitative study of student teachers' lesson planning perspectives. *Journal of Education for Teaching*, 17(3): 301–20.

John, P.D. (1996) Understanding the apprenticeship of observation in initial teacher training: exploring student teachers' implicit theories of teaching, in G. Claxton, T. Atkinson, M. Osborn and M. Wallace (eds) *Liberating the Learner: Lessons for Professional Development in Education*. London: Routledge.

John, P.D. (1996) The subject method seminar and the role of the teacher educator, in J. Furlong and R. Smith (eds) *The Role of Higher Education in Initial Teacher Training*. London: Kogan Page.

John, P.D. (in press) Student teachers' lesson planning: the dominant model and some alternatives. *Cambridge Journal of Education*,

Kounin, J.S. (1970) *Discipline and Classroom Management*. New York: Holt, Rinehart and Winston.

Kuhn, T. (1970) *The Structure of Scientific Revolutions*, 2nd edn. Chicago, IL: University of Chicago Press.

Leinhardt, G., Weidman, C. and Hammond, K. (1987) Introduction and integration of classroom routines by expert teachers. *Curriculum Inquiry* 17(2): 135–76.

Marland, P. (1977) 'A study of teachers' interactive thoughts', unpublished PhD thesis, University of Alberta, Edmonton, Canada.

Marland, P. and Osborne, A.B. (1988) 'Classroom theory, thinking and action', unpublished paper, James Cook University, Queensland.

Ober, R.L., Bentley, E.L. and Miller, E. (1971) *Systematic Observation of Teaching*. Englewood Cliffs, NJ: Prentice Hall.

Peterson, P.L. and Comeaux, M.A. (1977) Teachers' schemata for classroom events: the mental scaffolding of teachers' thinking during classroom instruction, *Teaching and Teacher Education*, 3(4): 319–33.

Polanyi, M. and Posch, H. (1975) *Personal Knowledge in Meaning*. London: University of Chicago Press.

Schön, D.A. (1983) *The Reflective Practitioner*. New York: Basic Books.

Schön, D.A. (1987) *Educating the Reflective Practitioner*. San Francisco, CA: Jossey-Bass.

Schön, D.A. (1991) *The Reflective Turn*. New York: Teachers' College Press.

Schutz, A. (1963) Common sense and scientific interpretation of human action, in N. Natanson (ed.) *Philosophy of the Social Sciences: A Reader.* New York: Random House.

Schutz, A. and Luckmann, T. (1974) *The Structure of the Life World.* London: Heinemann.

Shavelson, R.J. and Stern, P. (1981) Research on teachers' pedagogical thoughts, judgments, decisions and behaviour. *Review of Educational Research,* 51: 455–98.

Spradley, J. (1979) *The Ethnographic Interview.* New York: Holt, Rinehart and Winston.

Tom, A. (1994) *Teaching as a Moral Craft.* New York: Longman.

Wittgenstein, L. (1953) *Philosphical Investigations* (trans. G. Anscombe). Oxford: Blackwell.

Yinger, R.J. (1986) Examining thought in action: a theoretical and methodological critique of research on teaching. *Teaching and Teacher Education,* 2(3): 263–83.

Yinger, R.J. (1987) Learning the language of practice. *Curriculum Inquiry,* 17(3): 293–317.

Zeichner, K.M. and Tabachnik, B.R. (1981) Are the effects of university teacher education 'washed out' by school experience? *Journal of Teacher Education,* 32(3): 7–11.

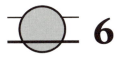 **6**

The role of intuition in mentoring and supporting beginning teachers

Elisabeth Lazarus

> The rational and the intuitive are equal partners, each providing the
> context within which the other can operate; neither makes sense alone.
> (Agor 1989: 119)

Introduction

In recent years, mentoring for beginning teachers has gained in importance
concurrent with a trend towards school-based teacher education in many
national contexts. There has been a plethora of studies, books, articles, practical guides and handbooks focusing on aspects such as conceptions of mentoring (e.g. McIntyre *et al.* 1993); the management of mentoring (e.g. Glover and
Mardle 1995); the role of mentors (e.g. Yeomans and Sampson 1994); mentoring and student teacher development (e.g. Furlong and Maynard 1995);
the mentor's scaffolding of learning (e.g. Edwards and Collison 1996); mentoring skills and strategies (e.g. Hagger *et al.* 1993); the effect of mentoring on
schools (e.g. Shaw 1992; Wilkin 1992); and developing reflective strategies
through mentoring (e.g. Tomlinson 1995). With the notable exception of
Tomlinson (1995), explicit reference to the role that intuition plays in mentoring is rarely found. This chapter attempts to redress the balance and aims
to demonstrate that within a specific professional domain – namely, initial
teacher education and training – mentors use many different strategies when
supporting beginning teachers.

According to Edwards and Collison (1996: 27–8), mentors are involved in
a range of interrelated tasks and behaviours such as:

- listening to students;
- modelling teaching and general classroom management;
- analysing and discussing their own practice;
- observing students;

- negotiating with students their own learning goals;
- supporting students as they teach;
- encouraging focused observations of classroom events;
- encouraging focused student self-assessment;
- providing constructive criticism for students;
- highlighting what students can learn from an analysis of practice.

These different role dimensions require the mentor to react and respond to beginning teachers in a variety of ways and to make use of different forms of intuition. Having an awareness and understanding of how intuition operates, and how it affects both mentors and protégés may bridge the divide between doing and knowing *why* one is doing. 'Intuition takes many different forms in science and mathematics, though all forms of it have certain properties in common: the suddenness of their origin, the wholeness of the conception they embody and the absence of conscious premeditation' (Medawar 1984: 108). This interpretation could also hold true for mentors in the educational field who are likely to experience a number of facets of intuition. The intuitive 'ways of knowing' discussed earlier by Guy Claxton (see Chapter 2) which seem most pertinent to mentors are:

- *Expertise* – most mentors are selected because of their expertise which may well be demonstrated by what Berliner describes as 'an intuitive grasp of [a teaching] situation and a non-analytical and non-deliberative sense of the appropriate response to be made' (1994: 110). In order to explain intuitive practice to the beginning teacher, however, the mentor is required to step back from a given way of teaching in order to try to articulate why a particular technique or strategy was employed.
- *Sensitivity* – mentors also rely upon their intuition when they appraise the optimum advice, support and challenge that beginning teachers in their charge require. They need to be sensitive to what they should say, how they should say it and when the most appropriate time would be to say it.
- *Judgement* – when assessing beginning teachers, mentors need to rely on objective criteria as well as their intuitive judgement.
- *Implicit learning* – an awareness and understanding of the intuitive nature of the strategies employed by the protégé may help the mentor understand the implicit learning that beginning teachers rely upon.

This chapter explores ways in which mentors and beginning teachers interact and tries to address the following questions:

- How can mentors best be prepared to share their implicit knowledge as well as their explicit knowledge?
- How does the mentor know what to say or how to react?
- How can mentors be 'trained' to focus on intuitive and cognitive domains?
- How do trainees gain knowledge and know-how about teaching?
- At what rate and at which stages should support be offered?
- What role does intuition play in the relationship between mentors and trainees?

- How does the effort to impart their own expertise impinge on mentors' own professional development?

In addition to the very wide-ranging literature on mentoring available, the content of this chapter draws on a number of small-scale qualitative and quantitative studies conducted by practitioners and researchers (including myself) in the UK and Malaysia.

How can mentors best be prepared to share their intuitive and explicit knowledge and know-how?

Mentoring conversations: making the implicit explicit?

A key feature of mentoring is allowing beginning teachers access to the 'craft knowledge' of mentors. Mentors need to be prepared for this process of articulation as they may not have needed to talk about their beliefs and implicit views of teaching and learning for some time. Internal monologues may have served them very well but mentoring requires them to express their views. Similarly, Medawar (1984) claims provocatively that 'scientific methodology is understood intuitively by scientists and needs to be propounded only for the benefit of other people' (p. 80–1).

Mentors are usually selected because of their experience and ability, not necessarily because they can articulate knowledge. Jerome Bruner suggests that we frequently know how to do things long before we can explain conceptually what we are doing or normatively why we should be doing them (Bruner 1996). Tomlinson proposes that mentors, as experienced teachers, may have become 'so intuitive they find it difficult to articulate what they are in fact doing' (1995: 18). If this is the case we cannot assume that the process of articulation will either be easy or spontaneous. Edwards and Collison (1996) described in their study of mentor–protégé talk how mentors focused particularly on the student teachers' successful task-setting and on the demands of the curriculum of the training institution. The student teachers in the study did not seek or receive explicit 'general learning principles' or theory from their mentors (Edwards and Collison 1996: 43). Furlong and Maynard (1995) found that the mentors they studied were able to talk about the content of their knowledge, but they found discussing how they applied this knowledge in the classroom much more problematic. They found it easier to talk about the knowledge that they may have acquired explicitly through formalized learning than the experientially acquired application of this knowledge. Metaphors and gestures were cited as tools to help the articulation process. The use of metaphors, drawings and images to help communication between mentors and protégés is currently being studied by Ramlah (in preparation), who is a member of the Teacher Support Team in Kuala Lumpur. Lucy Atkinson, earlier in this book (see Chapter 3), has also referred to the importance of non-verbal communication. Encouraging mentors and protégés in this process may well prove useful where finding words may be difficult, in line with Sartre's observation that 'words are only the support of knowledge. It is the image which is the intuitive "filling in" of the meaning' (1991: 83). In order to support beginning teachers, mentors need to develop the ability to articulate beliefs, views, knowledge and know-how, which may be implicit or intuitive, in a way that suits both the mentor and the protégé.

The mentor as model

Mentors may act as role models to trainees, allowing novices to observe their classroom teaching. This demonstrating of teaching techniques and behaviours is very beneficial to the protégé but becomes much more so through a process of discussion and questioning. It has been shown that beginning teachers hold very strong beliefs about teachers and teaching (John 1996a, 1996b). Mentors need to be aware of this and provide opportunities when such views can be challenged or questioned in a supportive environment. A way to link observations of experienced teachers with experiential learning for student teachers is through team or collaborative teaching activities. These focus attention on practical outcomes that are negotiated and discussed. This gives the novice a chance to contrast carefully constructed plans with the reality of practice in the classroom and can help highlight where an experienced teacher's intuition suggests a change of plan, teaching strategy or activity. It creates an ideal platform for discussion.

However, collaborative teaching is time-consuming and demands interaction between mentor and protégé. A study in Malaysia has shown that there may be significant discrepancy between rhetoric and practice. Despite the fact that 95 per cent of mentors surveyed believed collaborative teaching to be highly beneficial for the trainees, only 10 per cent of mentors were prepared to participate in any form of team teaching (D'Silva 1998). This may be due to the recent introduction of mentoring or because teachers may view a trainee in the classroom as a threat and equate observations with a judgemental process. This view of the protégé as threat can, I believe, be overcome, if the purposes of observations and collaboration become transparent and a professional culture is fostered. A small-scale study of 15 experienced modern languages mentors in Bristol indicated that mentors felt totally comfortable with the presence of student teachers in the classroom (Lazarus 1999). This contrasts with Berliner's findings from the late 1980s (Berliner 1994), where expert teachers demonstrated feelings of inadequacy, anger and distress when observed and were highly critical of their own performance as teachers, while less experienced teachers in the study did not indicate such a strong affective involvement. This would suggest that the process of opening our classroom doors to colleagues or trainees has become part of the educational culture.

The supervisory cycle

Mentors must be much more than mere role models. They are involved in the supervisory cycle of discussing lesson plans, aims, intentions and resources with their protégés. They observe lessons and provide written and oral feedback. This process is fundamental for the development of the student teacher. It allows mentors to develop their own interpersonal and communication skills, as my study indicates (Lazarus 1999). Knowing what to say to trainees and how to say it calls for experience and intuition.

Assessing trainees

School-based mentors also play an important role in assessing student teachers against formally prescribed criteria. The shift from critical friend to assessor is not always easy or comfortable but there will continue to be an intuitive dimension to the assessment process, as noted by Patricia Broadfoot in her chapter on intuition and assessment (see Chapter 12) and exemplified in the chapter by Curtis, Weeden and Winter and that of Brawn (see Chapters 13 and 9). An important function of mentor training is therefore to validate the role of intuitive judgements alongside formally derived ones based on the application of objective criteria.

The training of mentors

Legislation in England and Wales requires mentors to be 'trained' in order to participate in initial teacher education. Such training may focus on the administration and management of mentoring procedures or on developing a shared understanding of mentoring and mentoring strategies (Lazarus 1994). In an age that seems training driven, one has to consider whether the training that mentors receive supports or hinders the expert, intuitive fluid performance of the mentor as teacher. One strategy for encouraging mentors to use a range of feedback strategies is for them to watch trainees on video and take notes on what they would say and what they would write down for the trainee. Differences of view can then be aired in whole group discussions. From experience, some mentors have been surprised how perceptions of 'good teaching' or how trainees 'learn best' vary within such a homogeneous group of experienced practitioners. Such exercises in trying to make the implicit explicit (Lazarus 1999) seem to allow mentors to explore how they use their professional intuition.

How you word a critical observation and when it is best said may influence how the trainee 'hears' the comment. One of the Bristol mentors tried to summarize how she felt about the importance of feedback. She considered that choosing appropriate words in feedback to student teachers placed a huge responsibility on the mentor as 'the impact could be dramatic' if the mentor misjudged the situation. Role-play among mentors may also offer opportunities to investigate strategies which engage mentor and protégé in discussions. If such role-plays also focus on the shift from tacitly and implicitly held views to trying to be explicit, then they can also engage the mentors in explorations of the function of their professional intuition. Mentor training and development needs to address the different roles played by a mentor – for example, being a good listener, a critical observer or a person who encourages and challenges the trainee to reflect on different aspects of teaching and learning. Mentoring relies heavily on the development of professional and personal relationships as most work is carried out on a one-to-one basis. This aspect of the work should form part of mentor training and development. Mentors are likely to hold tutorials and seminars which may revolve around a theme specified by a training institution or which has been determined by the mentor–protégé dyad. Books and articles, lectures and seminars may well be discussed.

Mentors are likely to benefit from an understanding of different models of how beginning teachers develop and how mentoring strategies are best adapted to this. The training of mentors needs to move beyond providing guidelines of procedures to a theoretical understanding of the process. School mentors, like their colleagues in training institutions, may well be operating according to strongly-held beliefs about how protégés learn best, possibly drawn from their own circle of experience (Lazarus 1996). These beliefs may not correspond to those held by the designers of mentor training and support programmes. If, like Monaghan and Lunt (1992: 261), one believes that 'the mentor is not out there awaiting discovery but, on the contrary, mentors are constructed', one has to query who is doing the constructing and what materials and which templates are being used. A question worth exploring is whether conventional training may be undermining intuition in the experienced teacher or whether value is placed on allowing mentors to become comfortable with and confident about applying their professional intuition in working with trainees.

Training or intuition?

In the educational sphere, intuition has been viewed with scepticism by some and been linked to a restricted view of professionality. Hoyle (1974), for example, claimed that one difference between restricted professionality and extended professionality in teachers revolved around the fact that the restrictive professional perceived 'teaching as intuitive', while the extended professional viewed 'teaching as a rational activity'. This view stands in sharp contrast with that of Berliner (1994) or Tomlinson (1995), for example. Trusting one's intuition can of course be difficult and even misleading. Inexperienced or untrained mentors may feel very vulnerable without training and, as one study in Malaysia highlighted, may distrust their intuition when supporting protégés. Mazlina's small-scale study in Johor showed that one quarter of mentors felt that due to their lack of training they were 'guided purely by intuition'. This created a sense of frustration and a feeling of inadequacy that was summed up by one mentor as: 'unless you are trained, you are not advanced, of course you are in the blur [unclear]. Anything you have to do, you have to be trained to do' (Mazlina 1998: 56). Intuition was perceived by the mentors as only second best to 'proper' training. Mistrusting intuition and relying too much on training (which is expensive and often delivered through an ineffective cascade model in developing countries) may not be the best approach. It is interesting to note that mentors may well feel unclear about their roles and responsibilities due to lack of communication or training, but nevertheless be perceived as doing a very good job in supporting protégés (Saleena 1998) because of how they apply common sense, professional experience and intuition.

What kind of knowledge delivers maximum facilitation for beginning teachers?

Knowledge from different domains

Beginning teachers are interested in knowledge that is practical and can be applied in the classroom. However, providing protégés with tips alone is likely to be highly unsatisfactory as this 'simplifies the decision making in ways that do not take into account the fact that so many teachers' decisions are reactive and creative in the complex contexts that are classrooms' (Edwards and Collison 1996: 17). What protégés require is a sound pedagogical knowledge base (Carré 1993) which can be gained from different knowledge domains – for example, from schools, training institutions, research and readings (Furlong and Maynard 1995) – and which takes their previous experience and stage of learning into consideration. Bruner points to the importance of getting the balance right between theoretical understanding and practical application. He states that 'a skill can be improved with the aid of theory, as when we learn about the inside and outside edges of our skis, but our skiing doesn't improve until we get that knowledge back into the skill of skiing. Knowledge helps only when it descends into habits' (Bruner 1996: 152). As any skier will tell you, you ski best when you rely on previous experience, knowledge of the terrain, good equipment and a firm trust in your intuition. A smooth descent would be interrupted if you tried to stop and question every turn or every decision; however, asking a beginner to follow my tracks without making my movements or decisions explicit would be most unproductive. The analogy with teaching is not far-fetched.

Knowledge gained through observing experienced teachers

In schools, observations of skilled practitioners offer beginning teachers a key focus for learning. 'If you want to find out anything from the theoretical physicists about the methods they use,' said Albert Einstein, 'I advise you to stick closely to one principle: don't listen to their words, fix your attention on their deeds' (Medawar 1984: 79–80). This advice may be seductive but only provides partial answers in the classroom. Teachers may profess certain views (such as a strong belief in equality of opportunity) but these may well not be demonstrated in the classroom. Beginning teachers initially find it very bewildering to 'see' (Furlong and Maynard 1995) in the classroom as 'the expert appears to have uncanny abilities to notice things, an "instinct" for making the right moves, an ineffable ability to get things done, to perform in an almost effortless manner' (Berliner 1994: 107). Mentors need to be aware that 'the more embedded the subaction, the more tacitly and intuitively done by those with experience and the more difficult it is for those who observe to pick it out' (Tomlinson 1995: 29). Deconstructing a fluid performance, to help the protégé make sense of what he or she has observed is a key function of mentoring. Trainees can be helped in the process by using observation schedules and tasks prepared by mentors and tutors (see Lazarus 1999). The know-how and intuition which a proficient teacher demonstrates (Berliner 1994) can be accessed to some extent through a series of structured observation tasks followed up by discussions.

Many teachers do not necessarily relish the prospect of being observed but agree that the principle behind observation is sound. In Malaysia, where mentoring in primary schools has been implemented since 1996 and is slowly developing in secondary schools, mentors have been found who profoundly agree with the importance of observation in principle, but who do not allow beginning teachers access to classrooms in practice (Nur Anuar 1997; Mohamed Abd. Razif 1997). One study found that although collaboration between mentors and beginning teachers is now a compulsory part of the training curriculum, in practice this collaboration revolved around having discussions before lesson observations and during the feedback sessions after the lessons. Trainees were rarely welcomed into mentors' lessons or encouraged in team teaching. One trainee tried to articulate why her mentor was like this: 'she was not happy that I had to observe her as she thinks that she is not perfect' (D'Silva 1998: 90).

Observing others can provide a very rich experience for trainees, especially if linked to explication of practice, but the most important piece of the puzzle will be practical teaching.

Trainees being observed

An uncomfortable but highly effective way of sharing knowledge is for the trainee to teach while the mentor is observing. This can be a very daunting experience at first. It requires tact and intuition on behalf of the mentor if this fundamental process of experiential learning is to be valuable and not merely traumatic. A Malaysian study with 46 student teachers and their corresponding 30 mentors (Saleena 1998) showed that both mentors and trainee teachers felt that they gained considerably from the process of observation and feedback, even though this created a high level of anxiety in at least 80 per cent of the trainees. The observation cycle was perceived to be strongly assessment-driven and did not allow student teachers to exploit the teaching practice as an opportunity to experiment. Bristol student teachers have indicated that they consider being observed and receiving feedback on their teaching as absolutely crucial to their development as classroom practitioners.

Learning from feedback

Saleena's study (1998) also provided an interesting finding regarding the dominance of the mentor in feedback sessions. Mentors seemed to talk between 60–80 per cent of the time; nevertheless the student teachers seemed encouraged by the feedback they received. Over 90 per cent of mentors and trainees suggested that the feedback had been a mixture of positive and negative comments, and they felt that the observation–feedback cycle had had a very profound influence on the developing teacher. The trainees suggested to the researcher that they would like to be more involved in developing a focus for observation. They also wanted access to any notes or forms completed by the observer. They suggested that they should be allowed to comment on their lessons first and then be encouraged by mentors to participate to a greater extent in the post-observation discussions. As a group, they stated that they liked a directive approach to mentoring (which provides a puzzling contrast to wanting more involvement and more of a say in the process) and were looking for constructive criticism from their mentors. Mentors and trainees felt that the most helpful topics for discussion were:

- classroom management;
- teaching strategies and techniques;
- lesson planning;
- progress in the student teacher's teaching;
- attitude/personality;
- use of teaching aids/resources;
- reflective practice;
- personal matters/problems.

The way feedback is presented can directly affect the mentor–protégé relationship and the willingness of trainees to engage fully in the process. Mentors will need to use their intuition in order to know when to be critical, when to withhold support and when advice is necessary. Student teachers in Bristol indicated that they felt they had benefited very much from an ongoing constructive dialogue with their mentors (Lazarus 1999; see also Atkinson 1996; John 1996a, 1996b; Lazarus 1996). They were looking for feedback which was honest, focused and critical and which provided opportunities to explore alternative methods or approaches. They liked being given space to experiment and explore. Not surprisingly, criticism alone was seen as most unhelpful, as was vagueness, lack of tact and insensitivity in mentors and suggestions which were perceived as unrealistic by the student teachers.

Support which is valued

There have been numerous studies looking at the problems and needs of beginning teachers. The findings of predominantly western literature suggest that beginning teachers are very concerned about class management and maintaining discipline in lessons (e.g. Veenman 1984; Tickle 1994), whereas studies in South East Asia (Cooke and Pang 1991; Rajeswari 1997; Goh 1998) indicate that these are much less pressing issues. Cultural and social differences may account for this. Nevertheless, other areas of similarity can be found which seem unconstrained by culture or nationality. For many beginning teachers the concern with the 'self' overrides all other considerations (Fuller 1969).

Goh's study found the perceived needs of Malaysian novices to be developing ideas, teaching suggestions and materials, and help, advice, support and guidance. They wanted a mentor who could demonstrate teaching strategies and resources and who would help them develop their confidence. They wanted homogeneous classes, more materials, books and equipment, more space and smaller classes. Lee (1998) found that opportunities to observe more experienced colleagues were non-existent.

Some Malaysian mentors are clearly sceptical about whether intervention and support is really beneficial to beginning teachers as the following quote demonstrates: 'Let them be independent, not like helping them all the time. If we do collaborative teaching, they'll know that we will always go and help them and it won't motivate them at all' (D'Silva 1998: 76). The autonomy that many mentors or heads of department in Malaysia allow trainees and beginning teachers can easily develop into frustration and anger: 'When I come, I don't know anything. Nobody tell me. They think like I know what to do. I think they already know what to do, and they think I know also. Like now I know. But when I come, I don't know. I wish they have somebody to tell me. I mean not special treatment. But somebody to tell me what format of lesson plans, where the books to teach [are], how to make exercises, and things like that' (Goh 1998: 87). The importance of the affective domain in the development of beginning teachers and in the mentoring process should not be overestimated. One Malaysian beginning teacher made this abundantly clear: 'It is very difficult to ask teachers. I am very shy to ask. Scared afterward they say how come you don't know? You never learn in college? So I just try and do it on my own and sometimes I do it right. But sometimes it was no good' (Goh 1998: 88). Of course in many developing countries key concerns of policy makers and schools relate to finding enough qualified teachers, resources and classrooms. Where school-leavers are employed as teachers without formal teacher training, they will have a different set of mentor support requirements (see Rani 1997; Yang Oi Lin 1997) to that of student teachers. Mentors have to consider whether a novice needs emotional support – for example, boosting of confidence or critical acclaim or practical tips. By using their intuition and drawing on experience they will know what form of support is required.

At what rate and in which stages should support be delivered

A fundamental principle of mentoring concerns the different stages of development that beginning teachers pass through on their road to reaching professional status. Furlong and Maynard (1995) contend that five stages of progression can be detected:

- early idealism;
- survival;
- recognizing the difficulties;
- hitting the plateau;
- moving on.

Other writers have established similar developmental progressions both for teachers in training and those in their early career (Fuller 1969; Berliner 1994; McIntyre and Hagger 1996). Advice, support and criticism provided by mentors for beginning teachers need to be sensitized to the stage of development of the recipient. This will demand that the mentor is aware of and in tune with the protégé's development. Here the mentor's intuition, shaped by experience, may well lead him or her to decide when support should be withdrawn and when challenge or dissonance may provide better learning opportunities. If these intuitive faculties are not exercised or trusted, mentor and protégé may focus their concern too much on the what and how of teaching and less on pupils' learning or student teachers' learning (Tomlinson 1995).

How does the effort to explicate their own expertise impinge on mentors' own professional development?

'Teaching can be quite a private affair. You communicate your own ideas, strategies to your students. I welcome the idea [of inviting trainees into the classroom and collaborating with them] but not the whole year round because I have to admit it, it affects my teaching, my planning and of course, my students' (D'Silva 1998: 68). Mentors who have had no say in whether or not they want to participate in the mentoring process may resent having to explain their teaching, actions and thinking to an outsider. This has been noted by Berliner (1994), among others. Other mentors claim that having to articulate their actions to another person has sharpened up their thinking and made them re-evaluate much of their unconscious or implicit assumptions. Furlong and Maynard (1995) suggest that teachers draw upon their existing resources of experience and skills to frame teaching situations and to modify their actions. They consider this form of intelligent action or knowing-in-action as intuitive and tacit. A recent Bristol study (Lazarus, in preparation) shows that the majority of mentors felt that the presence of student teachers as observers made them much more aware of what they were doing in lessons. They enjoyed talking to student teachers about teaching and did not find that the flow of the lesson was disturbed by their presence. They considered trainees generally as good listeners. All of them found that mentoring had had a positive effect on their teaching and for all but one, it had given them an opportunity of re-evaluating their teaching: 'Being obliged to reflect on my own practice, ideals and so on, in order to convey them to another' had allowed one mentor 'to regain [her] enthusiasm'. They liked to share their experiences and knowledge with the student teachers and suggested that mentoring was a form of 'back door INSET [in-service education and training]'.

Of course not all mentors share this enthusiasm. Mentoring is very time-consuming and some mentors perceive their trainees as poor teachers and not as learners. Mentors may well lack confidence in the trainee's subject knowledge and abilities. This can affect both mentor and trainees: 'Student teachers feel uncomfortable and not confident when the mentor is around. Asians are shy people. We are not open to criticism. They think that if you go and observe them you're trying to find out the mistakes, their weaknesses' (D'Silva 1998: 85). Mentors may feel reluctant to give up their classes to those whose knowledge they question.

Mentors and beginning teachers may experience conflicts of perceptions and clashes of views which can be debilitating but which can also be the trigger for learning (Mazlina 1998). Trainees may feel that the knowledge domains of schools and training institutions offer contrasting, even conflicting visions of teaching and learning. One Malaysian trainee stated: 'the mentor did not agree with pair work and she prefers drilling rather than [the] communicative approach – We have different views [about] class control – The method used by the mentor is not the right method and she asked me to follow her way' (D'Silva 1998: 89). This trainee felt very unhappy to be caught up between perceptions of good teaching (that which the college transmits) and outdated methods which she felt she had to follow in schools. Many trainees will have experienced similar circumstances and will very likely have relied on tact and intuition about how to act before being able to seek advice from higher education tutors. This clash of perceptions may be very uncomfortable, even threatening to some mentors. Mazlina (1998) found that the most significant problems and tensions between mentors and protégés emerged from conflicts of ideas and differences of opinion, lack of cooperation (from the mentor), lack of confidence (by the protégé), mentors not devoting enough time to protégés and lack of cooperation from the pupils.

Conclusion

There seems to be a significant relationship between intuition and reflection in terms of how mentors and protégés interact and interrelate. As this chapter has shown, mentors act as role-models, teachers, trainers, coaches etc. They are acting intuitively as expert teachers within the classroom, while being observed by beginner teachers. They may react to the class in an intuitive way, which only later discussion with the trainee brings to light. If mentors change pace, activities or strategies, for example, they may do so because it 'felt right', arising from an 'intuitive knowing' of the mood of the class. Such actions remain implicit or tacit unless explicitly addressed in dialogue. We have seen that such dialogues can be of great benefit to both partners. They provide the trainees with an understanding and awareness of the importance of intuitive knowing in classrooms and may make them more willing to consider the process.

Mentors are also required to draw on their professional knowledge and intuition when providing feedback for trainees. They have to consider the what and the how of feedback in order to render it as effective as possible. They need to consider the needs of trainees and the stage of development that they have reached in both affective and cognitive domains. Mentors will use intuition in the process of evaluating and assessing professional competence. Most importantly, mentors need to realize that to rely on their trained intuition is a sign of professional confidence and competence and not a second-rate tool.

References

Agor, W.H. (ed.) (1989) *Intuition in Organizations*. Newbury Park, CA: Sage.

Atkinson, T. (1996) Teacher mentors and student teachers: what is transmitted? in G. Claxton, T. Atkinson, M. Osborn and M. Wallace (eds) *Liberating the Learner: Lessons for Professional Development in Education*. London: Routledge.

Berliner, D. (1994) Teacher expertise, in B. Moon and A. Shelton Mayes (eds) *Teaching and Learning in the Secondary School*. London: Routledge/The Open University.

Bruner, J. (1996) *The Culture of Education*. Cambridge, MA: Harvard University Press.

Carré, C. (1993) The first year of teaching, in N. Bennett and C. Carré (eds.) *Learning to Teach*. London: Routledge.

Cooke, B.L. and Pang, K.C. (1991) Recent research on beginning teachers: Studies of trained and untrained novices. *Teaching and Teacher Education*, 7(1): 93–110.

D'Silva, M. (1998) 'A survey on the role of collaborative teaching during the DPM practicum 3: Perceptions of school mentors and student teachers in Malaysia', unpublished MEd dissertation, University of Bristol.

Edwards, A. and Collison, J. (1996) *Mentoring and Developing Practice in Primary Schools*. Buckingham: Open University Press.

Fuller, F. (1969) Concerns of teachers: a developmental conceptualization. *American Educational Research Journal*, 6(2): 207–26.

Furlong, J. and Maynard, T. (1995) *Mentoring Student Teachers: The Growth of Professional Knowledge*. London: Routledge.

Glover, D. and Mardle, G. (1995) *The Management of Mentoring*. London: Kogan Page.

Goh, L.H. (1998) 'Perceived concerns and needs of newly-qualified English language teachers', unpublished MEd dissertation, University of Bristol.

Hagger, H., Burn, K. and McIntyre, D. (1993) *The School Mentor Handbook*. London: Kogan Page.

Hoyle, E. (1974) Professionality, professionalism and control in education. *London Educational Review*, 3(2): 13–19.

John, P.D. (1996a) Understanding the apprenticeship of observation in initial teacher education: exploring student teachers' implicit theories of teaching and learning, in G. Claxton, T. Atkinson, M. Osborn and M. Wallace (eds) *Liberating the Learner: Lessons for Professional Development in Education*. London: Routledge.

John, P.D. (1996b) The supervisory process in teacher education: learning event or learning bind? in G. Claxton, T. Atkinson, M. Osborn and M. Wallace (eds) *Liberating the Learner: Lessons for Professional Development in Education*. London: Routledge.

Lazarus, E. (1994) Partnership in initial teacher training between schools and universities: some reflections on the training of school-based mentors. Paper presented at the ATEE conference, Prague, August.

Lazarus, E. (1996) Teacher trainer and student teacher: sources of divergence in perceptions of learning? in G. Claxton, T. Atkinson, M. Osborn and M. Wallace (eds) *Liberating the Learner: Lessons for Professional Development in Education*. London: Routledge.

Lazarus, E. (1999) The role of mentoring in the professional development of teachers. Paper presented at the Malaysian Educational Research Association Conference, Malacca, 1 December.

Lee, T.E. (1998) 'A survey of the relationship between the needs of newly qualified teachers and their experiences of induction in selected secondary schools in Malaysia', unpublished MEd dissertation, University of Bristol.

McIntyre, D. and Hagger, H. (eds) (1996) *Mentors in Schools: Developing the Profession of Teaching*. London: David Fulton.

McIntyre, D., Hagger, H. and Wilkin, M. (1993) *Mentoring: Perspectives on School-Based Teacher Education*. London: Kogan Page.

Mazlina bt. Azhar (1998) 'Conflicts between school mentors and student teachers during the 1998 KDPM practicum 3 in Malaysia', unpublished MEd dissertation, University of Bristol.

Medawar, P. (1984) Induction and Intuition in Scientific Thought, in *Pluto's Republic*. Oxford: Oxford University Press.

Mohamed Abd. Razif (1997) 'The reality of mentoring in primary schools in the state of Pahang: perceptions of mentors and ESL student teachers', unpublished MEd dissertation, University of Bristol.

Monaghan, J. and Lunt, N. (1992) Mentoring: person, process, practice and problems. *British Journal of Educational Studies*, 40: 248–63.

Nur Anuar Mutalib (1997) 'The perceptions of ESL co-operating teachers on classroom observation responsibilities during the teaching practicum', unpublished MEd dissertation, University of Bristol.

Rajeswari V.S. Pillai (1997) 'The induction of newly-qualified English Llanguage teachers', unpublished MEd dissertation, University of Bristol.

Ramlah bt. Salim (in preparation) 'The role of the Teacher Support Team', unpublished MEd dissertation, University of Bristol.

Rani D/O Parasuramen (1997) 'The dilemma of untrained teachers: a quantitative and qualitative study of the needs of untrained teachers, their current support and the implications for induction', unpublished MEd dissertation, University of Bristol.

Saleena C.A. (1998) 'The reality of classroom observations and feedback discussions during the 1998 Diploma Perguruan Malaysia Practicum 3: Perceptions of student teachers and school mentors in Malaysia', unpublished MEd dissertation, University of Bristol.

Sartre, J.P. (1991) *The Psychology of Imagination*. Secaucus, NJ: Citadel Press.

Shaw, R. (1992) *Teacher Training in Secondary Schools*. London: Kogan Page.

Tickle, L. (1994) *The Induction of New Teachers*. London: Cassell.

Tomlinson, P. (1995) *Understanding Mentoring: Reflective Strategies for School-based Teacher Preparation*. Buckingham: Open University Press.

Veenman, S. (1984) Perceived problems of beginning teachers. *Review of Educational Research*, 54(2): 143–78.

Wilkin, M. (1992) *Mentoring in Schools*. London: Kogan Page.

Yang Oi Lin (1997) 'A survey of the professional needs of untrained temporary second-ary school teachers in the districts of Mukah and Dalat and its implication for men-toring', unpublished MEd dissertation, University of Bristol.

Yeomans, R. and Sampson, J. (1994) *Mentorship in the Primary School*. London: Falmer Press.

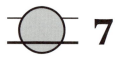 **7**

Elaborated intuition and task-based English language teacher education

Arlene Gilpin and Gerald Clibbon

Introduction

The other chapters in this book focus on the role of intuition in professional practice, and the need to offer opportunities in courses of professional education for the development of this kind of thinking and being. In this chapter we begin by looking at some of the reasons why intuition can let one down, leading to inappropriate conclusions, actions or states of mind. We draw on research into thinking, insight, problem-solving and creativity. We then examine whether these ways of 'being wrong' suggest that there are different levels of intuition: naive levels which may frequently lead to unsound judgements, and elaborated levels that are more reliable. We consider the possibility that one of the main purposes of professional education courses is to engage the participants in activities that require the externalizing of implicit beliefs and ways of thinking, with the result of allowing more elaborated ways of being and doing to become, in their turn, implicit and routinized. Continuing professional development can then be conceptualized as an iterative process between the implicit and the explicit, with each iteration permitting greater elaboration. There is no end to the process, merely a continuing elaboration of the resources of the individual. In teacher education for English language teaching (ELT), many educators now make use of what could loosely be called a task-based approach to training/education. We shall examine what this means, and show how it is an approach that has great potential for the development of the intuitive side of teaching.

One of the difficulties of working with the concept of intuition is the range of interpretations it has. Guy Claxton, in Chapter 2, notes the features most commonly associated with it: that it is unarticulated thinking, holistic, problem identifying, based on a solid foundation of both knowledge and experience; it takes place most fruitfully when a situation is characterized by a lack of tension, is unconscious, and usually has a feeling of 'rightness'. This last point is perhaps one of the hallmarks of expertise: you do not simply know *how* to do something, you do it with confidence in its appropriateness. Put together like this, the various definitions of intuition look very like a definition of expertise. We do not, however, accept that novice teachers are *less* intuitive in general than experts in any one sense; however, they are likely to be more naive professionally, and have a more restricted range of implicit options available to them. The job of professional development at all levels – whether initial training or in-service – is to search for ways to make the implicit repertoire more elaborated, more fine-tuned, and more responsive to context.

In order to try and think of ways in which novice teachers might be helped to develop a more elaborated set of intuitions, we begin by outlining some of the reasons why naive intuitions can be fallible. In adopting this approach we follow that of Schooler *et al.* (1996).

Problem identification

Depending on the level of expertise, one possible cause of fallibility in conscious problem-solving may be the failure to recognize the problem at the outset, or searching the wrong space to identify what the nature of the problem is. Failure to recognize the problem may arise from an overemphasis on irrelevant clues, underemphasis of relevant ones, or an inability to act outside a range of prescribed instructions (Dreyfus and Dreyfus 1986; Schooler *et al.* 1996). Heuristic and analytical processes may be identified as typical approaches to problem-solving. When a person is trying to solve a problem, pre-attentive, *largely automatic*, heuristic processes select certain aspects of the problem as potentially relevant to a solution. Analytical processes may then work on these but will be confounded if the problem is incorrectly recognized. If it is true that the identification of the problem space is often an implicit process anyway, then work to externalize the nature of this process may be helpful.

There are two aspects to this facet of fallibility: knowledge, including experience, and observation. We cannot see or hear what we do not know, and we often as a consequence do not see and hear the right things. This is further discussed below when we look at different types of knowledge. The ability to perceive in the broad sense of seeing and hearing through watching and listening may be a potent aid to intuition, as Lucy Atkinson suggests in Chapter 3. Equally, underdevelopment of these skills will create impasses.

Thinking

Here we take thinking to mean the kind of reasoning known as 'everyday' (Garnham and Oakhill 1994: 122). Garnham and Oakhill make a distinction between formal reasoning, of the kind taught on philosophy courses, and the thinking we do in everyday life, one of the main differences being a tendency to give less consideration to both sides of an argument in everyday thinking (Perkins 1985 cited in Garnham and Oakhill 1994: 257). There is a good deal of evidence for the partial nature of routine thinking and two causes of faulty everyday conscious reasoning are: confirmatory bias (pursuing your own prejudices or looking at only one side of an argument); and not establishing the correct problem space. This has also been called 'fixatedness' by other researchers (e.g. Duncker 1945), and has been identified as a barrier to creativity and problem-solving.

Relatively little research has been done into everyday conscious reasoning (see Garnham and Oakhill 1994: 259) for a number of methodological reasons. However, the research which has been done has often focused on work-based problems, and so is relevant to the arguments in this volume. Kuhn (1991), for example, used discussion activities to see how her groups of professional subjects managed argument. Kuhn found that the majority of her subjects (two thirds) took a single viewpoint and did not offer alternative accounts. They were also poor at weighing the evidence on the two sides. Kuhn considers what skills are needed, and points particularly to the need for metacognitive skills – that is, for the need to make the thinking and argument processes explicit. She maintains that people have an implicit command of these skills but need to make them explicit if they are to apply them appropriately in real time. Interestingly, Kuhn found that philosophers (undoubtedly trained in formal reasoning) were better at managing arguments than other groups of subjects, including teachers, and were able to generate evidence, alternative theories, counter-arguments and rebuttals. This is an intriguing hint of evidence that if discrete skills are thoroughly practised and learnt they become implicit and available for use in real time.

Therefore, in addition to fallibility arising from wrong identification of the problem, another set of causes may arise from too narrow a consideration of alternatives or a mind set that predisposes us to such narrowness, coupled with a lack of awareness of this.

Holistic perception

Here we are reminded of the expertise of the chess players, technicians, radiologists and physicists studied by Lesgold (1988). He found that these four groups exhibited a number of common characteristics, one of which was to see 'bigger chunks' and so free up working memory for other purposes: the novices tended to focus on single aspects of the whole, while the experts saw sequences together (see also Chapter 2). This is explained by saying that extensive practice can lead to 'compiling procedures', enabling the expert to take in a more holistic view of things, what Dreyfus and Dreyfus (1986: 28) refer to as 'holistic similarity recognition'. One could say that the expert stores data and procedures on a kind of mental compact disk which permits multiple pattern matching and then the matching of these patterns to routines, again multiple. On the other hand, the novice has everything stored on old '45' record and can only access one item at a time.

As well as lack of practice in establishing routines, there is also an apparent need for observation skills, and perhaps the hint that they can be built up through organized practice. It is clearly reiterated by a number of researchers that the expertise of chess players, for example, is the result of at least ten years of intensive practice. Interestingly, this practice is a holistic kind of practice, and much of it is based around studying chess game plans. The intuitive, holistic understanding of the expert is built on situated problem-solving experience. But as Dreyfus and Dreyfus (1986: 32) point out, this 'does not require calculative problem-solving, but rather involves critically reflecting on one's own intuitions'.

Knowledge and experience

Much of the research into thinking and reasoning, into insight, intuition and creativity, mentions the need for a knowledge and experiential base for these processes. The claims for intuition do not deny the need for knowledge. However, it is interesting to look at what we mean by knowledge. On the first programme of *Start the Week* to be hosted by Jeremy Paxman on Radio 4, one of the guests was Marilyn Butler, the Cambridge academic. The focus of part of their discussion was the burgeoning sources of information now available to us all. Professor Butler made the point that there is a difference between information and knowledge, and the difference is that knowledge is *information put to use*. Teacher education courses that do not enable information to be put to use are likely to produce teachers who cannot access information appropriately and quickly in the situations demanded by everyday teaching activity. Transmitted information that remains unprocessed is therefore a likely barrier to swift intuition.

This is an interesting reinterpretation of technical terms which is of significant importance for teacher education. The informational aspect of knowledge is what Griffiths and Tann (1992) and others refer to as 'public theory' or 'received knowledge'. Another aspect of knowledge derives from practice, and is variously called 'private theory', 'personal knowledge' or 'craft knowledge'. This is referred to below. Yet another aspect of knowledge might be what Johnson and Badley (1996) referred to as 'taken for granteds', a particularly appropriate name for something implicit and relatively unexamined. A final aspect of knowledge is what is known as 'articulated knowledge', where private knowledge is combined with received knowledge and can be used to evaluate one's 'taken for granteds'. The knowledge that Professor Butler referred to would be known as 'articulated theory or knowledge' in the lexicon of teacher education. Thus a compendium of received knowledge on its own would not facilitate expert practice because it would have no forged links with private knowledge (Ramani 1987).

However, over-reliance on experience or private knowledge may be another potential source for failed or faulty intuition. Here we are not only thinking of the practical experience gained from actual teaching but the general experience of learning that we all have. Such a set of implicit private theories of learning and teaching will have arisen from years of experience, some being implanted at an extremely early age. Teachers, therefore, bring to a course of professional development a host of 'taken for granteds', many of which may be inappropriate and may cloud perception. Unless the course enables the examination of beliefs and attitudes then these may remain unelaborated and may continue to inhibit holistic perception.

Tension

Here we refer to emotional tension of a negative kind, the kind that would set in place what Krashen (1982, 1985) called a *'high affective filter'* – that is to say, affective factors that may block learning, or, in this case, intuitive restructuring. It is easy to assume that the novice teacher might have more frequent occasions to experience this kind of tension in class, but the experienced teacher is not immune to it. Negative tension may be provoked by lack of familiarity with context, poor judgement in relation to decisions made about routine, students, self or language, and by external pressures such as workplace relationships, examinations or one's social context. Some of these sources of tension are closely related to the other sources of fallibility outlined here. In addition, in reflective intuition of the kind mentioned by Guy Claxton (see Chapter 2), perhaps the resolution of sources of tension depend on a common element, metacognition: being able to stand back and examine one's thinking processes, beliefs and feelings. Metacognitive strategies have already been identified as important for everyday thinking. If there is a kind of musing as a relaxed way of intuiting, then this must be related to the ability to see one's thoughts, feelings and actions from the outside and make them the objects of thought, and to do this calls for the development of a suitable form of language (Griffiths and Tann 1992: 81).

The ability to react without conscious thought

The most widespread definition of intuition may be the expert's ability to reach a conclusion, see a problem space and make decisions at lightning speed and below the level of consciousness. Here intuition is a close sister of insight, insight perhaps being the knowledge side of the family and intuition the process side. As with views about insight, there is a continuum of beliefs about this version of intuition, ranging from those who say that there is no such thing as exotic processes such as intuition and insight, through to those who seem to take a 'wizard Merlin' view of intuition as something almost magical. A middle road might be that of Wallas (1926) cited elsewhere in this volume (see Chapters 2 and 11), where insight and intuition depend on 'a prepared mind' (Seifert *et al.* 1996). There are potential causes of fallibility at each of Wallas' four stages. At the preparation stage, one may not use all of the knowledge one has, or it may be used inappropriately. This compares with Perkins' (1985) notion of confirmatory bias, and Kuhn's (1991) findings mentioned above. The incubation phase may not be allowed for, as Terry Atkinson points out in Chapter 4, or may be blocked by negative tension. Any one of these, or a combination of them, may lead to a block in the development of intuition.

Classrooms are immensely complex. As Gilpin (in press) puts it: 'Classrooms are places where we find the three Rs, routines (Breen 1985; Prabhu 1990, 1991), rituals (Coleman 1987) and recipes [John, this volume]. All three are jointly constructed by teacher and learners . . . the complexity of the routines, rituals and recipes, all of which are interwoven in a minute by minute decision-making process, reminds one of Reder's (1993) description of "polycontextuality" or multi-tasking'. This description of complexity reminds us of what makes intuitive, rapid reaction so essential in teaching: there is simply no time to stop and deliberate. The constituents are separately described as routines (regular procedures), rituals (lessons as socio-cultural events) and recipes (ways of doing things), but it is their interwoven nature and mutual construction that demands the quick responses, and results in the myriad exchanges noted by MacLeod and McIntyre (1977), Brown and McIntyre (1993), John [this volume] and others. For teachers, work is classically multi-tasked – that is, they have to attend to numerous tasks simultaneously and sometimes disjunctively, leaving one task to attend to something else and then returning to the first.

We have seen above that there are a number of factors that can stand in the way of developing what we call elaborated intuition. At this point, it may be worth listing these:

- identification of the 'wrong' problem space;
- knowledge, including experience, inappropriately accessed;
- information rather than knowledge;
- narrowness of observation (both visual and aural);
- confirmatory bias: not exploring all sides of the problem/argument; dominance of 'taken for granteds';
- lack of practice in establishing routines;
- negative affects;
- metacognitive strategies not made explicit;
- acceptance of initial solutions (lack of verification in Wallas' (1926) terms).

We have touched on the concept of intuitive restructuring which we see as changes in careful practice which, through the development of metacognitive strategies, investigate information, beliefs and attitudes about language, learning and strategies for language teaching. These return to the intuitive unconscious later, subsequently aiding the ability to perceive more holistically, thereby enabling more appropriately-focused observation and decision making in relation to one's practice. Thus, to develop intuitive ability practitioners need 'to use patterns without decomposing them into component features' (Dreyfus and Dreyfus 1986: 28). The restructuring of private theory results in more elaborated forms of intuition.

We turn now to a consideration of how, in initial teacher education, we might aid the examination of intuitive processes, combat those factors which inhibit the elaboration of intuition and assist the gradual development of understanding and expertise.

Task-based teacher education for ELT

Teacher education for ELT has seen a growing use of tasks as vehicles for teacher learning. Task-based approaches arose from a generally perceived need to allow teachers to work on the different levels of knowledge outlined above, and to provide opportunities for reflection. They also derive from task-based approaches to learning languages which combine opportunities for implicit learning through communicative tasks and explicit learning through the use of language analysis activities where the focus is on form and accuracy. Ellis (1986) lists tasks as one kind of learning activity among many others (lectures, readings, essays and so on). What is particularly useful about his conception is the link between task and data: a task's essential element is an activity with data to work on or with. It is not simply a matter of having a discussion: there must be a focused task, or plan of action related to a goal or outcome, and data on which to operationalize the plan. The data can comprise any relevant material provided by the trainer – such as videos or transcripts of lessons, readings, ELT textbooks and so on (Ellis 1986: 93) – or provided by the trainee, such as schematic knowledge. The activity can involve listing elements of some kind in the data, comparing, contrasting, completing, sorting, categorizing and so on.

The claim made for such tasks is that they are a 'halfway house' to experiential work: they require the learners to do something with the data – in other words, to put information to use. This is an example of what is known in Teaching English as a Foreign Language (TEFL) as 'awareness-raising'; a slippery expression, as Ellis (1986: 92) concedes: 'The assumption that underlies the use of awareness-raising practices, however, is that the practice of actual teaching can be improved by making teachers aware of the options open to them and the principles by which they can evaluate the alternatives. We do not know to what extent this assumption is justified . . . It would be comforting if there were some clear evidence to support this assumption.' However, phrased in terms of the argument presented above, such tasks will aim at encouraging the restructuring of professional thinking first by promoting the articulation of private theory.

Let us examine this assumption by looking at a task 'in action'. This one is taken from Willis (1990: 6–9). In it the student teachers' task is to make up their minds about the truth for them of a number of statements about language teaching and learning. Their activity is to rank their agreement with a set of statements about language learning, the data being the statements and the current private and received knowledge of the students. For the purposes of this illustration we shall use only two of the eight statements.

> Work in groups of three or four. Look at these statements. Decide whether or not you agree with each one. Mark each according to the following scale:
>
> 4 – strongly agree
> 3 – agree
> 2 – disagree
> 1 – strongly disagree
>
> (a) Some people learn to use a second or foreign language very well without having any formal lessons.
> (b) You cannot speak a foreign language unless you know the grammar of the language.

Trainees should begin by looking through the task sheet individually and deciding for themselves how they feel about each of the statements. After this they move into group discussion.

Here we have an opportunity for the students to reflect on their own learning and on their views concerning language learning. They then engage with others in exchanging views, and are exposed to possibly very different opinions about the points in question. Although justification of viewpoint is not stated in the instructions, the format makes this likely. At the end of the activity each group may have to present their 'findings' on one of the points, and so part of the discussion process is a summary in preparation for this. Consensus is not the aim – rather, it is important to explore a range of views.

Willis (1990: 7) goes on to outline the various lines of argument that might emerge from the group discussion. This takes place in what he calls an open session: what we would call feedback.

> I always begin by making a grid to record the conclusions reached by the groups, and to highlight areas of agreement and disagreement. The next stage is to ask a spokesperson from selected groups to explain the thinking behind their decisions. It is valuable at this stage to highlight the views of groups who do not hold the consensus view. This provokes further discussion in the open session. You may also ask for minority views . . . If you are working with a group of experienced teachers try to get them to illustrate the points they are making. If you are working with new trainees, encourage them to examine their own language learning experience. Throughout the open session try not to give the impression that there are right and wrong answers to all of these questions . . . There may be a sense in which we must 'know' the grammar of a language. The important thing is to tease out what we mean by 'knowing' the grammar in this context.
>
> Although there are not clear cut answers to many of these questions,

there are a number of ways in which we can help trainees formulate their own answers and perhaps seek to modify their teaching in the light of these answers. First there are a number of useful concepts which may help them to grapple with the arguments [gives some examples]. The discussion will also oblige trainees to focus on a number of issues which are central to a great deal of ELT theory.

What appears to be happening here is a 'scaffolding' of the processes of problem identification and argument. The trainer is concerned to allow as many points of view as possible to be heard. He also urges the use of experience and private knowledge, and the linking of instances of this to the points being made. He also states that the task permits opportunities to consider theoretical concepts within the feedback stage, an instance of information being converted into knowledge.

Willis (1990) lists a number of perceived benefits of the task-based approach. It permits students to explore their own 'mental set' (private theory), and it highlights the need for conceptual understanding: if their own experience is difficult to put into words, then this provides a framework for understanding theory and its relevance to them. The discussion makes them examine their own experience and interpret it. In addition, working in small peer groups is relatively unthreatening, and the public phase has the authority of the whole group and not an individual. In terms of our list of barriers to intuition this particular episode would appear to begin to address several: knowledge, including experience, inappropriately accessed; information rather than knowledge; confirmatory bias: not exploring all sides of the problem/argument; dominance of taken for granteds; negative affects; acceptance of initial solutions (lack of verification in Wallas' (1926) terms). It is not the task itself which provides for this richness, but the combination of task and feedback. Tasks of this kind, supported by scaffolded feedback from the tutor, provide the context for establishing routines for thinking about professional practice.

The task format also has a second major strength. The initial work is a structured activity around a set of data. It is therefore 'out there' and so not so bound up with beliefs that these get in the way of thinking. Beliefs are called into play at the second level of the task: in the justification phase. Here it is easier to objectify beliefs because there is an evidence base on which to work: this is awareness-raising at its best; where the evidence provided by the task and data are provided on which to externalize one's beliefs and knowledge. That this process can be useful in helping teachers talk about their beliefs is further exemplified by Gipps *et al.* (1996), who found that giving teachers lists of statements with which to agree or disagree as part of their interviewing procedures produced very much richer data and revealed a great deal about teachers' theories of teaching. Here we see a parallel to the task-based approach, where having concrete evidence to work with enables teachers to see their practices more clearly.

Woodward (1988) varies the task-based approach by using tasks that mirror (or model) good classroom practice. An example might involve using a technique such as 'divided reading' in which the participants are made to go through the processes as 'learners', and the input materials have as their topic the technique itself. They would thus be set a problem to solve about, for example, an aspect of teaching reading. Information would then be divided among them in the form of different readings, and through sharing their readings, and their own experiences as readers, they would engage in discussion to address the problem. Again an important element is the feedback, led by the tutor. The results of this type of activity are similar to those outlined by Willis (1990), with the addition that discussion also focuses on the technique itself. As well as the method, the feelings and attitudes it arouses can also be examined, again with the evidence of the task to focus on.

Both variants of task-based teacher education are not only seen to be working on the assumption that practice in tasks will enable better practice; they both offer opportunities to externalize inner thought and link it to knowledge. They also provide the deep involvement that some talk of as being essential (Benner 1986; Dreyfus and Dreyfus 1986). One could argue that such task-based teacher education will result in better intuitions in the future, given that it allows the participants with their tutor to address some of the barriers to intuition we outlined above.

Observation

One element is so far missing, however. Most writers comment on the importance of perception in intuition: the unconscious pattern-noticing that stimulates intuitive decision making. We noted above the importance of observation in intuition. Task-based teacher education can incorporate the element of observation, overtly included around the activities themselves (Gilpin 1990).

In this case class-based tasks are used as the basis for building up observational skills, through regular practice. Observation tasks focus on a particular aspect of the 'content' task or teaching procedure adopted by the tutor; the data is the ongoing lecture or discussion. Participants are led to explore their own learning in that particular environment, beginning by observing and describing the events of the sessions. Observers, selected in rotation, are invited to observe different events, and then report back at a later point in the session. Typically they work in supportive pairs, and their reports are then discussed by the class. Observation begins with very concrete, easily observed (low inference) phenomena (who talks to whom, how many times does x occur, etc.) and gradually develops to include aspects of events that are much less easy to describe (high inference), such as what kinds of roles people are playing in a discussion or what the aims of activities are. At each stage of development of the observation tasks, it is the tutor and their procedures which are the first focus of observation, or, at least, at each stage where the focus might be face-threatening to any participants. Three points are important here: first, the observation tasks gradually increase in complexity and inference level, from few features and low inference to more features and high. Second, the results of the observations are discussed as part of the feedback session. Third, the whole class is also the focus of observation tasks from time to time.

In the example of 'divided reading' in the previous section, one could slightly vary the instructions given to different groups. Some might be told that on no account must they *show* their readings to other group members, they must only explain what is in them. Other groups might then be given no such instruction. The appointed observers might be asked to observe their groups and make simple sociograms of turn-taking. They might also be asked to note how much time the activity takes, and to note what the group did when they had completed the task. Feedback on these points would then enrich the pedagogical discussion at the content feedback stage by providing some evidence. It might reveal, for example, that turn-taking is more equal when nobody is allowed to see another's paper and lead into a discussion of how one can involve all interlocutors using other techniques.

Many of the awareness-raising tasks that are widely used on teacher education courses depend on video, tape, print or remembered experiences of teaching and learning. These are all useful, but they lack the multi-tasked nature of the real world. One way to increase complexity is to use the current context (i.e. the lecture room, the tutor's sessions, and other learning experiences) as the focus of the observation: they are immediate, shared, equally complex. This has the added benefit of being less affectively threatening for the students, since the focus is someone else's sessions and not their own. For the tutor there are affective risks, certainly, but the benefits far outweigh these in terms of the gains in self-knowledge and increased interpersonal engagement with meaning construction for the participants.

Observation can thus be introduced as an element in any procedure used on the course. Tasks are the main building blocks of the course, and mediate between input through lectures and readings, in an attempt to create knowledge from information, and to open up participants' ways of thinking, seeing and doing for examination – in other words, to develop metacognition. A typical cycle might begin with a task (activity, plus data) followed by feedback; input could then be provided in the form of readings or lecture; this would be followed by another task where the focus might be on application (for instance, listing the different kinds of reading activities in a textbook) followed by adapting materials for use. Each stage is followed by feedback in which the tutor engages with the students in discussing both the content and the processes of the procedure or activity. This focus on processes is as crucial as the focus on content. Any stage can be accompanied by an observation task, typically done by appointed observers who have a specific brief to observe a particular phenomenon and report back to the class in the second feedback stage. During a course each student would have many opportunities to be an observer, and all would participate in feedback sessions on what had been observed.

The addition of observation tasks to the approach ensures that the barriers to intuition are brought within the approach: narrowness of observation (both visual and aural) and making metacognition explicit.

Conclusion

Very little research has been done to test the assumptions that we are making in this chapter. What we are saying is that the development of intuition can be assisted by taking an approach to teacher education that attempts to address what are seen to be causes of blocks to rapid intuitive action. In this we find support in what Easen and Wilcockson (1996: 672) say:

> How may this [intuition] be considered to have a rational basis? We would argue that this can be understood by extricating the different rational components contributing to the intuitive process. There are several elements fundamental to intuition. Of primary importance is a sound, relevant knowledge base and the ability to recognize patterns in the presenting problem. Such pattern recognition is rooted in past decision-making and experience is essential for linking of past similar events with the present. Embedded within the intuiter's performance is the implicit thinking and the use of professional know how.

We do not set out to teach intuition, nor do we say that it is the same as conscious thought. It is clearly different, in ways that reflect the difference between real-time professional behaviour with its polytextuality, and the isolated training event. Intuition is polytextual in the sense that it requires the operation of a number of processes simultaneously. Our contention is that intuition can, however, be learnt through an iterative process of restructuring, where naive intuitions are refined by conscious examination through task-based learning. Practice and repeated analysis in increasingly complex situations can enable this process to be a continuing one. It is an approach which honours the information content needed – the public knowledge – and one which provides the contexts of use to convert information into personal knowledge.

References

Benner, P. (1984) *From Novice to Expert: Excellence and Power in Clinical Nursing Practice.* Wokingham: Addison Wesley.

Breen, M.P. (1985) The social context for language learning: a neglected situation? *Studies in Second Language Acquisition,* 7(2): 135–58.

Brown, S. and McIntyre, D. (1993) *Making Sense of Teaching.* Buckingham: Open University Press.

Coleman, H. (1987) Teaching spectacles and learning festivals. *ELT Journal,* 41(2): 97–103.

Dreyfus, H. and Dreyfus, S. (1986) *Mind Over Machine: The Power of Intuition and Expertise in the Era of the Computer.* Oxford: Blackwell.

Duncker, K. (1945) On problem solving. *Psychological Monographs*, 58(5).

Ellis, R. (1986) Activities and procedures for teacher training. *ELT Journal*, 40(2): 91–9.

Easen, P. and Wilcockson, J. (1996) Intuition and rational decision-making. *Journal of Advanced Nursing*, 24: 667–73.

Garnham, A. and Oakhill, J. (1994) *Thinking and Reasoning*. Oxford: Blackwell.

Gilpin, A. (1990) *English Studies 3: Using Observation Sheets on Teacher Training Courses*. London: The British Council.

Gilpin, A. (in press) A framework for teaching reflection, in H. Trappe-Lomax (ed.) *Theory in Language Teacher Education*. London: Longman.

Gipps, C., McCullum, B. and Brown, M. (1996) Models of teacher assessment among primary school teachers in England. *Curriculum Journal*, 7(2): 167–84.

Griffiths, M. and Tann, S. (1992) Using reflective practice to link personal and public theories. *Journal of Education for Teaching*, 18(1): 69–84.

Johnson, R. and Badley, G. (1996) The competent reflective practitioner. *Innovation and Learning in Education: The International Journal of the Reflective Practitioner*, 2(1): 4–10.

Krashen, S.D. (1985) *The Input Hypothesis: Issues and implications*. Harlow: Longman.

Kuhn, D. (1991) *The Skills of Argument*. Cambridge: Cambridge University Press.

Lesgold, A. (1988) Problem solving, in R.J. Sternberg and E.E. Smith (eds) *The Psychology of Human Thought*. Cambridge: Cambridge University Press.

MacLeod, G. and McIntyre, D. (1977) Towards a model for micro-teaching, in D. McIntyre, G. MacLeod and R. Griffiths (eds) *Investigating Micro-teaching*. London: Croom Helm.

Perkins, D.N. (1985) Reasoning as Imagination. *Interchange*, 16: 14–26.

Prabhu, N.S. (1990) There is no best method: why? *TESOL Quarterly*, 24(2): 161–76.

Prabhu, N.S. (1991) The dynamics of the language classroom. *TESOL Quarterly*, 26(2): 225–42.

Ramani, E. (1987) Theorizing from the classroom. *ELT Journal*, 41(3): 3–11.

Reder, L.M. (1993) Watching flowers grow: polycontextuality and heterochronicity at work. *The Quarterly Newsletter of the Laboratory of Comparative Human Cognition*, 15: 116–25.

Schooler, J.W., Fallshore, M. and Fiore, S.M. (1996) Epilogue: putting insight into perspective, in R.J. Sternberg and J.E. Davidson (eds) *The Nature of Insight*. Cambridge, MA: MIT Press.

Seifert, C.M., Meyer, D.E. and Davidson, N. (1996) Demystification of cognitive insight: opportunistic assimilation and the prepared mind perspective, in R.J. Sternberg and J.E. Davidson (eds) *The Nature of Insight*. Cambridge, MA: MIT Press.

Wallas, G. (1926) *The Art of Thought*. New York: Harcourt Brace Jovanovich.

Willis, D.J. (1990) Task-based teacher training. *ELT Review*, 11: 6–9.

Woodward, T. (1988) *Loop-Input: New Strategies for Teacher Training*. Canterbury: Pilgrims Publications.

 **Part 3**

Intuition and continuing professional development

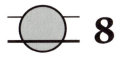 **8**

The development of professional intuition

Agnes McMahon

> Teachers and heads are at the heart of our drive to raise standards. They
> above all hold the key to improving performance and remedying under-
> achievement.
>
> (DfEE 1997: 45)

Introduction

Teacher education is under scrutiny. Programmes for initial teacher education
have long been tightly monitored by government but now its very delivery
and the continuing professional development (CPD) of teachers are increasingly centrally controlled. Improving the quality of the teacher force is seen
as the key means of raising student achievement in schools, and raising standards has become a national goal: 'Education is the Government's number
one priority. There is no more important task facing our nation than raising
standards in schools' (Blunkett 1998: ii). Little is being left to chance in pursuit of this goal. All teachers now have to engage in some CPD and the priority areas for training and even the style of training are largely nationally
determined.

The central question to be explored in this chapter is whether the
approaches to teacher professional development now being adopted recognize the importance of developing intuition and reflection as well as the
acquisition of practical skills and rationally-based knowledge. Three issues
will be considered: first, the relationship between rational problem-solving,
intuition and reflective practice; second, the nature of the national standards
for professional development being introduced by the Teacher Training
Agency (TTA); third, some research data about teacher perceptions of professional development will be reviewed to see if it provides any evidence that
teachers draw upon intuitive feelings about teaching when engaging in
professional development. Finally, some conclusions will be drawn about
the extent to which the current approaches to CPD are likely to promote the

use of reflection and intuition and, if not, what might be done to change this situation.

Rational problem-solving and intuition

As John Furlong highlights in Chapter 1, the traditional dimensions of teacher professionalism, knowledge, responsibility and autonomy are now being challenged. This challenge is evident in the model of the effective teacher which is being promoted from the centre, one which emphasizes rational problem-solving rather than reflective practice. Yet it is now well accepted that expert practitioners possess a complex personal knowledge base which they draw upon intuitively. This knowledge base is acquired through training and experience but individuals may not be able to articulate why they do what they do. In Schön's definition, a reflective practitioner possesses a tacit way of knowing which is intuitive rather than deliberate: 'although we sometimes think before acting, it is also true that in much of the spontaneous behaviour of skilful practice we reveal a kind of knowing which does not stem from a prior intellectual operation' (Schön 1987: 16).

Guy Claxton's definition of intuition in Chapter 2 is congruent with Schön's notion of reflective practice. Claxton describes intuition as 'a loose-knit family of "ways of knowing" which are less articulate and explicit than normal reasoning and discourse'. These ways of knowing include expertise, implicit learning, judgement, sensitivity, creativity and rumination. Intuition is a broader concept than reflective practice but, like reflective practice, it is grounded in prior learning and experience. To argue that teachers behave intuitively for some of the time is not to suggest that their behaviour is irrational. Nor should it imply that teaching is a mysterious practice which cannot be properly examined. Dunkin (1987), considering whether teaching was an art or a science, cited Gage's argument that teaching was an art, but, 'a useful or practical art' rather than an aesthetic one. Gage (1978) had suggested that certain features of teaching – for example selecting materials, pacing a lesson or interacting with students – provided opportunities for the teacher to demonstrate intuition, expressiveness, improvisation and creativity. Nevertheless he saw the need to establish a scientific basis for teaching and for research which would attempt to identify relationships between certain teaching behaviours and student learning.

Rational or deliberative processes (Eraut, 1997) and reflective approaches need not be polarized. Hargreaves (1996) argued for an evidence-based approach to teaching but saw this as compatible with the notion of the reflective practitioner. Reynolds (1998) takes the argument a step further, suggesting that teachers should be regarded as technologists who are able to research in their schools, to use the empirical rational model to create knowledge about effective practices. He makes a case for research on effective teaching practices so as to develop an applied science of teaching: building up a body of knowledge about the kind of teaching behaviours that are more likely to lead to student achievement. Again, this does not necessarily challenge the notion of reflective, intuitive practice. For instance, the effective behaviours that Reynolds cites include: instructional variety, high student time on task and using and incorporating pupil ideas. These are widely recognized as desirable practices but they are not easy to implement. Selecting appropriate strategies that will engage a group of students, judging when to move from presentation to questions etc. demands fine judgements on the part of the teacher, judgements that on some occasions will be made intuitively. One characteristic of expert practitioners is that they regularly review and revise their practice. The challenge surely is to provide teachers with knowledge and experiences which will prompt them to question their tacit beliefs about teaching, for as Guy Claxton notes in Chapter 2, intuition can be fallible. This is something also recognized by Eraut (1997) who argues that we should regularly evaluate both the public and the personal knowledge that we use in professional work.

Do the national standards for teachers disregard intuitive ways of knowing?

The rational approach to teacher development is most clearly spelt out in the professional development framework which has been developed by the TTA (1998). The framework contains a set of standards for teachers at various points in the profession:

- National standards for qualified teacher status (the entry qualification);
- National standards for subject leaders;
- National standards for special educational needs coordinators;
- National standards for headteachers, which underpin the national professional qualification for headteachers (NPQH).

The standards set out the professional knowledge, understanding, skills and attributes that are considered necessary to carry out the key tasks associated with each of these roles. Expectations for teachers in all aspects of their role are listed but the focus is upon the need to improve student achievement and to implement national educational priorities (e.g. developing the use of information technology). The standards are intended to be used by teachers in planning their own professional development, by providers of professional development in planning training, and by headteachers and others in making assessments of teacher performance. Though the term competency is not used, the standards are in effect a competency framework for teaching. However, it is recognized that propositional knowledge (Eraut 1994) alone cannot make an effective teacher. For example, the standards for the award of qualified teacher status include this statement: 'Professionalism, however, implies more than meeting a series of discrete standards. It is necessary to consider these standards as a whole to appreciate the creativity, commitment, energy and enthusiasm which teaching demands, and the intellectual and managerial skills required of the effective professional' (TTA 1998: 24).

Each set of standards lists the required professional knowledge and under-standing in considerable detail but desirable skills and attributes are also included. The teachers are expected to demonstrate the skills of leadership, decision making, communication and self-management and to possess a daunting range of personal attributes, namely:

• personal impact and presence;
• adaptability to changing circumstances and new ideas;
• energy, vigour and perseverance;
• self-confidence;
• enthusiasm;
• intellectual ability;
• reliability and integrity;
• commitment.

In a further development, the government has introduced a new category of 'advanced skills teacher', designed as a means of recognizing and reward-ing excellent teachers who want to stay in the classroom rather than move into managerial roles. These 'super' teachers are to be assessed in terms of student outcomes but also on their teaching capacity:

> Aspiring Advanced Skills Teachers must understand and use the most effective teaching methods to achieve the teaching objectives in hand; display flair and creativity in engaging, enthusing and challenging groups of pupils; use questioning and explanation skilfully to secure maximum progress; be able to provide positive and targeted support for pupils who have special educational needs, are very able, are from ethnic minorities, lack confidence, have behavioural difficulties or are disaffected; maintain respect and discipline; and be consistent and fair.
>
> (DfEE 1998: 7)

These dynamic, interactive skills seem far removed from the notion of a teacher technician who has merely mastered a set of discrete competencies. The models of the effective teacher that are embodied in the TTA standards and in the criteria for the advanced skills teacher may place a heavy empha-sis on professional knowledge and on student achievement outcomes but it is hard to see how they are incompatible with the concept of the reflective prac-titioner. However, the standards are intended to guide provision for teacher professional development and it is in the way that they are used that they will influence the ways in which teachers think and act.

Is there any evidence that teachers behave intuitively in relation to their own professional development?

In considering this question I returned to data that I had gathered in a study which focused on secondary teacher perceptions of CPD (funded by the Leverhulme Trust 1995–7). As part of this study, interviews were conducted with 24 teachers (12 women and 12 men) in three case study schools, one in each of three local education authorities. The teachers ranged in age from the early 20s to about 50, in experience from 1 or 2 years' teaching to 26 years and in responsibility from those who had no responsibilities other than their specific teaching duties to deputy headteachers. The main research question was: 'How do secondary teachers understand, experience and value CPD?' Though the teachers were not asked explicitly about their use of intuition, the data illustrated that the majority did not use a rational planning model when considering their own professional development. They had strongly-held views about what it meant to be a professional and what would help them to become better practitioners, views they were not always able to articulate. They seemed to have an intuitive understanding of their development needs.

Being a professional

All the teachers saw themselves as professionals. They did not hold a clear, shared definition of what this meant but spoke about being a professional in terms of respecting a set of standards of behaviour and always trying to do one's best in the job. These standards were rarely explicitly stated: 'it [standards] is to do with the way you are with people, not taking things personally, you try to be objective in your dealings with people' (female head of humanities faculty, 40s); '[There are] certain accepted norms that go with being a professional, norms of behaviour, expectations, values, simple things like dress' (male senior teacher, 40s). Several teachers spoke about the importance of knowledge and the responsibility of keeping up to date in their teaching subject area: 'You need to be well prepared for lessons and need to have a very good subject knowledge . . . you need to be fair and firm to all students and you need to give 100 per cent' (female physical education teacher, 20s).

Purposes of professional development

How do teachers acquire/learn these norms and standards? To what extent are they shared? Are they acquired implicitly through working with and observing fellow teachers in the workplace?

The teachers' understanding of professional development was rather instrumental: it was the training and experiences that were needed to enable them to do their job. Few of those interviewed spoke of engaging in professional development activities for their intrinsic value; the activities were assessed in terms of their potential to influence the work that the particular teacher was responsible for in school. A number of them drew a distinction between professional development to help them with their teaching tasks and other forms of training (e.g. management courses) which were geared to career development and promotion.

The younger and newly-qualified teachers were concerned to gain practical training which would help them become more effective classroom teachers: 'I regard the training as providing me with strategies for coping, helping me to cope with the load effectively and helping me ensure that the children get the best out of their time' (male newly-qualified languages teacher, 30s). However, the more experienced teachers also believed that the purpose of professional development was to help them in the classroom: 'I have to enjoy my teaching and my students have to enjoy it too . . . I've got to be changing, always making it more interesting and finding new ways to make it more interesting' (female art teacher, 40s); 'I tend to think of my professional development as two strands, what I do in the classroom and what I need if I am to move into more senior positions as I move up the managerial side . . . at the moment I am more interested in and feel I need to know more about how to improve the classroom side of things' (female recently-qualified history teacher, 20s).

One of the things that is striking about these statements is that the teachers' comments are self-referential, rooted in an implicit understanding of what might help them to cope in the classroom or make their teaching more interesting. Of course their views will have been influenced by their ideas about what is required for promotion (e.g. possession of a Masters degree) or perhaps by formal appraisal, but the reference point is their own sense of what they need at a particular time. As Taylor (1987: 482) noted, teachers develop theories about teaching not only from the influences and constraints of the work context but also 'out of beliefs about themselves, beliefs about how they learn to be more effective, and what it is that renders constant improvements in their performance'.

Identifying professional development needs

All three case study schools had notional systems for teacher appraisal (evaluation) in place since this is now a legal requirement, but in each of the schools the appraisal system had ground to a halt for a variety of reasons. Consequently, teachers largely took responsibility for identifying their own needs. Frequently, these arose directly from their teaching and administrative responsibilities. Asked how she identified her professional development needs, one teacher responded: 'By what they ask me to teach next year . . . you are aware sometimes that you may be becoming out of date . . . we have gone through a lot of new initiatives so in fact my needs have been forced upon me . . . I know I have to develop that area because I have to teach it' (female business studies teacher).

Other teachers identified their needs in terms of a career goal: 'I would like to go into [school] management . . . that's what prompted me to take the Open University course [a distance learning Master's degree which she was paying for herself]' (female history teacher).

Sometimes a teacher was prompted to engage in some development activity by another teacher (e.g. the head of department): 'I don't think I actually did [identify a development need], it was somebody, perhaps my head of department, who saw an opportunity for me and gave me that opportunity' (male business studies teacher). This teacher's head of department, speaking about identifying CPD needs said: 'I think it's about self-awareness and basically trying to keep proactive in actually seeking out opportunities not just for me but for my colleagues as well'.

Knowing when to seek development

It proved difficult to separate discussion of professional and career development since the teachers saw the two being closely linked. It became clear from the interview data that the majority of the teachers did not consciously plan their careers in the profession. They had very varied routes into teaching and the manner in which their careers developed seemed to have as much to do with happenstance as with deliberate choice on their part. A key variable was the extent to which the school was in a position to provide new professional challenges when the teacher felt in need of them. Several teachers in their 40s reported that they had worked contentedly in their subject area and had only begun to consider career development later, sometimes because of a crisis in their personal life.

One woman had taught in one school for 19 years but then a number of things had gone wrong in her personal life and she had been prompted to move: 'because I wasn't particularly ambitious I kept staying because I liked the kids and I'd say, oh I'll see this crowd out. I got totally involved in what I was doing' (female geography teacher, 40s). This attitude wasn't uncommon: 'My career has just sort of evolved as it has gone along . . . I am enjoying my work now, if at some point in the future I find I am not enjoying it I will look to change it but I don't try to plan at all' (female art teacher, 40s). A male design teacher in his 40s in the same school also said that he had been very engaged with his classroom teaching: 'My view of a career path is that there doesn't seem to be a path. You just go into it and take the opportunities as they come along'.

The picture that emerges here of teachers engaged with their work in the classroom, responding positively to some opportunities but not others, looking for a change of job when they feel they need it, is very different from a rational model in which a goal is identified at an early stage and individuals work towards it systematically.

Positive experiences of professional development

Most of the in-service training that these teachers had experienced had come in the form of short training courses, either external or school based and rarely lasting more than a day, often less. Although they reported that some of these experiences had been very positive, when they were critical of the provision they raised similar points. Either they had not perceived the training as relevant for their needs or, if the topic was relevant, the training was not pitched at an appropriate level. The style of training often did not suit them or was just generally of poor quality.

Descriptions of positive experiences of professional development were quite different. Factors that were cited were: training that was seen as practical; which took account of individual learning needs; and which took place over time:

> It was good because it gave me very practical ideas on how to set out the gym and the tutor also asked what ideas the participants wanted help with.
>
> (Female physical education teacher)

> One of the good things was that it [training] took place over a period of time and wasn't just a one-off, so you had a commitment to it and the people teaching it had a commitment to you . . . also the way it was taught, you had the theory but you also had the practical and they were linked together very well. Different styles of teaching and learning were used so you might be lectured at, you might work in small groups, you might work on your own using videos, there was a variety of ways of learning which was helpful. Also it was made relevant to what you were doing in your own school so we learned about flexible learning by writing study guides for example . . . You were being trained for a purpose so you could see the reason in it.
>
> (Male English teacher)

Most of the teachers' comments referred to short training courses which was all that the majority of them had experienced. However, a minority of older teachers in their 40s had experienced a period of secondment and for them this had been without doubt their best professional development experience. Their memories of it remained vivid even though the experience might have taken place several years previously.

Asked what had been his most valuable professional development experience, one teacher in his 40s said: 'undoubtedly it was the year out doing the degree [10 years ago]. One reason was that I had a considerable amount of choice about what I did. I found the whole course extending, interesting and valuable . . . it had been divorced from practical work in school but it hadn't made it difficult to come back.' A second teacher of similar age, in a different school, expressed a similar view when asked whether studying for his higher degree 12 years before had been a good experience: 'Brilliant . . . it's a completely different experience from doing an MA part-time. A lot of colleagues that I know have done a part-time MA which is obviously weekends and after work, they've got work to do before that and they can't immerse themselves in the culture of learning . . . it was good for me personally and I think it was good for the school.'

A female business studies teacher who had been on secondment to industry for a week had also found this a very valuable experience: 'It made me realize what it was like out there, you quite forget because you become quite isolated. It was nice to be with a different group of adults . . . they don't have the tension of having children there as well. It was invaluable [for the job] because I've written case studies about what I saw and the information I gathered.' Another woman had been given unpaid leave of absence from school for five weeks to go on a climbing expedition in Nepal – not something that would seem to be linked to her work in school: 'It has been a tremendous five weeks . . . it made me feel valued because I didn't think they would let me go . . . when I came back my geography teaching in relation to Third World countries just jumped tremendously because I had actually seen some of these places.'

The level of in-school support for teacher professional development was very variable. Although all three schools had arrangements for induction and appraisal there were no systematic arrangements for mentoring, peer observation, job rotation etc. However, departmental groupings of teachers could be very supportive of one another and this could lead to a very productive learning environment:

> I've learned a lot from my head of department and she engages everyone in the team . . . we are constantly learning things from each other.
>
> > (Female art teacher)

> I think we are a well-integrated faculty, we share things in the broadest sense. If things aren't going well we are able to talk about it. We are comfortable talking about work-related issues. More than that we are able to say to each other, I can't do such and such and support each other.
>
> > (Head of design faculty)

Some teachers had benefited from the fact that a colleague had assumed an informal mentoring role and provided them with guidance and support on a regular basis:

> From the beginning my head of department has been incredibly supportive and helpful. For example, when the post of second in the department came up she said to me I think that you can do it, I'd like you to do it. When the opportunity came to apply for the role on the head of department committee she spent a lot of time with me, looking at my CV and helping me with my letter of application. No one asked her to do it, she just did it.
>
> > (Female recently-qualified history teacher)

> In the five years that I've been here I've been given lots of opportunity and I've been in the right place at the right time. I've been able to develop from a professional point of view and I'm very grateful to the school for that. They've identified their needs, they've seen my potential, they've put the two together and taken it from there.
>
> > (Male business studies teacher)

How can intuition be developed?

Guy Claxton suggests in Chapter 2 that certain situational and psychological conditions are required for the expression and development of creative intuition: first, you must not be experiencing pressure and stress of any kind. Second, you need a personal disposition which enables you to tolerate uncertainty, to have confidence that answers to problems will emerge, to let questions and problems stew around in the unconscious mind rather than rush to solutions. While recognizing that people will differ in their ability to draw upon and use their intuitive skills, Claxton suggests that intuition can be developed through explicit instruction and modelling and through the epistemological culture of professional education and training. Eraut (1997) suggests that the quality of skilled behaviour can be improved by a variety of means which prompt you to question your assumptions (e.g. getting feedback from an observer, engaging in action research on one's own practice). Fullan (1993) argues that teachers must combine inner and outer learning and notes the importance of periods of solitude which provide space for personal reflection.

Conclusion

How likely is it that the approaches to professional development that are being adopted nationally will help teachers to strengthen their intuitive skills? It is difficult to be confident that they will. If we accept the definition of intuition as a family of 'ways of knowing' including rumination, which Guy Claxton refers to as 'the practice of chewing the cud of experience in order to extract its meanings and its implications' then it is hard to see when teachers will find time to do this. The teachers interviewed during the Leverhulme study often complained that they had no time for reflection on their work, meaning they had no time to consciously think back over their experience. Still less did they have the opportunity for the more leisurely focusing on experience that rumination would seem to require. Teaching is widely recognized to be a high stress profession (Crawford 1997). The workload is heavy: a 1996 survey (School Teachers' Review Body 1997) revealed that the average weekly hours of work for a secondary teacher was 50.3, for a teacher with middle management responsibilities 53, and for headteachers 61.7.

Not only do teachers lack the time for reflection, but the majority of the professional development activities that are currently available for them are short half-day or one-day training courses that do little more than raise awareness of innovations. Follow-up activities are very rare. Not many teachers receive opportunities to go on longer courses; very few obtain a secondment to enable them to engage in further study and, if they do, the focus will almost certainly be on an organizational priority which may or may not match their personal learning and development needs. Evidence is accumulating (e.g. Little 1993; Hargreaves 1995) that using a narrow model of training that is designed to develop particular skills may work well for technical innovations but is unlikely to provide teachers with the skills and abilities that they will need for the future. Moreover, even the learning of new technical skills is problematic. Thus, Joyce and Showers (1988) have argued that the model of training required to help teachers acquire complex skills is a 'theory-demonstration-practice-feedback' combination in which feedback is provided by coaches and mentors in the classroom. But, mentoring for teachers is not widely available and periods of secondment or study leave are practically unobtainable.

Given this situation it is hard to avoid the conclusion that, although the broad aims of government policy on teacher professional development, as exemplified by the TTA's national standards, are not in themselves inimical to the concept of the reflective, intuitive teacher, the ways in which professional development is being implemented will limit the development of a teacher's more intuitive and reflective skills. If teachers are to be supported in developing their creative and intuitive capacity then a number of things will need to happen: ways must be found of reducing the high levels of workplace stress and of providing continuing professional development which promotes personal growth.

References

Blunkett, D. (1998) Secretary of State's foreword, in *Department for Education and Employment and Office for Standards in Education: Departmental Report*. London: HMSO.

Crawford, M. (1997) Managing stress in education, in T. Bush and D. Middlewood (eds) *Managing People in Education*. London: Paul Chapman.

DfEE (Department for Education and Employment) (1997) *Excellence in Schools*. London: HMSO.

DfEE (Department for Education and Employment) (1998) *The Advanced Skills Teacher: Note by the DfEE*. London: DfEE.

Dunkin, M.J. (1987) Teaching: art or science? in M.J. Dunkin (ed.) *The International Encyclopedia of Teaching and Teacher Education*. Oxford: Pergamon.

Eraut, M. (1994) *Developing Professional Knowledge and Competence*. London: Falmer Press.

Eraut, M. (1997) Developing expertise in school management and teaching, in L. Kydd, M. Crawford and C. Riches (eds) *Professional Development for Education Management*. Buckingham: Open University Press.

Fullan, M. (1993) *Change Forces*. London: Falmer Press.

Gage, N.L. (1978) *The Scientific Basis of the Art of Teaching*. New York: Teachers' College Press.

Hargreaves, A. (1995) Development and desire: A postmodern perspective, in T.R. Guskey and M. Huberman (eds) *Professional Development in Action*. New York: Teachers' College Press.

Hargreaves, D. (1996) *Teaching as a Research-based Profession: Possibilities and Prospects* (Teacher Training Agency annual lecture). London: TTA.

Joyce, B.R. and Showers, B. (1988) *Student Achievement through Staff Development*. New York: Longman.

Little, J.W. (1993) Teachers' professional development in a climate of educational reform. *Educational Evaluation and Policy Analysis,* 15(2): 121–51.

Reynolds, D. (1998) *Teacher Effectiveness* (Presentation at the Teacher Training Agency corporate plan launch 1998–2001). London: TTA.

Schön, D. (1987) *Educating the Reflective Practitioner.* San Francisco, CA: Jossey-Bass.

School Teachers' Review Body (1997) *School Teachers' Pay and Conditions.* London: HMSO.

Taylor, P.H. (1987) Implicit theories, in M.J. Dunkin (ed.) *The International Encyclopedia of Teaching and Teacher Education.* Oxford: Pergamon.

TTA (Teacher Training Agency) (1998) *National Professional Standards for Teachers and Headteachers.* London: TTA.

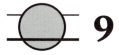 **9**

The formal and the intuitive in science and medicine

Richard Brawn

Waste not your time, so fast it flies;
Method will teach you time to win;
Hence, my young friend, I would advise,
With college logic to begin.
Then will your mind be so well brac'd,
In Spanish boots so tightly lac'd,
That on 'twill circumspectly creep,
Thought's beaten track securely keep,
Nor will it, ignis-fatuus like,
Into the path of error strike.
Then many a day they'll teach you how
The mind's spontaneous acts, till now
As eating and as drinking free,
Require a process; – one, two, three!
In truth the subtle web of thought
Is like the weaver's fabric wrought,
One treadle moves a thousand lines,
Swift dart the shuttles to and fro,
Unseen the threads unnumber'd flow,
A thousand knots one stroke combines.
Then forward steps your sage to show,
And prove to you it must be so;
The first being so, and so the second.
The third and fourth deduc'd we see;
And if there were no first and second,
Nor third and fourth would ever be.
This, scholars of all countries prize,
Yet 'mong themselves no weavers rise.

Mephistopheles, in Goethe's *Faust*, translated by Anna Swanwick
(from Heisenberg 1989: 158–9)

Introduction

The science teacher and the general practitioner both operate with a formal science training in a social science world where the methods and language of analysis and expression may be very different. The communication of ideas, the assessment of situations and people and responses to them – even perhaps thought and action – will be shaped by the norms and traditions of both the science and social science cultures. This represents at the very least an interesting situation, and in the context of this book a potentially fascinating one.

In this chapter, I want to begin by exploring the special nature of scientific thinking, taking as my starting point the rather specialized cognitive domain which school science represents for both teacher and learner, and wonder aloud if it is, in the long term, damaging for the mental process skills which characterize expert professionals. I will examine, through interview analysis, how science teachers and general practitioners use formal and informal methods in their assessment of presenting cases, situations, patients and pupils, and try to unpick the role of intuition and the responses of each group to it. Although it is the science classroom that is the primary focus, I also intend to draw on the medical literature – from nurse education in particular – to see whether we can learn from the allied medical context (in terms of cultural totems), where intuition has been discussed more openly. Finally, I want to explore how intuitive skills might be developed – taught is too strong a word – and look at the implications for science educators, whether they are teachers in the classroom or those tutors who help them get there. I will also suggest that an emphasis on more intuitive and personal responses to science may in the long term be an important step in revitalizing what has become a rather moribund subject in the secondary school curriculum, often presented in the form of homogenized packets of information; 'long-life' rather than lifelong learning.

The science mind

The scientific community places a premium on (indeed celebrates) certain modes of thought which might be loosely classified as hypothetico-deductive, the significant features of which are claimed to be dispassionate observation, rational analysis, logical deductions, the formulation and testing of hypotheses, and, by these means, the generation of theoretical statements about the natural world.

As Claxton (1997), Marton *et al.* (1994) and others have pointed out however, an important dimension in the progress and development of science and medicine is that of intuition. Scientific endeavour is replete with examples where the origins of significant advances have been in imaginative and creative leaps (in the sense of novel thinking about a problem) as well as by dint of painstaking, logical, step-by-step analysis of the already known. As Claxton says, the way of knowing that is most conducive to idea generation is leisurely, poetic and unpremeditated. Consider for example the stories of Kekule discovering the molecular structure of benzene in a dream of a snake swallowing its tail, of Feynmann seeing the way to atomic electron orbital understanding in the act of watching a plate spinning, or of Epstein following a hunch for years before isolating the cancer-causing virus which bears his name. These serve to illustrate that intuitive thoughts – and I extend this to feelings and emotions – play an important part in the scientific enterprise, despite the rhetoric which appears to deny it.

Yet I would wish to argue that a subliminal, almost poetic dimension to science is very much the preserve of the expert scientist who is steeped in the nuances of the subject. For most students of science (which will include the future teachers of science, and doctors) the reality may be very different. As Walpert (1993) has argued, much of science is counter-intuitive, does not sit happily with everyday beliefs and frequently explains the familiar in unfamiliar ways. Often it is not amenable to common-sense reasoning, as neither the procedures of science nor the ideas fit with everyday experience and expectations. While this is also a critique of education in general, in science the divorce from everyday experience and reasoning is often very marked.

In Solomon's (1997) words, students of science are like anthropologists watching alien people and being helped to see the world in a different way. And as she says, students soon discover that good imitations of a teacher's culture are rewarded. And what is this culture? Predominantly one of abstract thought often articulated in mathematical language. Learners and practitioners thus inhabit a world where common-sense thinking is resisted, quantitative rigour is promoted, feelings and opinions are devalued and learners are urged to abandon basic beliefs and adopt uncomfortable modes of thought. And this for the promised land where science can be appreciated for its beauty, elegance, simplicity, power and economy (even parsimony) of expression. That many never arrive is testimony for some critics of school science to the sterile and disconnected nature of the enterprise. Learners of science, they would claim, operate by and large in a denuded cognitive environment which, despite the rhetoric, offers few opportunities for social discourse, philosophical and ethical explorations, the bargaining and trading of ideas and the sense of collective enterprise which are features of scientific endeavour in the real world and most other subjects in the secondary curriculum. This denuded cognitive environment and, in its worse excesses, almost algorithmic approach to science would seem to favour the development of – at best – a forensic rather than a holistic mind set. My intention here is not so much to point to the shortcomings of the school science curriculum but to suggest, in the context of this book, that a likely outcome is one where imagination, emotional involvement, opinion and other expressions of intuitive and creative thought are not encouraged, and may even be insidiously suppressed. School science, in short, may lead to the erosion of cognitive qualities which are the characteristics of expert practitioners in any field.

The teaching context

Teaching is a complex business and teachers have many roles. Indeed the seven domains which Benner (1984) used to classify nursing competencies could also be used to classify dimensions of a teacher's activities:

- the helping role;
- the teaching–coaching function;
- the diagnostic and patient (pupil) monitoring functions;
- effective management of rapidly changing situations;
- administering and monitoring therapeutic interventions;
- monitoring the quality of practice;
- organizational and work-role competencies.

Teachers are also engaged in the processes of cultivation and modelling of the 'ways of knowing' that characterize the discipline they teach.

In some of these dimensions (in particular those of assessment and cultivation/modelling 'ways of knowing') the relationship between the intuitive and the rational/formal is problematic, with teachers of science finding themselves in an interesting dual bind. Science teachers deal with a subject which makes particular demands on them and their pupils. They have been trained, like doctors, to 'think scientifically' about issues. It might be expected that this training, or 'acculturation' in dominant modes of thought, pervades all aspects of their experience. This leads to the central question addressed in this chapter: how do the 'ways of knowing' (and thinking and learning), in which teachers have been steeped by virtue of their disciplinary study, influence the way that they approach the balance between intuition and reason in areas of their professional practice? Does the hard-nosed, formal, evidence-driven approach extend into 'non-scientific' areas such as assessment? In coming to a judgement about a pupil's ability or potential, what importance do science teachers place on the less tangible, less formal aspects of the process?

In Chapter 12, Patricia Broadfoot describes the territory and makes the point that much effective assessment in the school setting *is* intuitive in nature. How is this manifest, and what store is put on the outcomes of such assessment? In particular, does a science background inhibit intuitive responses to questions about individuals and lead teachers to undervalue intuition as part of the 'ways of knowing' that real scientists rely on?

In order to probe these issues and gain an understanding of the balance and interplay between formal and informal assessment modes, a series of taped semi-structured interviews was held with members of two professional groups: science teachers and general practitioners. While the former were the primary focus, the latter served as an interesting reference group in seeking answers to the question of whether the professional culture and training of science teachers leads them to adopt a different attitude towards intuition to that of another professional group. A comparison rendered more valid since both groups are called upon to use their scientific knowledge and expertise in complex social settings. Of interest too was whether the science teaching community could learn anything about the intuitive domain from the practices and ethos of medicine.

Interviews were transcribed and analysed for common themes and insights into the assessment processes routinely used. Typically, interviews lasted 40 minutes and conversations centred on respondents' understanding of intuition, their use of non-conscious thought processes in diagnostic assessment, their feelings as scientists towards this cognitive operational mode and, with the teachers, on the impact of the curriculum on the development of intuitive skills in learners of science. All the respondents were experienced practitioners and all were concerned with the training of novices in their respective professions.

There is an inherent difficulty in describing thought processes. Articulating the link between thought and action on a moment by moment basis – particularly when many of the thought processes are non-conscious ones – is very hard. Guy Claxton develops this theme of the fine-grained essentials of thought slipping through the coarse mesh of expression in Chapter 2 where he examines another impediment to easy conversations about intuition – namely, the slipperiness and inclusiveness of its definition. Given the limitations of language for describing intuition, it is perhaps not surprising that respondents frequently found difficulty in articulating the reasons why they took specific actions or came to decisions. Almost invariably, intuitive thoughts were described as 'feelings', 'hunches' or as 'just knowing'. There was often some discomfort, too, with the lack of precision attached to the word intuition. While this points up the difficulty or even impossibility of accounting for practice, it also has implications for the reliability of the data gathered during the conversations. This, together with the number of respondents in each group (eight), means their responses should be taken as illuminative rather than representative. I have used their comments, where quoted, to help make a point. Further research would be necessary before more global inferences could be drawn.

The formal and informal in practice

The science teaching context

It was clear from the conversations that the teachers in this survey had built up intelligence about groups and individuals within them, typically taking several months before a differentiated view of the teaching group was reached. The evidence base which these teachers developed was derived from many sources: writing (homework, classwork and tests), speaking (direct and indirect questioning and conversation), reading aloud about science, doing (practical skills observed) and by observing facial expressions and other forms of body language. This evidence had been recorded in formal and informal ways and appeared to include episodic storage in memory. Much of it was generated by working closely (or at least engaging) with individual pupils.

Formal test results exercised significant influence in shaping the more administrative elements of teaching (for example in setting, moving children between sets, determining levels of entry in public examinations etc.). Informal and often intuitive assessments of children (based on collected histories and the 'on-line', non-conscious and certainly unrecorded assessment outcomes mentioned earlier) played a big part in determining the more immediate, moment by moment diagnoses of children's understanding, conceptual difficulties and needs, as well as enriching the personal stories each teacher could tell themselves about a child's developing science understanding. The tension between these two modes was evident in some circumstances, as was the institutional view on the validity of such judgements:

> they've basically got where they are by their written assessment . . . you know, how well they've done in tests etc. It is very difficult, on your intuition, to move a child from one group to another, into perhaps a place where in fact it would be more suitable for them . . . but to try to get a child to understand that or parents to understand that is very difficult. You've got to have the information on paper. You can't just go on your intuition – it's just too abstract.

Some respondents worked in departments which relied almost solely on the results of formal assessment methods, where computer-processed inter-group comparisons drove decision making about children's learning trajectories. In other cases, the sharing of intuitive feelings about children was encouraged at a departmental level. Respondents felt that within their school science community such feelings were valued and seen as 'professional judgement' – i.e. a judgement based on the teachers' knowledge of pupils and not necessarily supported by formal evidence.

This intuitive sense of a child's understanding and level of attainment seemed very secure in the minds of the teachers. All felt that such judgements were based on a sound and extensive evidence base, even though that evidence was memory-located rather than formally recorded. Most expressed great confidence in the judgements they made in this non-conscious way. They saw no conflict between the use of subjective data and their training and status as scientists, although the potential discomfort was acknowledged – in several cases respondents qualified their belief in such feelings by claiming that although they felt they were good teachers, they didn't feel they were very good scientists. In only one case was a scepticism of purely intuitive judgements displayed, but even that was expressed within what might be interpreted as a typical scientist's outlook on the nature and value of evidence generally and was not a specific attack on intuitive feelings *per se*. The conversation was centred on whether intuitive feelings about individuals were trusted: 'No . . . no. I think you just . . . I . . . you trial it and see if it responds . . . I don't trust any evidence . . . I always have to . . . question it and review it and the more repeatable it becomes . . . the more it keeps happening and I keep getting the same messages.' And later: 'I think you'd have to stand up and say, intuitively, I don't trust evidence . . . I intuitively don't trust evidence unless I see it repeated. I don't trust a one-off sample. As I said to you before, if I see evidence in a positive sense that something has been achieved I mark it as achieved. If I see evidence of someone achieving highly, then that's evidence I've got to take on board.'

Within this group at least, intuitive judgements are firmly held and are powerful determinants of action. They may not be wholly trusted, as we saw above, but they exert significant influence on the shaping of expectations. What happens when this personal sense of a child's understanding is at odds with the results of more formal tests? How do discrepancies like this modify the confidence with which such intuitions are held?

I tend to trust my own intuition . . . I just think it's been right so often in the past and all that [the discrepancy] does is put a question mark in my head and then I look for further evidence of what a child is capable of.

I would tend to trust my feeling, but if it's a wide range of evidence – not just a diagnostic test – if the evidence is all of a subjective nature it's difficult to know where I would go . . . I would be tempted to go back and say there's something wrong here . . . I need to get my evidence sources coming together a bit more. They don't usually stay apart all the time.

In that case, I go . . . I look for more formal information about them. So if I've only got in front of me their . . . say, their science scores and I'm thinking no, I do not feel that is a true reflection of what this child is capable of . . . 'cos it's usually that way round, I usually find that these are lower than what I think they should be doing – I will then go into SAT scores, VRQs just to see if my intuition has got any grounding here at all.

There are two significant factors in this trust of professional judgement. The first is a sense of reliability based on past successes in making similar judgements in similar contexts. The second is a mistrust of formal written assessments. Paradoxically, although great store appeared to be placed in the outcomes of formal testing, particularly for pupil setting and reporting to parents, there was a widely-reported suspicion of the outcomes of such tests. While the validity of more modern test instruments like SATs (standard assesment tasks) was acknowledged (in terms of their ability to assess understanding rather than recall), their perceived unreliability was clear. Often this was reported as a feeling that the child knew more than the test revealed, and for several reasons:

quite often they don't read the question or don't understand the questions and quite often put down the first thing that comes into their heads. If you then sit down and put the question in another form, then you'll get the answer – I'm sure lots of kids perform badly in their GCSEs – even A levels.

they're positively disturbed by them. The tests positively upset them. You watch them push the tests away across the desk. Question 1 just has a word in it they can't read and . . . they switch off. It's a 0 out of 10 on the test . . . the next bit can get easy, but they won't read Question 2.

> because your understanding is sometimes based upon criteria which aren't assessed in the tests, which can't be, such as their creativity, their ability to plan, predict . . . they're not assessed; often the assessment is based on pure fact.

Generally, high marks in formal tests were accepted more readily than low ones. When the result was a high mark, it often served to reinforce the intuitive judgement and reassure the teacher, but in cases where such a performance was at odds with the teacher's intuitive judgement, this served to alert them to seek further evidence: 'Sometimes you get a child who produces a very good test result and you think "I didn't think they would achieve that" and you think "right, I'll keep an eye open for them, and see how they perform in future". You don't actually think that, but you make a kind of mental note.'

It was in the responses to poor performance in tests where this stimulus to seek further evidence was most marked. Low scores were mistrusted where they were at odds with the teacher's judgement. In some cases this response was driven by the discrepancy itself, but in others it was based upon a more fundamental mistrust of low performance: 'I don't trust low scores in tests of performance. It's like saying I don't trust a blank exercise book because the kids haven't done any work – that doesn't tell me what they've done. But a full exercise book of original work tells me a lot about the way they're working.'

The medical context

General practitioners are also the product of scientific training and are expected to be thoroughly familiar with an extensive science knowledge base. They use that knowledge and respond to their training in a complex, personal, emotional setting where the stakes are high. Like teachers, general practitioners are required to make rapid decisions or diagnoses of need in a limited time. Unlike teachers, who 'live' with their client community for long periods, their decisions and diagnoses are made on the basis of information gleaned during a consultation which, on average, lasts about eight minutes. This knowledge is supplemented by a patient history recorded in a formal way. A number of decisions must be made during this time – decisions related to diagnosis of condition, to the appropriateness and efficacy of treatments, to whether or not a pharmaceutical intervention is called for, to the risks of polypharmacy, or to whether further research into a condition, investigation of the patient or support from a colleague is required. Other questions which may impinge at this time will be related to factors which may not be so clear-cut – the real reason for a visit or the degree of patient expectation for medication, for example. Some decisions may be capable of resolution on the basis of the doctor's declarative knowledge of diseases, conditions or pharmaceuticals, and superficially these may seem relatively straightforward. Others appear to require more subtle information, less easily gathered and more difficult to describe or quantify:

I make a clinical impression of the needs of the child because the child isn't the initiator of the encounter – the mother is, so I'm thinking not only of why is the child here clinically, but why is the child here socially, and that's down to the mother and not down to the child. So one has to exercise one's mind beyond just the temperament and the poorliness of the child, one has to go beyond that and consider the competence or attitude of the mother.

The dataset on which decisions are made thus comes from formal and informal means. The formal would include the asking of direct questions, the conscious focusing on observable symptoms and the balancing of probabilities amidst considerable uncertainty. Less formal means, which tune in to the nuances of situations are both difficult to describe and difficult to distinguish:

I mean one of the interesting things is . . . the sort of feelings that a person can give rise to . . . those feelings are really very important . . . but again, I wouldn't actually describe those as being intuition . . . I would regard it very much as picking up the, well maybe this *is* what you describe as intuition . . . but picking up the feelings that somebody engenders in me by the way in which they're talking to me, by the way they're presenting their story to me, by the way they're sitting and by the expression on their faces. All those sorts of things that one picks up and reads, all at the same time but really scarcely consciously. But I'm not sure that this is any different to my listening to the story and somebody telling me well, two days ago I tripped over and hurt my ankle. Now is the way in which I receive that information in any way different to the information provided by the expression on their face, or the way they ask their questions or the way they cross their legs or the way they put their hand on my hand or something like that?

This difficulty of distinction and description is also evident in trying to separate intuitive thought from conscious pattern recognition or semi-algorithmic responses based upon previously encountered situations:

My difficulty comes . . . in that I'm not sure, sometimes, whether I can actually distinguish between what is intuition and what is pattern recognition . . . because I think pattern recognition is very much . . . has it's origins in logical thought processes . . . but it's a short cut when one sees a patient with a particular sequence of symptoms and physical signs when you're examining them, and you say 'Aha, I know what this is, it's the sort of situation where I prescribe such and such', rather than going through the formalities of making a diagnosis.

Thus there are many processes which might be classified legitimately under the label of intuition. Pattern recognition, an awareness of the subjective response to patients, the sequential (or even simultaneous) elimination of possibilities and the seemingly non-conscious reading of signals from many sources, as described earlier and dealt with in more detail in Claxton's chapter on the anatomy of intuition, are all evident in the transcripts of the conversations with general practitioners. They are all widely reported in the medical literature too. However described, there is no doubt that, just as we saw in the teacher sample, the more subjective and certainly less formal channels of communication play an important part in assembling the dataset on which decisions are based. Intuition therefore appears to complement more conscious rational processes, as Elstein and Bordage (1979) maintain. They suggest that the intuitive component of diagnosis either helps to limit the range of possibilities so that a more manageable analytic approach may be adopted, or it leads to the early generation of hypotheses (often based on a limited dataset) which can then be confirmed or refuted by a more focused set of questions. In this way the global question of what is wrong with the patient is turned into a more manageable (and rational and sequential?) search for confirming or denying evidence. This is similar in many ways to that sense of intuition as the 'first impression' that kick-starts more analytic problem-solving processes (Bruner and Clinchy 1972).

In any event, the intuitive dimension to skilful decision making was both recognized and appreciated by the general practitioners in this small survey, although there was evidence of a tension between the more artistic or aesthetic aspects of general practice and the scientific medical culture in which general practitioners are trained. This was evident in the degree of comfort expressed by different practitioners in using more subjective data in decision making, as well as in the balance between the two paradigms of practice:

> general practice is a combination of art and science, but I think we've probably gone too far down the road with the art, belief in the art, and less in the way of the science. We've really got to be a bit more accountable and structured.

> I think the other thing is patterns of education as well, because I mean, certainly when I was a medical school student it was very frowned on to use your feelings as a basis of judgement about what was wrong with patients and what to do about it. You were supposed to be the hard-nosed scientist – medical scientist – for whom clinical detachment was very important indeed, and so you made your decisions in terms of rigorously examining the evidence which had to be of a fairly hard-nosed sort in relation to the patient and that particular problem. Whereas I think nowadays people are more aware of the importance of feelings in determining the doctor's response to the patient's problems and the importance of the doctor being aware of these feelings and how this can actually enhance or inhibit the therapeutic relationship.

Discussion

Arguably, a teacher's intuition, and the actions which stem from it, are the biggest determinants in deciding expectations of a learner's future performance, achievement and progress. It would be worrying if this intuitive assessment was no more than a prejudiced view based on ignorance of the quality of a learner's thinking and an assumption that 'teacher knew best'. The evidence from this small study is reassuring on several fronts. The exercise of intuition seems, at its heart, to be the integration of multiple evidence – much of it transient, some of it defying description – into a holistic mental representation which is constantly added to and refined. In Solomon's (1997) terms again, the 'webbishness' of a teacher's knowledge of individuals is enhanced by a process of accretion of evidence from all sources. The approach of the teachers in this study was one of backing up their intuition by seeking more substantive and potentially valid evidence. In a similar fashion to that described by Curtis, Weeden and Winter (see Chapter 13) in their analyses of teachers' assessment processes in art, mathematics and geography, intuitive feelings tended to be the first response of confident teachers who then used more objective criteria to confirm their judgements, especially when those judgements needed to stand up to external scrutiny. Such a loop process will inevitably shape the intuitive 'feeling' for a child's progress as the new assessment information becomes assimilated. It is interesting to note that none of the respondents were claiming that their intuitive judgement was beyond question – indeed the opposite inference could be drawn. Neither were they flying by the seats of their intuitive pants. All were actively (although not in a conscious way) seeking to calibrate their mental mark books, update their pupil intelligence and continually refine the picture they had of a child.

However, such a process would appear to require a substantial degree of 'next to' assessment methods. Both the general practitioner and the teacher need to spend time listening to, talking to and watching their clients, as well as relying on more formal test and examination evidence (and in the case of teachers, on semi-formal evidence such as classwork, homework and projects). In order for science teachers to develop reliable and valid internal 'feelings' for pupils, they need to spend time 'living' with them, engaging with them in science ideas, and by these means informally and intuitively assessing them. The general practitioner seems to have the advantage in terms of dedicated time with the client, for in the typically busy science lesson, one-on-one time is fleetingly brief. On the other hand, the teacher might appear to be better placed for long-term, cumulative growth of knowledge about individuals. Whether or not this longitudinal process leads to a confirmatory bias[1] has to remain an open but extremely important question, however. While intuitive 'internal pictures' of clients seem to be powerful modifiers of more formal judgements, the reverse calibration is also required if subjectivity is to be avoided. An open mind would thus seem to be a professional requisite. Looked at positively, intuition in the cases examined appears to be the engine of more formal validation and further evidence-seeking as well as the unconscious manifestation of such activities. In this respect both groups (doctors and teachers) were, as Patricia Broadfoot points out in Chapter 12, engaging in the complex use and interpretation of evidence and in the integration of diverse sources of qualitative and quantitative data. As she goes on to say, although much of the process of interpretation is intuitive or at least based on an implicit learning about the patient or pupil, the judgements made are rigorous in the sense that they have many referents.

In passing, we might note that pupils too can use their science knowledge intuitively only when the concepts and skills are secure and practised. Both of these requirements (for the development of teachers' *and* pupils' intuitive knowledge) need time and therefore have implications for the content to be taught in science and the methods to be used. Teachers in the survey frequently expressed the view that the concept-heavy and content-laden science National Curriculum rarely allowed time for pupils to play with ideas rather than (simply?) accumulate them, and the science situation was unfavourably compared with other subjects in this respect. They were all pessimistic about increasing opportunities for pupils to use their restricted knowledge-set in investigative, imaginative and creative ways. They foresaw fewer opportunities for teachers to spend more time alongside, rather than in front of, pupils. The latter approach leads to an oversimplification of science teaching (or any other), reducing it to the transmission of facts, some of which stick, many of which don't. We also risk ending up with pupils who, when looking back over the journey through secondary science see, in the memorable words of a sixth-former who had chosen not to study science further, 'a debris of half-baked ideas' rather than a coherent and intuitively accessible framework of concepts. If the nature of science teaching is such that it is damaging to the development of teachers' intuitive grasp of pupils' understanding, then the reliability and validity of teachers' personal judgements will be further weakened. If it is also corrosive of the ability of pupils to process their science knowledge in intuitive ways (and intuitively, I believe it is), then we will come to regret it – we possibly are already – as more and more choose to leave science behind.

Tuition for intuition?

In order to represent more accurately the science enterprise in the classroom, to make science lessons potentially more interesting and in order to develop real-life learning competencies in learners, we may need to change the culture of school science. This is not a new argument, but I repeat it here in the context of developing an intuitive understanding of science. How science is taught is inevitably shaped by the curriculum of what is to be taught. Making more space for children to develop the quality of their thinking and for teachers to assess that quality will require us to teach less. Teaching approaches are also modified by the values held by those doing the teaching, and the training phase is a powerful determinant of these, as we saw in the general practitioner interviews.

The influence of the training process on the future behaviour of professionals is well-known. Whether it is in the realm of declarative knowledge (e.g. the stability of a doctors' personal drug formulary) or practices (a teacher's reliance on particular teaching methods), the effects can be long-lasting. Degrees of dysfunctionality inadvertently introduced at the training stage (or earlier), can take years to eradicate, if they are eradicated at all.

Perceived deficiencies in the education and training of professional groups have led to changes in curricula which, in rhetoric at least, reflect a move away from content-oriented courses towards ones which place more emphasis on the skills of using such knowledge in problem-solving contexts and on the skills of 'information mining'. Such developments are underpinned by an ethos which promotes lifelong learning and continuing professional development. Recommendations for changes in the training of doctors, lawyers, solicitors and teachers have all, to one extent or another, recently followed such principles. Central to these changes is the blend of experiential learning with more theoretical approaches. Experience can only be gained, not given, yet as Kahneman and Tversky (1990) have pointed out, ten years' experience can consist of that period of continuous development or ten years of the same experience repeated. If experience is all it takes then why, as others (Smith and Alred 1993) have asked, aren't schools full of expert teachers and surgeries full of expert doctors? Clearly, experience *per se* is not the sole determinant of expertise. Intuitive processing of information is often posited as another hallmark characteristic of expert practitioners and in this survey at least, we have seen evidence of that. Yet even experts can make poor intuitive judgements, suggesting the potential unreliability of the intuition/experience mix. Two questions are provoked:

- Is the presence of an intuitive processing dimension the key factor which facilitates the progression from novice through competence and proficiency to expert?
- Is it possible for an intuitive disposition to be fostered in the trainee practitioner in order to accelerate this progression? Could intuitive CASE (cognitive acceleration in science education), materials be developed, for example (Adey *et al.* 1989)?

Several authors on intuition in the medical (particularly nursing) field believe that intuition can be fostered in the novice practitioner by paying attention to the kinds of learning environments provided and the teaching methodologies adopted (Pyles and Stern 1983; Benner 1984; Rew 1990; Ruth-Sahd 1993). Central to their ideas are strategies for clarifying, differentiating and analysing intuitive episodes described by nurses. By giving time in the training process to thinking about such experiences, they suggest that nurses learn to reflect on the advantages and disadvantages of basing decisions on such feelings. Such processes would have the additional advantage of highlighting the fragility or transience of some evidence which might otherwise go unheeded. It would also illustrate that some decisions risk being made on the flimsiest of evidence or even none at all.

They suggest that intuition can be fostered in the novice by educators in several ways:

- By raising the status of intuition as a component of expert decision making in courses of professional education. This could be achieved by more overt references to different ways of knowing in conventionally-taught programmes.
- By sharing intuitive experiences with students in group settings so that the differences and similarities of perceptions of presenting situations are highlighted.
- By trusting the validity of ambiguity and encouraging the philosophy that there is usually more than one answer to certain clinical situations.
- By encouraging students to assess the available objective data alongside the perceptual data furnished by their intuition. In this way, both the power of intuitive judgements as well as the fallibility of acting on feelings alone might be demonstrated – the harnessing of intuition as the engine of rational thought rather than the replacing of it. This is perhaps the key component in highlighting the interplay between formal and informal assessments.
- By designing learning objectives that emphasize the process of decision making rather than the decisions themselves in order to make the thinking processes more tangible.
- By encouraging students to trust and act on intuition within a safe, legal and ethical framework.
- By focusing on pattern recognition through encouraging a perspective which emphasizes a holistic view of situations.

Science educators, too, may have much to learn from strategies which work from the inside out as well as from the outside in. Of course, many of the strategies which these writers suggest will be familiar to those engaged in teacher education. Others appear to place a greater emphasis on the subjective as a legitimate channel for data acquisition in the context of decision making, assessment and evaluation. An unfortunate aspect of many science teacher education programmes is the separation of those approaches which foster the toleration of uncertainty and the science itself, which often promotes the opposite. Perhaps if the importance of science teachers' intuition was highlighted in more overt ways when dealing with assessment and teaching matters at the training stage, we might be increasingly successful in creating the more elastic and less rigid culture of science teaching in which creativity can flourish. By extension, we might argue for similar methods to the ones described above in order to create the same climate in the school science laboratory and classroom. An unfortunate aspect of recent curriculum pronouncements for initial teacher training in science, which read more like an aircraft maintenance manual than guidance on how to fly, is that we may be reinforcing the orthodoxy rather than loosening it.

Conclusion

Both groups in this survey – science teachers and general practitioners – value and employ intuitive processes, and there appear to be far more powerful influences than a science background in steering them towards the formal and away from the intuitive – for example, the professional training process and the working cultural context. There are external pressures too which lead to the disablement of intuitive responses (see Broadfoot, Chapter 12). The differences within and between groups may lie in their confidence as clinicians and in the way they use intuition – in particular, in the triangulation of this data with other, more objective and defensible data. In both medical and science teaching contexts, intuition appears to drive the probing, guide the questions and shape the instruments of assessment. On the one hand we might wish to celebrate this less formal, unrecorded mode as not merely a back-up for more verifiable knowledge. On the other, as Eraut (1994) points out, we need to be careful that judgements don't end up being based on remembered encounters selected for their accessibility rather than significance or representativeness. The literature is replete with examples of the contaminants of human judgement based on memory, and so assessments of pupils or patients based on holistic, intuitive, memory-based data needs to be buttressed (but not replaced) by more formal assessments. One encouraging aspect of this work is that while the significance and trust placed upon intuitive judgements seemed secure in the sample interviewed, the importance of the interplay between formal and informal assessment methods came across strongly.

Note

1 In the sense that it results in convergent expectations where one sees what one expects to see, rather than in the opening up of possibilities.

References

Adey, P., Shayer, M. and Yates, C. (1989) *Thinking science: The Curriculum Materials of the Cognitive Acceleration through Science Education (CASE) Project*. London: Macmillan.

Benner, P. (1984) *From Novice to Expert: Excellence and Power in Clinical Nursing Practice*. Menlo Park, CA: Addison Wesley.

Bruner, J.S. and Clinchy, B. (1972) Towards a disciplined intuition, in J.S. Bruner *The Relevance of Education*. London: George Allen & Unwin.

Claxton, G. (1997) Science of the times: a 20-20 vision of education, in R. Levinson and J. Thomas (eds) *Science Today: Problem or Crisis?* London: Routledge.

Elstein, A.S. and Bordage, G. (1979) Psychology of clinical reasoning, in G. Stone, F. Cohen and N. Adler *Health Psychology: A Handbook*. San Francisco, CA: Jossey-Bass.

Eraut, M. (1994) *Developing Professional Knowledge and Competence*. London: Falmer Press.

Heisenberg, W. (1989) *Physics and Philosophy*. New York: Pelican.

Kahneman, D. and Tversky, A. (1990) The simulation heuristic, in D. Kahneman, P. Slovic and A. Tversky (eds) *Judgement Under Uncertainty: Heuristics and Biases*. New York: Cambridge University Press.

Marton, F., Fensham, P.J. and Chaiklin, S. (1994) A Nobel's eye view of scientific intuition: discussions with the Nobel prize winners in physics, chemistry and medicine (1970–86). *International Journal of Science Education*, 16(4): 457–73.

Pyles, S.H. and Stern, P.N. (1983) Discovery of nursing gestalt in critical care nursing: the importance of the gray gorilla syndrome. *Image*, 15(2): 51–7.

Rew, L. (1990) Intuition in critical care nursing practice. *Dimensions of Critical Care Nursing*, 9(1): 30–7.

Ruth-Sahd, L. (1993) A modification of Benner's hierarchy of clinical practice: the development of clinical intuition in the novice trauma nurse. *Holistic Nurse Practice*, 7(3): 8–14.

Smith, R. and Alred, G. (1993) The impersonation of wisdom, in D. McIntyre, H. Hagger and M. Wilkin (eds) *Mentoring: Perspectives on School-based Teacher Education*. London: Kogan Page.

Solomon, J. (1997) School science and scientific culture, in R. Levinson and J. Thomas (eds) *Science Today: Problem or Crisis?* London: Routledge.

Walpert, L. (1993) *The Unnatural Nature of Science*. London: Faber & Faber.

 **10**

Complex decision making in the classroom: the teacher as an intuitive practitioner

Laurinda Brown and Alf Coles

Introduction: orienting

How are the many decisions which fill a single lesson made by both teacher and students? Teachers are continuously making rapid, subtle decisions about how to respond to the dynamic, complex environment that classrooms constitute. Yet they often reach these decisions with seemingly little in the way of conscious reasoning and decision making. So, how do they do it? In particular, what is it that keeps them 'on track' in the midst of all this uncertainty and complexity?

We have investigated this in our own practice. Alf Coles is a teacher of mathematics to 11–18-year-olds in the UK and Laurinda Brown a mathematics teacher-educator. We work together in Alf's classroom, Laurinda an intermittent visitor, each with our own questions and agendas. Laurinda's questions are concerned with ways of working with teachers in training and those new to the profession to develop effective practice. Alf's questions are concerned with developing his own practice as a teacher and the learning of mathematics of the pupils in his classroom. Inevitably questions and themes emerge where our thinking overlaps and finding ways of describing an intuitive practitioner is one common theme. Our work looks at the detail of practice – what we do – using the strategy of giving 'accounts of' (Mason 1994) significant incidents for us and reflecting on, or accounting for those incidents to probe our motivations and implicit beliefs and theories (Claxton 1996). Our approach is situated within and draws upon what Bruner (1990: 16–17) called a 'culturally sensitive psychology', which 'is and must be based not only upon what people actually do but what they say they do and what they say caused them to do what they did. It is also concerned with what people say others did and why . . . how curious that there are so few studies that [ask]: how does what one does reveal what one thinks and believes'.

We have developed an approach which gives a central place to a rather special sense of the word 'purposes'. Let us state our central contention and then unpack and illustrate it. Purposes are a mechanism for staying with the complexity of classroom interactions to develop a range of educated intuitions. These educated intuitions accrue somatic markers (Damasio 1996: 173) which support complex decision making in the moment.

How do purposes and complex decision making manifest themselves as aspects of the practice of a teacher? After an example of a less complex space to illustrate the links between purposes and intuition, we will discuss in some depth what we mean by purposes and intuitions separately. We will then show how we apply our central contention to complex decision making through an analysis of classroom vignettes.

Theorizing

The relationship between intuition, rational analysis and 'purposes' can be most clearly illustrated in contexts which are somewhat simpler and less hectic than the normal classroom. We can also demonstrate something of our 'research methodology' in such contexts. Take the solving of cryptic crosswords for example. Here is Laurinda reflecting on the rather different processes whereby she came to solve three such clues:

> I have recently, after a gap of four years, started to do cryptic crosswords with a friend. The statement 'I haven't got your ability to know what to fiddle with' intrigued me. Of course, doing cryptic crosswords is not always a matter of fiddling. Sometimes the answer to the clue comes with a sort of inspiration. Consider:
>
> Shepherdess and other people keeping it to hit back (6, 2–4)
>
> What is it that made 'Little Bo-Peep' appear in my head? The analysis took me some time and acted as a check on this immediate response: anagram of 'people' with 'it' and 'belt' reversed inside: L(it*tle B*)o-Peep. But this was not an example of 'knowing what to fiddle with'. A better example would be:
>
> Meat cooked with mast from trees (8)
>
> An anagram of 'meatmast' looking for something to do with trees. The word 'stemmata' was not known to me but was created from fiddling with the clue. I confirmed that the word did exist and meant something to do with trees by looking it up in a dictionary. I knew somehow that 'cooked' meant I had to do an anagram even though anagrams are not always clued by 'cooked'. Another example:
>
> Run a horse in the West (6)
>
> What informs my work on the answer here? There is a curious mixture of intuitions and analysis where some of the intuitions are what I call educated, in that although the answer seems to come automatically, in the moment, I am using a lot of previous experience and learning which is

capable, nonetheless, of adaptation. I am not simply using memory. For instance, I could memorize lots of words which could clue an anagram in a crossword, but I have a category 'look for anagrams' which means that 'cooked' becomes a signal for anagram even if I have never seen the word used in that form before. In this clue I am aware that 'run' could mean different things. This is another educated intuition since, from past experience, I know that the compiler will try to mislead! I could look for a small word for horse and place this inside (in) West. Here's where the analysis and intuition combine: 'nag' inspired 'manage', a different interpretation of 'run' than that more usually linked to horses. I checked back, using analysis to confirm the connection to 'West': ma(nag)e. 'Mae', ah! Mae West was an actress. I did quite rightly 'know' what to fiddle with. This does not always bring the reward of the answer to the clue however!

Why talk about solving cryptic crosswords? Because it is possible to watch the effects of doing the same tasks repeatedly in these simple and quite bounded cases. Neither analysis nor intuition is privileged in this activity, both are active and complementary. Such a category as 'look for anagrams' we would describe as a purpose. It is not a goal, as in finding the answer to the clue, nor a motivation such as wanting to get better at cryptic crosswords. If I become interested in solving cryptic crosswords it is likely that someone will explain how to 'look for anagrams'. At this early stage I may forget their advice or start finding myself getting better at looking for anagrams.

The dictionary (*Chambers Twentieth-Century*, 1976) definition of purpose reads 'idea or aim kept before the mind as the end of effort; power of seeking the end desired'. The words 'effort' and 'power of seeking' locate purpose within the realm of energy release. There is nothing here about actually getting to the end, although that is not precluded. The situation is more complex than, for example, a simple urge to scratch which is then accomplished in the moment. Here the urge to scratch and scratching could well be automatic and need not be consciously attended to at all. With purpose, however, we give ourselves the motivation to make effort in relation to some 'idea kept before the mind'. Initially the idea is consciously considered, but an expert crossword solver would 'look for anagrams' without conscious deliberation and simultaneously with many other purposes.

Often purposes are associated with more transformative ideas. Richard Feynmann, a physicist, once said during a television documentary about his life and work: 'I have spent all my life looking for the problem that I will spend the rest of my life trying to solve.' The learning is not in the attainment of the goal but in the process. The purpose of trying to solve a problem is a strong motivational energy for him which leads to learning.

Csikszentmihalyi's (1992) notion of a 'flow experience' seems to be what Feynmann experienced in relation to solving problems in physics. There is a direct relation to purposes:

Creating meaning involves bringing order to the contents of the mind by integrating one's actions into a unified flow experience . . . People who find their lives meaningful usually have a goal that is challenging enough to take up all their energies, a goal that can give significance to their lives. We may refer to this process as achieving *purpose*. The goal in itself is usually not important; what matters is that it focuses a person's attention and involves it in an achievable, enjoyable activity.

(Csikszentmihalyi 1992: 216)

However, in using the word purpose within our current work we are not assuming that all teachers and learners of mathematics will find their life goal in the activity of learning mathematics, although some might. Our purposes are smaller things. What seems important is that purposes are removed in some way from the current action by being longer term. Feynmann's search for his problem is different from his actual doing of the physics. The search for the compiler's strategies for clueing anagrams is removed from the act of solving the anagram itself.

As I start to consciously use a purpose such as 'look for anagrams', I will begin the process of accruing experience of ways in which anagrams are clued. A range of behaviours will develop, connected to this purpose (e.g. reading each word of a clue separately), and depending on whether I am successful or not, I will feel positively or negatively about using that strategy again. Damasio (1996) calls these emotions positive or negative somatic markers. Over time, as my behaviours associated with a purpose become more skilled and more varied, they become what we call 'educated intuitions' – distilled past experiences which fall into patterns but with the possibility of extending and adapting the pattern. Somatic markers act to simplify the decision as to which behaviour to try. Negative somatic markers mean that the behaviours do not even come to mind as possibilities for action. A positive somatic marker means that the behaviour becomes one of a number available for use. The complexity of cryptic crossword solving ensures the continuing coming to know about anagrams, a never-ending process since compilers will always clue anagrams in new contexts. It is possible for educated intuitions to lose their flexibility and descend into habits but in general the person whose educated intuitions are open to adapting to circumstances will continue to learn.

Purposes are a mechanism for beginning the process of learning about crosswords without being inhibited by images of ourselves (positive or negative) in relation to the doing of crosswords (e.g. 'I'm hopeless at them'). What also happens, over time, is that through using the mechanism of purposes, my image of myself in relation to crosswords, my 'emotional orientation' (Maturana 1988) towards crosswords, may change. Such dearly-held central images of self such as 'can't do cryptic crosswords' are difficult to shift but get modified through experiences and actions.

Purposes seem to be in a middle position, both influencing central images over time and allowing the development of effective behaviours, while not being identified with the actual behaviour itself. They are simply stated ('look for anagrams') but ongoing foci to support learning. For an expert crossword

solver there would be many of these purposes but they would be unconsciously and instantaneously applied. Only in reflection after the crossword
has been finished might a comment arise such as 'that was a fiendish way of
clueing the anagram in 12 across' which would give some insight into new
extensions to old categories.

Purposes in our current work

When Laurinda worked as a curriculum developer with groups of teachers
she noticed that in discussing their teaching it was rare for established practitioners to talk in terms of the details of their behaviours in the classroom in
response to particular events. No two events or responses are ever quite the
same and past experience allows seemingly automatic adaptation to events.
As a teacher educator she observed that this fluency of decision making made
it hard for student teachers to see what an experienced teacher was doing.
When she suggested the use of a particular behaviour to a student teacher she
often got the response 'Well that didn't work when I tried it'. It was as if they
were trying to apply a technique blindly without taking the complex context
into consideration. What is it possible to offer as a teacher educator which
might support the development of these student teachers?

What teachers do seem to articulate are purposes. For instance, they
wonder about how to know what their pupils know. For example, at the start
of a topic or theme how can you find out what the individual pupils in your
class know and where they find problems so that you can make decisions
about what to offer? (How do I know what they know?) Established practitioners would have a whole variety of possible strategies which they could
choose to adopt to carry through such purposes. Which one of these they
would use in a given situation would depend on the many factors within a
classroom to which they would have to adapt and they would decide how to
act without conscious reflection.

Beginning teachers need to temper idealistic goals with a realistic assessment of how much skill might be required to achieve them. Engaging with a
student teacher in debate on a philosophical level (about their central images
of mathematics and/or mathematics teaching) did not seem to allow practical
development or change of these images, implicit theories or attitudes. Nor did
giving 'tips for teachers' at a behavioural level do much for their developing
sense of who they might be becoming as a teacher. Discussions at the level of
purposes, however, did seem to be effective in allowing a group of student
teachers to begin to collect together a range of strategies for use.

Laurinda had started to think in terms of three layers of communication
where 'purposes' lay somewhere between detailed behaviours and abstract
beliefs and philosophies, when she came across Nisbet and Schucksmith's
(1986) book *Learning Strategies* and was struck by the similarities between
their framework and hers. In their writing about a hierarchy of learning strategies they refer to central, macro- and micro-strategies. The 'central strategy'

at the top of the hierarchy relates to attitudinal and motivational factors and hence is the most difficult to affect. Laurinda saw her task as working with the student teachers to modify their central strategies and adapted the full model as a way of talking about learning to teach mathematics:

> the central strategy [refers] to teachers' images of mathematics and mathematics teaching, giving an overall sense of direction to their work. Such philosophical and attitudinal perspectives (implicit learning theories and theories of self – Claxton 1984, 1989) build up over time and are certainly not easily transferable, but do inform the decision making necessary to apply lower order strategies. Next I associate macro-strategies with the teacher's purposes. For a particular purpose the teacher often has a range of strategies which could be used at differing times and in differing circumstances. Micro-strategies are identified with these specific behaviours.
>
> (Brown with Dobson 1996: 225)

Such a hierarchy is discussed again in the work of Rosch described in Lakoff (1990). Rosch reported that basic-level categories are 'the generally most useful distinctions to make in the world' (p. 49). Having been shown the picture of a dog we are able to recognize it as such and most people would use the word 'dog' to describe the picture. There would be some individuals who might know that particular dog and so use its name as a descriptor and be able to give details of that dog's individual characteristics and behaviours (interactional properties – see Lakoff 1990: 51). There are also people who would describe a dog in a more general, technical way (superordinate categories – see Lakoff 1990: 51).[1] We were interested in the parallels (Table 10.1) across these hierarchies and started to see purposes as the most useful and most easily expressed distinctions which described and motivated teaching actions. There was, as with the basic-level categories, the feeling of being between detail and abstraction.

When we started to work together Laurinda had been looking for someone, not trained by her, with whom to work with using the purposes model. Alf

Table 10.1 Comparison of hierarchies from abstract to most detailed layers

	Rosch categories	*Nisbet and Shucksmith learning strategies*	*Brown teaching strategies*
Abstract layer (mind)	Superordinate	Central strategies	Teachers' images of mathematics and mathematics teaching
In-between layer (most useful distinctions in the world)	'Basic-level'	Macro-strategies	Purposes
Detail layer (actions)	Interactional properties	Micro-strategies	Behaviours

had recently done his one-year teacher training. For the work to happen there needed to be the identification of a purpose for us to work with in the classroom. This teaching agenda would be generated by Alf. Laurinda encouraged him to look back on the year and think of times when he felt comfortable teaching mathematics in a classroom. This provoked two 'brief-but-vivid' (Mason 1994) anecdotes:

> (1) During an A level lesson on partial fractions I was going through an example on the board, trying to prompt suggestions for what I should write. Some discussion ensued among the pupils, which ended in disagreement about what the next line should be. I said I would not write anything until there was a unanimous opinion. This started further talk and a resolution among themselves of the disagreement. I then continued with the rule of waiting for agreement before writing the next line on the board.
>
> (2) Doing significant figures with a Year 9, I wrote up a list of numbers and got the class to round them to the nearest hundred or tenth . . . Keeping silent, I wrote, next to their answers, the number of significant figures they had used in their rounding. Different explanations for what I was doing were quickly formed and a discussion followed about what significant figures were.

Without any prompting from Laurinda, Alf suddenly made an energetic statement: 'It's silence, isn't it? It's silence.' 'Using silence' was the first purpose that we worked with in Alf's classroom. He had recognized a response from the pupils which he valued – i.e. 'the use of silence forced students to think for themselves about what I was doing and put the onus of explanation on them' (diary entry 1995; Brown and Coles 1996). Our work involved joint planning where we thought through a range of strategies to support and develop this learning environment. What is striking is the large amount of work that has to be done in this early stage of teaching to develop a flexible range of educated intuitions or behaviours different from the novice teacher's own experiences of being taught. There are initially few positive somatic markers outside the comfort range of 'how it was done to me' and yet holistic unconscious analogy (see Chapter 2) is a trap. Working with the purpose of 'using silence' allowed Alf to move away from the use of teaching strategies which had been used on him but which did not seem effective for him in engaging the pupils he taught in mathematics. He developed new teaching strategies and also extended his images of mathematics and mathematics teaching practically rather than philosophically.

Without purpose 'action by itself is blind, reflection impotent' (Csikszentmihalyi 1992: 226). Purposes give the focus which allows the noticing of difference in effectiveness of teaching strategies – e.g. I can sense whether I know more about what they know using different strategies or whether I know in different sorts of ways. The strategies then acquire positive and negative somatic markers for their various applications. In using the word 'purpose' we mean a complex interrelationship of ideas giving the motivational energy for learning and, through the development of somatic markers, allowing complex, fast decision making.

Intuition

In *The Relevance of Education* Bruner (1974) said 'that nothing is known about the training of intuition and that very likely we are still too unclear about what is intended by the word to devise proper educational procedures' (p. 89). This was after the Woods Hole Conference in 1959 which had identified 'intuitive and analytic thinking' as an area for study so that 'education in science might be improved in our primary and secondary schools' (Bruner 1966: vii). This conference led to some important questions and statements for future exploration but progress in developing them proved to be slow to non-existent.

At this conference statements were made such as:

> In mathematics intuition is used with two rather different meanings. On the one hand, an individual is said to think intuitively when, having worked for a long time on a problem, he rather suddenly achieves the solution, one for which he has yet to provide a formal proof. On the other hand, an individual is said to be a good intuitive mathematician if, when others come to him with questions, he can make quickly very good guesses whether something is so, or which of several approaches to a problem will prove fruitful (pp. 55–6) . . . The good intuiter may have been born with something special, but his effectiveness rests upon a solid knowledge of the subject, a familiarity that gives intuition something to work with (pp. 56–7) . . . Intuition implies the act of grasping the meaning, significance, or structure of a problem or situation without explicit reliance on the analytic apparatus of one's craft. The rightness or wrongness of an intuition is finally decided not by intuition itself but by the usual methods of proof . . . What is involved is transforming explicit techniques into implicit ones that can be used almost automatically (p. 60).
>
> (Bruner 1966)

By 1974 Bruner had listed the features of intuitive thinking as 'activation [energy for getting started], confidence, visualisation, nonverbal ability, the informal structuring of a task, and the partial use of available information' (p. 83), and was thinking through the links between intuitive and analytical thinking: 'Intuition is an invitation to go further – whether intuitively or analytically. And it is with the training of people to go further in this way that we are concerned here' (p. 88).

Fischbein (1982: 12) takes the ideas further:

> In its anticipatory form, intuition offers a global perspective of a possible

way of solving a problem, and, thus, inspires and directs the steps of seeking and building the solution. In its conclusive form the role of intuition is to condense – again in a global compact manner – an analytic solution previously obtained. In this form, too, the role of intuition is to prepare action. That final concentrated interpretation is destined to make the solution directly useful in an active, productive, thinking process.

The notion of intuition is therefore multi-faceted and complex. Our intuitions are developed through experiences. These concentrated, condensed interpretations can, of course, sometimes lead to wrong action and so need to be brought into question. What we are interested in developing for ourselves are not just 'condensed interpretations' but educated intuitions that are flexible and adaptable to each new circumstance.

All teachers are intuitive in that they have a set of more or less flexible educated intuitions which guide their behaviours. Whatever novice teachers *do* in response to their classes creates educated intuitions and it seems important that they therefore are not simply trapped by holistic unconscious analogy (see Chapter 2) into becoming by default an amalgam of the teachers who taught them. We become what we do. Often student teachers express concern at their behaviour not being like their image of themselves and, on reflection, report that a particular teacher of theirs used to do that in such a situation.

For student teachers of mathematics, with their range of central strategies (images of mathematics and mathematics teaching), purposes seem to serve a function in allowing them to work together independently of their philosophical stances through a focus on whether the children in their classrooms are learning. The continued sharing of examples of strategies, related to common purposes, allows for a developing range of educated intuitions which creates choice in the moment of decision making and holds off the sometimes dysfunctional automatic response. To act in this holistic sense, working with what the pupils bring and allowing their development, seems to entail another facet of intuition from the typology in Chapter 2, the 'holistic perception of the elements of the problem in relationship'.

The idea is analogous to working on a golf swing in that attention can be given to separate facets of the process (e.g. weight transfer) while still hitting the ball. The expert, however, must put aside the awareness of the separate facets of the swing in order to swing fluently. If the shot is not played well there might be a sense that more attention could be paid to an aspect of the process in reflection afterwards. Similarly, although attention was given to the use of silence in Alf's teaching this was done while still working with the interaction in the classroom. The expert teacher is in the act of teaching, nothing more, nothing less.

In using the idea of purposes we are aware that in the doing of the teaching they are unconscious but provide, as with the many facets of a golfer's swing, different lightings which can be reflected on after the event. The recognition of purposes is again only apparent in reflection after the event and often only if some new learning has taken place for the teacher or something has gone wrong and the condensed, educated intuitions need to be brought into question. One aspect of how an intuitive practitioner might work is in the relationship between reflection and action. It is in reflection (or rumination) after classroom interaction and before the next interaction that different lightings of events can be considered.

The image of an intuitive practitioner that we are developing is of a teacher able:

- to 'stay with the complexity' of the situation;
- to adapt their lessons to the contributions of their students;
- to provide the grit in the oyster and then work with the consequences; and
- to subordinate their teaching to their pupils' learning.

We have found Gattegno's (1987) writing on intuition useful to remind us of this holistic sense of mathematics teaching, not offering simplistic algorithms nor pre-digested lesson structures but travelling with the pupils on a journey, taking different lightings to a problem as they offer ideas, with analysis being used as a tool in this process. Gattegno's definition of intuition as a way of knowing states that it is:

> needed when encountering complexity, and one wants to respect it, to maintain it. In the past, intuition has been called in as a fleeting activity of the mind needed to open doors through which the analytic mind would enter to do the only job that is serious: that of analysis or verification (p. 73). . . Once we become aware that we can function as an intuitive person, we find that all (other ways of knowing) are renewed and capable of serving us as they never have before.
>
> (Gattegno 1987)

Intuition in action

Educated intuitions are formed from what we do and the related positive somatic markers make for fast decision making. Recently however, within the teaching of mathematics, the advent of the National Curriculum has provoked a fragmentation of the curriculum and schemes of work into attainment targets (ATs) (such as number, algebra, handling data) and (initially) of these ATs into statements of attainment. Many schemes of work became the statements of attainment divided up throughout the years of schooling to ensure coverage. It used to be possible to teach something called mathematics where there would be aspects of number, shape, space and algebra in one activity. Connections were made. Instead, a spurious simplicity was found through focusing teaching on single statements of attainment, but problems also arose with this approach. A later version of the curriculum in mathematics encourages focus on working, say, 'from Level 5 to 7' rather than assuming that it is possible to teach each level in turn. Mathematics has always had a negative image in the minds of many adults and children. This is often linked to the way it is taught dualistically rather than relativistically (Copes 1982). Such fragmentary teaching has reinforced this algorithmic approach with a focus on answers being either right or wrong. We are trying to stay with the complexity of the subject and to allow pupils to make connections.

We will illustrate our current thinking about these ideas through an analysis of a series of vignettes from one lesson with a Year 9 group in a comprehensive school, but some insight will be given into what happened in the lessons leading up to and following the lesson in question. We have chosen a lesson characterized by whole class interaction to highlight the differences between this approach and more traditional lessons where pupils are asked to practise a method for solving a problem given by the teacher. The text is taken from a transcript of a tape recording of the lesson and the analysis follows each section of dialogue. The headings for each section are given as particular types of intuition based on categories derived from the earlier discussion in this chapter and from Claxton's typology (Chapter 2).

Activation: 'energy for getting started'

> Alf: I will say that once more. Can you think of two numbers such that when I double the first number and add on the second number I get the answer 48? Just write down your answers . . . OK. Can someone give me an answer?
> Pupil: 12 and 24.
> Alf: Can someone give me another one?
> Pupil: 20 and 8.
> Alf: Yes.
> Pupil: 22 add 4.

> (This sequence continues for some time with Alf writing the responses on the whiteboard as coordinates, e.g. 12, 24).

The pupils are immediately engaged in offering to Alf their meanings in relation to what he has asked them. He does not give an explanation of how to respond to the task but works with their feedback. He chooses to write the responses as coordinates, but otherwise is engaged in the task of collecting what is said and noticing what is happening for individuals within the group. After the offer of the first response there were expressions of surprise from some pupils since their solution was different to that which had been articulated. Were they expecting only one 'right' answer? There is the possibility of developing an awareness of an infinite number of solutions to this statement. The collection of responses began the process of the pupils' mobilization of their own energy and their own sense-making in relation to the task. The teacher holds off the temptation to 'know' what to do next and lets events emerge.

Increasing the complexity to encourage a holistic perception of the elements of the problem in relationship

Alf: Could you give me one other condition, tell me something else which could be true about the two numbers so that it would narrow it down so that just one of those answers would work for both conditions? I'll give you a minute to think about that on your tables. [Working noise] OK. Let's see if anyone's come up with anything from there. Could someone give me a neat way of writing my first condition?

Pupil: 2x + y = 48.

Alf: So when you're giving me your second condition you might want to use x and y perhaps to express it. OK. Can someone give me another condition to narrow it down to one solution?

Pupil: The first number has to be . . . and then double that gives you the second number.

Alf: Right, so can you express it in terms of x and y?

Pupil: 2x = y?

Alf: 2x = y. Would anyone like to tell me the solution that works for both of those?

Alf offers an activity which allows the pupils to experience links with their previous mathematical work. The pupils' responses to the initial task were fine and so he increases the complexity inherent in the problem. This was something that had been planned but is contingent on what the pupils do. It only emerges in this lesson because the pupils have not encountered a difficulty. The pupil who Alf asked to give a neat way of writing the first condition was someone he knew was comfortable with expressing ideas algebraically. The complexity of the task is increased further as all pupils are then invited to express their conditions in this form. This is another point where, had no one been able to express the first condition algebraically, the lesson would have taken a different form. Again the pupils are not being told how to work or respond – it is their job to make sense of the task and Alf uses feedback to adapt the situation to enable the pupils to stay in touch with their own meaning-making.

Judgement/creativity

Alf: OK still with our first condition, can someone give me another condition?

Pupil: 2x – y equals 48.

Alf: Can you try and work out the solutions to both those equations? [Some time is given for students to work on this. After a conversation with the whole group about whether there can be an answer and whether zero is a number, the correct solution (x = 24, y = 0) is offered by a student. Someone else then offers 25 and –2 as another solution. Alf picks this up] Could we try that out? Does that work in both equations? So, if x is 25 and y is –2 what is 2x + y?

Pupil: 48 [Lots of murmurings of this].

Alf:: Can you explain why it's 48?

There were some problems with working with negative numbers and Alf decided to focus on articulations of rules for working with directed numbers. The rest of the lesson was spent working on these. Where did this decision come from? It seems to have been an instantaneous decision in the moment related to the second solution to the pair of simultaneous equations being offered. Yet at the same time it is dependent on all Alf's knowings in relation to his past experiences with this group of students over two terms. There is the heightened attention to detail and flexibility referred to as sensitivity in the typology of Chapter 2. The lesson is created through judgements of what it might be useful to focus the pupils' attention on.

After Alf asks 'Can you try and work out the solutions to both those equations?', he is waiting to make a decision about what to do next. But this decision is subordinate to and contingent upon what is happening in the classroom. When the second solution of the pair of simultaneous equations is generated the possibilities inherent in this for working on negative numbers with the students become apparent. Alf is attending to the students and yet aware of waiting for possibilities to emerge while not forcing them to do so. He seems to be like the man 'capable of being in uncertainties, mysteries, doubts, without any irritable reaching after fact and reason', with 'negative capability' as mentioned by Guy Claxton quoting Keats.

'Working on a specific skill' is a purpose for Alf under which he has developed a variety of strategies, behaviours and skills. In deciding to work on negative numbers with this group these skills, in the form of educated intuitions, are immediately available for use in restructuring the lesson. The fact that a particular choice of action arose in Alf's mind as a possibility showed it carries a positive somatic marker from successful previous experiences of doing something similar.

The focused work on negative numbers emerged out of a complex space at a point where pupils seemed to be experiencing confusion. There was therefore an immediate purpose for the pupils in looking at negatives in isolation and the particular awarenesses that arose from this were linked back to the broader context when the group returned to simultaneous equations. The pupils are supported in making connections between areas of mathematics. Alf does not see his task as giving the class an algorithm or explanation to help them through their difficulty but instead offers a mechanism to help them complexify their understanding of negative numbers. Pupils in this environment do not comment that mathematics is hard or boring or meaningless.

As we saw earlier, approaching cryptic crosswords with the purpose 'look for anagrams' allows the possibility of an entry into the activity free of the disabling effect of negative self-images about solving crosswords. Similarly, the purposes for the pupils emergent from the classroom interaction allow an entry into work on negative numbers, without them being caught up in ideas such as 'I can never do negatives'. The pupils here are not expressing doubts about their abilities, despite getting stuck or confused. There is a broader context in which the work on negatives is embedded, a situatedness which supports sense-making.

Planning

So where did the original offer of the task come from? One aspect of an intuitive practitioner is that no two lessons will ever be the same. The start may indeed be the same but what happens after the start will depend on the pupil's responses. Alf used the identical start with the same group a year later. A pupil offered a second condition with a quadratic term in it and the class worked on ways of finding solutions to one linear and one quadratic equation. The teacher's decision making in the moment is informed by their awareness of everything that has happened within the group for different individuals and on the story of the mathematics which is developing in the classroom. The function of the teacher here seems to be to hold the memory of the group. In planning, the teacher might rehearse a number of scenarios and possible developments but not become attached to any particular one. In fact, in planning for the lesson described here, the possibility of the need to rework negative numbers had been discussed, since Alf had been aware that whenever these arose some pupils had problems. Here the energy generated from the response of the pupils led to more focused work on directed numbers as part of the flow of the lessons.

Given that the teacher is not giving the 'same' lesson, the start has to be created from their awareness of what the group has been doing mathematically and the particular skills of the pupils. Planning includes thinking through what happened in the last lesson and getting senses of direction so that it is then possible to wait for the task to emerge in the classroom, often spontaneously as a sort of insight. In planning for this type of lesson we have developed educated intuitions as to what kinds of activities lend themselves to rich possibilities of adaptation in response to pupils. Principles for such starts include:

- getting some feedback from the pupils to work with; focusing on differences in the feedback; having an action to invite the pupils to do and describe;
- having a sense of a developing story of the mathematics within the idea, gaining both in complexity and abstraction.

These principles have emerged in the work of this one teacher through working with the idea of purposes. It seems important to note that although such criteria may be useful to share with other teachers these are not principles which would necessarily govern the teaching of every teacher nor, necessarily, the teaching of every lesson by any particular teacher. The principles develop through the work with particular groups of pupils and become educated intuitions. This is what makes it so hard to copy the approach of another teacher! You do not have their educated intuitions. What we consider to be important is that the teacher adapts to the responses of the pupils and that the structures of the lesson emerge rather than being imposed.

Pupil purposes

Although our work initially focused on our own practice as teachers, this was in relation to the pupils and we have been increasingly aware of the similarity between ourselves as learners and the pupils as learners. As part of a project funded by the Teacher Training Agency (TTA), we are currently exploring the effects of our using the purpose of 'being a mathematician' to motivate the learning of a class of Year 7 pupils, particularly in relation to their algebraic awareness. As they work they enter a 'community of practice' (Lave and Wenger 1991) where their behaviours such as 'looking at simpler cases' or 'testing a theory' become their own purposes which are similar in effect to 'looking for anagrams' in that they are at a distance from the actual doing of the problem. They also develop a range of educated intuitions to try out for their purposes.

We have evidence from writing by these pupils that working in this way develops positive images of mathematics which has become a meaningful activity. The question 'what have you learnt?' was put to the Year 7 class after one month at secondary school. Some examples of their responses are given below:

> I have learnt it is OK to make mistakes . . . maths is more exciting in secondary school because you can write on the board and make suggestions and talk about the work and write in your books.

> I have learnt . . . you've got to jot little theories down. On a lot of theories you have to write why. You've got to correct your mistakes. You've got to confirm things . . . explain your findings.

> I have learnt that mathematicians write things down even though they might not be true and then they see if the statement is true.

There is a sense of these pupils learning through a process of coming to know rather than the culture implied by their comments of 'it not being all right to make mistakes'. We have also been excited by what they have produced in terms of algebraic ideas seen as one way of proving 'theories' and so still linked closely to the context of the problem as Figure 10.1, written after some eight lessons working on a problem called '1089', illustrates.

Conclusion

The thesis here is that the intuitive practitioner deals primarily with wholes, interacting with the pupils to adapt the whole of their previous experiences of teaching to the flow of the lesson and the story of the mathematics. The pupils

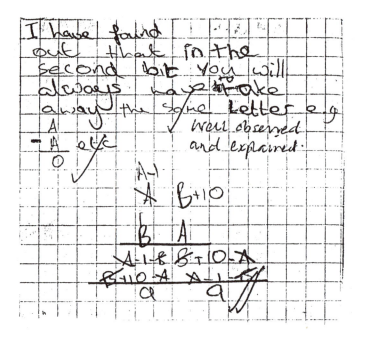

Figure 10.1 Year 7 pupil proving a 'theory'

experience mathematics holistically and 'in flow'. Predigested algorithmic teaching with logical exposition has no place in this world since the focus is on meaning-making; by the pupils of the mathematics and by the teacher of the meaning the pupils are making of the mathematics. However, how does an individual, learning to be a teacher, develop these skills? Classrooms are complex spaces and many decisions are taken – there must exist some principles on which the teacher bases these decisions which happen very quickly, in the moment.

Purposes such as 'how do I know what they know?' developed by the novice teacher can provide an orientation through which rich patterns of behaviours can be organized. We call these behaviours 'educated intuitions' and they carry with them positive or negative somatic markers (Damasio 1996) which help simplify decision making while staying with the complexity of the classroom, as the teacher becomes comfortable teaching those pupils in the classroom and addressing their problems rather than being attached to a preconceived structure. In this model individual pupils also develop their senses of doing mathematics in a connected and holistic manner. Proof, rigour and analysis are parts of mathematics, and important parts, but are not the whole. Problem-solving skills and synthesis are also important. This work creates classrooms where pupils do not see mathematics as an alien and difficult subject and where they are able to work energetically both to solve problems and develop their skills in the subject.

Note

1 Thank you to David A. Reid of Arcadia University, Canada, for this example used in a seminar in the UK, summer 1996.

References

Brown, L. and Coles, A. (1996) The story of silence: teacher as researcher, researcher as teacher, in L. Puig and A. Gutiérrez (eds) *Proceedings of the Twentieth Annual Conference of the International Group for the Psychology of Mathematics Education*, Vol. 2, pp. 145–52. Valencia: Universitat de València.

Brown, L. with Dobson, A. (1996) Using dissonance: finding the grit in the oyster, in G. Claxton, T. Atkinson, M. Osborn and M. Wallace (eds) *Liberating the Learner: Lessons for Professional Development in Education*. London: Routledge.

Bruner, J.S. (1966) *The Process of Education*. Cambridge, MA: Harvard University Press.

Bruner, J.S. (1974) *The Relevance of Education*. London: Penguin.

Claxton, G. (1984) *Live and Learn: An Introduction to the Psychology of Growth and Change in Everyday Life*. London: Harper & Row.

Claxton, G. (1989) *Classroom Learning*, Open University Course E208, Exploring Educational Issues, Unit 13. Milton Keynes: The Open University.

Claxton, G. (1996) Implicit theories in learning, in G. Claxton, T. Atkinson, M. Osborn and M. Wallace (eds) *Liberating the Learner: Lessons for Professional Development in Education*. London: Routledge.

Copes, L. (1982) The Perry development scheme. *For the Learning of Mathematics*, 3(1): 38–44.

Csikszentmihalyi, M. (1992) *Flow: The Psychology of Happiness*. London: Rider.

Damasio, A.R. (1996) *Descartes' Error: Emotion, Reason and the Human Brain*. London: Macmillan.

Fischbein, E. (1982) Intuition and proof. *For the Learning of Mathematics* 3(2): 9–18.

Gattegno, C. (1987) *The Science of Education: Part 1: Theoretical Considerations*. New York: Educational Solutions.

Lakoff, G. (1990) *Women, Fire and Dangerous Things*. Chicago, IL: University of Chicago Press.

Lave, J. and Wenger, E. (1991) *Situated Learning: Legitimate Peripheral Participation*. Cambridge: Cambridge University Press.

Mason, J. (1994) Researching from the inside in mathematics education: locating an I-you relationship, in J. da Ponte and J. Matos (eds) *Proceedings of the Eighteenth Annual Conference of the International Group for the Psychology of Mathematics Education*, Vol. 1: pp. 176–94. Lisbon: University of Lisbon.

Maturana, H.R. (1988) Reality: the search for objectivity or the quest for a compelling argument. *The Irish Journal of Psychology*, 9(1): 25–82.

Nisbet, J. and Schucksmith, J. (1986) *Learning Strategies*. London: Routledge & Kegan Paul.

 **11**

Developing intuition through management education

Gill Gregory

Introduction

> After submitting a sealed bid of $165,000 for the Stevens House, a
> Chicago hotel, Hilton awoke with a hunch that he should make that
> $180,000. He did and the second highest bid turned out to be $179,800.
> The Stevens House is now the Chicago Hilton.
>
> (Nadel 1990: 64)

Senior executives readily acknowledge the use of intuition in decision making
(Agor 1989). Isenberg (1984) conducted a study into how senior managers
think about complex or novel problems. He found that they relied more on
their intuition than on logic to guide them, even though they felt a rigorous,
systematic, analytical approach was expected of them. In a study of creative
business innovators – for example, Bill Gates of Microsoft – it was found that
one of the characteristics they had in common was intuition (Landrum 1993).
Intuition is clearly a significant factor in achieving corporate success.

However, though intuition is a characteristic shared by successful business
leaders, it does not appear on any formal management education agenda.
Instead what does appear is a set of competencies designed to cover the functional aspects of a manager's job, which include managing operations, information, people and finance. This is the core content of a management
vocational qualification. This competency framework offers guidelines to help
a manager achieve best practice. The framework focuses on performance criteria, knowledge and understanding which the manager can demonstrate
explicitly by the production of evidence and reasoned argument. However,
the framework does not accommodate the action and knowledge which managers rely on throughout their working day and which they are unable to
articulate. Polanyi (1967) calls this knowledge 'tacit' – that which we know
but cannot explain. If intuition is a characteristic of successful leaders but does

not feature in a manager's learning, then those concerned with the education and development of managers need to reconsider the content of the management education agenda.

Thus, in the context of intuition and management education,[1] there are three issues which need to be considered. First, the role of a manager is evolving. It is important to consider the context in which managers are now operating and why intuition may be a useful ally. Second, the complexities of intuition, with its many varied forms and definitions, need to be discussed. And third, but most important, is this question: can intuition be developed and if so does everyone have the potential to do so? If evidence can be found to support this notion then there are clearly implications for management education.

My focus on management is predominantly in the commercial sector, but clearly the discussion here is of relevance to the education sector. With the rise of a managerialist approach to education, schools are now being run along the lines of a small business enterprise. Therefore, parallels can be drawn between the role of a headteacher and a senior business executive.

The changing role of the manager

Since the Second World War, the role of the manager has been researched extensively, leading to an abundance of management theories and models. One such theory, which has formed the bedrock of modern management, is that expressed by Henri Fayol (1949), a French mining engineer. He asserted that there were five areas of management activity: planning; organizing; commanding; coordinating; controlling. The model shows them as a wheel, starting with the planning activity, then rolling on to organizing and so on, until the planning phase is reached again and the cycle recommences. This theory encouraged managers to adopt a military efficiency, which favoured a 'command and control' directive style of working. This management style, which is still widespread today, values a systematic, analytical approach towards achieving results with little or no room for creativity or personal initiative. Thus management education has focused on developing Fayol's five key areas, a trend that continues currently.

Parikh *et al.* (1994) and others, however, paint a rather different picture of the manager's role. In today's economic climate organizations are experiencing continual rapid change. Managers find themselves operating in an uncertain and unstable environment. They have to make faster decisions about new and more complex problems. In the past, problems have been solved by analysing all available information and choosing the best solution. For example, if a company wanted to purchase new personal computers, they were faced with a fairly limited range of suppliers. Today, the number of personal computer suppliers is vast and growing all the time. Choice becomes more and more difficult as the differentiating factors are limited. Nowadays, there is an overload of information available and often there is more than one solution to the problem. Even though technology enables information to be processed faster and more effectively, there is always the unnerving prospect that perhaps the chosen solution is not the best one and that there may be more relevant information that has not been considered. Managers are therefore required to be more creative, more innovative, more efficient problem-solvers and more effective decision makers. They cannot rely on previous skills and techniques; they need new ways of dealing with these complexities. Thus management activity today is not solely characterized by Fayol's progressive, five-step model. It is more complex and far less routine. Therefore, managers need to develop new ways of working which will help them to meet current business demands. As previously mentioned, Isenberg's study (1984) showed that managers rely on their intuition as well as logic to help guide their decisions. If this is so, what is being done to help managers develop that intuition? However, before we can tackle that question, we need to be clear about what, in this context, is meant by intuition.

Forms of intuition

The problem with intuition is that it has many forms and definitions. Different disciplines treat intuition differently. Guy Claxton (see Chapter 2) warns of the mystical connotations of intuition. He suggests that there are two variants of this mystical sense which still pervade twentieth-century thinking. One is of a supernatural nature and associated with precognition and clairvoyance. The other is one that totally rejects any form of scientific explanation and rationality and prefers to believe that decisions and judgements can only be based on intuition.

However, it is not the world of mysticism that concerns us here. Claxton offers a family of 'ways of knowing' that have a psychological and cognitive basis. They are not in contrast to reason but work alongside it. These ways of knowing inform our everyday thoughts and actions but are difficult to articulate and explain. Claxton's family includes expertise; learning; judgement; sensitivity; creativity and problem-solving; and incubation. These words which describe the various forms of intuition are certainly more acceptable and credible in the business world. They are concepts and words which managers use every day. It is conceivable, however, that when a manager is, for example, making a judgement, he or she is not consciously aware of being intuitive or does not openly admit to it. Referring back to Isenberg's (1984) study of senior managers, there appears to be a disparity between the rhetoric and the reality. On the one hand, managers use their intuition to help them make decisions, but on the other hand when they are challenged about the process they have used, it is the rational, systematic approach which appears to take precedence in their explanation. Management education continues to build upon the public rhetoric rather than the private reality. Business people and management educators need to be convinced of the connection between intuition and management activity before its use will be encouraged openly in the workplace. We shall now look at how these links can be made explicit by relating Claxton's terminology to business applications.

Expertise and learning

Management expertise and learning are inextricably linked. To become a manager is often seen as a career advancement. In my experience of working in the field of management development, it is often the case that managers do not receive any training until they are well into their management career. Prior to any training, they describe their style as 'flying by the seat of their pants' or 'gut feel'. Managers do not have any benchmarks or frameworks to use. In Chapter 7, Gerald Clibbon and Arlene Gilpin describe a model of professional competence which places intuition on a continuum. At one end is 'naive intuition' where the novice practitioner is not consciously aware that they are being intuitive and at other the end is 'elaborated intuition' where the expert practitioner is consciously using intuition. In contrast to this model of professional competence is the one offered by Dreyfus and Dreyfus (1986). They say that intuition is only used when one attains the level of expert. They make no reference to intuition at the novice level, in fact they say that the novice would be 'adhering to taught rules or plans' (see Eraut 1994: 124). This would appear to contradict the reality and experience of novice managers. While the model of Dreyfus and Dreyfus is useful when describing the development of certain professionals, like computer programmers and surveyors, where a set of rules and maxims are taught at the beginning, and their naive intuition is marginalized, the model is too rigid when looking at the role of a manager. The culture of management is such that managers just slip into a management role and are often left to get on with it. They learn by trial and error. As they have no rules or maxims to adhere to, their naive intuition develops into elaborated intuition covertly. It is not until later in their career, when they may receive some training, that they will be taught some rules and procedures. However, the training usually aims to develop and proliferate the systematic, explicit approach to managing rather than encouraging the manager's already elaborated intuition, thus striking an overt balance between the use of intuition and reason in the workplace.

Judgement

Guy Claxton has alluded to the fact that professional judgement is often intuitive. This is supported by the research into how senior managers think and make decisions (Agor 1989; Parikh *et al.* 1994). However, as Isenberg (1984) has highlighted, there is a tension between the private and public world of the manager's thoughts and actions. Judgement is often prefaced by the notion of having a 'hunch'. When faced with making a decision, even in the light of all relevant data, a manager may decide to take a contrary course of action to what might be expected and call it an intuitive decision based on a hunch or gut feeling. In management terms, hunches and gut feelings can be a risky business but equally they can bring great rewards, especially if the stakes are high – for example, Hilton's bid to purchase what is now the Chicago Hilton hotel. Rowan (1986) provides many anecdotal examples of hunches that can pay off in business settings. He describes many situations where executives have relied on their intuition which have resulted in a successful outcome. For example, Ray Kroc and the expansion of the McDonald's fast-food chain; John Teets and the rise of the Greyhound Corporation in America. Claxton (1997) stresses the fact that hunches can sometimes turn out to be right and sometimes wrong. There are therefore two issues: how to legitimize the use of intuition and how to improve the quality of intuitive thinking and decision making.

Sensitivity

Claxton describes sensitivity as the way in which a person can 'extract the maximum amount of significance from the available information'. One may be sensitive to the subtleties and nuances of the problem, which, to the unintuitive mind could go unnoticed but which could provide the key to solving the puzzle.

In organizational terms, 'scanning the environment' is akin to Claxton's concept of sensitivity. This process could involve piecing together what is happening in a particular sector of the market or looking at what the competition is doing. It might involve examination of trends and historical data. While analysis plays a key role in evaluating the data, intuition provides that feeling of certainty towards a particular course of action. An example of this sensitivity is provided by Goldberg (1983) who recounts how in 1971 a toy manufacturer had an inexplicable urge to increase the production of panda dolls. The following year Richard Nixon made a historic trip to China where he was given two pandas, thus creating a market for these toy items. If managers can learn to sensitize their intuitive antennae and get better at picking up the clues, their skill and judgement in decision making will increase.

Creativity, problem-solving and incubation

It is hard to make a distinct division between these three processes. When managers are solving problems, they often have to employ a creative approach, especially if the problem is novel. Incubation, which Claxton describes as 'rumination', is part of the problem-solving process. The expression 'sleeping on it' describes how one can foster the process of incubation and allow the unconscious mind to get to work. Sometimes a change in routine, which diverts the conscious mind away from the problem at hand, is all that is needed for a solution to emerge. Often a solution may come 'out of the blue' from an intuitive insight. This insight is sometimes referred to as the 'ah-ha' factor, an experience which could be likened to a revelation, like Archimedes' cry of 'Eureka!'

Morgan (1988) advocates that managers need to break from routine to foster a spirit of innovation. This requires managers to distance themselves from the immediate problem and work on something completely different. However, this flexible approach to time is at odds with the cultural norm. While groups are often given a controlled amount of time for participation in creative thinking processes like quality circles, the individual who takes time out to reflect, ponder and search for meaning is frowned upon for not appearing to be productive. The business attitude towards time and productivity needs resolving before intuition can be seen as a credible business ally.

One definition of creativity offered by Kaufmann (1988: 105) is:

Creativity is most intimately linked to problem solving that results in high novelty solutions. However, novelty in thought product does not constitute a sufficient condition for defining creativity. The weird ideas of a psychotic person may rank high in originality and novelty, but we would hardly regard them as creative. To justify the term 'creative thinking', a thought product also has to satisfy the criterion of having some *use* or *value*.

Creativity to a manager means generating novel solutions to new or existing problems that are of use or value to the business. New ideas are the lifeblood on which businesses survive, from strategic business planning through to improving new working practices on the factory floor. Brainstorming is a technique which is widely used and encouraged in business settings to generate new ideas. One of the key factors in the early stages of brainstorming is to postpone rational judgement and logic until the later evaluation stage so as to allow ideas to flow freely (Osborn 1963). However, problems with this technique have been identified and documented (Dennehy *et al.* 1991). As brainstorming takes place in a controlled and forced environment and usually within a group setting, a variety of factors can contribute to the loss of idea generation; for example, the worry that ideas will be negatively evaluated by others, working less due to shared responsibility and ideas being forgotten in the midst of other ideas being generated (Diehl and Stroebe 1986). New ways of idea generation are clearly called for. Finke *et al.* (1992) recommend an individual approach to idea generation, away from the problems of the group setting. Once the ideas have been formed, they are then subjected to critical evaluation in a traditional group setting. This sense of creativity can be achieved independently of a group and is within the grasp of individual managers. It offers a refreshing alternative to the well-worn technique of brainstorming. It is this independent approach which needs to be fostered and developed by managers and adds strength to the debate for including intuition within management education programmes.

Thus far, I have considered the various forms of intuition and their management application. But for intuition to be accepted as a legitimate management process, the following questions now need to be answered. Why do people differ in their use of intuition? Can intuition be developed? Does everyone have the potential to develop their intuition? In what follows, my sense of intuition fits within the realms of creativity, problem-solving and incubation, as described above.

Why do people differ in their use of intuition?

There may be a number of reasons why people differ in their use of intuition. Many of those reasons will be cultural or environmental. Those aspects, while acknowledged as important and contributory factors, will not be discussed here. Instead, I now explore a number of questions which provoke differing views of intuition, views which, by their very nature, impact on the educability of intuition. The five questions listed below form the central theme of a research programme being undertaken by the author and some of the issues, therefore, are speculative due to the research being in its formative stage:

1 Is intuition a personality trait?
2 Is intuition a disposition?
3 Is intuition a skill?
4 Is intuition a state of mind?
5 Is intuition problem-specific?

To consider intuition as a personality trait paints a very 'black and white picture', where the individual exerts little or no control over their psychological make-up. A trait is a personal characteristic that is presumed to stay relatively fixed across different contexts and over time. If this concept of a trait is valid it suggests that some people are intuitive and some people are not, in the same way that some people are cheerful and some are not. This view offers little support to the educability notion, as a personality trait is relatively stable within the individual and is unlikely to change.

If intuition is viewed as a disposition, then this suggests that some people may be more inclined to use it than others. Unlike a trait, which is more stable, a disposition could change over time and across contexts. Answers need to be found to questions like, what factors predispose people to use intuition or not; what are the settings in which intuition is more likely to be used; what type of person uses intuition; what characteristics does a person display when they are using intuition? However, this view of intuition lends itself more to the notion that intuition can be developed, if the right conditions prevail.

To consider intuition as a skill invites us to believe that it is more likely that everyone has the capacity to learn how to use it. However, as with most skills, there are levels of attainment or competence. People who might be regarded as unintuitive, may, in competence terms, actually be 'novice intuitives', whose intuition is not yet fully developed, whereas people who are regarded as highly intuitive could be considered to be 'expert intuitives', whose intuition is very finely-tuned. This view of intuition increases the probability of developing intuition if the appropriate personal and environmental conditions coexist.

Can intuition be linked to a particular state of mind, which can be accessed when the individual, emotional and environmental conditions are right or where the individual may be able to temporarily shut off the outside world and focus their attention inwardly, paying attention to and being aware of their inner thoughts and images? Viewed this way, intuition appears more likely to be educable since individuals could be taught to recognize the mental and physical conditions needed to access an intuitive state.

So far, the focus has been on the individual and personal characteristics that could determine why people differ in their use of intuition. If we now change the focus to the problem itself and consider whether intuition is 'problem-specific' it gives us a different perspective of intuition. This view suggests that intuition might be triggered when people are faced with solving certain types of problems. As the emphasis is on the nature of the problem rather than the person, it implies a likelihood that intuition can be used by anyone. In this instance the learning would need to focus on problem recognition and knowing when, rather than how, to apply intuition.

What we will now consider is the evidence, or lack of it, to support or refute these different views of intuition and, hence, the degree to which intuition may or may not be educable.

Jung (1923) says that intuition is one of four basic, mental functions. It is a way of perceiving information in a holistic way, via the unconscious mind, which is in opposition to sensing, which perceives information through the five senses. It is the habitual prevalence of one of these functions (thinking, feeling, sensing and intuiting) which produces a corresponding personality 'type'. Jung asserts that everyone can use all four functions, but by nature of their polarity, not at the same time. As thinking is opposite to feeling and sensing is opposite to intuition, a person cannot be using sensing and intuition at the same time. Jung says it is the overdevelopment of one function that constitutes our psychological 'type'. Hence 'intuitive types' have a more developed intuitive function. Jung's theory would seem to offer more support to the notion that intuition is likely to be a relatively fixed characteristic, which is stable over time and contexts. As yet, there seems to be no evidence to refute the idea that if intuition is an underdeveloped function, it could, with help and encouragement, be developed.

In addition to the four mental functions that constitute our psychological type, Jung (1923) found that people have either an inner or outer orientation to the world, thus giving us the terms 'introvert' and 'extrovert'. This gives an extra dimension to the four basic types: there can be introverted intuitive 'types' and extroverted intuitive 'types'. A study conducted by Westcott (1968) into how people use intuition found that there was a relationship between intuition and introversion. Westcott's definition of intuition, which is relevant to the notion of problem-solving discussed here, is: 'intuition occurs when an individual reaches a conclusion on the basis of less explicit information than is ordinarily required to reach that conclusion' (1968: 97).

Westcott's subjects were given a set of problems to solve. The experimental variables were how much information they needed to solve the problem, success in solving the problem and their confidence rating on their success. Westcott categorized those people who required a low amount of information to successfully solve the problem as 'intuitive thinkers'. He carried out a series of psychometric tests to find out what intuitive thinkers had in common and found that one of the characteristics they shared was a tendency towards introversion. It would be unwise to dismiss extroverted intuitives as poor problem-solvers or to make the assumption that all introverts are intuitive as a result of the Westcott experiments. Clearly further research is required before comparisons can be made. However, Westcott's research supports the notion that intuition could be linked to personality type.

Based on the work of Carl Jung, the Myers Briggs Type Indicator (MBTI) is a psychometric instrument which purports to measure, among other things, intuition. In MBTI terms, intuition is viewed more as a preference, but one which is more stable and developed. The MBTI, however, focuses on the definition of intuition as holistic perception: people take in information by seeing the big picture, focusing on the relationship and connection between seemingly unrelated events. They want to grasp patterns and are especially good at seeing new possibilities and different ways of doing things (Briggs and McCaulley 1985). While the MBTI's definition of intuition focuses on holistic perception, there is a relevance to the sense of intuition being discussed here, as relationships and connections between unrelated events can often trigger novel solutions to problems.

Another psychometric instrument which purports to measure someone's preference for intuition is one developed by Agor (1992), whose research was gathered from the business environment. While the Agor Intuitive Management survey (AIM) definition is different again, it does have a relevance to this context of problem-solving and decision making. It claims that people who have a preference for intuitive thinking 'have the ability to base decisions on unknown possibilities. [They] have the potential to apply ingenuity to problems, to see how best to prepare for the future and can tackle difficulties with zest. [They] are more likely to prefer management situations that are unstructured, fluid and spontaneous' (Agor 1992: 11).

The MBTI and the AIM would seem to support the disposition theory, as people are predisposed to use intuition in preference to something else. While this preference does not appear to be as fixed as a trait, there is a certain stability implied by the MBTI theory, which, after all, is based on the work of Jung. Myers and Myers (1980: 174) say there is a necessity for choice between opposites, which suggests an either/or approach towards the preference: 'People cannot hear an intuition if their senses are dinning in their ears, and when listening for an intuition, people cannot get information from their senses. Neither kind of perception is clear enough to be interesting or worth sustained attention.' This implies that 'sensing types' should concentrate on developing their sensing function at the expense of their intuition and 'intuitive types' should concentrate on developing their intuition at the expense of their senses. If, as a result of the author's research, evidence can be found to show that 'sensing types' can develop their intuition effectively, this raises questions for the usefulness of the MBTI.

In further support of the view of intuition as a disposition, Vaughan (1979) claims that everyone has the potential to use intuition. She suggests that while it might be more developed and available to some people it is possible for everyone to cultivate their intuition. However, what seems to be lacking from Vaughan's claim is any empirical evidence. Vaughan says key factors that influence the development of intuition are self-awareness and choice. She says that if a person has the inclination to develop their intuition, they can. While the claims made by Vaughan support the educability notion, they offer a rather simplistic view. If developing intuition was that easy, why isn't everyone doing it?

Noddings and Shore (1984) also believe it is possible to enhance intuition. They say important criteria are acknowledgement of intuitive capacity, its existence and the sharing of intuitive experiences. They advocate that these discussions should be part of the psychology of learning and teaching, which would help to bring intuition into the public domain. If this began to happen it would help to resolve the disparity between the rhetoric and reality of business decision making, which Isenberg (1984) discovered. Management educators would do well to heed this advice by reflecting on whether their actions and attitudes adversely affect or positively influence the acceptance of intuition by the management world.

Many management educators and managers are preoccupied with teaching and learning new skills. While the Dreyfus and Dreyfus (1986) model of professional competence referred to earlier was unhelpful when looking at intuition as a form of expertise, it is helpful in illustrating a progression in skill acquisition. The model shows that a learner progresses through five stages: novice; advanced beginner; competent; proficient; expert. This is in line with Clibbon and Gilpin's continuum of naive through to elaborated intuition (see Chapter 7). While there appears to be no empirical evidence to prove or disprove that intuition is a skill, the Dreyfus and Dreyfus model offers a useful framework to show that a person's ability to use intuition could develop incrementally. It would give a learner more encouragement to see themselves as a 'novice intuitive' with the possibility of progression, rather than being classed as 'unintuitive' with no opportunity to change the situation.

Many of us know people who are considered to be highly intuitive, which is seen as a gift or a talent. In certain domains people who display exceptional skill performance are termed 'gifted' which implies that the person has an innate talent for, say, playing golf or playing the piano. While historically these talents may have been seen as 'gifts bestowed by the gods', recent research into expert performance has revealed that attainment of peak performance is due to such mundane factors as practice, structured training and environmental conditions (Ericsson and Charness 1994). This finding contests the view of intuition as a special talent available only to an élite group of people. Their evidence helps to establish the possibility that intuition could be available to anyone who has the motivation and determination to learn to use it, which coincidentally supports Vaughan's (1979) views on the development of intuition.

Practitioners who believe intuition can be developed focus strongly on developing the powers of visualization. Vaughan (1979) asserts that human intuition can be experienced at four levels, one of which is the mental level where imagery and visualization feature. Parikh *et al.* (1994) have developed a model to help business leaders with strategic planning which encourages the use of imagery, symbolism and visualization. One benefit often attributed to meditation is a clarity of thought which might help the receptivity of intuition into the conscious mind. While these factors do not presume that intuition is a state of mind, the evidence suggests the necessity for certain personal and environmental conditions to exist.

So far I have concentrated on intuition within the domain of the individual. I now turn to the question of whether intuition could be triggered by a particular type of problem. Mayer (1995) states that problems can be categorized into two types, routine and non-routine. He describes routine problems as those which the problem solver has solved in the past; they therefore have a known procedure for generating a solution. Non-routine problems are those with which the problem solver is unacquainted; they therefore do not have a procedure to apply to find a solution. The former type of problem would encourage an approach which would rely on past experience and memory, a concept Mayer calls 'reproductive thinking'. The latter type of problem, for which no previous procedure exists, would require the problem solver to generate a novel way of solving the problem, which involves 'productive thinking'.

Claxton (1997) offers another way of defining types of problems – that is, by the number of solutions which exist for the problem. There are those problems which have one correct answer and could be similar to what Mayer calls routine problems. A process of logic and analysis would be an appropriate strategy to these problems. Then there are those problems which by nature are more ill-defined and open-ended and do not necessarily have one correct answer, which are similar to Mayer's non-routine problems and to which Claxton advocates a more intuitive approach. As previously mentioned, incubation can assist the problem-solving process and might be helpful to solve the non-routine or open-ended type of problem. Interestingly, the problems used by Westcott (1968) in his experiments were constructed in a way that meant each problem had only one right answer. If evidence can be found to support the view that intuition is problem-specific, then this might question whether intuition was a critical factor in Westcott's study or whether there was another type of intuition being used, which was different to Westcott's definition.

We have reviewed some hypothetical questions as to why people may differ in their use of intuition and the implications raised concerning the educability of intuition. If management education is to play a role in the development of intuition, learning opportunities need to be exploited so that managers can be exposed to a variety of initiatives.

Developing intuition

There are three types of management education: formal courses leading to recognized qualifications, in-company training programmes and on-the-job experience. During their business lives, managers may experience some or all of these types. Management educators need to consider how to maximize the range of opportunities so that managers can learn to develop their intuition, irrespective of the development route managers choose.

Management qualifications can be gained either through the academic degree route of an MBA or the competency route leading to a Management NVQ (National Vocational Qualification). Typically, as has been mentioned, both of these cover functional subjects such as managing people, information and resources. These functional aspects of a manager's job feature those components which can be analysed, broken down into discrete parts and taught explicitly. If management educators explicitly featured intuition on the agenda in the same way that a subject like finance is featured, it would help first to acknowledge the existence of intuition and second to raise the profile of intuition as a legitimate management process. If managers were made aware of the role of intuition by using the business language of creativity, problem-solving and decision making, its acceptance would be more credible in the management world.

Less formal management education takes place via a variety of methods, including workshops, computer-based training, books, videos, distance learning, projects, secondment and in-company training programmes. These programmes usually take the form of short courses and are usually specific to the organization. They have a company cultural flavour in that skills and knowledge are taught with company policies and procedures in mind. Here again, material on intuition can be made available and explicitly offered to managers, but using the recognizable language of creativity, problem-solving and decision making, so that intuition can start to have an impact on management activity. However, in my experience, new ways of developing managers are not necessarily readily accepted and are often considered just a new 'fad'. Radical shifts in mind sets and attitudes are needed, not only by management developers, but by managers too, if a culture is to develop that allows intuition to coexist alongside reason and analysis. In my opinion these shifts in attitudes and values have to start at the top of an organization. It would seem from the evidence so far that senior managers do not need to be convinced of the value of intuition – as we know, they are well acquainted with it. Perhaps senior managers' education has to be directed towards an acceptance of the applicability of intuition at every level in the organization.

Finally, there are many managers who have never attended, or will never attend any form of management education, either through choice or lack of opportunity. They gain their expertise from doing the job and learning from experience. Arguably there is nothing that management educators could do here, as there is no opportunity for any kind of learning intervention. However, if we accept Clibbon and Gilpin's notion of naive and elaborated intuition, managers need first to be made aware that intuition is an acceptable strategy and second that raising the use of intuition to consciousness will help to validate its use in business. The role of management educators here is to promote this awareness and instead of taking managers away from the job to teach them about intuition they can offer a supporting role as a coach or mentor, using the experience of the job to help the manager to learn. Jung's (1923) notion of the collective unconscious, a form of blueprinting inherent in a species, passed on unconsciously through each generation, suggests that a management mind set that values intuition as a credible resource might ultimately exist.

Summary

Evidence exists to show that intuition is used by senior successful managers in their decision-making processes. However, currently intuition is not included in a manager's education, formal or otherwise. There are many forms and definitions of intuition and to help make intuition credible in the business world it is important to discriminate between the mystical forms and the psychological and cognitive forms. These latter forms can be of legitimate use in the field of management and are the subject of current research by the author. It is hoped that evidence may be found which may help to shed some light on these key questions: why do people differ in their use of intuition; is intuition available to everyone and if so is intuition educable? Earlier in the chapter I suggested parallels could be drawn between senior executives and headteachers. I hope that this chapter has shown the importance of intuition, whether the focus be 'educating managers' or 'managing educators'. Raising awareness of the value of intuition can be achieved through learning interventions, through the development of an organizational culture that encourages intuitive thinking and decision making and, most importantly, through providing role models of intuitive practice.

Note

1 In the context of this chapter the author views management education and management training as interchangeable.

References

Agor, W.H. (1989) *Intuition in Organizations: Leading and Managing Productively.* Newbury Park, CA: Sage.
Agor, W.H. (1992) *Intuition in Decision Making: How to Assess, Use and Develop your Intuitive Powers for Increased Productivity.* El Paso: The University of Texas at El Paso.

Briggs, M.I. and McCaulley, M. (1985) *A Guide to the Development of the Myers Briggs Type Indicator*. Palo Alto, CA: Consulting Psychology Press.

Claxton, G. (1997) *Hare Brain, Tortoise Mind: Why Intelligence Increases When You Think Less*. London: Fourth Estate.

Dennehy, E.B., Bulow, P., Wong, F.Y., Smith, S.M. and Aronoff, J.B. (1991) 'A test of cognitive fixation in brainstorming groups', unpublished manuscript cited in R.A. Finke, T.B. Ward and S.M. Smith (eds) (1992) *Creative Cognition: Theory, Research and Applications*. Cambridge, MA: MIT Press.

Diehl, M. and Stroebe, W. (1986) Productivity loss in brainstorming: toward the solution of a riddle. *Journal of Personality and Social Psychology*, 53: 497–509.

Dreyfus, H.L. and Dreyfus, S.E. (1986) *Mind over Machine: The Power of Human Intuition and Expertise in the Era of the Computer*. Oxford: Blackwell.

Eraut, M. (1994) *Developing Professional Knowledge and Competence*. London: Falmer Press.

Ericsson, K. and Charness, N. (1994) Expert Performance: Its Structure and Acquisition, *American Psychologist*, August: 725–47.

Fayol, H. (1949) *General and Industrial Management*, trans. C. Storrs. London: Pitman.

Finke, R.A., Ward, T.B. and Smith, S.M. (1992) *Creative Cognition, Theory, Research and Applications*. Massachusetts: MIT Press.

Goldberg, P. (1983) *The Intuitive Edge*. New York: Putnam Books.

Isenberg, D. (1984) How senior managers think. *Harvard Business Review*, November–December: 81–90.

Jung, C.G. (1923) *Psychological Types Or the Psychology of Individuation*, trans. H. Godwin Baynes. London: Kegan, Paul, Trench, Trubner & Co. Ltd.

Kaufmann, G. (1988) Problem solving and creativity, in J. Henry (ed.) *Creative Management*. London: Sage.

Landrum, G. (1993) *Profiles of Genius: 13 Creative Men Who Changed the World*. Loughton: Prometheus.

Mayer, R. (1995) The search for insight, in R.J. Sternberg and J.E. Davidson (eds) *The Nature of Insight*. Cambridge, MA: MIT Press.

Morgan, G. (1988) *Riding the Waves of Change*. Oxford: Jossey-Bass.

Myers, I. and Myers, P. (1980) *Gifts Differing*. Palo Alto, CA: Consulting Psychologists Press.

Nadel, L. (1990) *Sixth Sense: How to unlock your Intuitive Brain*. New York: Prentice Hall.

Noddings, N. and Shore, P.J. (1984) *Awakening the Inner Eye: Intuition in Education*. New York and London: Teachers' College Press.

Osborn, A.F. (1963) *Applied Imagination*. New York: Scribner.

Parikh, J., Neubauer, F. and Lank, A.G. (1994) *Intuition: The New Frontier of Management*. Oxford: Blackwell.

Polanyi, M. (1967) *The Tacit Dimension*. London: Routledge.

Rowan, R. (1986) *The Intuitive Manager*. Aldershot: Gower.

Vaughan, F. (1979) *Awakening Intuition*. New York: Doubleday.

Westcott, M.R. (1968) *Toward a Contemporary Psychology of Intuition*. New York: Holt, Rinehart & Winston.

 **Part 4**

Intuition and assessment

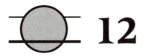 **12**

Assessment and intuition

Patricia Broadfoot

> 'Where is the wisdom we have lost in knowledge?
> 'Where is the knowledge we have lost in information?
>
> (T.S. Eliot, 'The Rock' 1928)

Introduction

And where is the information we have lost in data? asks Priestly (1996). We live in a world obsessed with data; with the collection and dissemination of performance indicators, statistics, measures, grades, marks and categories. In a world in which it is assumed that quality can be defined, compared and cer- tified. And a world in which what cannot be perceived, explained and measured is deemed to be either unimportant or non-existent. The result is what Charles Handy calls the 'Macnamara Fallacy':

> The first step is to measure whatever can be easily measured. This is OK as far as it goes. The second step is to disregard that which can't easily be measured or to give it an arbitrary quantitative value. This is artificial and misleading. The third step is to presume that what can't be measured easily really isn't important. This is blindness. The fourth step is to say that what can't easily be measured really doesn't exist. This is suicide.
>
> (Handy, cited in Madans 1994: 219)

The Macnamara Fallacy is the subject of this chapter. In it I explore some of the historical reasons why we now find ourselves in a global culture that conforms to Handy's analysis; a culture in which 'the myth of measurement' (Broadfoot 1996b) pervades the prevailing discourse to the extent that an obsession with 'measurement' not only dominates the *means* we choose to achieve our ends, but is increasingly becoming *the end* itself. A world in which what cannot be measured in a systematic way is deemed not to exist. Thus the way in which the business of educational assessment is currently conceived represents one of the most powerful manifestations of the tension which forms the heart of this book: the tension between cognition, logic and rationality on the one hand and the complex, subliminal, mental processes we call 'intuition' on the other. Of the many different aspects of the intuitive practitioner that this book explores, none is more central than issues of assessment which have the power both to define 'quality' and the ways in which it should be demonstrated. If some aspects of professional practice cannot be readily defined, quantified or observed, they cannot easily be assessed by conventional means. The result is likely to be that they are not valued. How much does this matter? That is the subject of this chapter.

In the chapter I present three main arguments. First, I argue that there is now overwhelming evidence that we collectively pay a high educational and social price for our obsession with measurement. The high educational price, I suggest, is the failure to mobilize for individuals some of the most powerful potential ingredients of effective learning. Second, I set out to demonstrate that the emphasis on a 'measurement-driven' pursuit of higher standards that has characterized education policy in many countries in recent years has not been successful in raising overall standards of student achievement. Equally it may be argued that it has not been successful in enhancing the quality of teacher education and professional development more generally whether indirectly through the relentless pressure of 'league tables' of school performance or directly in the application of defined 'standards' of competence. Last, but by no means least, I shall argue that the prevailing obsession with the pursuit of 'objective' measurement has constrained education to a point where fundamentally important, but necessarily more amorphous, forms of learning are becoming excluded. This is likely to have potentially profound implications on our wider cultural and social life. In short, it may well be that prevailing forms of assessment influence how learning is encouraged, and the focus and quality of that learning, in ways that can be shown to be significantly out of step with changing social needs. In the light of this analysis, the chapter concludes with a sketch of what an alternative, more balanced, approach to assessment might look like and the potentially powerful effects this could have both on education in particular and on society as a whole.

Already the stirrings of such a change in our thinking about assessment are becoming evident. Increasingly powerful voices are being raised on both sides of the debate so that the present time represents something of a paradox. For while on the one hand the obsession with assessment seems to be becoming daily more powerful, on the other there is increasingly articulate opposition to a society held in thrall by an obsession with mechanistic judgements. There are signs that the breaking down of modernist culture more generally is eroding the blind acceptance of the power of science as the key to human progress and opening up the possibility of new perspectives and debates (Castells 1998). However, it is ironic that, as Wiliam suggests, 'what saved the "scientific" project was that just as psychological "measurement" was discarding inconvenient aspects of human behaviour in order to move towards science, "hard" science was heading in the opposite direction, giving increasing attention to "social" constructs such as the community of scientists (Kuhn 1962) or positive and negative heuristics' (1994: 4).

Thus in education, the prevailing hegemony of 'measurement' has yet to be seriously challenged. What is urgently needed now is the beginnings of an active search for a more humanistic, even intuitive, approach to educational assessment which is more in keeping with the spirit and needs of the times. This chapter represents a contribution to what I hope will rapidly become a substantial arsenal of scholarly ammunition, sufficient to initiate and sustain such a struggle on a scale that can challenge the contemporary worldwide obsession with established forms of educational assessment.

But what might such an alternative perspective look like? The question is not easy to answer because it centres fundamentally on issues of purpose. There are times, of course, notably with regard to the use of student assessment data for purposes of selection, when assessment is 'high-stakes'. In such a situation the emphasis must remain on the pursuit of assessment techniques which are as objective as possible so that they reduce bias to the minimum and provide for comparability of results. Such techniques are central to the pursuit of fairness. Indeed the desire to find an objective means of identifying individual merit was historically one of the main sources of motivation behind the search for 'scientific' techniques that could 'measure' educational achievement. We should not abandon such a concern with the provision of equal opportunities lightly.

The issue is more one of redressing the balance; of fitness for purpose. As I argue in what follows, we now find ourselves increasingly in a situation in which it is the many *other* potential roles for assessment that need to become pre-eminent. Just as the reformers of the nineteenth century recognized the need of their society for a system of impartial judgements of individual competence and relative merit, and for the quality control of institutions, so today it is important to recognize the *new needs* that our contemporary society is generating. These require not only a different technology of educational assessment, but also a fundamentally different conceptual discourse. Increasingly now there is a need to harness the dynamic power of educational assessment to motivate and empower learners. In the more developed countries, we no longer live in a situation where facilities for learning need to be rationed as they were in the nineteenth and early twentieth centuries. Rather the situation is one in which each individual's capacity to take advantage of the opportunities on offer is likely to be increasingly vital to both their own quality of life and that of society as a whole.

Central to such a project is the preparation of students with the necessary skills and attitudes that they will need to meet the challenges of a rapidly changing world. These include self-awareness as the basis for individual target-setting; the capacity to choose rapidly and effectively between a variety of options in order to function in a complex and unpredictable environment; and creativity – the capacity to generate new solutions to problems and to be self-reliant when established procedures are found wanting. Many of these qualities may be subsumed within the broad term 'intuition' which is the subject of this book.

'Intuition' has many potential meanings and is not easy to define. This in itself may reflect the lack of explicit scholarly attention it has received from conventional psychology (Claxton 1996). Contemporary western society's relative lack of understanding of this important area of mental activity compares poorly with that of many other cultures whose technological simplicity belies a high level of sophistication concerning other kinds of understanding. Indeed we have arguably moved so far away from such insights in the contemporary western world that we are hardly aware of what we have lost or the conceptual structure that would be needed to begin to create such forms of understanding.

In his contribution to this book (see Chapter 2), Guy Claxton defines intuition as 'forms of knowledge or senses of knowing that come without explicit justification or explanation, but which can be shown to have utility and validity . . . including expert performance, implicit learning, judgement and choice, problem-solving and creativity; which are holistic, creative and emotional'. This chapter explores the implications of these kinds of learning and performance for assessment. What new approaches might be needed to collect valid evidence of the quality of such insights and what are the new assessment concepts which might be the basis for a more appropriate assessment discourse? The chapter argues that we urgently need to reconceptualize the whole business of education in order to bring it into line with the needs of a rapidly-changing world; to recognize, as part of such a project, the contribution to learning of a range of different functions of the brain including the emotions and a variety of unconscious processes, as well as cognition (LeDoux 1998), and so to challenge the latter's current domination as the almost exclusive focus of our educational efforts.

The chapter's specific focus is the scope for a more 'intuitive' approach to assessment as a means of liberating learners (Claxton *et al.* 1996) from the sometimes disastrous effects of what Foucault has described as the 'disciplinary power of normalizing judgement'. It is to the development of educational assessment that we must attribute much of the form and content of our current educational provision, since it was the advent of public examinations that underpinned the development of classes and grades, syllabuses and school subjects, as well as all the conventional paraphernalia of school organization. It is therefore to change in this respect that we must look if educational institutions are to be released from the stranglehold of assessment's pervasive influence. Not only would such liberation greatly enhance the effectiveness of *current* approaches to teaching and learning; it will be essential to the full realization of the many *new* possibilities of the 'Learning Age'.[1]

Where did we go wrong? Assessment: a modernist obsession

It has become a cliché to say that we live in times of change. As we approach the millennium, the implications of the transition from a modernist to a postmodernist culture are the subject of intense scrutiny in every aspect of life. Central to such change, and to the future we anticipate, is education. If it is true that we are entering the much-vaunted 'Learning Age', we must antici-pate radical new developments in the organization and practice of education. This means more or less fundamental changes in the familiar structure of those institutions – schools, colleges and universities – which have evolved to provide for learning in the modern age. It means major changes too in cur-ricula and teaching methods as new technologies provide opportunities for more dynamic and interactive learning, liberating learners from dependence on the traditional, more 'linear' sources of teachers and books.

Perhaps most significant of all, it means a radical change in the orientation of students themselves to the business of learning. Not since the notion of compulsion to attend school became established as the norm during the industrial era of the nineteenth century has there been such a potentially sig-nificant development. With the benefit of hindsight we can now look back on the history of education in the first millennium as the struggle for learning to survive in the 'dark ages' of militaristic, and frequently anarchic, societies. By contrast, the second millennium witnessed the gradual development of insti-tutions devoted to learning and a growing recognition of the desirability of providing systematically for the development of scholarship and the associ-ated processes of teaching and learning.

The establishment of the major European universities in the early medieval period was a testimony to the spirit of the age. It was also the foundation for the emergence of educational practice as we have come to know it today. Our contemporary curriculum priorities and our assumptions about teaching and learning are arguably still profoundly shaped by the learning culture and edu-cational practices that developed in the early universities. As we enter the third millennium, we need to recognize the fundamental changes currently taking place in our increasingly global society, changes which are rapidly making obsolete these traditional approaches if only we had the benefit of hindsight to see it.

However, even more influential in shaping contemporary educational prac-tice has been the grafting of formal assessment procedures onto the model of education which gradually evolved over the centuries of the second millen-nium. The advent of formal university examinations at the end of the eight-eenth century[2] signalled the beginning of a new era in which educational assessment has gradually came to dominate and shape every aspect of the teaching–learning process from the motivation of students at one extreme to the management of institutions at the other.

Fundamental to this growing domination has been the development of a discourse rooted in a rationalist vocabulary of scientific measurement – of standards and scales; of objective judgements and comparisons. It is a pro-foundly modernist discourse, the product of an age committed to a belief in the power of science and rationality to lead to social and economic improve-ment. Thus it is possible to link the steadily increasing significance of the role of educational assessment with the modernist project more generally and its domination by notions of rationality. The paraphernalia of modern systems of management – such as 'planning, quantification, accounting of revenues, outcomes, performance review, productive and societal contribution – all these are symptoms of modernity' (Barnett 1994: 4), or as Giddens (1990) terms it, 'high modernity'. High modernity is associated with the further strengthening of the techniques associated with modernism including, for example, rationality, scientific legitimisation and accounting.

Assessment has become integrally connected with teaching and learning as we know it in contemporary educational practice simply, yet fundamentally, because in its broadest sense of evaluation (to make reference to a standard) assessment is one of the most central features of the rationality[3] that underpins advanced industrial society itself. Assessment procedures are the vehicle whereby the dominant rationality of the corporate capitalist societies typical of the modern western world were translated into the structures and processes of schooling. As Cherkaoui (1977: 233) suggests, the forms of assessment that emerged with mass education systems must be understood as 'organically connected with a specific mode of socialisation' – a mode of socialization in which preparation for a division of labour, bureaucracy and surveillance were dominant characteristics.

These changes reached their apotheosis in the major scientific, religious and political movements which marked the end of the Middle Ages: the Enlightenment, the Reformation and the French Revolution respectively (Harrison 1998). The most central theme in the changes taking place was that of individualization – individual rights, individual responsibilities and individual opportunities. These three great social movements which both reflected and reinforced the change from a predominantly communalist basis for social integration to one based on a more individualist orientation are of crucial importance in any attempt to understand the contemporary role of educational assessment. This is because it was this new orientation that made possible changes in the whole range of social institutions – notably, politics, religion, law and education. It changed the underlying social values, the cultural discourse that made particular ideas and practices seem right – even inevitable.

One of the central themes of these changes was the growth of a particular kind of rationality. Gordon (1980) suggests that the dominant theme in philosophy from the end of the eighteenth century concerned the nature of rational thought, a theme which constituted the heart of the Enlightenment. Quoting Foucault, Gordon identifies this preoccupation with rationality as: 'the search to identify in its chronology, constituent elements and historical conditions in the moment when the West first affirmed the autonomy and sovereignty of its own mode of rationality, the rationality of the Lutheran reform, the "Copernican revolution", Cartesian philosophy, the Galilean mathematisation of nature, Newtonian physics' (Gordon 1980: 106). This is the rationality of science, of logic, of efficiency and of individual rights and responsibilities.

Thus, the progression from feudalism to capitalism and, in particular, from entrepreneurial to corporate capitalism, may be seen as one in which the ever-increasing power of technical–scientific rationality structures not only the ideology and organization of production, but is more and more pervasive in the ideology and organization of social life as a whole including, notably, education. Reimer (1971: 19) puts the point with some force:

> School has become the universal church of a technological society, incorporating and transmitting its ideology, shaping men's minds to accept this ideology and conferring social status according to its acceptance. There is no question of man's rejecting technology. The question is only one of adaptation, direction and control. The role of the school teacher in this process is a triple one combining the functions of umpire, judge and counsellor.

Thus Foucault argues, like Marcuse, that with the coming of 'modern' society, there is a:

> Proliferation of 'judges' who take the form of technical experts – teachers, doctors, psychologists, guards, social workers. As they operate in a sphere well protected from judicial or popular intervention, an antithesis has developed between discipline and democracy. Disciplinary power coexists with democratic forms and undermines them from within. The roots of discipline are so deep in the organisation of modern society that the subordination of discipline to democratic control is increasingly difficult.
>
> (Sarup 1982: 24)

It is the prominence of individualism and rationalism which has made *thinkable* the concept of assessment as we know it; which underpins a system in which, not only do 'experts' have the power to 'judge', but they are expected and required to do so; in which they are provided with 'tools' which are regarded as scientific and therefore fair and dependable.

Perhaps the clearest example of this rationale and its apotheosis is the advent of intelligence testing in the late nineteenth and early twentieth centuries. In a recent editorial of a special issue of the journal *Intelligence* entitled 'Mainstream science on intelligence: an editorial with 52 signatories, history and biography' Gottfredson (1997) and his colleagues review the research relating to intelligence as measured by intelligence tests and conclude that it is fixed, measurable and probably racially distributed. The vigour with which the protagonists of this view in the USA and their opponents continue to conduct the argument concerning the nature of intelligence[4] provides a very good illustration both of the powerful legacy of nineteenth-century developments in educational assessment and of the dangerous capacity of science to play the role of apparently neutral handmaiden in a debate that is profoundly politically charged.

Another salient contemporary example of this is provided by the fashion for conducting international surveys of student achievement. Despite the acknowledged technical limitations of such surveys in achieving genuine comparability (Atkin and Black 1997) and the even greater difficulty of attributing explanations for the apparent differences between countries (Fletchers and Sabers 1995), politicians and the mass media appear to have little time for such niceties and are more than ready to act on the apparent verdict of 'science' (e.g. see Budge 1997).

I have suggested that the systematic use of formal educational assessment procedures was a defining feature of the education systems which emerged as a response to the new social, economic and political characteristics of the modernist era. Moreover, these procedures embody a typically modernist belief in the power of science and rationality. Educational assessment has played a core role in providing for, and regulating, the competition between both individuals and institutions that resulted from the opening up of the new opportunities which the modern era made possible. To this end it under-pinned the requirement to demonstrate competence by means of some formal evaluation and merit, rather than birth or influence, as a more rational basis for selection.

However, the implicit belief in the possibility of measuring social phenom-ena and in the validity of manipulating such data which was necessarily associated with such developments, has lent to educational assessment all the legitimating power of science. This makes it also an immensely powerful potential means of control over both individuals and educational institutions and systems, for the verdict of data generated in this way is likely to be diffi-cult to contest (Broadfoot 1996a).

Rooted as such practices are in modernist assumptions about the power of science to be the basis of progress, they constitute a powerful inhibitory force to the development of alternative understandings and practices, alternatives that are increasingly being called for in the postmodern 'Learning Age'. More-over, as evaluative data becomes more and more the currency of the edu-cational 'market' (Ball 1998; Whitty and Edwards 1998), assessment activities become associated with powerful new functions that serve further to rein-force their iron grip on education. The mechanisms used to define quality – typically marks, grades or levels – acquire a significance and a degree of trust which belies their fundamentally social origin. They become subsumed beneath the legitimating power of a more or less spurious 'rationality of judgement' (Broadfoot 1984).

So, contemporary society is dominated by assessment. Alongside the now familiar practices of student assessment which are part of formal educational provision, have grown up other applications of assessment, other procedures for collecting, interpreting and judging evidence in relation to criteria of qual-ity in almost all spheres of social and economic life. Activities such as appraisal (of staff performance); institutional evaluation, inspection and audit; pro-vision for accountability and 'league tables' of comparator scores have become an integral part of the contemporary cultural scenery.

The driving force for the increased attention now being given to various kinds of assessment, monitoring and evaluation, appears to be a concern for, on the one hand, providing for maximum dependability of assessment infor-mation and, on the other, both ensuring and demonstrating value for money.

It is also possible to trace a third source of motivation behind many of the current assessment initiatives, notably the reporting of results in terms of a range of 'performance indicators' in comparative 'league tables'. This third source of motivation is based on a belief in the value of competition between both individuals and institutions as a valuable spur to improvement.

In short, it would seem that assessment activity of one kind or another is increasingly being regarded as a management 'panacea' – the key mechanism for both monitoring, and indeed enhancing, quality of all kinds and at every level of activity. Such use of assessment information is necessarily based on the modernist assumption that it is possible to 'measure' quality by applying criteria to the available evidence and, on the basis of this evidence, to form a judgement.

It is further typically assumed that it is both appropriate and desirable to express such judgements in the form of grades or marks; ranks, percentages or levels – that is, quantitatively, or 'categorically,' rather than descriptively, in order to provide a common basis for comparison. This belief – that it is meaningful to identify objectified *standards*, and desirable to use these in order to compare some aspect of institutional or individual performance such as a university's research activity or a school's value for money, on a common, objectified scale – is a characteristic feature not only of contemporary educational *practice*, but of current approaches to educational management as well as of educational policy itself.

Thus schools, and the teachers who work in them, find themselves obliged to pursue the demonstrable quality and excellence which underpin an increasingly consumerist orientation and a market ideology. They find themselves creating a learning environment that emphasizes 'performativity' (Lyotard 1979). This is an approach to learning that has profound long-term consequences both for individual learners and for society as a whole – a point to which I shall return later.

Assessment is, in short, central to the discourse of our contemporary culture, so central indeed that, as Wittgenstein (1965) has pointed out, we find ourselves in a 'linguistic prison'; we have been 'bewitched' by the concepts of educational assessment that emerged during the modernist era to such an extent that even what we are able to think is constrained by the boundaries of that conceptual language. We are in a 'catch-22' situation since

> Our errors are so entrenched in our tradition that it is not possible for us entirely to escape from them. For example, if you wish to criticise the Western idea of reason your criticisms will take no force unless they take the form of rational arguments . . . which therefore will have the effect of confirming it rather than undermining it. So you cannot win. You fight the enemy only with the weapons of his choice, and by your use of them you acknowledge that he has won because you have conceded his right to define the rules.
>
> (Cupitt 1987: 6)

Referring more explicitly to educational assessment, Wiliam (1994: 6) makes a rather similar point:

The fact that construct validation has for so long been taken to be value-free testifies to the power of the discourse in which it has been conducted. Indeed Gramsci's notion of 'hegemony' as a situation in which any failure to embrace wholeheartedly the prevailing orthodoxy is regarded as irrational or even insane, seems to describe the situation rather well.

It is difficult to see a way out of this impasse for, as Winner (1986: 40) suggests, once a 'technological development has been set in motion, it proceeds largely by its own momentum, irrespective of the intentions of its originators'. We are prisoners of our own cultural tools (Wertsch 1901). The artefacts that we ourselves created to serve the needs of a particular time and place now hold us in thrall, like computers which have run amok, and we cannot escape from their insidious power.

'Running against the walls of our cage is perfectly, absolutely hopeless' says Wittgenstein (cited in Priestly 1996). Whether this is so or not, there does now seem to be a groundswell of international opinion in favour of new developments in educational assessment which can be applied in a more valid way in relation to real-life performances and tasks . It is profoundly to be hoped that the very awareness of the chains that bind our contemporary thinking will constitute the key to unlocking them, so that as a society we may gradually come to see that radically different perspectives are possible; that we may begin to evince the beginnings of a vocabulary which is not dominated by the arrogance of scientific assumptions. Not only will this allow us at last to admit the limitations of educational assessment, it will also reveal important new perspectives about the business of learning more generally in which, formally or informally, assessment plays such a central part.

But perhaps most important of all, it will allow us to revive an area of debate which has for too long been silenced by the domination of a technicist discourse of efficiency. Here I refer to fundamental questions concerning the goals of education, questions which themselves need to be rooted in a more general discussion about the nature of 'the good life' and the kind of society we aspire to at the beginning of the third millennium.

The high price of our obsession with outmoded forms of assessment

The misplaced trust

The next part of my argument rests on two core propositions. The first is that educational assessment does not deserve the claims made for it, the weight put upon it. As I shall set out to demonstrate, it is a frail and flawed technology which, although it has a range of legitimate uses, needs to be cut down to size. The second proposition is a more general one. It is also concerned with redressing the current lack of balance in our education system, this time by asserting the urgent need to put 'wholeness' back as a core focus of education, especially with regard to curriculum and assessment. I shall suggest that our current overwhelming preoccupation with a particular approach to assessment has insidiously redefined our understanding of what education is, to the point at which it has become almost synonymous with vocational preparation and economic competitiveness. The consequences of this development, I suggest, are of profound significance both for individuals, as they face the challenge of a very different future, and for society as a whole.

Writing over ten years ago, Malcolm Ross, a leading protagonist for education in the arts, deplored a situation in which:

> Assessment – more precisely 'examination' – is rapidly becoming the sole objective, so it would seem, of education . . . Increasingly our education system at all levels is succumbing to the pernicious doctrine . . . a pestilence caught exclusively off managerial moguls. Emotional enfeeblement and moral degeneration could become the defining characteristics of our society by the turn of the century as today's school children take on the executive role . . . Those of us who resist the march of the assessors do so on the grounds that the loss of happiness is too high a price to pay for a spurious legitimacy.
>
> (Ross 1986: ix)

At that time it was hardly possible to envisage the exponential growth in assessment activity that has characterized the ensuing decade. In schools in England, for example, this includes the advent of comprehensive national testing at frequent intervals throughout the course of compulsory schooling; the regular publication of 'league tables' of examination results; the obligation for schools and local education authorities to engage in detailed target-setting; and a punitive inspection system that provides arbitrary and public judgements of school quality, including naming and shaming those deemed to be failing. For higher education it has meant the advent of the research assessment exercise – formal assessment of each institution's research quality; teaching quality assessment; the introduction of standards for newly-qualifying teachers, as well as attempts to regulate initial and in-service training more generally, and a range of other provisions for audit and the monitoring of quality. Indeed, as the language of performance indicators and audit, quality control and review becomes daily more pervasive in all sectors of education, it is clear that Foucault's 'hierarchical authority' and 'normalizing judgement' have become one of the definitive characteristics of contemporary provision.

This elaborate edifice is built on the rationalist assumption that the data so produced are accurate and meaningful despite the now enormous body of research literature documenting the inherent vagaries of what is, inevitably, a process shot through with human subjectivity. Satterly (1994: 54) for example, documents the many potential sources of 'error' in what has traditionally been regarded as the most rigorous form of assessment – external examinations.

Although assessment can be carried out in many ways, using different modes of presentation and response which yield a number of outcomes, all share at least one common feature: each is based on only a sample of the performance of interest from which the assessor and other users of the result wish to generalise to the invariably much larger domain which it is assumed to represent . . . Research in the psychology of assessment has consistently demonstrated that small changes in task presentation, in response mode, in the conditions under which assessment takes place, in the relations between assessor and assessed and within students on different occasions all have an effect on the performance.

Both from the point of view of the assessor who collects and interprets the data, and from that of the assessee who seeks to demonstrate their level of performance in the way that will gain them the highest marks, the process is one of human interaction. That this is so is well recognized by both students in their adoption of various strategies that will maximize their marks (Miller and Parlett 1984) and institutions who, faced with external assessment, are well aware of the need not only to achieve a high standard in relation to the criteria laid down, but even more importantly, to be able to show it through the appropriate documentation.

Thus Hanson (1993) argues that tests to a significant degree produce or fabricate the personal constructs they purport to measure; that 'reality' is constructed by culture and that tests act to transform, mould and even create what they supposedly measure'. 'Tests', he suggests, are not 'valid irrespective of human expectation, ideas, attitudes and wishes' but control and dominate these (p. 52). The notion of 'absolute' standards which can provide the basis for inter-subject comparability or for the comparability of a particular examination over time has been accepted by those who work in the examinations business as unrealistic (e.g. Cresswell 1998). It has also been demonstrated by historians to be an unobtainable chimera (Aldrich 1998).

But if it is now widely acknowledged by experts in the field that educational assessment is at best a rough and ready process, some might want to argue that it is nevertheless better than the possible alternatives. Whether this is so must be weighed in the light of three factors. First, in broad terms, there is little sign that efforts to raise educational standards through the application of more or less punitive, summative assessments, have had the desired effect. With regard to educational institutions, for example, there is little evidence that approaches which emphasize quality control through various measures of their effectiveness coupled with the stimulation of competition, have been effective. Much more effective arguably, has been the institution of quality assurance procedures which emphasize the incorporation within ongoing institutional arrangements of provision for more formative and dynamic assessment and monitoring procedures. Where there is evidence of improvement, this tends to be in very specific areas. 'We should be clear about cause and effect' writes Wilby (1988: 11), reviewing the available UK research. 'We shall attain precise, narrow targets because we have set precise, narrow targets – not because of any wider reforms. In the past decade billions of pounds have been spent trying to improve our schools. Almost all of it has been wasted. Research on standards from the NFER [National Foundation for Educational Research] suggest that it has had almost no effect.'

Second, more recent studies have shown that such policies result in a widening gap between schools serving rich and poor communities rather than a general increase in standards. Third, and arguably even more important, however, is that such assessment pressures detract from the much more important goal of addressing the new challenges facing education.

The missed opportunities

In the introduction to this chapter it was suggested that we are currently poised on the brink of an era of unprecedented change. Central to these changes is the advent of what is frequently termed the 'knowledge society' and the information and communication revolution. Schools are already changing and will need to change much more in ways that we can as yet barely envisage. One vision is provided by Hanson (1993: 223):

> Schools may have to reconstruct their role in society as the co-ordinating centres of electronically-based learning systems and networks which are open and flexible to inputs from learners faced with the task of constructing their own futures . . . The idea that the outputs of learning can be determined independently of pupil inputs, and pre-specified in terms of clusters of trained abilities linked to a set of stable and unchanging productive enterprises, is already becoming obsolete as a basis for curriculum design and being replaced by the idea of a core of generic personal abilities; cognitive, interpersonal and motivational. The individualisation process in advanced societies challenges schools to develop an education which enables pupils to take active responsibility . . . to locate the development of their natural talents within a personally constructed vision of a life worth living.

Abbott (1997: 2) enlarges on this vision:

> The nature of the changes, whether in the development of learning skills, the practice of teaching and the development of new forms of community – does not represent a comfortable, sequential development; this is not a simple 'step at a time' process but an intrinsic part of a paradigm shift. This is not easy stuff. Practitioners, theoreticians and especially policy-makers have to live both within the here and now (where they have to make present arrangements work as best they can), whilst also preparing themselves to give practical leadership in introducing and cultivating a whole new set of arrangements . . . this is as much to do with the creation of new forms of community as it is to do with children's learning. The old structures of decision-making are constraining the formulation of new ways of doing things.

Clearly the implications of these developments are enormous but at the heart of them, as is becoming increasingly widely acknowledged, is the cultivation of more intuitive approaches to learning, approaches which, in terms of our earlier definition emphasize the cultivation of 'expert performance, implicit learning, judgement and choice, problem-solving and creativity; which are holistic, creative and emotional' (see Chapter 2). Indeed, Stevenson and Palmer (1994: 24) draw a clear distinction in this respect between explicit and implicit forms of learning and their implications:

> Learning may be either implicit or explicit. Implicit learning is found in all animal species and occurs without conscious awareness. Through such learning we come to respond to the regularities of the world in consistent ways. The knowledge gained through implicit learning is itself implicit and inaccessible to conscious awareness. We use the knowledge to act in the world but we cannot describe that knowledge. The ease and rapidity with which we use language and act in the world reveal the extent of our implicit knowledge. Explicit learning is unique to humans and enables us to think deliberately and consciously about what things mean, about how to solve problems and about how to remember things. That is, explicit learning occurs through understanding, problem-solving and memorisation.'

Existing approaches to assessment are almost exclusively concerned with explicit learning, with measuring what has been consciously learned and reproduced in a formal setting. However the goals of learning are likely in the future to centre increasingly on the acquisition of attitudes, skills, and personal qualities since the acquisition of knowledge, formerly the core of the curriculum, is likely to become more and more irrelevant by its universal availability at the push of a button. It is the ability to know what knowledge is needed, to know how to look for it and to be able to apply it, that is likely to become central. Moreover, as Terry Atkinson points out in his contribution to this book (see Chapter 4), a similar tension exists between implicit and explicit knowledge. The intuitive practitioner who is the subject of this book arguably functions primarily by making use of implicit knowledge, using explicit knowledge only for particular purposes such as problems or exceptional situations.

Perkins (1995) identifies three distinct kinds of intelligence: the fixed neurological intelligence linked to IQ tests; the specialized knowledge and experience that individuals acquire over time; and reflective intelligence – the ability to become aware of one's own mental habits and to transcend limited patterns of thinking. Although all of these forms of intelligence function simultaneously, it is reflective intelligence, Perkins suggests, that affords the best opportunity to amplify human intellect. For 'reflective intelligence' read 'self-assessment'. It is the ability to engage in the metacognitive monitoring of one's own learning that is likely to be a central feature of successful learning in the future. Learners will need to be able to monitor their level of application and effort; to set themselves appropriate and achievable learning targets and to review their efforts. The recognition that this is so is well expressed in a recent UK government document:

> It is recognised that individuals will need to be equipped with the core skills involved in managing their own learning such as reviewing achievement, action-planning and self-presentation . . . Many people are increasingly likely to live so-called 'portfolio lives', constantly needing to update their skills and knowledge in order to take advantage of opportunities as they arise. Their skills need to be transferable. The concept of 'qualifying' is changing too. In place of a one-off preparation for employment, which many expected to last a lifetime, we need to encourage the idea of continuous qualifying, a more flexible approach in which continuing, rather than completing, our learning becomes the norm. This changing world will thus place much greater emphasis on individuals taking responsibility for reflecting on what they have already experienced, setting future learning goals and preparing plans for how these will be achieved in order to improve their contribution and their employability.
>
> (DFEE 1997: paras 1.8–1.10)

Moreover there is mounting evidence that herein lies the key to raising standards. In a recent review of the relevant research literature, Black and Wiliam (1998) establish a clear connection between standards of student achievement, even as measured by conventional tests, and the use of 'formative assessment'. For low-achievers especially, the gains can be equivalent to several examination grades. Explanations for why this should be so are not hard to find in the research on learning. They bring us back once again to the importance of intuition:

> The evidence suggests that intuitive theories and beliefs can interfere with learning and may be resistant to change through explicit tuition. However, as if this were not serious enough . . . people also hold intuitive theories of intelligence, and these seem to determine the goals that people set themselves, the way they interpret their own actions and the views they hold of themselves and of others. In short, intuitive theories may underlie people's self-concepts in a way that determines their motivation to learn and the likelihood that they will attempt to learn at all.
>
> (Stevenson and Palmer 1994: 132)

There has long been a well-established body of research available to inform practice on the factors that influence learning but it seems to have had relatively little impact in practice compared to the more common-sense attraction of the apparent capacity of competition to enhance effort. Perrenoud (1993) describes the stranglehold that evaluation currently has on schooling. He claims that it absorbs most of the energy of teachers and pupils; that pupils work for marks and that it encourages war, rather than cooperation, between teacher and pupil. Furthermore he argues that the necessity for comparability encourages a conservative pedagogy with closed, structured activities that lend themselves to traditional assessment techniques because they are readily measurable, rather than higher-order skills which are less so. Change, he suggests, is urgent and needs to encompass a number of different fronts: the evaluation of teaching; teacher–pupil relations; the curriculum; the organization of classes and courses; and selection.

The most important concern of all

The need for change is pressing if we are to make the learners of the future more effectively and more appropriately equipped to cope with the complex challenges of both work and life that they are likely to face. However, the most important concern of all is not a pragmatic one of this kind. Rather it concerns issues of the most fundamental kind regarding the type of society to which we aspire and the part that education needs to play in building it. Earlier I suggested that one of the effects of our current obsession with 'measurement' in education is that it has tended to elevate efficiency to being the goal of education, as well as one of the means of achieving it. It has underpinned the evolution of a discourse which now almost completely excludes discussion of these more fundamental questions about goals. Charles Darwin, who according to his autobiography, seems to have been an early victim of the rationalizing power of science, provides a poignant insight into the implications of a life dominated by such instrumentalism:

> In one respect my mind has changed during the last twenty or thirty years . . . Formerly pictures gave me considerable, and music very intense, delight, but now I have almost lost my taste for pictures or music . . . My mind seems to have become a sort of machine for grinding general laws out of large collections of fact . . . The loss of these tastes, this curious and lamentable loss of the higher aesthetic tastes, is a loss of happiness, and may possibly be injurious to the intellect, and more probably to the moral character, by enfeebling the emotional part of our nature.
>
> (Darwin cited in Ross 1986: ix)

The same ennui has arguably infected education. Here too, minds are increasingly being implicitly regarded as learning 'machines' – at least by policy makers. The magic and mystery of emotion which can bring the whole process alive is subsumed to the necessity of covering the syllabus and doing what is required for the exam. As both Claxton (Chapter 2) and Brown and Coles (Chapter 10) argue in their contributions to this book, contrary to many common-sense assumptions about the source of motivation, most satisfaction seems typically to be derived from meaningful engagement and activity which is divorced from any sense of final reward. Indeed, Brown and Coles cite Csikszentmihalyi (1992), a work that reveals a loss of interest in an activity when it becomes formally rewarded rather than being voluntary. Thus, as Sylwester (1995), points out: 'By separating emotion from logic and reason in the classroom, we've simplified school management and evaluation, but we've also then separated two sides of one coin – and lost something important in the process. It's impossible to separate emotion from the important activities of life. Don't even try.'

The growing number of organizations[5] committed to raising the profile of the emotions in education, and to a more holistic vision, testifies to the steadily increasing awareness that education in the twenty-first century needs to be very different to that of the last century and a half.

Conclusion

At this point in the chapter, readers might be becoming justifiably critical that 'intuition' has become something of a conceptual chameleon that changes its shape to represent any of the shortcomings of contemporary educational organization and practice, and that the analysis has strayed a long way from the more specific definition offered at the beginning. But if this is so, it is not for want of conceptual clarity in the argument. Rather it is because it is indeed the case that at the heart of many of the problems that currently challenge us in education is the issue of intuition – the recognition that human beings are a profoundly complex mixture of different kinds of intellectual processes, some overt, some covert; some cognitive, many not, and that effective education starts with this recognition. Equally it follows that attempts to pretend that a human being's achievement, or even more, their potential, can be unambiguously measured, are doomed from the outset. Assessment is a powerful tool for good or ill; used in ill thought-out ways it condemns those in its power to the at best mechanistic, at worst fruitless, pursuit of arbitrary goals. Against this, it can be the key to releasing the measure of individual engagement that could transform many different aspects of our society.

Moreover, to recognize the importance of fostering intuition is also to recognize that much of the effective assessment that is currently done is itself intuitive, as other chapters in this collection illustrate. For example, Wolf (1995), referring to the learning of vocational competencies, suggests that the assessment of individual tasks is a matter of the complex use and interpretation of evidence. However, it is rigorous since, although much of the process of interpretation seems to be intuitive, or at least implicit, there are many referents for the judgements made. Indeed, though teachers can be shown to be very effective in making such assessments, where they are forced either to make this process explicit – to articulate it – it produces many problems since so much of the judgement being made rests on 'intuitive' 'guild' knowledge acquired during the course of professional practice (Sadler 1989; Maxwell 1996). By the same token, Allal (1988: 42) argues that classroom evaluation 'needs to be approached more as a process of decision-making than as a process of measurement'. She suggests that, typically, teachers integrate diverse sources of qualitative and quantitative evaluative data in reaching a judgement and allocating scores, partly because of their intuitive concerns about reliability.

In short, teachers are already very effective at undertaking 'intuitive' assessment but the continuing domination of concerns for more apparent objectivity is inhibiting the growth of a willingness to trust such judgements:

> the gains for educational and psychological 'measurement' in being based on physical measurement were therefore marginal at best, and almost certainly more than negated by the distortions necessary to make them fit . . . the pioneering work of our best teachers (in relation to 'hermeneutic' assessment) has run far ahead of the available theory, and I believe the lack of theoretical support from the academic community for these innovative practices has made it much easier for politicians to deride and dismiss any assessment practice that does not meet their own aims . . . what we need are ways of talking about what is going on, a language that enables us to demonstrate that these alternative assessment paradigms are no less rigorous or dependable ways of describing the attainment of young people. It is time that educational assessment stopped trying to be a science and found its own voice.
>
> (Wiliam 1994: 7)

Up to this point, I suggest, the vast industry that has grown up around educational assessment in all its various guises has been based on the search for 'continually-improved means to carelessly-examined ends' (Merton 1964: 117). In this search we seem to have convinced ourselves that science can and should extend its methodological grip to the judgement and categorization of learning progress. We have made some gains as a result. In most, but by no means all countries, we have replaced nepotism by merit in the allocation of life chances. We expect people to demonstrate their competence before we allow them to practise. We have been able to introduce a measure of coherence and progression into what might otherwise have been very disorganized educational provision of very variable quality. But we have also paid a high price. As Poincaré said, 'the purpose of proof is to legitimate the conquest of the intuition'. Our pursuit of scientific rigour has taken us almost to the point of forgetting the powerful role of the intuitive in facilitating learning; in judging it; and above all in helping to define the nature of the good life.

Many of those things which are of most value to us cannot be communicated through direct language at all. Kierkegaard, for example, argued that, 'all communication of the spiritual, of the arts, of anything that has value must be through indirect and not direct language' (Priestly 1996: 8). If schools, and indeed all other conventional educational institutions, are not to become what Durkheim referred to as 'museums of modernity' we urgently need to rediscover intuition and to engage with the challenge it presents for education. Only by so doing can we exchange the discipline of 'the assessment society'[6] for the liberation of the learning community.

Notes

1 I use this term which is the title of the British Government's 1998 Green Paper on support for lifelong learning since it effectively captures the scale of the revolution in learning and education of which I believe us to be currently on the threshold.
2 Cambridge University, for example, introduced marks for the Tripos examination in 1784.
3 'Rationality' is taken here to refer to both forms of logic and ideology.
4 Gottfredson, L.S. (1997) Editorial: mainstream science on intelligence: an editorial with 52 signatories, history and biography. *Intelligence* (special issue on intelligence and social policy) 24(1): 1–4. A clutch of articles in support of Hernstein and Murray (1994) argues that intelligence is fixed, measurable and probably racially distributed.
5 For example, Antidote: Making the Case for Emotional Education, London; Remembering Education, Learning by Heart: The Role of Emotion in Raising School Achievement, Brighton: Education 2000 and the 21st Century Learning Initiative, *http://www.21learn.org/test/newstxt.html*.
6 This is the title of a forthcoming book by P. Broadfoot and A. Pollard which explores some of the issues of this chapter at more length.

References

Abbott, J. (1997) Education 2000: The 21st century learning initiative. *Education 2000*.
Aldrich, R. (1998) Standards in historical perspective. Paper presented to British Academy Seminar, London, 8 June.
Allal, L.K. (1988) Quantitative and qualitative components of teachers' evaluation strategies. *Teaching and Teacher Education*, 4(1): 41–51.
Atkin, J. and Black, P. (1997) Policy perils of international comparisons: the Timms case. *Phi Delta Kappan*, 79(1): 22–8.
Ball, S. (1998) Big policies/small world: an introduction to international perspectives in education policy. *Comparative Education*, 34(2): 119–31.
Barnett, R. (1994) *The Limits of Competence: Knowledge, Higher Education and Society.* Buckingham: SRHE and Open University Press.
Black, P. and Wiliam, D. (1998) Assessment and classroom learning. *Assessment in Education*, 5(2): 7–75.
Broadfoot, P. (1984) 'The rationality of judgement', unpublished PhD thesis. The Open University.
Broadfoot, P. (1996a) *Assessment, Education and Society.* Buckingham: Open University Press.
Broadfoot, P. (1996b) The myth of measurement, in P. Woods (ed.) *Contemporary Issues in Teaching and Learning.* London: Routledge in association with The Open University.
Broadfoot, P. and Pollard, A. (forthcoming) *The Assessment Society.* London: Cassell.
Budge, D. (1997) Maths failure lingers after curriculum revolution, *Times Educational Supplement*, 13 June: 20.
Castells, M. (1998) *The Information Age: Economy, Society and Culture*, Vols 1–3. Oxford: Blackwell.
Cherkaoui, M. (1977) Bernstein and Durkheim: two theories of change in educational systems. *Harvard Educational Review*, 47(4): 156–66.
Claxton, G., Atkinson, T., Osborn, M. and Wallace, M. (eds) (1996) *Liberating the Learner: Lessons for Professional Development in Education.* London: Routledge.

Cresswell, M. (1998) Issues in the comparability of standards. Paper presented to British Academy Seminar, London, 8 June.

Cupitt, D. (1987) *The Long Legged Fly*. London: SCM.

DfEE (1997) *National Record of Achievement Review: Report on the Steering Group 1992*. London: DfEE.

Fletchers, T. and Sabers, D. (1995) Interaction effects in crossnational studies of achievement. *Comparative Education Review*, 39(4): 455–67.

Giddens, A. (1990) The Consequences of Modernity. Cambridge: Polity Press.

Gordon, C. (ed.) (1980) *Power and Knowledge: Selected Interviews and Other Writings by M. Foucault 1972–1977*. Brighton: Harvester Press.

Gottfredson, L.S. (1997) Editorial: mainstream science on intelligence: an editorial with 52 signatories, history and biography. *Intelligence* (special issue on intelligence and social policy) 24(1): 1–4.

Hanson, F.A. (1993) *Testing Testing: Social Consequences of the Examined Life*. Berkeley, CA: University of California Press.

Harrison, P. (1998) *The Bible, Protestantism and the Rise of Natural Science*. Cambridge: Cambridge University Press.

Hernstein, R.J. and Murray, C. (1994) *The Bell-curve: Intelligence and Class Structure in American Life*. New York: The Free Press.

LeDoux, J. (1998) *The Emotional Brain*. London: Weidenfield and Nicolson.

Lyotard, J.F. (1979) *The Post-Modern Condition: A Report on Knowledge*. Manchester: Manchester University Press.

Maxwell, G. (1996) *Processes of Judgement of Standards, in Educational Assessments*. New York: AERA.

Merton, R.K. (1964) Foreword, in E. Jacques (ed.) *The Technological Society*. New York: Vintage.

Miller, H. and Parlett, M. (1984) *Up to the Mark*. London: SRHE.

Perkins, D. (1995) *Outsmarting IQ: The Emerging Science of Learnable Intelligence*. New York: The Free Press.

Perrenoud, P. (1993) Touch pas a mon evaluation: pour une approche systemique du changement. *Mesure et evaluation en education*, 16(2): 107–32.

Priestly, J. (1996) Spirituality in the curriculum. Hockerill Lecture. London: Hockerill Foundation.

Reimer, E.W. (1971) *School is Dead: An Essay on Alternatives in Education*. Harmondsworth: Penguin.

Ross, M. (ed.) (1986) *Assessment in Arts Education*. Oxford: Pergamon.

Sadler, R. (1989) Formative assessment and the design of instructional systems. *Instructional Science*, 18: 119–44.

Sarup, M. (1982) *Education, State and Crisis: A Marxist Perspective*. London: Routledge.

Satterly, D. (1994) Quality in external assessment, in W. Harlen (ed.) *Enhancing Quality in Assessment*. London: Paul Chapman.

Stevenson, R. and Palmer, J. (1994) *Learning: Principles, Processes and Practice*. London: Cassell.

Sylwester, R. (1995) *A Celebration of Neurons: An Educator's Guide to the Human Brain*. Alexandria, VA: ASCD.

Wertsch, J. (1991) *Voices of the Mind: A Socio-cultural Approach to Mediated Action*. Cambridge, MA: Harvard University Press.

Whitty, G. and Edwards, T. (1998) School choice policies in England and the United States: an exploration of their origins and significance. *Comparative Education*, 34(2): 211–29.

Wilby, P. (1998) Why not try old ideas, smaller classes, more books? *Times Educational Supplement,* 13 February.

Wiliam, D. (1994) *Towards a Philosophy of Educational Assessment.* Oxford: British Educational Research Association.

Winner, L. (1986) A national testing system: manna from above? An historical/technological perspective. *Educational Assessment,* 1(1): 9–26.

Wittgenstein, L. (1965) Lecture on ethics. *Philosophical review,* l: xxiv.

Wolf, A. (1995) *Competence-based Assessment.* Buckingham: Open University Press.

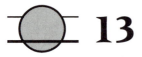 **13**

Measurement, judgement, criteria and expertise: intuition in assessment from three different subject perspectives

Roger Curtis, Paul Weeden and Jan Winter

Introduction

This chapter looks at the role of intuition in assessment from the perspectives of three tutors working in teacher education. We all have extensive classroom experience in secondary schools and the opportunity to work with teachers at different stages in their careers. Our subject backgrounds are art, mathematics and geography and we became interested in the similarities and differences in teachers' practices in assessing their pupils in these three curriculum areas. What are the issues teachers face when assessing pupils' learning? Should intuition play a part in assessing pupils' work, both the product and the process of 'doing' art, mathematics or geography? What role does intuition play in the process of making judgements? Do teachers develop an intuitive sense of potential performance?

We investigated these and other questions in different ways, each adopting an enquiry approach suitable to our circumstances and the contact we had with teachers. The resulting three case studies, while differing in format, tackle the same main questions and issues and give rise to interesting pointers which can tell us much about the effects of recent changes in schools and how teachers have worked with them. Patricia Broadfoot's chapter (see Chapter 12) provides us with a powerful argument on which to base a claim that much of what we want to teach in schools cannot be measured but yet is nonetheless valuable in itself and capable of being assessed. The compelling range of evidence she quotes is supported by our case studies in which the teachers express their own security and strength in their knowledge of their pupils. Their assessments are not always measurements, but they are no less valid for that.

The introduction of National Curriculum assessment in England and Wales in the late 1980s and early 1990s required teachers to review their assessment procedures and to come to terms with using national frameworks of assessment for the first time. The prevailing ethos of accountability and rigour is perhaps encouraging us to lose sight of the role of the professional with 'craft knowledge' which cannot always be simply expressed. While the National Curriculum structure has encouraged a clearer focus and more objectivity in assessments, the new systems resulted in many teachers feeling disempowered and no longer trusted to know about the performance of their pupils.

In considering the conceptual framework for intuition outlined by Guy Claxton (see Chapter 2), there are many aspects of these teachers' work which tally with his definitions of intuition. Teachers deploy a wide range of strategies in order to 'know' their pupils and thus direct their teaching. The idea of intuition as *expertise* is one aspect of most experienced teachers' practice: they do not interrogate every insight and look for evidence to support it because their experience has shown them that they can rely on their insights. They have developed *sensitivity* which allows them to understand the world in which they work and the responses which they get in different circumstances from their pupils. They are often told they should use 'professional *judgement'* – does this mean judgement in Claxton's sense? If so, teachers have every right to feel aggrieved when their professionalism is then doubted and undermined by the conflicting requirement for accountability. Some of the complex and subtle judgements they make cannot easily be opened up for scrutiny to a lay audience – after all, it has taken most teachers many years to *learn* everything they use in their daily work.

These issues will all be examined in the rest of this chapter. Each case study begins with a broad introduction of its context and purposes, followed by the major findings. These findings, which are largely illustrative rather than 'hard' evidence, are organized under four headings:

- intuition in the current climate;
- dealing with work which doesn't 'fit' the criteria;
- the risk of bias in intuitive judgements;
- how teachers' use of intuition changes with experience.

The chapter then ends with a summarizing section which examines the similarities and differences between the situations in these three school subjects. We try to draw out the main lessons which we think can help teachers to examine their own use of intuition in order to make it, and their pupils' learning, more effective. One further lesson that is explored is how to develop intuitive 'expertise'.

The role of intuition in the assessment of art (Roger Curtis)

The context

Patricia Broadfoot's analysis of the recent history of education with its emphasis on the scientific, rational and explicit strikes a familiar chord with arts educators who tend to feel that the education system has restricted opportunities for young people to explore their own feelings and sensations, thereby restricting their ability to cope effectively with the world.

The Gulbenkian Foundation Report, *The Arts in Schools* (1982) claimed that 'Society needs and values more than academic abilities. Children and young people have more to offer. The Arts exemplify some of these other capacities – intuition, creativity, sensibility and practical skills. We maintain that an education in these is quite as important as an education of the more academic kind and that *not* to have this is to stunt and distort their growth as intelligent, feeling and capable individuals'. This is, unfortunately, a far cry from the reality of many art rooms where work is often prescriptive and the outcomes preordained. Tom Davies (1995: 24) claims that 'examination success is largely the manipulation of formulae (teaching) and pupils are directed to the production of acceptable evidence'. There are many possible reasons for this: public accountability; a lack of time; the pressure for examination success; a fear of risk-taking and the need to manage often quite large teaching groups. However, this is not the whole picture. I have visited many art departments where there is a diversity of work, and students, particularly in examination classes, are encouraged to explore ideas and media in considerable depth and produce highly personal work.

How then do teachers on the ground carry out assessments in art? What are the qualities they are looking for? Does intuition have a part to play in the assessment process? In order that I might find some answers to these questions I invited a number of teachers and examiners, with a range of experience, to complete a questionnaire related to various aspects of their practice. In addition, two meetings took place with a small group of teachers in which responses to the questionnaire and some of my initial thoughts about the role of intuition in art and its assessment were discussed.

Intuition in the current climate

The role of intuition in assessment of students' art work presents particular problems as the tensions between the subjective and objective, and the intuitive and explicit, are unavoidable. Eisner (1996: 111) suggests that, 'There has always been an uneasy relationship between art education and evaluation and assessment' which he believes 'puts a premium on predictability, rationality, and precision, features that are not typically associated with the emotional, unpredictable, and ambiguous features of the artistic process.'

As a way of establishing the main strategies used in assessing art work I asked teachers to describe the methods they employed to build up a picture of the relative abilities of pupils. These included: observing how students handled materials; observing their reactions to success or failure; noting their comments about their own work and that of others; observing the different ways in which they developed ideas; looking out for the unpredictable response; looking for evidence of the ability to work independently and evidence of understanding in their practical work, in sketchbooks and written evaluations; noting levels of participation in group work and evidence of enthusiasm and involvement. These responses suggest that art teachers are as interested in *how* pupils work as much as *what* they produce. They appear to be looking for indications of more than that which is immediately apparent.

When asked what specific characteristics they were looking for in pupils' work the teachers included: creativity and imagination; technical ability; energy and enthusiasm; the ability to explore ideas in depth; evidence of divergent thinking; the ability to 'play with ideas' and experiment with media; aesthetic judgement and response; the ability to follow their own lines of enquiry and make connections; self-expression and understanding and awareness of the work of others. This suggests that the qualities which teachers regard as important are those which are associated with students working in an innovative environment, with a significant degree of independence, producing work in which they have opportunities to respond to personal issues and enthusiasms.

One of the main difficulties encountered in assessing art lies in the nature of art itself. A work of art acts as an interface between the artist and the viewer. Artists may not fully understand what they produce. They have intentions and work within the context of their experience, but making art involves a range of conscious and unconscious processes. Art which is predictable is rarely satisfying. The road that many artists travel is rarely a smooth one and includes frequent blind alleys. Intuition is central to this journey. It might be seen as the lubricant which unlocks creativity and enables the artist to discover unexpected solutions to problems. A work of art seldom matches the artist's original intentions.

Similarly, the process of responding to art is also far from straightforward or predictable and by its very nature cannot be adequately conveyed in words. Perkins (1994) maintains that appreciating works of art requires time and effort and needs to be 'thought through'. This process involves different kinds of cognition which he claims can lead to 'better thinking'. It is a process in which new layers of meaning are revealed by intense and informed looking, allowing the work to 'speak' for itself.

My own experience should help to illustrate this point. When I visit a gallery I usually move through the collection quickly, making a mental note of exhibits which 'catch my eye'. I then return to them and spend time 'getting to know them'. My first encounter will be largely governed by an immediate, instinctive, intuitive response. Other factors will affect my choice such as personal preferences and prejudices, the influence of other people's opinions (friends, critics, artists etc.) and my mood at the time, but without the oxygen of the intuitive response my interest might never be ignited.

It would seem, therefore, that the experience of making and viewing art can unleash powerful sensations and that intuition is profoundly implicated in both processes. These feelings, sensations or gut reactions may be deeply felt but are difficult to pin down, describe or explain. In this case, how are these qualities recognized in the current climate?

Somewhat surprisingly, the National Curriculum order for art makes no mention of intuition. The programmes of study require that pupils should be given opportunities to 'develop visual perception . . . creative and imaginative skills' and 'express ideas and feelings' but intuition fails to surface (DfE 1995: 6).

The requirements which 'describe the types and range of performance the majority of pupils should characteristically demonstrate by the end of the key stage' do not mention intuition, innovation, exploration or risk-taking – the qualities which one might readily associate with experience in the arts. The descriptions suggest that assessment in art should be based only on what can be objectively identified, analysed and quantified. The criticism of this approach is that it can lead to somewhat predictable, preordained responses. Is this the result of pragmatism or is it the reflection of a deeper malaise?

Arthur Hughes (1998: 41) maintains that, 'As we move towards the Millennium, we are still delivering art curricula in our schools predicated largely upon procedures and practices which reach back to the nineteenth century – procedures and practices which cling to a comfortable and unpretentious view of art and its purposes.' The orthodoxy of approach which, he suggests, exists throughout secondary education may owe much to the current climate which appears to be dominated by league tables and accountability. This is a climate in which there are few opportunities for risk-taking and the development of genuinely individual and innovative work, in which students have opportunities to deal with difficult and challenging issues.

The fact that art teachers 'play safe' is not surprising when one considers the context within which they are working. Contemporary art is dominated by contentious, provocative and often shocking imagery which may only be understood by an élite band of critics and ardent 'gallery goers'. On the other hand 'school art' is buoyant and apparently successful. Intuition might simply be one of the casualties of art teachers being prepared to play the assessment game.

Dealing with work that doesn't fit the criteria

One of the issues which arose from my discussions with teachers was the difficulty of dealing with the idiosyncratic students whose work did not match examination requirements. These students are often considered to be very able but fail to meet assessment requirements as their work lacks a logical and coherent pattern of development. They encounter many 'false dawns' and the connections they make may lack clarity and direction but they are capable of 'making instinctive leaps'. Their work might contain moments of sheer inspiration or imagination and have qualities of completeness which are difficult to define. One teacher recently summed up these qualities as *synthesis*: the coming together of ideas, media and images which simply 'feel right and indicate a deeper level of understanding and genuine innovation'. These students tend to rely heavily on their intuition to guide the direction and outcome of their work. As one teacher remarked: 'Current assessment doesn't cope with students who start with the material or who find objects and work intuitively with these – but they are probably nearer to the "true artist" '.

I came across twins who excelled in every subject and who exhibited qualities which could readily be associated with genius. The art department decided to enter them for A levels with two different boards as they had an immense body of coursework. They both gained A grades with the first board but were awarded B and C grades by the second. Asked to explain this discrepancy, the teacher said that although they had this tremendous innate ability, their work did not fit the usual conventions associated with work at this level. Genuinely innovative work has qualities which are difficult to pin down and assess.

The risk of bias in intuitive judgements

The example above clearly illustrates the subjective nature of the assessment process even when using apparently objective criteria. In contrast, Mary Figg (former SEG GCSE chief examiner) stated in response to my questionnaire that we cannot count on intuition 'because there is no agreed coherent aesthetic policy or understanding of philosophical concepts behind the intuitive response'. Similar views were expressed by teachers – for example, 'I have no idea how you would begin to implement the role of intuition in assessment. Every time you feel anyone is on the same wavelength a different person makes a completely different observation and the moment of understanding and empathy is gone.'

But perhaps the greatest risk is not taking the risk. However difficult, a far more conscious effort is required to find the language to define the qualities associated with intuition. Rachel Mason (1996: 115) refers to the 'extreme difficulty of constructing vivid images with words' experienced by art teachers which she attributes to inadequate English teaching and reflects on 'the enormous hold that technocratic or instrumental thinking has on ordinary language in everyday life'.

On a more positive note, Andrew Stibbs (1998: 204) maintains that 'art rooms are linguistically special as work places. They are theatres for thinking, both aloud and silently, for collaboration, evaluation, celebration, and – to move to finer detail – hypothesising, checking, correcting and reassuring'.

How teachers' use of intuition changes with experience

Given that intuition plays a significant role in making and responding to art but that assessment criteria fail to recognize its importance, how do teachers reconcile these tensions when marking work? Binch and Robertson (1994: 107) claim that assessment objectives are 'rarely used systematically as they were intended', and that 'GCSE assessment is subjective, with reference to the assessment objectives only when there is a dispute'. My experience of working with teachers in moderation meetings is somewhat different. Generally, assessment criteria are used in a fairly systematic manner but other considerations are clearly operating. Often there is an immediate recognition of 'quality' by teachers when work is first presented for assessment and this is particularly marked when work by the most able candidates appears. There is also a sense in which first impressions 'carry the day'.

When asked whether first impressions were important teachers made comments such as: 'Yes, the first impression I feel is usually a good indication of the final mark', and 'Impact and impression is an important part of art, so yes'.

A related issue is that of the skills developed through experience. Eisner (1996) uses the term 'connoisseurship'. This appears to refer to a range of skills developed by expert practitioners who have effective perceptual understanding, are knowledgeable, sensitive to contextual considerations and able to take account of qualities which go beyond what is immediately apparent.

When asked to comment on whether experience resulted in teachers being more or less likely to use their intuition in making judgements, responses were far from conclusive. A typical comment was: 'Far more likely – less experienced teachers usually have that understanding too but lack the confidence in their intuition.' A counter view to this was: 'Probably less, since, if pushed, most judgements will be rationalized by reference to criteria and experience.' Opportunities of working with examiners and teacher markers over a considerable number of years suggest to me that the ability 'to take into account qualities which go beyond what is immediately apparent' is as much to do with confidence, empathy and appreciation of the context in which the work was produced as it is to do with experience.

Conclusion

Guy Claxton (Chapter 2) has described environments in which the qualities associated with intuition might best be nurtured as 'convivial, playful, cooperative and non-judgemental, as well as being purposeful and professional'. These qualities can be found in many art studios. Many teachers recognize that intuition is an important element in the making of art and in their formative assessment of pupil performance but are far less sure about its role in summative assessment. Nevertheless, making effective use of intuitive judgements requires art teachers to have the confidence to use objective criteria as a means to an end, rather than an end in itself. They need to create environments in which genuine innovation can occur and where imagination, flexibility and the unpredictable response is applauded; where failure might be viewed as a step on the road to success and where there is a shared excitement about learning.

The role of intuition in the assessment of mathematics (Jan Winter)

The context

The assessment of school mathematical achievement has sometimes been thought to be unproblematic – a question of right or wrong. This reflects a common popular belief that mathematical achievement is all about 'product' – the mathematical facts and skills – rather than about 'process' – the decision making and reasoning abilities which are fundamental to the effective use of any skills. Discussions with teachers show that the issues are much more complex than is often recognized and that the ways teachers make judgements about pupils needs careful scrutiny in order to establish what teachers value and what evidence they consider to be useful. A group of four teachers, of varying length of experience, discussed these issues with me and I quote from them in what follows. I asked them to consider assessment in a wide-ranging discussion in which the issue of intuition was not introduced by me until halfway through. I took part in the discussion in preference to adopting the role of 'interviewer' as this was a group of teachers I knew well and had worked with for a considerable time in varying contexts.

Intuition in the current climate

Mathematics was one of the first subjects to be prescribed by the National Curriculum and, in many ways, what was proposed was not a radical departure from teachers' previous practice. For secondary teachers it was as though GCSE requirements, with which they were becoming familiar, were being introduced lower down the school with a compulsory assessment at the end of Year 9 which mirrored many aspects of GCSE assessment. What was new, at GCSE too, was an increased emphasis on the assessment of the *processes* of mathematics in addition to the traditional assessment of knowledge and skills. This required teachers to think about assessment in new ways and to collect evidence of a different type. The quotes that follow reflect teachers' concerns about their ability to do this against the criteria presented in the National Curriculum. They felt that their knowledge of pupils' achievements was not always represented by the evidence that they were able to collect – their intuitive knowledge could not always be 'pinned down'.

While teachers have always assessed pupils, the emphasis in recent years has shifted towards evidence. This included 'ephemeral evidence', an idea which accompanied some of the National Curriculum attainment targets that did not seem so amenable to formal assessment. This proved difficult for teachers to either understand or implement and the focus has shifted away again somewhat. This leaves the question of how National Curriculum assessment can encompass the 'measurement' of all that a teacher knows as a result of contact over perhaps hundreds of hours (see Paul Weeden's comments on holistic-level descriptions in the geography section, page 231).

In discussion, teachers (T1, T2 etc.) commented on the criteria in the National Curriculum attainment targets:

T1: I feel constrained by them.
T2: They're all I've ever known . . .
T1: They're all I've ever known but I still feel constrained by them. Go back to the kid who was at the bottom of set one all the time – for

two or three years in fact – who submitted coursework that was like proofs of why odd and even numbers are odd and even. Because it didn't fit into 'they've done this and they've done that', and because it was extremely random it was very difficult for me to assess . . .

T3:: It can be a hindrance, can't it, that the actual references that you are using to make your assessment can hinder the assessment?

T4: And you pass it on to the kids as well. I think it can militate against allowing kids to show a bit of flair because everybody's now got these criteria in the back of their minds. We must all train the kids to make up a table, make a prediction . . .

This has implications for professional judgement since high-stakes assessments will discourage teachers from operating intuitively. GCSE assessment is now high stakes not only for pupils but also, given the importance attached to league tables, for teachers. The need to be able to justify one's judgements with tangible evidence can make teachers feel unsure about those judgements unless the evidence is absolutely secure:

T4: I think with assessment being a lot more tied down now through things like the National Curriculum, GCSE criteria and so on, there's more and more feeling that unless someone's producing something tangible, on paper, actually it isn't worth as much. So someone [*a pupil*] can say something incredibly intuitive and show a great deal of understanding but somehow it's not the same because it isn't something tangible.

Dealing with work that doesn't 'fit' the criteria

In mathematics, as in the other two subjects dealt with in this chapter, pupils' work is often difficult to categorize in terms of the restricted criteria which seem central to a national assessment scheme. The reliability (i.e. making assessment standards repeatable and consistent) requirements of a scheme being implemented by tens of thousands of teachers with hundreds of thousands of pupils mean that validity (i.e. assessing what you really value) is a possible casualty. Combining this with all the other demands on teachers' energies and teachers' wishes to do justice to their pupils' achievements leads to teachers feeling confused about the value of the criteria they are working with:

T1: What's intriguing is what T4 was saying about the mathematical content. I have found that sometimes what I consider to be mathematically difficult, done in coursework, doesn't show on the criteria, which makes me think the criteria are wrong in that instance.

T3: Yeah.

T1: But then I'm stuck by that because I think that's showing some

insight that can't be assessed under that criteria which makes me
think, oh no, what can I do about that?

T3: I tend to ignore the criteria personally.

The teachers were able to act in fairly autonomous ways within the constraints imposed on them although they did feel the impact of these on their
practice and, in many cases, resented it.

The risk of bias in intuitive judgements

One teacher was aware of some of the underlying difficulties which more
intuitive judgements allow – those of bias, prejudgement or simply poor
judgement:

T4: But there is a danger with this 'gut feeling' that it is very subjective.
I mean if you like work that is beautifully presented and has lots of
coloured in diagrams, you're going to value something that's
presented in that way.

This concern links closely with the issues of reliability and validity raised
above. Teachers recognized the problems of subjectivity and bias but were
confident in the judgements they made – see, for example, the long quote
later in this section from T1. However, they were sceptical of judgements
made in a similar way by other teachers, perhaps indicating some uncertainty
of the way in which other teachers might be using (or abusing) the criteria by
which they felt constrained.

How teachers' use of intuition changes with experience

Bruner (1972: 99) (writing about children's learning), says they need to be
able 'to proceed intuitively when necessary and to analyse when appropriate'.
The same is just as true for teachers, so the balance and use of the right technique at the right time is crucial. This is a skill learned over time and teachers
feel that they develop more expertise as they build up experience:

T4: You sort of build up a bank of past experiences of how pupils in the
past have reacted and maybe you're in a better position to make
comparisons. I mean that's basically how people do things like
predicted grades, isn't it? It's from past experience.

T2: That was so difficult in the first few years . . .

T4: That's right.

T3: It gets much easier, doesn't it?

However, along with this increased familiarity, teachers expressed a belief
that they lost some degree of spontaneity and self-belief which they had had
in their early days of teaching:

T1: I was thinking of my first year of teaching when I had a top set year
seven and there was a girl there who consistently came at the

bottom of any assessment that we formally did and there were many rows about the fact that she should be moved down at least one if not two sets. I maintained she had a real pizzazz about her in terms of how she did the maths when I worked with her, and wouldn't let her go. At that point I couldn't see why all this formal assessment was being used as ammunition, at least that's what it felt like, when I'd only just started teaching. Now she has won many awards and is in our year eleven top set and likely to be an A/A* pupil. I felt then that was uncluttered, I think what T4 was saying was true for me. I didn't have all the pointers, if you like, I couldn't have picked out a lot of in-between scales on assessment scales, I couldn't have done a sort of mental rank order which I might be able to do more now, but I could certainly pick out the anomalies. Whereas I now feel a lot more pushed by the outside too. Because I can do a mental rank order I'm tempted to think, well those people who are at the bottom might well not have much potential, but it's because of experiences like that girl that I have to keep holding on to the first year of my teaching.

In saying that 'intuitive structures are essential components of every form of active understanding and of productive thinking', Fischbein (1982: 10) implies that 'analytic' assessment techniques can't work alone. He also says that 'the essential function of intellectual intuition is to be the homologue of perception at the symbolic level, having the same task as perception: to prepare and to guide action (mental or external)' (p. 11). In the mathematical context he describes three types of conviction: through formal argument, through empirical evidence and through intuition. The second and third relate closely to assessment – do we believe we're convinced of something when we've collected enough empirical evidence? If so, what is enough and what is 'good' evidence? Intuition can overcome these problems but then leaves the question of the acceptability of such evidence and the problem of standardization. Again these questions hinge on confidence, both of the teacher making the initial judgement and then of the wider community in that teacher's judgement. The quote from T1 above indicates her confidence in her own judgements and her willingness to stand by them as well as her recognition of the need to 'hold onto' that experience and not forget it.

Conclusion

Is intuition a kind of knowledge which is of a similar form to analytic knowledge but of which the analysis which has formed it is not consciously available to us and therefore not subject to checking? (A bit like computer-based proofs of mathematical theorems – we can't check them and can't know whether there is some undetected bug in the system.) This inaccessibility does matter, but is it any more of a fundamental flaw than some of those apparent in other, checkable, forms of assessment?

In conclusion, this group of mathematics teachers used a wide range of sources of evidence on which to base their judgement (similar to the case considered by Watson 1995). They built up a wide-ranging picture through discussions, written and oral work, practical tasks and observation of interaction between pupils. They were, in the main, confident of the judgements they made even when they could not offer firm tangible evidence to support them. They learned through experience to make better assessments in which they have more confidence but still wished to hold on to the clarity and 'unclutteredness' which they felt characterized their early practice.

The role of intuition in the assessment of geography (Paul Weeden)

The context

Geography as a subject bridges the divide between the sciences and the social sciences and is eclectic in its use of methodologies and discourses from a wide range of disciplines. Geography teachers have always used a range of evidence for formative purposes but over the last 30 years both the work being assessed and the assessment methodologies have changed radically. In the past, summative assessment was largely limited to students' recall of factual knowledge and their ability to organize an argument through the product, usually an essay (Hall 1986). Recently, however, it has been extended to include assessment of the process of 'doing geography' through a range of other tasks that demonstrate both thinking skills and ability to carry out enquiries. I suggest this shift has resulted in increasing both reliability and validity in summative assessment but does not address the concern that we only assess the easily measurable areas of pupils' performance, and has not decreased the need for intuitive approaches as described by Patricia Broadfoot in Chapter 12.

Since 1990 I have been involved with the introduction of National Curriculum Geography (NCG) for Key Stage 3 (Grades 7–8) in England and Wales in a variety of roles. My experience has been that the introduction of the National Curriculum assessment system(s) initially caused many teachers to doubt their previous, often intuitive, expertise. This had enabled them to make judgements about pupils and their work in a range of contexts using their sensitivity to clues and ephemeral evidence. Now, many have re-examined their methods and beliefs about assessment. The evidence for this is derived from the extensive literature about the introduction of NCG as well as from my observations and conversations with teachers and geography 'experts' since 1990, in particular with more than 20 teachers during the process of writing and trialling Key Stage 3 geography optional tests and tasks. In addition, I also draw on questionnaires/conversations with two groups of 15–20 teachers (Group A: 'experts' – experienced teachers, and Group B:

'novices' – a group of PGCE students) who were being trained in the use of the optional tests and tasks.

However, my major focus throughout the period of data collection was not on the place of intuition in assessment; instead, it was on the practicalities of creating manageable assessment instruments that gave reliable and valid assessment data and on developing the consistency of teachers' judgements. Here I now reflect on the issues that arose and reconsider and illustrate the tensions that exist when the pressures of high-stakes assessment and account-ability require judgements to be made using criteria and when the process of data gathering requires intuitive leaps in the dark of the sort described by Richard Brawn in Chapter 9.

Intuition in the current climate

As with Jan Winter's account of the introduction of National Curriculum mathematics, the introduction of NCG assessment in England and Wales has been problematic, and the story of the last ten years has been of teachers attempting to understand, interpret and implement novel, complex and changing systems of assessment in a climate of rapid and uncertain imposed change.

I believe that there were two major reasons for teachers questioning and doubting their often intuitive judgements of students' performance. First, the twin messages of National Curriculum assessment – to improve pupil per-formance and to make schools and teachers more accountable – appeared to be making assessment increasingly high stakes and focused on a more limited curriculum, as described by Patricia Broadfoot in Chapter 12. This placed enormous stress on many teachers who wanted to ensure they 'got it right'. Second, the pace of change was so rapid that teachers were forced to specu-late about what they were being required to do. A common comment was, 'We're waiting for someone to tell us what to do.'

Dealing with work that doesn't fit the criteria

The original NCG proposals focused on content more than skills or processes and, although intended to describe competence, could be interpreted at so many different levels that both teachers and 'experts' were confused. Graves *et al.* (1990: 4) used the Statement of Attainment (SoA) 'Understand the main characteristics of a range of types of farming, including their location' to demonstrate that this SoA, typical of most, didn't help teacher assessment because it was open to so many different interpretations. How many charac-teristics? To what depth? How many types of farming? How many locations? Does this imply case studies or not? Teachers were forced to use previous expertise in making judgements but lacked confidence that this would be the same as colleagues in other schools.

In 1994, the Dearing Report addressed some of the curriculum and assess-ment issues that had been identified as problematic in the original order

(Bennetts 1994: 60). The revised curriculum gave teachers yet another new assessment system to use – level descriptions which gave 'fuzzier' criteria but contained a coherent system of progression. How far does the guidance from SCAA (1996: 2) about using these level descriptions '(the essential function of level descriptions is to help you [teachers] make rounded summative judgements at the end of the key stage)' match a definition of intuition as being 'a confidence in one's ability to operate with insufficient evidence' (Bruner 1972: 98)? Maybe only partially because, SCAA (1996: 2) go on to say, 'By the end of the key stage, you will have built up sufficient knowledge about a pupil's performance across a range of work, and in a variety of contexts, to enable you to make a judgement in relation to the level descriptions. When judgements are made at the end of the key stage, you should decide which description best fits a pupil's performance.'

Does the above statement imply that teachers can only collect the required evidence in a systematic and logical way, and does this preclude intuition? My experience suggests that intuition is required because one of the major problems with assessing pupils against the NCG is that pupils' work often doesn't fit the narrowly defined National Curriculum criteria. Teachers, in assessing pupils' work, found they couldn't give credit for some aspects of the work because they didn't fit the criteria, so teachers either ignored them or intuitively used their professional judgement as described in the SCAA/ACAC statement above.

The risk of bias in intuitive judgements

Before the introduction of the National Curriculum, geography criteria for assessing work tended to be informal. Hence, a handbook for geography teachers written in the 1960s had to encourage teachers to be objective in their marking and to use formal mark schemes:

> [Where a question requires a map] the mark scheme would set aside 5 marks for the map. These should then be awarded in a standard way, e.g. 1 for an accurate outline, . . . 1 for a named river and 2 for other locating features . . . It must be realised that if an outline is not well drawn the accuracy of the whole map is affected; for this reason some would prefer to allow 2 marks as giving greater scope for the subtleties of accuracy. If, within the poor outline, the information is placed relatively correctly, the child should not be penalised again.
>
> Long and Roberson (1966: 346–7)

Despite the detail, this mark scheme is capable of being interpreted in a wide variety of ways and the assumption that experienced teachers were consistent in their assessments was challenged by some:

> A-level schemes of assessment fall into two broad categories. At one end of the spectrum is the 'broad' view: this supposes that all assistant examiners (and teachers in schools) possess a common shared understanding

about quality . . . At the other end of the spectrum is the 'narrow' view, which is suspicious of assumptions that the examiners enjoy a consensus about quality, and argues for greater control over the definition of quality.

(Hall 1986: 262)

That there is a risk of bias if criteria are not explicitly spelt out has been recognized for years: 'The essay, for example, can be notoriously unreliable: not only may different examiners award markedly different marks for the same essay, but a marker may give widely different marks for the same essay when assessed at different times' (Jones 1986: 240). In geography it is often necessary to allow some leeway in the interpretation of answers because pupils can and do draw on a wide range of valid experiences in describing places or attitudes to them. We could require assessments to be narrow and focused but this would preclude the creativity, imagination and learning that comes from responding to more open-ended tasks.

A further risk is that presentation can unduly influence assessment. This was illustrated by the use of pupils' work derived from the Key Stage 3 geography optional tests and tasks trial, conducted with both experienced and novice teachers. When asked to rank three pieces of work on first impressions, the word-processed piece with a picture downloaded from a CD-ROM was almost universally ranked first. However, on more considered analysis it was discovered that although the product looked good the geographical content was poor, so it is clear that snap (intuitive?) judgements may sometimes be poor indicators of quality, an interesting contrast to the comments made by art teachers earlier in the chapter.

How teachers' use of intuition changes with experience

'I used to initially scan through them, without marking them and sort them into three piles, top, middle and bottom, and then I would mark them thoroughly. More often than not I would find that I had got them just about in the right place' (Ann, experienced geography GCSE marker).

For many teachers this accurately describes the process that they use when marking a large quantity of pupils' work. Does this mean that their marking is being prejudiced by those initial judgements or that their experience allows them to accurately predict the quality of the product – do they intuitively *know* the quality from a relatively cursory inspection? Teachers usually find the initial stages of marking difficult. Students' responses to questions vary and yet can be quite valid, particularly where extended writing is involved. Even where there is a precise mark scheme it is possible to interpret the possible answers in a variety of ways. Until several answers have been marked the process can be slow and tortuous as the marker grapples with the questions, the answers, the mark scheme and the criteria. Over time, knowledge of the range of possible answers develops and the process speeds up until eventually it becomes almost automatic – unless a student gives an answer that is more problematic. At this point the marker either has to refer back to the mark scheme or think more carefully using the criteria available.

My experience has been that teachers' expertise in making judgements was disrupted by the introduction of the National Curriculum. During INSET (in-service education and training) sessions on the introduction of optional tests and tasks, teachers almost universally expressed a lack of confidence in using the new level descriptions. In order to test how quickly they learnt to use level descriptions to assess pupils' work, 'experiments' were conducted with two different groups of teachers, experts and novices.

Group A (experienced teachers) expressed initial doubts about the meaning of the level descriptions. However, after marking three or four pupils' work, they were able to relate the performance to their previous knowledge and to make accurate and consistent judgements of pupils' performance using the level descriptions. Although these criteria are open to considerable differences in interpretation, a measure of consistency was achieved by means of discussion. However, it became clear that many teachers were making intuitive judgements of quality which were then justified by reference to the criteria.

Group B (PGCE students) were given opportunities to develop their understanding of level descriptions by marking pupils' work. The exercise was done three times: first, a quick judgement was made; second, they had time to consider their answer; and third, there was a discussion of the differences in their judgements. They showed close agreement in the rank order they assigned but it was clear that many felt unsure and lacked confidence in their initial, more intuitive, judgements because they couldn't justify them. At the end of the session they still lacked confidence even in their more considered judgements. An issue for teacher trainers therefore is how to develop the assessment expertise of trainees so that they can make accurate judgements about pupils' work. Most trainees require considerable practice in using explicit, objective criteria or mark schemes to develop their understanding of this intricate, skilled process.

Conclusion

Geography teachers have considerable expertise in assessing a range of pupils' work in a range of contexts using different methodologies. However, it has always been easier to assess products such as accurate factual knowledge than more intangible qualities such as creativity, imagination, enquiry, values and attitudes. The process of making judgements about performance has an intuitive element and this became particularly apparent when the introduction of the new National Curriculum assessment criteria caused teachers to doubt their expertise in making judgements using limited evidence.

Summary: what role does intuition play in the assessment of art, mathematics and geography?

This chapter has looked at the use of intuition in assessing three different subjects. We have shown that while assessment methods may vary considerably between the subjects there are still common themes emerging about assessing products, the process of 'doing' the subject and potential performance. At the beginning of the chapter we asked four questions to which we now turn along with the new questions that now present themselves.

What are the issues teachers face when assessing pupils' intuitive learning? Bruner's (1960: 58) image of intuition tackles the dividing-up of knowledge into small 'assessable' chunks: 'intuitive thinking tends to involve manoeuvres that seem to be based on an implicit perception of the total problem'. Teachers' understandings, arrived at intuitively, seem often to be based on the 'whole' child rather than being specific about one aspect of learning. It is a 'derived form of knowledge' accomplished by synthesis rather than analysis. The National Curriculum requires teachers to make holistic 'best fit' summative judgements about pupils' performance against criteria, and this implies that teachers must use intuition in these judgements because much of the evidence they have collected will be ephemeral. Why then is intuitive knowledge perhaps less formally valued now that the curriculum is closely prescribed in detail and pupils' achievement within it must be matched to specific criteria?

Should intuition play a part in assessing pupils' work, both the product and the process of 'doing' art, mathematics or geography? We suggest that the illustrative evidence of our work with teachers indicates that intuition is important and often plays an unacknowledged role in assessing pupils' work. Uncritical intuition may result in bias when the criteria used aren't clear, agreed or followed consistently and reliability. This can be a problem because there can be substantial variation in the judgements made. However, the 'high stakes' summative assessment context of the National Curriculum, with its emphasis on data for accountability and reliability purposes, has resulted in a trend towards easily measurable, limited assessments. In all three subjects there is a tendency to play down areas such as creativity, imagination and even intuition, that are much more difficult to assess. Is there a danger that increasingly we are teaching 'to the test' and losing sight of many important areas of learning that are more difficult to assess?

What role does intuition play in the process of making judgements? Teachers have to make holistic judgements about performance using the relatively 'fuzzy' National Curriculum assessment criteria in art, geography and mathematics Attainment Target 1. These judgements are often intuitive because teachers develop sensitivity to ephemeral evidence about pupils' work, such as creativity, and use this in conjunction with more objective evidence. However, assessing whether pupils are 'good' artists, mathematicians or geographers can be problematic because the processes involved in 'doing' the subjects are often difficult to pin down and teachers may find it difficult to justify what makes for good performance. Over time, teachers develop expertise (ways of intuitively knowing quality and standards). The introduction of the National Curriculum both focused their attention on their assessment practice and caused them to doubt their own understanding of standards. The process of developing expertise, so that consistent judgements are made, is one of interest to teacher trainers. Beginning teachers struggle to 'know' what appropriate standards are. They need practice using criteria, and opportunities to discuss how work matches criteria, if they are to develop their assessment expertise and begin to trust their judgements. How do teachers learn to make judgements about work?

Do teachers develop an intuitive sense of potential performance? Teachers still use 'expert' knowledge in their daily interactions with pupils and in their decision making about learning activities. These formative purposes are 'low stakes' unless potential performance is affected. One example is decisions about set placements which in mathematics can predetermine potential performance. However, the increasingly 'high stakes' nature of assessment at all levels means that intuitive understanding of potential performance by teachers may be restricted by lack of evidence. The nature of evidence therefore becomes an issue. Are teachers allowed to trust their expert 'intuitive' judgements or do they have to rely on the more narrowly focused and assessable?

References

Bennetts, T. (1994) The Dearing Report and its implications for geography. *Teaching Geography,* 19(2): 60–3.

Binch, N. and Robertson, L. (1994) *Resourcing and Assessing Art, Craft and Design.* Corsham: National Society for Education in Art and Design.

Bruner, J. (1960) *The Process of Education.* Cambridge, MA: Harvard University Press.

Bruner, J. (1972) *The Relevance of Education.* London: George Allen & Unwin.

Davies, T. (1995) *Playing the System.* Birmingham: Cascade Publications.

DfE (1995) *Art in the National Curriculum.* London: HMSO.

Eisner, E. (1996) *Evaluating and Assessing the Visual Arts in Education.* London and New York: Teachers' College Press.

Fischbein, E. (1982) Intuition and proof. *For the Learning of Mathematics,* 3(2): 9–18, 24.

Graves, N., Kent, A., Lambert, D., Naish, M. and Slater, F. (1990) Evaluating the Final Report. *Teaching Geography,* 15(4): 147–51.

Gulbenkian Foundation (1982) *The Arts in Schools.* London: Calouste Gulbenkian Foundation.

Hall, D. (1986) Advanced level examinations, in D. Boardman (ed.) *Handbook for Geography Teachers,* pp. 257–68. Sheffield: Geographical Association.

Hughes, A. (1998) Reconceptualising the art curriculum. *Journal of Art and Design Education,* 17(1): 41–9.

Jones, M. (1986) Evaluation and Assessment 11–16, in D. Boardman (ed.) *Handbook for Geography Teachers,* pp. 234–49. Sheffield: Geographical Association.

Long, M. and Roberson, B.S. (1966) *Teaching Geography.* London: Heinemann.

Mason, R. (1996) *Evaluating and Assessing the Visual Arts in Education.* London and New York: Teachers' College Press.

Perkins, D.N. (1994) *The Intelligent Eye: Learning to Think by Looking at Art.* Santa Monica, CA: The Getty Centre for Education in the Arts.

SCAA (Schools Curriculum and Assessment Authority) (1996) *Consistency in Teacher Assessment: Exemplification of Standards, Geography Key Stage 3.* London: SCAA.

Stibbs, A. (1998) Language in art and art in language. *Journal of Art and Design Education*, 17(2): 201–9.

Watson, A. (1995) Evidence for pupils: mathematical achievements. *For the Learning of Mathematics*, 15(1): 16–20, 28.

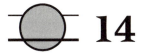 **14**

Intuition, culture and the development of academic literacy

David Johnson

Introduction

Much of the current research and writing on intuition has been from the perspective of what the individual knows or can do (O'Malley and Draper 1992; Clement 1994), and there is less evidence of attempts to probe the role of intuition in the cultural, historical and social contexts of human interaction. However, recent work in cognitive science is beginning to suggest that 'ways of knowing' have their roots in culture. There is a distinct move away from a perspective which assigns intuitive ways of knowing to the individual towards one which argues that, like other forms of cognition, they are socially situated (Wertsch 1995) or culturally implicit (del Rio and Alvarez 1995).

This chapter starts from the premise that understanding intuition, and indeed seeking to extend its potential for improving academic discourse (or the way in which members of the discourse community relate to each other through speaking, reading and writing), demands that we probe the social setting. To understand ways of knowing or forms of practice which do not always appear to have an explicit rationale, we must look at embedded cultural practices, rather than at individuals. Thus this chapter seeks to probe the roots of intuition from a socio-cultural perspective. This theoretical perspective maintains that meaning is made through people participating with others in a social environment (Vygotsky 1978, 1987) and that cognitive development has to be understood as taking place through interaction with other members of the society who are more conversant with the society's intellectual practices and tools for mediating intellectual activity. It argues that it is incomplete to focus on an aspect of individual cognition without concern for the cultural activity in which personal and interpersonal actions take place (Rogoff 1995: 141).

The chapter is concerned with the role intuition plays in professional settings, and the 'academic discourse community' is of specific interest. As we shall see later, the term, 'academic discourse community' is not without problems. However, it is used throughout this chapter to mean a professional setting in which there exists a shared (or at least an apparently shared) understanding between academics themselves and between academics and students, about the role and function of text (Ballard and Clanchy 1988).

Central to the way in which the academic discourse community functions is a set of implicit or intuitive understandings. At one level, students are thought to become full members of the community, and are allowed to graduate from it when they can demonstrate the capacity to use written language to perform those functions required by the academy at a level which is judged acceptable.

The notion of 'judgement' is important in this chapter. It is argued that judgements are made not on the basis of explicit indicators but intuitively. This does not imply however that these judgements are arbitrary or capricious. Rather, they are said to grow out of a set of implicit understandings that academics have about the function of language in higher education. These understandings shape literacy in higher education. They inform the way in which writing tasks (essay questions) are framed, they have a bearing on student responses and they are used to assess the eventual written product.

It is usually contended that most academics find themselves in broad agreement with these intuitive understandings about literacy – that they all for example, 'just know' how to set academic writing tasks (essay or assignment topics), or that they 'just know' what a successful piece of writing is. This chapter intends to show that while there is a broad understanding between individual academics about the nature of academic tasks, or assessment, these understandings are not always consistent. While the importance of individual ways of knowing in professional practice cannot be underestimated, we also need to understand how individuals function in interaction with each other to develop shared meaning and shared practice. The chapter argues that there is little evidence of a 'culture of practice' in academic settings which enables academics to share and to continue to develop new meanings and understandings. It proposes that it is only in what Lave (1997) calls a 'community of practice' that new academic staff or students ('newcomers' in Lave's terms) will both appropriate (Rogoff 1995; Wertsch 1997) and contribute to intuitive ways of knowing.

To summarize, this chapter sets out to argue that:

- Intuition is a product of social interaction rather than simply an element of an individual's cognitive behaviour.
- Intuitive ways of knowing underpin many of the activities of the academic discourse community, particularly the framing of writing tasks, the production of written texts and the activity of assessment. However, these practices are individual rather than shared.
- Developing intuition and intuitive ways of working, and building on intuitive practice to make that which is implicit explicit, can be achieved through reorganizing the professional setting and building a functional community of practice.

Perspectives in the study of intuition

Much has been written about intuition from a variety of perspectives. Guy Claxton (Chapter 2) reviews the anatomy of intuition and finds that the term has been used to refer to a multiplicity of phenomena. Claxton suggests that despite differences in our understanding of what intuition is, we can largely agree that intuition is a family of 'ways of knowing'. It is also broadly accepted that intuition is a different way of knowing. This seems to be a reasonable starting point, but if it is our task to enhance intuitive ways of knowing in the context of the development of professional practice, then it is necessary both to sharpen the definition and to consider carefully not only what intuition is, but how it is shaped.

Clement (1994) also contends that intuition has multiple meanings. According to him, the confusion that exists in understanding what it is arises from the application of the term to mean both elemental knowledge structures and complex non-formal reasoning processes. In looking at the role of intuition in subjects like physics, Clement finds it useful to separate the two meanings. He prefers to regard intuition not as a set of reasoning processes such as induction, analogical reasoning or heuristic strategies for problem-solving, but rather as elemental knowledge structures, seen as basic units of knowledge: 'a particular type of internal knowledge structure' (p. 211).

Unlike di Sessa (1983), who refers to certain kinds of intuition as 'phenomenological primitives' which are 'relatively minimal abstractions of simple common phenomena that stand without significant explanatory substructure or justification' (p. 15), Clement argues that intuition is a central part of the knowledge used by expert problem-solvers in science. He demonstrates through various experiments that intuition is not restricted to a 'start-up' role in a brief spell at the beginning of the problem solution, as suggested by Bruner (1990), but is deployed more strongly throughout the problem-solving activity.

A closely-related perspective on intuition is that it is a 'mental model'. Although there is not complete agreement as to what constitutes a mental model (according to Payne (1992), there are several competing theoretical positions in existence) there is some consensus that mental models are 'coherent structural representations' (Clement 1994: 204). O'Malley and Draper (1992), for example, argue that conceptual understandings in such domains as physics bear out the view that the intuitive knowledge possessed by 'novices' consists of a coherent set of ideas, some of which might be regarded as theories or models. Again, this is in stark contrast to di Sessa's (1983) proposition that intuitive physics consists of fragmentary knowledge which does not have the systematicity of a theory or a model.

Both the notions of 'knowledge structures' and 'models' are pertinent to the discussion of intuition and literacy in academic settings and there is a great deal of research on the importance of knowledge in the activity of writing (Bereiter and Scardamalia 1987, Scardamalia and Bereitor 1994). According to Purves and Purves (1986), there are three basic forms of knowledge which writers draw on in producing text. First, semantic knowledge, which involves knowledge of words and larger units of discourse. Second, there is knowledge of models, such as text models and other culturally appropriate formulaic uses of language. This would include, for example, knowledge of the general shape of a story, including that it has a particular structure such as a beginning, middle and end, which provides a frame that can be filled with various kinds of information and forms like plots, characters and settings. In addition, knowledge of models includes awareness of types of linguistic devices that belong in a particular kind of text. Third, there is knowledge of social and cultural rules governing when it is appropriate to write as well as knowledge of the appropriate procedures to use.

According to Purves and Purves (1986) all three kinds of knowledge are a prerequisite for constructing discourse. What is particularly important though is the emerging awareness that knowledge of text models, forms and structures, as well as knowledge of the cultural rules which govern what is written and when, is as important as knowledge of smaller units of discourse. Interesting too, is ongoing research in the field of contrastive rhetoric which is suggesting that our knowledge of text models, forms and structures is culturally determined. In the broader sense of the term 'culture', this means that a story, for example, derives its form from the history of a particular culture. It may have its own way of beginning, developing and reaching a conclusion, to such an extent that the eventual structure might seem alien to another cultural context, even where the same language is spoken.

In the narrower sense of the term, it is also true that culture determines the shape and function of a text. Academia, law or business, for example, will each determine what is written and how, mainly because of the existence of a set of cultural rules. Purves and Purves (1986: 193) make the point that: 'Most writing is done within the framework of a community, be it a rather restricted community such as a community of scholars in a particular discipline, or be it a broad community such as an educated citizenry in a nation state. This idea of a community is what we have called a culture.'

It seems plausible to conclude, from the above discussion, that intuition can be described as a particular kind of internal knowledge structure, which is applied to problem-solving activities (Clement 1994; O'Malley and Draper 1994), text production (Purves and Purves 1986; Bereiter and Scardamalia 1987), and a wide range of other professional activities (see Chapters 4, 5 and 8).

The next question we need to address is: how are these knowledge structures learned?

Knowledge of text models is learned implicitly, by and large, and is culturally and historically determined. So, for example, most children who have stories read to them learn the structure and form of a story and have a fairly good idea as early as the age of 2 (Bereiter and Scardamalia 1987) that stories contain plots, characters and settings, among other elements. Similarly, it is not difficult to see how a certain genre may be learned as part of a religious liturgy which individuals hear once or twice a week. However, very few of us have had bedtime 'arguments' read to us and we probably do not learn the structure and form and the linguistic and rhetorical elements associated with this genre until much later in life.

Models of stories or argumentation and other forms of reasoning have been described recently by some writers as 'cognitive tools'. According to Cole (1995), cognitive tools embody a culture's intellectual history. They have theories built into them, and users accept these theories – albeit unknowingly – when they use these tools. It is in invisible ways therefore that the history of a culture, which is inherently a social history, is carried into every act of cognition (Cole 1995). Even when there are no obvious tools involved, theories, implicit and explicit, both enable and constrain thinking. Thus, not only theories but ways of reasoning are socially determined.

Intuitive ways of knowing would thus appear to have their roots in cultural settings, and particularly settings where individuals interact with each other or with cognitive tools. O'Malley and Draper (1992) were interested in this question and studied the extent to which mental models were formed through interaction with computers as cognitive tools. They claim from their study that the development of intuitive models for application in practice does not result purely from internal goal-directed activity, but is more the result of an interplay between goal-directed activity and the actual physical and functional settings that users find themselves in. Thus, an understanding of the nature of interaction between a user and a device might provide us with a better understanding of what a user's mental model consists of.

Another perspective on learning models can be found in the work of Lave (1991). Lave argues that learning is not a process of socially shared cognition that results in the internalization of knowledge by individuals. Rather, it is a process of becoming a member of a sustained community of practice. Learning, both intuitively and explicitly is, for Lave, developing an identity as a member of a community of practice and becoming a knowledgeable partner in the process. Lave uses the term, 'legitimate peripheral participation' to describe a process by which 'newcomers' (students or new academic staff, for example) become 'oldtimers' through a social process of centripetal participation, which depends on legitimate access to ongoing community activity. Newcomers develop a changing understanding of practice over time, and move from legitimate peripheral participation to full participation in the socio-cultural practice of the community. Knowledge of the way in which the community functions (much of it being intuitive knowledge, and 'ways of doing things without being able to explain why') is developed in the process of assuming an identity as a practitioner, and eventually becoming a full participant – an 'oldtimer'.

An important aspect of this perspective is that it begins to characterize 'communities of practice' and learning environments. Lave demonstrates for example how Alcoholics Anonymous, Yucatek Mayan midwives in Mexico, Vai and Golan tailors, or butchers in the USA can be described as communities of practice. She documents the 'apprenticeship' process newcomers go through in these settings and how they eventually become 'oldtimers' through learning skills, but more pertinent to our discussion here, through intuitive models of practice.

The question we are now faced with is whether academic communities are actually communities of practice. Much has been written about the academy as a 'discourse community' and there is yet another body of literature which make reference to the fact that much of the practice in this community is intuitive. We would like to explore these issues here. First, we shall ask the question, are academic settings identifiable communities? We will then explore whether academics bring to these communities models of practice, intuitive ways of doing things, and we will ask of these models whether they are individual or shared. It is conceivable that members of an academic community bring to their professional practice intuitive ways of doing things (like setting academic writing tasks, or assessing students writing) that have been shaped in other cultural and social contexts. (Many academic staff for example might have been previously part of other communities of practice, such as education, business, law, etc.) The question remains as to whether intuitive ways of practice in the academic setting can be considered to be knowledge which has evolved, and continues to evolve, through shared practice.

The academic discourse community as an intuitive community

The notion of an academic discourse community, though it has been at the centre of recent debates in linguistics, is not accepted without question, unlike the related notion of a 'speech community' (Gumperz 1971; Hymes 1972), which is well-established in sociolinguistics. Harris (1989) argues that the term is vague and problematic and it cannot be presumed that the academic discourse community is the same as a speech community which describes an actual group of speakers living in a particular time and place. He argues that a group of actual readers and writers who are dispersed in time and place and who rarely meet each other cannot readily be identified as a community. As such, the term is nothing more than a hypothetical notion.

Swales (1990) on the other hand, suggests that a discourse community is identifiable and has a set of defining characteristics and a broadly agreed set of public goals which may be either formal or tacit. A similar argument is made by Faigley and Hansen (1985: 133), who argue that discourse communities are characterized by 'in house language and conventions of discourse'. The key expectation is that all participants in the discourse community possess a discourse competence to allow them to participate as a specialized group.

Further support for the notion of an academic discourse community comes from Ballard and Clanchy (1988); Hounsell (1988); Bizell (1982) and Bartholomae (1986), who all argue that universities and other institutions of higher education both shape and elicit a distinctive use of language which is inextricably linked to the particular cultural context of higher education.

Academic literacy, then, is a particular kind of literacy, one with its own rules and conventions – a code of its own. Becoming literate in higher education therefore involves learning to read the culture of the university or, as Hounsell (1988) describes it, learning to crack the code.

Most research into academic literacy makes the assumption that most academics intuitively understand the cultural code, and it is students who need to be inducted to become an integral part of a 'disciplinary' or 'rhetorical', discourse community (Bartholomae 1986; Bizell 1982; Purves and Purves 1986; Berkenkotter *et al.* 1988; Hounsell 1988; Harris 1989; Taylor 1989). In this regard, Bartholomae (1986: 134) makes the following point:

> Every time a student sits down to write for us, he has to invent the university for the occasion – invent the university, that is a branch of it, like history or anthropology or economics or English. The student has to learn to speak our language, to speak as we do, to try on the peculiar ways of knowing, selecting, evaluating, reporting, concluding, and arguing that define the discourse of our community.

That academics have an implicit understanding of the culture and rules of the community should however not be taken for granted. This assumption needs further investigation. In addition, we cannot be entirely sure that individuals, even in the same cultural setting, have the same idea of when a cultural or a text model is approximated. For example, one academic assessing a student's essay (be it an analysis, an argument, a report or a hybrid of two or more of these genres) may think the model has been approximated when all the ideas are set out in order. Another might think that it is when the ideas have been elaborated and a third might argue that it is only when the ideas are presented without a flaw that the model has been approximated. They may have differing ideas about the model itself, its linguistic and structural characteristics, as well as the sort of information that should be included in the text. The central argument here is that the culture shapes not only the nature and structure of texts, but also the processes by which we acquire them. It would be reasonable to expect, therefore, that academics who share the same cultural environment would have a shared understanding of discourse models. This assumption was investigated by Johnson (1994) and some of the findings are discussed in the next section.

Studies in intuition and discourse

Johnson (1994) conducted a series of related studies into the implicit understandings academics have about the way in which language functions in academic settings. The studies were interested in exploring the implicit models academics use in framing academic writing tasks and in assessing students' writing. The investigations took the form of a series of 'text-based experiments', carried out with a small group of ten academics.

Study 1: discourse models and implicit knowledge

According to Garner *et al.* (1986: 43), an important feature of text is structure, 'because it specifies the relationship between ideas'. The authors share the view of Kintsch (1982) that all texts share some structural properties and that such structural properties are genre specific. In other words, texts like persuasion, argument and analysis share similar structural features but such features are distinct from those of texts such as personal accounts, narratives and imaginative accounts.

In the first investigation, academics were given six texts to read. These had been classified previously by linguists independent of the study. The academics were asked to classify the texts as those which told some kind of a story (narration), those which gave information (exposition) and those in which issues were debated (argumentation). The results were surprising. Only half of the sample recognized narrative texts and only three lecturers identified those texts which belonged in the exposition genre. However, if Andrews (1989) is correct in thinking that expositional texts are 'inert' in that they borrow structures from narrative and argument in order to give themselves shape and direction, it is possible to see why most of the respondents assumed that this cluster of texts belonged in the argumentation genre. Indeed, identifying texts from the argumentation genre did not present lecturers with much difficulty. Those respondents who did not label these texts correctly confused them with expositional texts. It may be assumed that these lecturers were giving scant attention to the rhetorical or discourse structure of the texts and were attending rather to the content issues, or what writers were saying.

The results do not tell us much about whether lecturers have explicit or tacit knowledge of various rhetorical structures of text, nor whether this knowledge exists but for some reason is not applied here. However, they do begin to suggest that lecturers need a principled basis from which they can begin to distinguish between genres.

In a variation of this study (Johnson 1994), designed to establish what knowledge lecturers had of the discourse elements of texts, an interesting picture emerged. The same academics were asked to identify structural and rhetorical elements in the narration, argumentation and exposition genres. Structural elements in the narrative genre are 'characters', 'plot' and so on. According to Bereiter and Scardamalia (1987), knowledge of the structural elements of discourse is important in order to understand the differences between texts. In the narration genre, lecturers recognized a mean total of 19 elements out of a possible 160. The most elements recognized by a individual respondent was 4. Even more surprising however was the knowledge of rhetorical elements lecturers displayed in the exercise on 'argument'. Again a mean total of 19 discourse elements were recognized. The exercise on exposition further supports the suggestion made earlier about this genre: none of the respondents were able to identify any of the elements belonging to it.

In broad terms, the results have implications for the assumption that educators have a sound knowledge of the structural elements of genre. The study indicates that such an assumption is likely to be unfounded. However, the limitation of such investigations is the small sample size and the fact that the sample was not randomly selected. However, the study suggests that a similar result might well emerge if the study were to be replicated for a larger population. The issue of the representativeness of the sample remains open.

The implications of the findings may be weighed up in terms of the importance of a knowledge of genre which educators need in order to help their students develop their literacy skills. According to Connor (1990) teachers need to evaluate students' writing at various levels in their development of genre knowledge and 'a crucial factor affecting teachers as evaluators of student writing is the recognition by teachers of those features that define genre and are valued by the audience' (p. 74).

Study 2: is task setting an explicit or intuitive activity?

Contrary to the view that the difficulties writers have in grasping the expectations of academic writing tasks reside almost wholly in the writer, there have been several claims that the content quality and quantity of the academic essay are significantly affected by the nature of the question (Britton *et al.* 1975; Applebee 1982; Ruth and Murphy 1984; Hamp-Lyons 1988; Nightingale 1989).

Despite growing recognition that the nature of questions and how they influence writing is of particular importance, there is not much research on the topic. Nor, it would appear, is there much evidence that task setting in higher education is an explicit, research- and theory-led activity. For example, it is not clear why lecturers sometimes use key words like *'discuss'* and at other times *'critically discuss'*. This obviously raises the question as to what the difference between the two types of text is. It is also a problem with which students frequently have to grapple.

It is not clear whether the words used in task setting are specifically and consciously chosen to elicit a specific type of writing, or whether they are used intuitively to mean different things by different lecturers as a rough indication of what they expect, and which students are expected somehow to decode. Johnson (1994) interviewed ten academic staff about the activity of task setting. A sample of assignment topics written by these academics, and going back three years, was collected. During the interviews lecturers were presented with the essay questions that they had set, and were asked to comment on the way in which they used instruction verbs differently. What was of interest was whether lecturers interpreted the use of instruction verbs like 'discuss', 'critically discuss' or 'analyse' as intending to elicit different genres. A further concern was whether they had a clear framework within which to assess such different genres, or whether the instruction verbs were in fact all nominally intended to elicit a form of writing, which lecturers would recognize intuitively as analytical writing.

The study found that the academics did not appear to give much thought to the setting of academic writing tasks. The main problem seemed to be that lecturers did not consider carefully enough the instruction verbs they used. Lecturers appeared to adopt the position that there are only a few ways in which to ask academic writing questions and felt that by changing the order of the instruction verbs, enough variation is created to make questions look different. White (1988) lends credence to this argument. He writes: 'One of my friends remarked that, like plots of western novels, there are only 17 basic essay topics, and we just write a million variations' (p. 233).

The issue however is not so much about how many types of essay questions there are, but about the way variation is created. Hence, although it is arguable that there are only 17 basic essay topics, it is not so difficult to believe that lecturers generally seek to create variations in the questions they set. It has already been pointed out that the most preferred instruction verb in the academic setting is 'discuss' and the problem with creating a variety of 'discuss' questions, merely for the sake of creating variation in a question paper is the nub of the issue. Asking students in one question to 'discuss' an issue and in another to 'discuss the issue critically' creates more confusion than variety. Most lecturers who were interviewed seemed to agree that the use of different varieties of the same instruction verb did not come about as a conscious decision to elicit from students different genres. In so saying, they admit that they are not always absolutely clear about what they want the student writer to achieve in the essay. Lecturers admitted that they generally did not give much thought to setting writing tasks from the students' point of view. Just as students often 'just write', lecturers often 'just set writing tasks'. They usually 'just phrase a question and give it to the students'. Consider the point made by one of the interviewees in the following extract: 'usually you just tend to phrase the question and give the question to the students . . . hoping that the students will meet with the expectation.' The point made by the interviewee is consistent with the conclusions drawn by Hamp-Lyons (1988) with regard to task setting. She suggests that 'setters of essay test questions are themselves not conscious of some of the "messages" they are sending out, or that they have failed to convey exactly their intended "message"' (p. 37).

It is clear that the issue of task setting is problematic. The study reveals that lecturers set writing tasks intuitively, and that they rarely use an explicit framework which is itself based on shared knowledge and verified approximations of a variety of genre types.

Study 3: intuition and assessment

Intuitive judgements play an important part in the assessment of literacy and there is evidence that intuitive judgements of reading (Owen 1992; Stierer 1994) and writing (Johnson 1994) are valid when compared to assessment scores on standardized tests. These judgements, however, are confined to the assessment of the 'global' aspects of text. In other words, broad notions about the writing in relation to the task set. What is less clear is how adequate such intuitive understandings are to the development of academic literacy. It would seem that in order to promote academic literacy, these intuitive judgements need to be made more explicit in such a way that they create the basis for a shared understanding about the role and function of text, between academics and student writers (Ballard and Clanchy 1988).

There is evidence that teachers have implicit knowledge of the structure of texts (Hyland 1990). But tutors appear not to be able to use this knowledge in providing guidance or support to students. Owen (1992) concludes from her study on reading that teachers as experienced readers have a powerful intuitive sense but found that they are rarely able to intervene at other than the word or sentence levels of texts. In other words, the only guidance tutors are able to provide is at the formal level of text – grammar, spelling etc.

In this enquiry, the ten academics involved were asked to assess a piece of writing produced by a student. The writing topic was general, and not related to any specific discipline. It required the student to consider the statement 'Boxing should be banned as a sport' and to write an argument either supporting or contesting the claim. Academics were asked to assess the writing and to decide whether, as an argument, the writing was successful or not successful. They were then interviewed about their implicit understandings of what constituted a successful piece of writing in this genre.

Six academics 'failed' the script while four 'passed' it. Discussions revealed that academics had some shared notions of what constituted a successful response. They shared such conventions as the need to provide evidence on both sides of the argument and the need to support claims. The problem was that each academic placed a different emphasis on what was deemed to be important. Thus, each had a different mental and cultural model of what most closely approximated an 'argument'.

Discussion

The series of studies above shows that activities such as task setting and assessment are based on intuitive practice. The knowledge base (at least that which was available to lecturers at a metacognitive level) which governs such practice is, it would seem, limited and fragmented. Thus, the current model of academia as a community is one where intuitive knowledge exists, some of which is shared and some not. Academics, it would appear, understand the rules and conventions in the community, but it is arguable the extent to which this implicit knowledge forms a common framework which is capable of governing the practices of the community. Aligned to this is the fact that implicit knowledge of the practices of the community are not made explicit. Thus newcomers to the community, both new staff as well as new students, have a difficult time becoming 'oldtimers'.

The challenge we face is finding ways to improve professional practice. There is no doubt that intuitive ways of knowing and doing are an integral part of the way in which we function as professionals but it would seem that relying simply on intuition in professional practice is not enough. We might have to find ways to make that which we know implicitly and do intuitively, both explicit and shared. The relationship between explication and sharing is an important one. There have been several attempts in professional settings to develop explicit 'markers' of practice. These are often contained in guides or templates – a standard way of doing things. The problem with much of this is that it is developed not by building on that which professionals know implicitly but on decontextualized understandings of what it means to improve professional practice.

What is perhaps more appropriate is to find ways in which we can develop the professional community (in this case, the academic community) as a community of practice in the ways suggested by Lave and Wenger (1991). Here, we would seek to engage with what is known and understood, and through shared participation in the community of practice, seek to reflect on knowledge and practice in an attempt to develop an appropriate set of principles to guide the activity of the community. In practical terms, lecturers and students would need to spend time working out what an 'analysis' is, for example. How is it approximated, how should it be elicited and what features are important in its assessment? Resulting models could be made explicit, but should never be fixed. They would offer the framework through which apprenticeship, guided participation and participatory appropriation, in Lave's terms, can continue to govern the practice of the academic community.

Conclusion

This chapter has set out to argue that intuition is as much a product of social interaction as an element of individual cognitive behaviour. Further, that intuitive ways of knowing are central to much of the activity of the academic discourse community, particularly the framing of writing tasks, the production of written texts and the activity of assessment. I have argued that intuitive practice is individual rather than shared and that developing professional practice is perhaps better achieved through shared practice. I have argued further that shared practice might be built on that which professionals know and do intuitively, but that through a process of reflection on what it is we know that we know, we develop models of practice built on explicit principles. It is these explicit principles which ought to guide the processes whereby newcomers to the academic community learn the rules and conventions. These principles help bring about, in Lave's terms, a 'transparency of the socio-political organisation of practice' (1991: 102). I have also argued that it is only through participation in the (transparent) practice of the community that professionals can both appropriate, but also transform, knowledge and practice.

References

Andrews, R. (1989) *Narrative and Argument*. Milton Keynes: Open University Press.
Applebee A.N. (1982) *Writing in the Secondary School*. Urbana, IL: National council for the teaching of English.

Ballard, B. and Clanchy, J. (1988) Literacy in the university: an 'Anthropological' approach, in G. Taylor (ed.) *Literacy by Degrees*. Milton Keynes: SRHE/Open University Press.

Bartholomae, D. (1986) Words from afar, in A.R. Petrosky and D. Bartholomae (eds) *The Teaching of Writing*. Chicago, IL: National Society for the Study of Education.

Bereiter, C. and Scardamalia, M. (1987) *The Psychology of Written Composition*. Hillsdale, NJ: Lawrence Erlbaum.

Berkenkotter, C., Huckin, T.N. and Ackerman, J. (1988) Conventions, conversions and the writer: Case study of a student in the rhetoric PHD program. *Research in the Teaching of English*, 22(1): 9–44.

Bizell, P. (1982) College composition: initiation into the academic discourse community. *Curriculum Inquiry*, 12: 191–207.

Britton, J., Burgess, T., Martin, N., McLeod, A. and Rosen, H. (1975) *The Development of Writing Abilities (11–18)*. London: Macmillan Education Ltd.

Bruner, J. (1990) *Acts of Meaning*. Cambridge, MA: Harvard University Press.

Clement, J. (1994) Use of physical intuition and imagistic simulation in expert problem solving, in D. Tirosh (ed.) *Implicit and explicit knowledge: an educational approach*. (*'Human development'* Vol. 6). NJ: Ablex Publishing Corporation.

Cole, M. (1995) Socio-cultural-historical psychology: some general remarks and a proposal for a new kind of cultural-genetic methodology, in J. Wertsch, P. del Rio and A. Alvarez (eds) *Sociocultural Studies of the Mind*. New York: Cambridge University Press.

Connor, V. (1990) *Coherence: Research and Pedagogical Perspectives*. Washington, DC: TESOL.

del Rio, P. and Alvarez, A. (1995) Tossing, praying and thinking: the changing architecture of mind and agency, in J. Wertsch, P. del Rio and A. Alvarez (eds) *Sociocultural Studies of Mind*. New York: Cambridge University Press.

di Sessa, A.A. (1983) Phenomenology and the evolution of intuition, in D. Genter and A. Stevens (eds) *Mental Models*. Hillsdale, NJ: Lawrence Erlbaum.

Faigley, L. and Hansen, K. (1985) Learning to write in the social sciences. *College Composition and Communication*, 36: 140–9.

Garner, R., Alexander, P., Slater, W. and Hare, V. (1986) Childrens' knowledge of structural properties of expository text. *Journal of Educational Psychology*, 78(6): 411–16.

Gumperz, J.J. (1971) *Language, Social Knowledge and Interpersonal Relations*. Berkley, CA: University of California.

Hamp-Lyons, L. (1988) Second language writing: assessment issues, in. B. Kroll (ed.) *Second Language Writing: Research Insights for the Classroom*. Cambridge: Cambridge University Press.

Harris, J. (1989) The idea of community in the study of writing. *College Composition and Communication*, 40: 1.

Hounsell, D. (1988) Towards an anatomy of academic discourse: meaning and context in the undergraduate essay, in R. Saljo (ed.) *The Written Word: Studies in Literature Thought and Action*. Berlin: Springer Verlag.

Hyland, K. (1990) A genre description of the argumentative essay. *RELC Journal*, 21(1): 68–78.

Hymes, D. (1972) Models of the interaction of language and social life: directions in sociolinguistics, in J.J. Gumperz and D. Hymes (eds) *The Ethnography of Communication*, pp. 35–71. New York: Rinehart and Winston.

Johnson, D. (1994) 'The effectiveness of a genre-based approach to academic literacy', unpublished PhD thesis. University of Bristol.

Kintsch, W. (1982) Text representations, in W. Otto and S. White (eds) *Reading Expository Material*. New York: Academic Press.

Lave, J. (1997) What's special about experiments as contexts for thinking, in M. Cole, Y. Engstrom and O. Vasques (eds) *Mind, Culture and Activity*. Cambridge: Cambridge University Press.

Lave, J. (1991) Situating Learning in Communities of Practice, in L. Resnick, J. Levine and S. Teasley (eds) *Perspectives on Socially Shared Cognition*. Washington, DC: American Psychological Association.

Lave, J. and Wenger, E. (1991) *Situated Learning, Legitimate Peripheral Participation*. New York: Cambridge University Press.

Nightingale, P. (1989) Language and learning: a bibliographical essay, in G. Taylor (ed.) *Literacy by Degrees*. Milton Keynes: SRHE/Open University Press.

O'Malley, C.E. and Draper, S.W. (1992) Representation and interaction, in Y. Rogers, A. Rutherford and P. Bibby (eds) *Models in the Mind: Theory, Perspectives and Application*. London: Academic Press.

Owen, P. (1992) Defining reading standards: establishing the operational validity of assessments, in M. Hayhow and S. Parker (eds) *Reassessing Language and Literacy*. Buckingham: Open University Press.

Payne, S.J. (1992) On mental models and cognitive artifacts, in Y. Roberts, A. Rutherford and P. Bibby (eds) *Models in the Mind: Theory, Perspective and Application*. London: Academic Press.

Purves, A. and Purves, W. (1986) Culture, text models and the activity of writing. *Research in the Teaching of English*, 174–97.

Rogoff, B. (1995) Observing sociocultural activity on three planes: participatory appropriation, guided participation and apprenticeship, in J. Wertsch, P. del Rio and A. Alvarez (eds) *Sociocultural Studies of Mind*. New York: Cambridge University Press.

Ruth, L. and Murphy, S. (1984) Designing tools for writing assessment: problems of meaning. *College Composition and Communication*, 35: 410–22.

Scardamalia, M. and Bereiter, C. (1994) Development of dialectical processes in composition, in B. Stierer and J. Maybin (eds) *Language, Literacy and Learning in Educational Practice*. Milton Keynes: The Open University.

Stierer, B. (1994) Simply doing their job? The politics of reading standards and real books, in B. Stierer and J. Maybin (eds) *Language, Literacy and Learning in Educational Practice*. Milton Keynes: The Open University.

Swales, J.M. (1990) *Genre Analysis: English in Academic Settings*. New York: Cambridge University Press.

Taylor, G. (1989) The literacy of knowing: content and form in students' English, in G. Taylor (ed.) *Literacy by Degrees*. Milton Keynes: SRHE/Open University Press.

Vygotsky, L.S. (1978) *Mind in Society: The Development of Higher Psychological Processes*. Cambridge, MA: Harvard University Press.

Vygotsky, L.S. (1987) *The Collected Works of L.S. Vygotsky: Vol. 1, Problems of General Psychology*, trans. N. Minick. New York: Plenum.

Wertsch, J.V. (1995) The need for action in sociocultural research, in J.V. Wertsch, P. del Rio and A. Alvarez (eds) *Sociocultural Studies of Mind*. New York: Cambridge University Press.

Wertsch, J.V. (1997) Collective memory: issues from a socio-historical perspective, in M. Cole, Y. Engstrom and O. Vasquez (eds) *Mind, Culture and Activity*. New York: Cambridge University Press.

White, R.V. (1988) Academic writing: process and product, in P.C. Robinson (ed.) *Academic Writing: Process and Product*. London: Modern English Publications/British Council.

 **Part 5**

The Intuitive Practitioner:
a critical overview

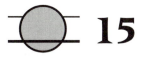 **15**

The Intuitive Practitioner: a critical overview

Michael Eraut

This book provides a fascinating case study of conceptions of intuition. The range of ideas about the nature of intuition is considerable and half the contributions contain empirical data about the role of intuition in professional practice. As befits its origin in a School of Education, the main emphasis is on teaching: which, together with its ancillary activities of management, assessment, teacher education and professional development, provides a rich context for explaining the nature of intuition, and its contribution to professional life. This concluding chapter provides a personal overview from outside Bristol of the range of understandings of intuition portrayed, and addresses five questions in turn:

- What range of phenomena can be properly described as intuitive?
- Where and when do they occur?
- What is their relationship to rational and reflective thinking?
- What is the significance of intuition for professionals, for their clients and policy?
- What are the implications for the development of future professional practice?

My personal preference is for clarity of definition wherever possible, but also for inclusiveness. Though my own preferred definition of intuition does not include all the phenomena described as intuitive by my co-authors, that does not detract from the points they are making. Thus I am generally, but not totally, in accord with Guy Claxton's excellent introduction of the term 'intuition' and I appreciate the cohesion it provides for this book. Having just finished an article on non-formal learning, implicit learning and tacit knowledge (Eraut 1999), my concern is about how *intuition* relates to *implicit learning* and *tacit knowledge*. All three terms refer to mental processes and their outcomes, none bypass the brain, and all three refer to phenomena which we experience but cannot explain. However, the terms are not interchangeable, not even, in my personal framework, overlapping.

Human learning is a process of which we may be conscious (explicit learning) or unaware (implicit learning). Its outcome is the acquisition of information (words, images, impressions, etc.) which, in its organized, usable form, we call knowledge. When that knowledge cannot be described or explained we refer to it as 'tacit knowledge'. We should note, however, that tacit knowledge can be acquired explicitly (as when learning to swim or ride a bicycle) as well as implicitly (as when you know somebody from a series of incidental encounters without ever having taken any deliberate action to get to know them). Explicit knowledge cannot be directly acquired implicitly but some, though not all, tacit knowledge can be quickly made explicit (as when constructing an identikit picture).

Learning is a process, while knowledge is an outcome of that process; but what is intuition? I concur with Claxton's preferred definition of intuition as 'immediate apprehension, without the intervention of any reasoning process', which clearly refers to a rapid process. The outcome of this process is typically referred to as a hunch, a feeling or an insight which may then be followed by a decision or an action; but what is the input? Two types of context readily come to mind. One is that of rumination, as Claxton likes to call it, when no significant new information is being received. The intuitive process then appears to involve selections from prior knowledge being brought together and suddenly being recognized as a significant combination for the problem in mind – Claxton refers to this as *creativity* and *problem-solving*. The second context involves decision making: new information is recognized as forming a familiar pattern and leading on to a familiar course of action associated with that pattern. Information acquired by 'reading' a new situation is recognized as matching *patterns* established for previous similar situations and the usual response is made, perhaps with some slight modification. The feature common to both contexts is the retrieval from memory of prior knowledge, its linkage to other knowledge (old or new) and immediate apprehension of what to do next.

Claxton, following Belenky *et al.* (1986), describes varieties of intuition as 'ways *of* knowing'; but if intuition is a process, would it not be better described as a 'way *to* knowing'? Alternatively, if learning is regarded as the acquisition of knowledge, intuition might be regarded as a form of knowledge use, with learning as a possible side-effect. In either case I have some difficulty in sustaining all six of Claxton's varieties. *Rumination*, for example, is not a separate variety of intuition but a facilitating factor in creative problem-solving. *Implicit learning* cannot be a form of intuition, because people know when they are having an intuition and do not know when they are engaged in implicit learning. What implicit learning contributes to intuition is tacit knowledge that can only be used intuitively, because using knowledge rationally requires that it be explicit rather than tacit. Claxton confirms my argument rather than his own when he refers to implicit learning as the acquisition of expertise by non-conscious means.

Ironically, the outcomes of 'intuitive thinking' described as hunches, feelings or insights are frequently reported in self-accounts of explicit learning. They refer to such phenomena as connecting different pieces of knowledge together (pattern notes and concept maps are used as mediating artefacts to facilitate this process), sudden understanding of an explanation ('the penny dropped') and developing personal models of the situation (sometimes facilitated by computer-based modelling tools). I would argue that the key feature of progressing from a surface-processing to a deep-processing approach to academic reading is ceasing to focus entirely on the written text and trying to create mental models to represent either the author's underlying intentions or your own preferred conceptual framework for the topic. A second aspect of learning which could be regarded as intuitive is the metacognitive control of one's attention: picking up key features of a text when skim-reading, sensing which references to follow up and which to ignore when reading a journal paper, finding new ideas by browsing in a library.

Claxton's notion of 'sensitivity' seems to be rather confused. Heightened awareness can arise either through metacognitive focus or through emotions that stimulate the production of adrenalin or drugs that have a similar effect. But the term 'sensing' is more likely to refer to non-verbal communication as a mode of learning about people and situations. The use of metaphors for such learning in non-academic contexts is particularly revealing: 'She read the situation'; 'You have to follow your nose'; 'He cannot see the wood for the trees'; 'I sensed that he was hiding something'.

The last two of Claxton's varieties are linked to decision making. *Judgement* normally refers to decision making in situations where there is disagreement or uncertainty, and time to deliberate and possibly consult. One feature it shares with problem-solving is the intuitive retrieval from memory of potentially relevant information. In both processes there is time to transform or reorganize this information in a conscious, explicit and purposeful manner. The other possibly intuitive element in judgement is a sense of fitness for purpose which goes beyond logical analysis. This may either help to resolve the uncertainty inherent in trying to combine different factors and interests or else cause judges to re-examine their initially favoured option because it did not 'feel quite right'. A deliberative process is likely to be called 'judgement' if the focus is on deciding between a small number of alternative options in a complex, uncertain situation. It is more likely to be described as 'problem-solving' if (a) there is an identified problem needing to be framed and analysed and (b) the focus is on finding a novel solution to that problem rather than deciding between already familiar alternatives.

Expertise is a rather difficult term to use. Psychologists in the last 20 years have conducted large numbers of 'novice–expert' studies but without using a consistent definition of the term 'expert': it has been used to mean any professional with a given amount of experience, a professional with a specialist role (e.g. a medical consultant), a person with an international reputation or a Nobel prizewinner. Psychologists have linked expertise to both rapid decision making and judgement. Claxton describes it best in his concluding section as 'the ability to function fluently and flexibly in complex domains without being able to describe or theorize one's expertise'. There is considerable variation in the extent to which experts can describe at least some of their expertise, but in rapid decision making it is clear that they do not use that expertise consciously at the time. Thus it fits my definition of an intuitive process, whereas when making deliberative judgements about situations, expertise will be used in a very explicit way. Expertise is not a process but a term used to describe the specialized knowledge of experts, both explicit and tacit. Judgement is a deliberative process which draws mainly on explicit knowledge, but rapid decision making is a largely intuitive process which draws almost entirely on tacit knowledge. Some of that tacit knowledge may be easily made explicit on later reflection, some with considerable difficulty and some not at all.

What enables rapid decision making is, first, the rapid reading of the situation with the aid of prior knowledge, and then, second, the rapid linkage of that situational understanding with an immediate course of action, using prior knowledge of what has worked before and possibly adjusting it to take quickly recognized situational differences into account. The demands for rapid action place limits on both the accuracy of the situational understanding and its match with situations previously encountered, not to mention the attribution of the success of previous action to that particular action. The terms 'complex' and 'flexible' are important here. Failure to describe fluent routinized actions in explicit terms justifies the description of tacit knowledge but does not make those actions intuitive – 'mindless' could be a more appropriate description of riding a bicycle around a track. Professional practice, however, rarely consists of routinized actions alone – such actions are punctuated by myriad rapid decisions, for example, how to respond to the client one is interviewing, how to handle a disruptive pupil, etc. It is these decisions which require intuitive responses, not the ongoing performance. This distinction is not always clear-cut. The comprehension and production of speech will be relatively routine, while the objectives, tone, timing and emotion may be adjusted to the developing situation.

Overall I have so far identified four contexts in which professionals use intuition: problem-solving, decision making, learning and assessing situations. The intuitive processes themselves have been described in the following terms: retrieval of knowledge from memory, insight through connecting different areas of knowledge, sensing new aspects of the situation, recognizing familiar patterns, rapidly deciding on an option to respond to a changing situation, feeling that a particular course of action or 'solution' best fits the situation/problem. All these processes, even that of sensing new aspects of the situation, are dependent on a professional's prior knowledge and experience, both that which has been explicitly developed and that which has been implicitly acquired. However, when quick decisions or rapid action are required, a large part of the knowledge synthesis process must have already occurred, perhaps over a series of fairly similar occasions. This ready-to-use 'action knowledge' is largely tacit: to have it in explicit form would make it too slow and cumbersome. When the process is more deliberative, explicit knowledge is likely to be consciously used, but the insight which leads to the solution of a problem or informs a difficult judgement may still be sudden and inexplicable. In this latter case rumination sometimes facilitates one's progress, but other situations such as consultation with others and thinking under pressure can also stimulate new ideas. 'Necessity', it is said, 'is the mother of invention.'

Before moving on to discuss the role of intuition in specific contexts, I wish to comment briefly on some of the theoretical issues raised by other authors. Gill Gregory, for example, raises the question of whether intuition is a personality trait, a disposition, a skill, a state of mind, and/or problem-specific. Having just identified six different intuitive processes, I would also ask whether intuition is process specific. Given my earlier definition, it would be illogical to consider intuition as a state of mind, though intuitive processes might be facilitated by certain states of mind (e.g. a more general version of the rumination hypothesis). My emphasis on prior knowledge would also suggest a great deal of problem specificity: so also would an increasingly massive body of research on expertise. The need for experience also suggests that dispositional factors will influence individuals' use of intuition and the significance accorded to it. Lucy Atkinson and Gill Gregory both refer to confidence in one's own judgement, which links with Bandura's (1982) emphasis on 'self-efficacy' and my own finding that confidence is an important factor affecting learning in the workplace (Eraut *et al.* 1998). Agnes McMahon refers to stress as an inhibiting factor, which I would classify as partly dispositional and partly situational. Several authors suggest that hyper-rational approaches to pupil assessment and teacher appraisal will cause intuitive processes to weaken from disuse. However, I do not believe that this would lead to people making less use of intuition in other, non-professional, aspects of their lives. Hence I find it difficult to entertain with any seriousness the idea of intuition as a trait. Nor can I respond with any enthusiasm to the idea of intuition as a skill, because it is a sudden, unexpected and rapid process. The use of intuition, however, is an important aspect of professional expertise. In conclusion, I would therefore argue that intuition is a domain-specific (not problem-specific) process and that the use of intuition is an important dimension of professional practice affected by dispositional as well as other factors.

The final theoretical issue I wish to resolve is the idea introduced by Gerald Clibbon and Arlene Gilpin (and followed up by several other contributors) of naive and elaborated levels of intuition. The general idea is interesting, but I think that it is wrong to attribute levels to the intuitive process itself, about which we know very little indeed. What becomes increasingly elaborated through professional experience and development is first the tacit knowledge base on which intuition relies and, second, the practice itself as the professional learns to make appropriate use of intuition and to take into account its potential fallibility.

Intuition in teaching

I found three of the papers on intuition in teaching particularly valuable in quite distinctive ways. Terry Atkinson's thinking is close to my own, but I like the way he persistently asks questions which challenge common 'taken-for-granted' assumptions. He points out (1) that learning to teach in a purely school-based programme is unlikely to lead to improvements in practice, and (2) that the outcome of the attempt to use reflection to reconstruct practice as a learning experience is likely to be personal knowledge about practice rather than ready-to-use practical know-how: 'Reflection on practice may lead to better understanding but not necessarily to better practice.' Would it be better, he asks, to use reflection as a 'tool for developing intuition'? 'Both reason and intuition can be viewed as tools having certain characteristics which make each more or less suitable for any given task. Teachers need to be able to use each tool and to know when to use which one or when and how to use both at the same time.' He cites the work of Elbaz and Clandinin on the guiding role of images of how good teaching should look and feel, arguing that images operate at a more holistic level than theory and can be used more readily by practitioners in the art of teaching itself. This is a further addition to my list of intuitive processes, one that operates (in my own view) at a metacognitive level. The other two intuitive processes Atkinson discusses are pattern recognition, which 'allows the teacher to read the context at a glance and to adapt the preconceived plan in the light of the changing context' and fluent performance, which depends on integrating routinized action with rapid decision making. Alongside these intuitive processes, Atkinson argues that teachers need analytic and objective thinking 'to plan for learning' and 'the reflective thinking that is crucial to monitoring and learning from experience'. His concluding case studies relate to developing 'intuitive skills' in student teachers. These are: seeing patterns, fluency, flexibility, coping with complexity, and being holistic and self-aware. I would prefer to call them 'attributes', but do not dispute their prime importance. I look forward to teacher educators taking up this challenge!

Peter John's excellent chapter presents data from post-lesson stimulated recall interviews with 15 student teachers. Of particular interest are his evidence for 'key moments' of reflection during the course of their lessons and for responses which anticipate future problems in the lesson rather than reacting to them after they have happened. His discussion notes that this flexible reframing-in-action is underpinned by an important sense of routine and also uses recipes culled from a wide range of sources. John then suggests for further research five models of intuition related to thinking. Two of these are proactive: problem avoidance and opportunity creation; and three are more reactive: interpretation of pupil cues, mood assessment and improvisation. He speculates that the more effective teacher may be one with 'a more highly-tuned and highly differentiated intuition for understanding and interpreting classroom life, and a wide repertoire of appropriate models for reacting to specific situations'.

Laurinda Brown and Alf Coles' evidence relates mainly to the teaching of Coles, a recently qualified maths teacher. The additional interest in this chapter is that doing mathematics is itself a form of problem-solving; and in the view of many mathematics educators engagement in authentic mathematical problems is the best way to learn mathematics. Their quotations from Bruner refer not only to moments of insight when a solution is actually achieved, but also to holistic understanding – 'Intuition implies the act of grasping the meaning, significance or structure of a problem or situation without explicit reliance on the analytic apparatus of one's craft' (Bruner 1966: 60) – and a good feel for what could be a fruitful approach to trying to solve a problem. They describe this as an anticipatory form of intuition.

Brown and Coles' image of an intuitive practitioner is of a teacher able to stay with the complexity of the situation and to adapt their lessons to the contributions of their students (both stressed by Atkinson), who can also 'provide the grit in the oyster and then work with the consequences' and 'subordinate their teaching to their pupils' learning'. These latter two purposes are concerned with developing pupils' own use of intuition in mathematical problem-solving. They give considerable attention to pupils' confidence and motivation as key factors facilitating pupils' learning, and provide some vivid classroom examples to illustrate their case. They also stress what John calls 'opportunity creation' and suggest that this is more likely to occur when planning is emergent rather than predetermined, i.e. having several possible courses of action in mind for a lesson and being prepared to use any one or more of them in order to 'go with the flow' and sustain the motivation generated by pupils' enquiry. This is facilitated by the use of middle-range purposes (I would call them sub-goals) as guides to teaching for various phases of a lesson. These purposes, they conclude from their experience, are the most appropriate level of discussion for encouraging teachers to share their practice and learn from each other. More general aims cause ideological debate, and detailed classroom behaviour is too personal and idiosyncratic; but middle-range purposes provide an excellent framework for exchanging ideas and developing practice, and also for emergent planning which enables the teacher to respond flexibly to developing classroom situations.

Intuition in the curriculum and assessment

The contributions in this area are of three kinds: those arguing that modernist approaches to curriculum and assessment are excluding opportunities for children to develop those dispositions and skills associated with independent learning, creativity and problem-solving which most analysts predict will be widely needed in the future; those arguing that the education of feeling and emotion is being neglected; and those arguing that the process of assessment itself has an important intuitive dimension, whose neglect is leading to education becoming increasingly controlled by hyper-rational theories of assessment which cannot possibly deliver the promised benefits. These arguments are linked in a number of ways, with authors varying in the contexts and priorities they address. Patricia Broadfoot attributes these threats to providing an appropriate education to the hegemony of the modernist project and its wilful denial of the significance of intuitive processes and implicit learning. Other authors focus rather more on the role of intuition in teacher assessment, both presenting empirical evidence of it and reporting that the current trend towards minimizing its role is having the effects on the curriculum described above.

The empirical evidence presented by Richard Brawn, Roger Curtis, Paul Weeden and Jan Winter covers science, art, mathematics and geography. They describe how teachers make use of multiple sources of evidence in assessing their pupils' progress and how they prefer to combine these different sources. Brawn describes how science teachers build up intelligence about individual pupils over a period of several months, deriving evidence 'from many sources – writing (homework, classwork and tests), speaking (direct and indirect questioning and conversation, reading aloud about science) and doing (practical skills observed, and also by observing expressions and body language)'. However, formal test results were dominant in 'shaping the more administrative elements of teaching (for example in setting, determining levels of entry in public examinations, etc.)'. These are often described as 'high stakes' decisions, whereas informal and often intuitive assessments of children play a big part in more immediate classroom decisions. This tension is created by the reluctance of schools or parents to accept evidence that could not easily be explicitly described or justified as free from bias. Nevertheless all eight science teachers interviewed expressed confidence in their intuitive judgements. Their concern is greatest when they felt particular pupils had underperformed in formal tests, which the teachers regarded as unreliable because of the way pupils were disturbed by the testing process. The teachers also expressed the view that the science curriculum was overloaded and gave little time for pupils to play with ideas, investigate or exercise imagination and creativity.

Similar problems arose in art, maths and geography. There was conflict between the assessment criteria which teachers were formally required to use and those that the teachers normally used and associated with the processes of 'doing the subject'. This lack of match weakened teachers' confidence in their own judgements, even when they were based on a wide range of evidence, and distorted the nature of their subject by playing down those areas which are more difficult to assess. The other critical issue is teachers' wish to assess pupils' potential performance by a wide range of process criteria and the quality of their best work, rather than accept the verdict of an inferior test performance. This finding is ironic, given that teachers are constantly accused of having too low expectations of their pupils. This sense of potential is a central aspect of teachers' intuitive judgement, and it is depressing to consider what might be the effect of extinguishing it. It is crucial that such judgements should be regarded as provisional and needing further confirmation; but should not that also apply to test results?

Developing intuition during initial training and continuing professional development

Lucy Atkinson's chapter focuses on the development of intuition in child-hood, arguing that a key feature of professional work is being able to trust in one's judgement – not blindly, but with sufficient confidence to act upon it rather than avoid the responsibility. Thus the disposition to make intuitive judgements may or may not be strong at the time of entering a profession. She argues that to develop an appropriate level of confidence in one's intuition, one needs a well-ordered environment, a high level of support and not too much external direction. Since most authors associate the development of intuition with experience, those whose childhood and youth have been characterized by low self-esteem and low self-efficacy will have acquired less experience of intuitive decision making and hence have a less well-developed intuitive capability. The implication of this analysis is that the counterpart of well-developed intuitive capabilities may not be hyper-rationalism but timid-ity, a quality which probably features quite highly in rejecting applications for training in professions like teaching. It is strange that none of the contributors mention selection for training or for jobs as an area where intuitive judge-ment features prominently!

Atkinson goes on to discuss the influence of structure, support and level of direction in training and working environments but at a rather general level. Gregory notes that senior managers recognize and use intuition in their decision making but tend not to encourage it in others (Atkinson might describe this as a low-support, highly-directed environment). She refers to Noddings and Shore's criteria for enhancing intuition: acknowledgement of intuitive capacity, recog-nizing the existence of intuitive processes and sharing intuitive experiences. Several authors draw attention to these ways of encouraging the disposition to use intuitive processes, but there is an equal desire to enhance intuitive capability by helping students to acquire greater critical control over their use of intuition. They need to recognize that intuition can be fallible, to avoid overconfidence, to know when to trust and when not to trust their intuition. Gregory even suggests putting intuition on the syllabus as a formal topic for study.

There is an unexplored tension in the book between encouraging people to share their experience of intuition in a free uncritical atmosphere (John refers to an open-ended, liberal, loose, non-analytic seminar environment) and a desire to give intuition status by discussing it in a more academic fashion. The looser approach is likely to be favoured by those whose main concern is countering the modernist agenda and empowering the students' voice, the more critical approach by those anxious to integrate evidence gained from both intuitive and rational processes. Brawn describes this as: 'encouraging students to assess the available objective data alongside the perceptual data furnished by their intuition. In this way, both the power of intuitive judge-ments as well as the fallibility of acting on feelings alone might be demon-strated – the harnessing of intuition as the engine of rational thought rather than the replacing of it'.

One solution might be to concentrate on awareness-raising of intuitive processes – for example, through peer group comparisons and student-initiated reflection early in training. This would enable the development of the language needed for talking about intuition. One might then move on to a discussion of fallibility and the integration of implicit knowledge with more explicit knowledge, once the significance of intuitive processes has been firmly established. Most contributors clearly believe that it is possible to be both intuitive and rational about intuition; and those who are mathematicians and scientists are arguing that in those disciplines one has to be both intuitive and rational about reason.

Terry Atkinson and Richard Brawn both recommend specific aspects of intuitive capability for development by teacher educators. These include

- recognizing patterns of behaviours in a class;
- awareness of multiple perceptions, ambiguity and complexity;
- seeking a holistic perspective of situations and one's own role in them;
- flexible lesson planning which can accommodate intuitive pacing and decision-making;
- coping with complexity;
- combining intuitively acquired and explicitly acquired evidence when using deliberative processes, e.g. in assessment;
- focusing on the process of decision making not just on the decisions themselves.

Elisabeth Lazarus concentrates on the intuitive processes used by mentors. One of the most important aspects is their modelling of ways of using intuition such as those listed above. This is particularly difficult and critical when giving students' feedback, and ultimately when assessing them. Mentors, she suggests, intuitively know (or don't know) what to say and how to say it; and when to withdraw or reduce the level of personal support. Linked with this and also to the problem of exploring one's own practice is sensing where the students are coming from, and what they are trying to say to you. Not surprisingly, this was my experience in reading this book. Perhaps one should read it first with an intuitive orientation, then adopt a critical orientation for the second reading?

Intuition and accountability

John Furlong's opening chapter positions intuition in the context of national debates about teacher accountability and professionalism. He rightly points out that judgements based on intuition are ill-suited for public justification; but who is advocating that judgements should be based mainly on intuition? My reading of this book is that its authors are making two main arguments. First, many processes integral to good teaching – flexibility, creativity, sensing children's understandings and dispositions, developing motivation to learn, even judging children's potential – have a strong intuitive dimension.

To try and remove this dimension would turn classrooms into cognitive and interpersonal deserts. To recognize it and develop critical awareness of it will help to develop good teaching. Second, both the assessment of students and the evaluation of teaching need to integrate several different kinds of evidence, some gained intuitively and some gained systematically and rationally. These arguments can be usefully evaluated in two ways: are they true, and whose interest do they serve? My personal view is that they are true and highly consistent with research into the nature of professional expertise. Intuitive processes play an important part in the four contexts I listed earlier: problem-solving, decision making, learning and assessing situations. But in every case, they have to be integrated with rational, and reflective thinking, and the outcomes evaluated after an appropriate interval, so that intuitive thinking can be shaped by evaluated experience using a wide range of criteria. The intuitive processes themselves are easily recognizable. Who does not recall from their life experience examples of retrieval of knowledge from memory, insight through connecting different areas of knowledge, use of mental models and imagery, sensing new aspects of the situation, recognizing familiar patterns, rapidly finding a decision option to respond to a changing situation or problem? These can hardly be excluded from schooling.

So, let me focus on the second evaluative question, that of whose interests are served by the recognition of these intuitive processes. One conclusion is that some degree of discretion has to be given to teachers in their own classrooms. There are limits to the degree of central specification that is compatible with retaining classrooms as humane and effective learning environments. Flexibility, personal respect, motivation and creativity are too important to be snuffed out by over-prescription. However, there will be considerable debate over when that level of control is reached. As teacher educators, the authors of this book have little to gain from recognizing limits to external prescription in schools, but something to gain from applying the same argument to central prescription of practice in teacher education. But the key to this question must surely be not whether proper recognition of intuitive processes will benefit teachers but whether it will benefit pupils. This will depend on the context and conditions in which it happens; and it is these that I now propose to examine.

The key distinction to be made from the outset is that between central prescription and professional accountability. My reading of post-war developments is rather different from Furlong's. Like him I believe in professional accountability, but unlike him I believe that the current increase in central specification was triggered by the professions' reluctance to take their accountability to their clients sufficiently seriously. Teachers' claims for autonomy were not based on arguments about any quasi-scientific knowledge base – they neither possessed one nor expressed any interest in developing one – but on their acquisition through experience of the process skills of teaching and their unique knowledge of their school context and of individual pupils. The brief hegemony of the 'ologies' in teacher education lasted less than 20 years in most departments, from the late 1960s until the early 1980s, and had very little impact on schools.

The dominant feature of the upward accountability of schools throughout the post-war era has been the problematic concept of 'good practice'. This is a socially constructed concept, and it would be impossible to write a plausible account of post-war education without studying the changes and variations in its meaning over time and across localities. Whose definition of good practice counted, where and when? The notion of good practice was virtually untouched by research, though not by examination results. It was extremely prominent in the reports of Her Majesty's Inspectors and local advisers/inspectors, and sustained more by notions of connoisseurship that those of systematic enquiry. Significantly it excluded non-professionals. Its crowning achievement was the creation of a mythological era of progressive education, which was adopted by primary HMI and many local education authority advisers in the early and mid-1960s. I use the word 'mythological' advisedly because the scarcity of 'progressive education' on the ground was revealed by nearly all the large-scale surveys conducted outside London in the 1970s (Bassey 1978; DES 1978; Galton *et al.* 1980). The impact of this myth was revealed by my own research into teacher–parent relations in 1977–9, which found that over 50 per cent of junior-school parents interviewed thought that their children were taught neither spelling nor tables, when in fact they had not only been taught in all the schools concerned but tested weekly. One barrier to the recognition of intuitive processes could be its improper identification with the discredited image of *laissez-faire* progressivism, the supposed (but in most places non-existent) cause of all our educational problems.

Ironically, teachers stood to gain rather than lose from opening up their classrooms to greater parental scrutiny and moving to more equitable relations with parents. Parental anxiety, fanned by their ignorance of what actually went on in school, was misinterpreted by many teachers as hostility. Fears of parent power led to the disregard of parent rights and a situation ripe for politicization (Becker *et al.* 1981). Many of the reforms of the late 1980s and 1990s were predictable. Instead of a relatively informal and equitable relationship between teachers and parents, constructed on mutual understanding, we have government representing the parents' interest by introducing highly formalized accountability mechanisms, incorporating an endless chain of policy initiatives, reduced local discretion and performance indicators. This policy is popular for reasons which go quite deep. The emphasis on the three Rs is popular with employers who do not need highly-skilled workers or prefer to train their own. Schooling is the last arena where strong intergenerational control survives intact and the psychological appeal of maintaining 'disciplined environments' for young people should not be underestimated. Professional distrust and scapegoating will remain popular until professional communication with the public improves dramatically. The vogue for hyper-rational 'solutions' reflects a fear of complexity and a continuing search for authoritative answers. The paradox is that hyper-rational policies are sustained by mainly irrational, unexpressed, intuitive feelings.

The current closing down of space for teachers to develop motivating approaches to learning key concepts and skills constrains one important aspect of intuition-facilitated teaching. But in the classroom penumbra of teacher–pupil and pupil–pupil relationships the intuitive, human processes of assessment and rapid response will become even more important. So also, I would argue, will the use of intuition in more open, responsive relations with parents. However, it is also important to consider future models of decision making and accountability in preparation for a time when the need to develop independent learning, problem-solving and creativity in schools is recognized once more. To avoid any confusion about the role of intuitive processes in that new context I suggest three guiding principles:

1 Intuitive processes need not and should not lead to undisciplined or *laissez-faire* practice. Intuitively derived ideas have to be checked out or tested in a disciplined, rational manner. But this evaluation should not be only on a short-term basis; significant risks need to be assessed early, otherwise premature evaluation can constrain creativity. This type of practice has been thoroughly researched in the field of medicine, particularly for the process of diagnosis (Eraut and Du Boulay 1999).
2 Learner motivation (short-term), knowledge of oneself as a learner (medium-term) and the disposition to learn (long-term) are the most important performance indicators for schools, and need to be extended also to out-of-school contexts in order to provide a foundation for life-long learning. This requires creative and imaginative teaching and the development in learners of the capability to use intuitive, rational and reflective thinking in a balanced and coordinated way. They need the confidence to take risks in learning and a sense of cognitive self-efficacy in a range of learning contexts.
3 Accountability for the long-term progress, motivation and well-being of individual learners is the central responsibility of teachers on which evaluations of practice need to focus. Although learning in schools and most other contexts is strongly influenced by the social environment, and classroom teaching involves a degree of batch-processing, this focus on outcomes for individual clients is critical. For me this implies the periodic review of each student's progress which brings together evidence of student performance with episodes from teachers' notes and episodic memory to gain some understanding of a pupil's achievement and potential, and to probe for teacher actions which might make a difference for that particular pupil. Accountability processes can only be justified if they benefit individual pupils, and decisions at the individual level must necessarily involve the integrated use of all possible kinds of evidence. (Eraut 1993).

The challenge for school management is how to build such reviews into their allocation of school time and extend them to include the pupils and their parents in the most appropriate way. The challenge for policy makers is how to use some of the huge amount of time taken up by assessment for formative decision making, and finding new ways of motivating students and developing their confidence in learning.

References

Bandura, A. (1982) Self-efficacy mechanism in human agency. *American Psychologist,* 37: 122–47.

Bassey, M. (1978) *Nine Hundred Primary School Teachers.* Slough: NFER.

Becher, T., Eraut, M. and Knight, J. (1981) *Policies for Educational Accountability.* London: Heinemann.

Belenky, M., Clinchy, B., Goldberger, N. and Taruk, J. (1986) *Women's Ways of Knowing: The Development of Self, Voice and Mind.* New York: Basic Books.

Bruner, J.S. (1966) *The Process of Education.* Cambridge, MA: Harvard University Press.

DES (Department of Education and Science) (1978) *Primary Education in England.* London: HMSO.

Eraut, M. (1993) Teacher accountability: why it is central to teacher professional development, in L. Kremer-Hayon, H. Vonk and R. Fessler (eds) *Teacher Professional Development: A Multiple Perspective Approach.* Amsterdam: Swets & Zeitlinger.

Eraut, M. (1999) Non-formal learning, implicit learning and tacit knowledge, in F. Coffield (ed.) *Informal Learning.* Bristol: The Policy Press.

Eraut, M., Alderton, J., Cole, G. and Senker, P. (1998) *Development of Knowledge and Skills in Employment* (research report 5). Brighton: University of Sussex Institute of Education.

Eraut, M. and Du Boulay, B. (1999) Developing the Attributes of Medical Professional Judgement and Competence, report to the UK Department of Health.

Galton, M., Simon, B. and Croll, P. (1980) *Inside the Primary Classroom.* London: Routledge.

Index

Abbott, J., 211
absolute standards, 210
academic discourse community, 239–40
    as an intuitive community, 244–5
academic literacy, 11, 239–52
accountability, 28–9
    intuition and, 264–8
acting on intuition, 8, 53–65
activation, 175
advanced skills teachers, 140
aesthetic sensitivity, 47
Agor Intuitive Management (AIM)
    survey, 190
aims, 90, 91–8 *passim*
Allal, L.K., 215
Alred, G., 70
Andrews, R., 246
anticipations, 89, 91–8 *passim*
Apple, M.W., 16
apprenticeship model, 2
argument, 124
    text structure, 242–3, 246
Arnheim, R., 40
art, 221–6, 236–7
articulated knowledge, 125
assessment, 11, 199–238, 261–2
    academic literacy, 248–9
    art, 221–6, 236–7
    geography, 231–5, 236–7
    high price of obsession with outmoded
        forms, 208–15
    maths, 226–31, 236–7

mentoring and, 111
misplaced trust, 208–11
missed opportunities, 211–14
modernist obsession, 202–8
raising profile of emotion, 214–15
science teachers and formal
    assessment, 155–6, 159
attainment targets, 174, 227–8
autonomy, 59–61
    crisis of professionalism, 16, 19–20
awareness, 9, 84–106
awareness-raising, 128

balance, 44–6
base-level categories, 170
Barnett, R., 17, 27
Bartholomae, D., 245
Bartlett, W., 20
Bastick, T., 40–1, 98
Beard, R.M., 59, 63
Bechara, A., 36
beginning teachers, 9, 107–21
Belenky, M.F., 34
beliefs, 130
Benner, P., 77, 152
Bereiter, C., 246
Berg, P., 47
Berliner, D., 110, 114
bias, risk of, 225, 229, 233–4
Binch, N., 225
Black, P., 213
Blunkett, D., 137

Bordage, G., 158
Bourner, T., 63
Bowers, K.S., 42
brainstorming, 187
Briggs, M.I., 190
Brown, J.D., 61
Brown, L., 170
Brown, S., 5, 6, 72, 73, 74–5
Bruner, J.S., 43, 54, 109, 229, 236, 261
    culturally sensitive psychology, 165
    self-confidence, 61
    theory and practice, 113
    Woods Hole Conference, 32, 172
Butler, M., 125

Calderhead, J., 71
Callaghan, J., 19, 28–9
career development, 142, 143
Carr, W., 26, 27
Carter, K., 86
Castells, M., 200
central control, 20
    and accountability, 265–7
    assessment, 206–14
central strategies, 169–70
Charness, N., 191
Cherkaoui, M., 204
Chicago Hilton, 182, 186
Clandinin, D.J., 72–3, 81
Claxton, G., 3, 41, 63, 150–1, 186, 192
Clement, J., 241
Clinchy, B., 43
cognition, 4
cognitive tools, 243
Cole, M., 243
collaborative teaching, 110
collective unconscious, 194
Collison, J., 107–8, 109, 113
communication, 4
communicative action, 27
communities
    academic discourse community,
        239–40, 244–5
    of practice, 179, 240, 243–5, 249–50
competence, 77, 182, 185, 191
competition, 207
complex decision making, 10, 165–81
complexity
    increasing, 176
    manager's role, 183–4

connoisseurship, 226
Connor, V., 247
consciousness, 6
    levels of, 22
consumerism, 206–7
content, 90, 91–8 *passim*
content analysis, 87–98
contextual cues, 98
continuing professional development, *see*
        professional development
control beliefs, 55
Coulson, M., 36
craft knowledge, 125–6
    mentoring, 109–10
    model of professional learning, 2
    teacher education, 73–4
creativity, 38–9, 40, 44, 45, 256
    complex decision making, 176–8
    management education, 10–11,
        186–8
    voices of intuition, 46–7
crisis in professionalism, 8, 15–31
    responding to, 21–7
criteria, 220–38
    work which doesn't fit, 224–5, 228–9,
        232–3
critical theory, 21, 26–7, 29
cryptic crosswords, 166–7
Csikszentmihalyi, M., 49, 167–8, 171,
    214
culturally sensitive psychology, 165
culture, intuition, 11, 239–52
Cupitt, D., 207
curriculum, 261–2
    National Curriculum, *see* National
        Curriculum

Damasio, A.R., 36, 166, 168
D'Andrade, R., 43
Darwin, C., 214
Davidson, J.E., 39
Davies, T., 222
Dearing review, 232–3
decision making, 257–8
    complex, 10, 165–81
deliberations, 89, 91–8 *passim*
Dennehy, E.B., 187
Descartes, R., 33
Dewey, J., 85
DfEE, 213

Di Sessa, A.A., 241
Diehl, M., 187
direction, 55–6, 57, 59–61
disciplined practice, 267
discourse, 27
    academic discourse community,
        239–40, 244–5
    models and implicit knowledge, 246–7
disposition, 188, 190–1
divided reading, 131, 132
domain specificity, 259
Draper, S.W., 241, 243
Dreyfus, H.L., 124, 125, 185, 191
Dreyfus, S.E., 124, 125, 185, 191
D'Silva, M., 110, 114, 116, 117, 118
Dunkin, M.J., 138

Easen, P., 133
Eccles, J.S., 61
educability of intuition, 48–9, 191
educated intuitions, 168, 178–9, 180
Edwards, A., 107–8, 109, 113
effective teaching behaviours, 138–9
Einhorn, H.J., 54
Einstein, A., 113
Eisner, E., 222, 226
elaborated intuition, 122–34, 185
Elbaz, F., 72, 74
Elliott, B., 71
Ellis, R., 128
Elstein, A.S., 158
emotion, 41, 214–15
    student teachers' awareness and
        feelings, 91–8 *passim*
English language teaching (ELT), 9,
        122–34
    task-based teacher education,
        128–33
Enlightenment, 204
environment, 48
    nurturing environments and trust in
        judgement, 55–64
    sensitivity to, 101
Eraut, M., 57, 73, 81, 139, 146, 163
    competence and proficiency, 77
    performance period, 75
    technical rationality, 5–6
Ericsson, K., 191
ethnographic analysis, 87–98
everyday conscious reasoning, 123–4

evidence, 227–8
    integration of multiple evidence,
        153–6, 159–60
evidence-based professionalism, 25
experience, 4, 41
    how teachers' use of intuition changes
        with, 225–6, 229–30, 234–5
    knowledge and, 69–70, 125–6
    on-the-job experience as management
        education, 193–4
    student teachers and, 74–8
experienced teachers, observing, 113–14
expertise, 35, 40, 108, 257–8
    and assessment, 220–38
    management, 185
explicit learning, 212
external examinations, 209–10, 227
extroversion, 189–90

Faigley, L., 244
fallibility of intuition, 42–3
    naive intuitions, 123–8
Fayol, H., 183
feedback, 70
    elaborated intuition, 129–30, 131, 132
    mentoring, 115
    outcome feedback, 57–8
feelings, *see* emotion
Fensham, P.J., 32, 44
Feynmann, R., 167
Figg, M., 225
Finke, R.A., 187
Fischbein, E., 172–3, 230
Fitzgerald, F. Scott, 38
Flammer, A., 55, 61
flow experience, 167–8
Flowers, S., 63
focused awareness, 85
formal-intuitive relationship, 10, 149–64
formal management education, 193
formal reasoning, 123–4
Foucault, M., 204, 205
French Revolution, 204
Fullan, M., 146
Furlong, J., 20, 25, 27, 63, 109, 117

Gage, N.L., 138
Garner, R., 246
Garnham, A., 123–4
Gattegno, C., 174

GCSE, 227
Gelernter, D., 41
Gendlin, E., 47
general practitioners, 152–3, 156–8, 159
genre, 242–3, 246–7
geography, 231–5, 236–7
Getzels, J.W., 49
Gipps, C., 130
Goh, L.H., 116
Goldberg, P., 186
good practice, 266
Gordon, C., 204
Gottfredson, L.S., 205
Grace, G., 19
Greenfield, S., 70, 77
Graves, N., 232
Greyhound Corporation, 186
Grolnik, W.S., 55–6
Gulbenkian Foundation, 222
gut feelings, 33–4, 42, 185–6

Habermas, J., 27
Hall, D., 233–4
Hamp-Lyons, L., 248
Handy, C., 199
Hansen, K., 244
Hanson, F.A., 210, 211
Hargreaves, A., 25, 64
Hargreaves, D., 29, 102, 138
Harris, J., 244
Hartley, J., 59, 63
high modernity, 204
Hilton Hotel, Chicago, 182, 186
Hirst, P., 17, 23–5, 29, 58
Hogarth, R.M., 54
holistic perception, 124–5
  complex decision making, 173, 176
holistic unconscious analogy, 43, 173
Hoyle, E., 16, 17, 18, 59–60, 112
Hughes, A., 224
Hughes, T., 46
humanistic approach to professionalism,
  28–30
hunches, 33–4, 42, 185–6
hypotheses, 43–4

ideal speech situation, 27
images
  and intuitive decision making, 72–3
  of self, 168

teachers' images and purposes, 170
implicit knowledge, 125–6
  discourse models and, 246–7
  mentoring, 109–10
implicit learning, 36, 40, 108, 212
  intuition, tacit knowledge and, 255–9
improvisation, 99–100
in-company training programmes, 193
in-school support, 145
incubation (rumination), 39–40, 186–8,
  256
individual learners, 267
individualization, 204
information
  overload, 183–4
  put to use, 125
information and communication
  revolution, 211
information processing skills, 86
initial teacher education, *see* teacher
  education
insight, 126
instrumentalism, 214
intelligence, 212
intelligence testing, 205
interactional properties, 170
international surveys of student
  achievement, 205–6
interpretation, 99, 100
interpretive tradition, 26
introversion, 189–90
intuition, 3–4, 8, 32–52, 172–4
  and accountability, 264–8
  in assessment, 261–2
  balance, 44–6
  in complex decision making, 174–9
  continuum, 126–8, 185
  in current climate, 222–4, 227–8,
    232
  in the curriculum, 261–2
  developing, 146, 193–4, 263–4
  educability of, 48–9, 191
  facets of, 40–2
  fallibility of, 42–3, 123–8
  how teachers' use of intuition changes
    with experience, 225–6, 229–30,
    234–5
  implicit learning, tacit knowledge and,
    255–9
  intuitions as hypotheses, 43–4

and learning to teach, 84–6
models of intuition-related thinking,
  98–101
perspectives in the study of, 241–4
rational problem-solving and, 138–9
and rationality, *see* rationality
and reflection, 81–2, 173–4, 260
in teaching, 260–1
training vs in mentoring, 112–13
tuition in, 160–2
variability of, 47–8, 188–92
varieties of, 34–40, 184–8
voices of, 46–7
intuition culture, 11, 239–52
intuitive restructuring, 127–8
intuitive thinking, 6–7
intuitive types, 190–1
Isenberg, D., 182, 184, 185

Jackson, P.W., 86
James, W., 41
Jastrow, J., 38
John, P., 16, 17, 18, 59–60, 110
Johnson, D., 245, 246, 247
Jones, M., 234
Joyce, B.R., 147
judgement, 18, 37, 40, 108, 240, 257
  complex decision making, 176–8
  management education, 185–6
  measurement, criteria, expertise and,
    11, 220–38
  risk of bias in intuitive judgements,
    225, 229, 233–4
  role in intuition, 53–6
  science teachers, 154–5, 159
  trust in, 8, 53–65, 215–16
Jung, C.G., 47, 189, 190, 194

Kagan, J., 61
Kahneman, D., 70, 161
Kaufmann, G., 187
Keats, J., 49
Kemmis, S., 26, 27
Kennedy, M., 26
key skills for intuitive practitioners, 80,
  81
Kierkegaard, S.A., 216
Kintsch, W., 246
knowledge, 4, 138
  craft, *see* craft knowledge

crisis of professionalism, 16, 17–18,
  21, 22–3, 26, 28
from different learning environments,
  113
and experience, 69–70, 125–6
implicit, 109–10, 125–6, 246–7
intuition as elemental knowledge
  structures, 241–4
intuition, learning and, 255–9
kinds that deliver maximum
  facilitation for beginning teachers,
  113–17
objective, 17, 26–7
professional common-sense, 102
structured nurturing environment,
  58–9
tacit, 182, 255–9
teacher thinking paradigm, 86
knowledge-in-action, 5, 22
knowledge-based teacher education, 70–1
knowledge society, 211
Kroc, R., 186
Kuhn, D., 124
Kuhn, T., 85

Landrum, G., 182
language, 4
  English language teacher education, 9,
    122–34
Lave, J., 240, 243, 250
Lazarus, E., 110, 111, 112, 117–18
Le Grand, J., 20
league tables, 206–7
learning, 35–6
  accountability and individual learners,
    267
  changing nature of and assessment,
    211–14
  implicit, *see* implicit learning
  intuition, knowledge and, 255–9
  management expertise and, 185
  motivation of learner, 267
  nurturing environments and trust in
    judgement, 55–64
  performativity and, 207
  perspectives on study of intuition,
    242–4
  postmodernist culture and, 203
  professional, models of, 2–3
  strategies, 169–70

learning by doing, 70
legitimate peripheral participation, 243
Leinhardt, G., 102
Lesgold, A., 124
lesson planning, 103, 178–9
    flexible, 74–7
lesson reconstructions, 91–8
lessons: how student teachers 'read'
    their own, 9, 84–106
level descriptions, 233, 235
Lewicki, P., 36
literacy, academic, 11, 239–52
Long, M., 233
Lorenz, K., 44
Lowell, A., 45
Luckmann, T., 102
Lunt, N., 112
Lynn, S.J., 47

Macnamara Fallacy, 199
macro-strategies, 169–70
magical intuition, 33–4
management education, 10–11, 182–95
    types of, 193–4
managers, changing role of, 183–4
Mangan, B., 41
market ideology, 19–20, 206–7
Marland, P., 87
Marton, F., 32, 44, 150
Mason, R., 225
mathematics, 261
    complex decision making in teaching,
        165–81
    intuition and assessment in, 226–31,
        236–7
maxims, 35–6, 104
Mayer, R., 192
Maynard, T., 63, 109, 117
Mazlina bt. Azhar, 112, 118
McCaulley, M., 190
McDonald's, 186
McIntyre, D., 5, 6, 72, 73, 74–5
measurement, 11
    judgement, criteria, expertise and, 11,
        220–38
    obsession with, 200–1, 202–8
Medawar, P., 109
medicine, 10, 149–64
    general practitioners, 152–3, 156–8,
        159

memory, 4
mental functions, 189
mental models, 241
mentoring, 103–4, 145, 147, 264
    beginning teachers, 9, 107–21
    and conflicting views, 118
    mentors' professional development,
        117–18
    mentors as role models, 110
    preparation of mentors to share their
        knowledge and know-how, 109–13
    student teachers, 77–8
    training of mentors, 111–13
mentoring conversations, 109–10
micro-strategies, 169–70
Mill, J.S., 33
Millett, A., 25, 28
models, knowledge of, 242
modernism, 202–8
Modes of Teacher Education research
    project, 21–2
Monaghan, J., 112
mood assessment, 100–1
Moore, H., 45
Morgan, G., 187
motivation, 267–8
Munby, H., 5
Mussen, P.H., 58
Myers, I., 190
Myers, P., 190
Myers Briggs Type Indicator (MBTI), 190

naive intuition, 122, 126–8, 185
    fallibility, 123–6
National Curriculum, 220–1, 236
    art, 223–4
    geography, 231, 232–3, 235
    maths, 174, 227–8
    science, 160
national standards, 10, 139–40
needs identification, 142–3
negative capability, 49
negative numbers, 176–8
negative somatic markers, 168
new rationalism, 21, 23–6, 29
'next to' assessment methods, 159
Nisbet, J., 169–70
Nixon, R., 186
Nobel science laureates, 44, 47
Noddings, N., 191

non-routine problems, 192
Nørretranders, T., 6
nursing, 161
nurturing environments, 55–64

Oakhill, J., 123–4
objective knowledge, 17, 26–7
objectives, 90, 91–8 *passim*
observation
    of experienced teachers, 113–14
    by mentors, 114
    student teachers' lessons, 87–98
    task-based language teacher
        education, 131–3
O'Hear, A., 19
O'Malley, C.E., 241, 243
on-the-job experience, 193–4
opportunity creation, 99
Osborn, A.F., 187
Osborne, A.B., 87
outcome feedback, 57–8
Owen, P., 249

Palmer, J., 212, 213
paranormal intuition, 33
parents, 266
Parikh, J., 183, 192
pattern recognition, 73, 256
pedagogical content knowledge, 86
Peirce, C.S., 38
perceptions, 89, 91–8 *passim*
performance, 6
performance indicators, 206–7, 209
performance period, 75, 76
performativity, 207
Perkins, D.N., 212, 223
Perrenoud, P., 213–14
personal attributes, 140
personal knowledge, *see* craft knowledge
personality trait, intuition as, 188,
    189–91
phronesis, 28
physical sensitivity, 47
Pirsig, R.M., 15, 29–30
planning, *see* lesson planning
Poincaré, H., 44–5
Polanyi, M., 35–6, 182
positive somatic markers, 168
positivism, 26
practical knowledge, teachers', 86

practical principles, 24, 58
practical wisdom, 28
practice
    communities of practice, 179, 240,
        243–5, 249–50
    knowledge and experience, 69–70
    new rationalism, 23–5
    theory and, 80–1, 113
presentation, 234
Prince, G.M., 48–9
private theory, *see* craft knowledge
problem avoidance, 98–9
problem identification, 123
problem-solving
    creativity and, 38–9, 41, 186–8, 256
    rational and intuition, 138–9
problem-specificity, 189, 192
producer capture, 19
productive thinking, 192
professional common-sense knowledge,
    102
professional development, 10, 137–48,
    263–4
    evidence for teachers' intuitive
        behaviour in relation to, 140–6
    knowing when to seek, 143
    mentors' 117–18
    national standards, 139–40
    needs identification, 142–3
    positive experiences of, 143–5
    purposes of, 141–2
    stages of development, 116–17
professional learning, models of, 2–3
professionalism, 59–61, 141
    crisis in, 8, 15–31
proficiency, 77
progressive education, 266
psychological types, 189–90
public theory, 125
pupils
    accountability and individual learners,
        267
    purposes, 179
    student teachers and awareness, 90,
        91–8 *passim*
purpose
    and assessment, 201
    intuition, rational analysis and,
        166–9
    pupil purposes, 179

purpose *continued*
    purposes and complex decision
        making, 165–72, 173–4
Purves, A., 241–2
Purves, W., 241–2

qualifications, management, 193

Ransom, S., 19
rational problem-solving, 138–9
rational thinking, 6–7
rationalism, new, 21, 23–6, 29
rationality, 267
    assessment, 203–5
    and emotion in learning, 214–15
    the formal and intuitive in science and
        medicine, 10, 149–64
    and intuition in professional practice,
        72–3
    intuition, rational analysis and
        purposes, 166–9
    technical, 5–6, 17–18, 204–5
reaction without conscious thought,
    126–8
'reading' a situation, 85
received knowledge, 125
research, 26
recipes, 98, 102, 127
Reder, L.M., 127
reflection, 3, 78
    intuition and, 81–2, 173–4, 260
    mentors and, 117–18
    structure in nurturing environments,
        58
reflection-in-action, 5, 22, 98
reflection-on-action, 22, 58
reflective conversation, 101
reflective intelligence, 212–13
reflective model of teacher education, 71
reflective practice, 21–3, 138–9
reflective practitioner, 4–5
    model of professional learning, 2
reflective thinking, 6–7
Reformation, 204
rehearsing, 6
Reimer, W., 205
reproductive thinking, 192
responsibility, 16, 18–19
reverie, 46–7
Reynolds, D., 138–9

Rhue, J.W., 47
rightness, feeling of, 41–2
rituals, 127
Roberson, B.S., 233
Robertson, L., 225
role models, 110
Rosch's categories, 170
Ross, M., 209
routine problems, 192
routines, 81, 98, 127
    types of in classroom, 102
Rowan, R., 186
rumination, 39–40, 186–8, 256
Russell, T., 5
Ryan, R.M., 55–6

Saleena, C.A., 114, 115
Satterly, D., 209–10
SCAA, 233
scaffolding, 129–30
Scardamalia, M., 246
scholastic model of professional learning,
    2
Schön, D.A., 85, 98
    reflective practitioner, 4–5, 22, 58,
        101, 138
    technical rationality, 17–18
school experience
    flexible lesson planning, 74–7
    how student teachers 'read' their own
        lessons, 9, 84–106
school improvement, 210–11
Schooler, J.W., 37, 39, 123
Schucksmith, J., 169–70
Schutz, A., 57, 102
science, 200–1, 241
    Nobel laureates, 44, 47
    rationality and intuition in science
        and medicine, 10, 149–64
science mind, 150–1
science teachers, 152–3, 153–6, 158–60,
    262
secondment, 144–5, 146, 147
self, images of, 168
self-assessment, 212–13
self-esteem, 61
self-monitoring, 81–2
semantic knowledge, 242
seminars, 103
sensing types, 190–1

sensitivity, 37–8, 40, 108, 177, 221, 257
   management education, 186
Shore, P.J., 191
short training courses, 143–4, 146
Showers, B., 147
silence, 171
skills
   intuition as a skill, 188–9, 191–2
   key skills for intuitive practitioners, 80, 81
Smith, R., 28, 70
social rules, knowledge of, 242
Solomon, J., 151, 159
somatic markers, 166, 168, 171–2, 180
Spradley, J., 87
stages of development, 116–17
standards
   assessment and, 207, 210
   national standards for teachers, 10, 139–40
   professionalism and, 141
state of mind, intuition as, 189, 192
statements of attainment, 174
Stevenson, R., 212, 213
Stibbs, A., 225
stimulated recall, 87–98
Stroebe, W., 187
structure
   nurturing environments, 55–6, 56–9, 62
   text and, 242–3, 246–7
student teachers
   how student teachers 'read' their own lessons, 9, 84–106
   lacking in confidence, 79–80
   observation of by mentors, 114
   very intuitive, 79
   see also teacher education
subjective knowledge, 27
subsidiary awareness, 85
supernatural intuition, 33
superordinate categories, 170
supervisory cycle, 110–11
support
   from mentor, 115–17
   in-school for professional development, 145
   nurturing environments, 55–6, 57, 61–3

Swales, J.M., 244
Sylwester, R., 214–15
synthesis, 224

tacit knowledge, 182
   intuition, implicit learning and, 255–9
tactical perspectives, 88, 91–8 *passim*
'taken for granteds', *see* implicit knowledge
task-based teacher education, 128–33
task setting, 247–8
taste, 47
Taylor, P.H., 142
teacher education, 9, 69–83, 263–4
   differences in student teachers, 79–80
   English language teacher education, 9, 122–34
   models of, 70–1
   reason and intuition, 72–3
   role of tutor/mentor, 77–8
   school experience, 74–7
   student teachers and awareness, 9, 84–106
   task-based, 128–33
   see also beginning teachers; professional development
teacher interpretation, 99, 100
teacher thinking paradigm, 86
Teacher Training Agency (TTA), 25
   national standards, 10, 139–40
teachers
   advanced skills teachers, 140
   evidence for intuitive behaviour in relation to professional development, 140–6
   how use of intuition changes with experience, 225–6, 229–30, 234–5
   observing experienced teachers, 113–14
teaching
   collaborative, 110
   dimensions of, 152
   effective teaching behaviours, 138–9
   intuition in, 260–1
   strategies, 170–2
technical rationality, 5–6, 17–18, 204–5
Teets, J., 186
tension, 126
testing, formal, 155–6, 209, 210
text-based experiments, 245–9

theory, 17–18
  and practice, 80–1, 113
theory-demonstration-practice-feedback
    model, 147
thinking
  fallibility of naive intuitions, 123–4
  how student teachers 'read' their own
    lessons, 9, 84–106
  levels of explicitness, 22
  models of intuition-related thinking,
    98–101
  processes, 6–7
  productive and reproductive, 192
  teacher thinking paradigm, 86
thought units, 87–98
Tomlinson, P., 109, 114, 117
touch-typing, 69–70
training of mentors, 111–13
trust in judgement, 8, 53–65, 215–16
tutors, role of, 77–8, 103–4
  see also mentoring
Tversky, A., 70, 161

unconscious, 41
  collective unconscious, 194
universities, 203
  academic literacy, 11, 239–52

values, 18
variability of intuition, 47–8, 188–92
Vaughan, F., 191, 192
visualization, 192
voices of intuition, 46–7
Vonk, H., 77

Wallas, G., 126–7
Walpert, L., 151
Wenger, E., 250
Westcott, M.R., 47–8, 54, 189–90, 192
White, R.V., 248
Whitty, G.D., 19
Wilby, P., 210–11
Wilcockson, J., 133
Wiliam, D., 200–1, 207–8, 213, 216
Willis, D.J., 128–30
Wilson, T.D., 37
Winner, L., 208
Wittgenstein, L., 85, 207, 208
Wolf, A., 215
Woods Hole Conference, 32, 172
Woodward, T., 130–1
workload, teachers', 146
writing tasks, 247–8

Young, C.E., 58